Consumer Reports

1998 NEW CAR *buying guide*

THE EDITORS OF CONSUMER REPORTS

PUBLISHED BY CONSUMER REPORTS
A DIVISION OF CONSUMERS UNION
YONKERS, NEW YORK

A SPECIAL PUBLICATION FROM CONSUMER REPORTS

CONSUMER REPORTS AUTO TEST DIVISION

CONSUMER REPORTS

CONSUMERS UNION

First printing, June 1998

Published by Consumers Union of United States, Inc., Yonkers, New York 10703.

Library of Congress Catalog Card No.: 88-15006
ISSN: 1044-3045
ISBN: 0-89043-890-0

Manufactured in the United States of America.

Consumer Reports

1998

NEW CAR

buying guide

Contents

CHAPTER 5 SAFETY & RELIABILITY

CHAPTER 6 THE PROFILES

CHAPTER 7 CARING FOR YOUR CAR

PREFACE

The *1998 New Car Buying Guide* is published by CONSUMER REPORTS, the monthly magazine best known for test reports, product Ratings, and buying guidance. We are also a comprehensive source of unbiased advice about services, personal finance, health and nutrition, and other consumer concerns. Since 1936, our mission has been to test products, inform the public, and protect consumers. Our income is derived solely from the sale of CONSUMER REPORTS magazine and our other publications and services, and from nonrestrictive, noncommercial contributions, grants, and fees. We buy all the products we test, just as you do. We accept no ads from companies, nor do we let any company use our reports or Ratings for commercial purposes.

PRODUCTS AND SERVICES FROM CONSUMER REPORTS

CONSUMER REPORTS. Published monthly, CONSUMER REPORTS magazine provides unbiased information on brand-name products, services, health, and personal finance. When you subscribe, you get the annual Buying Guide as well. To subscribe (12 issues, $24), write P.O. Box 53029, Boulder, Colo. 80322-3029.

CONSUMER REPORTS ONLINE. The CONSUMER REPORTS web site can be found at *www.ConsumerReports.org.* Free areas of the site give general buying guidance, a comprehensive list of product recalls, manufacturers' phone numbers, and other useful information. Members-only sections provide searchable Ratings of electronics, appliances, cars, and more, along with the current issue of CONSUMER REPORTS. Membership is $2.95 per month or $24 per year.

NEW CAR PRICE SERVICE. Our reports compare sticker price to dealer's invoice for a car or light truck, and for factory-installed options. Call 800 933-5555.

USED CAR PRICE SERVICE. Find market value and reliability summary for most 1989-1997 used cars and light trucks. Call 800 422-1079.

AUTO INSURANCE PRICE SERVICE. Compare the cost of insurance for the coverage you need; find the best price. Now available in Ariz., Calif., Colo., Fla., Ga., Ill., La.,

Nev., N.J., N.Y., Ohio, Pa., Texas, Va., and Wash. (As of July 1998, available in Conn., N.C., Tenn., and Wis.) Call 800 944-4104.

CONSUMER REPORTS CARS: THE ESSENTIAL GUIDE. This CD-ROM covers new and used cars, minivans, pickups, and SUVs. $17.95 postpaid. Call 800 331-1369, extension 171.

CONSUMER REPORTS BY REQUEST. Specially edited reports are available by fax or mail. Call 800 789-3715 for an index of what's available. The index costs $1.

CONSUMER REPORTS ON HEALTH. To subscribe (12 issues, $24), write us at P.O. Box 56356, Boulder, Colo. 80322-6356.

CONSUMER REPORTS TRAVEL LETTER. Monthly newsletter with travel values. To subscribe (12 issues, $39), write us at P.O. Box 53629, Boulder, Colo. 80322-3629.

ZILLIONS. Bimonthly magazine for kids ages 8 to 12. To subscribe (6 issues, $16), write us at P.O. Box 54861, Boulder, Colo. 80322-4861.

CONSUMER REPORTS TELEVISION. Produces TV specials; videos for home and school; and our nationally syndicated consumer news service, Consumer Reports TV News.

OTHER MEDIA. Information from CONSUMER REPORTS is available online through America Online, CompuServe, Knight-Ridder, and Nexis; on TV and radio around the country; and in columns appearing in more than 500 newspapers.

CHAPTER ONE

The 1998 cars

WHAT'S NEW THIS YEAR

The biggest news from Detroit in recent months was not about styling, prices, or safety equipment. It was about fuel tanks and tailpipes. U.S. automakers are finally talking about taking serious steps to reduce pollution from cars and other passenger vehicles.

Ford Motor Co. was the first of the Big Three to take the "green" line, stating that it would sell low-emission versions of its popular sport-utility vehicles next year. Two weeks later General Motors Corp. and Chrysler Corp. joined Ford in announcing that they would sell cleaner-running passenger cars and SUVs in 12 Northeastern and mid-Atlantic states next fall, and nationally within three years. The new national low-emission vehicles, or "N-LEVs," are expected to emit 70 percent less smog-producing oxides of nitrogen and 50 percent less hydrocarbons than cars now on sale.

The same day the automakers announced the N-LEVs, the Department of Transportation announced a government-industry partnership that will spend $100 million a year to increase automotive fuel economy by 50 percent by the year 2004.

These recent developments will help curb an unsettling trend: An ever-increasing number of vehicles—many of them low-mpg sport-utility vehicles—are worsening overall fuel economy and generating an ever-increasing amount of pollution. (Because SUVs are classed as trucks, they need not meet the same fuel-efficiency standards as passenger cars. As a result, SUVs have had a disproportionately harmful effect on fuel economy in the U.S.)

Credit the convergence of geopolitics, global economics, and environmental concerns for the move toward cleaner, more efficient vehicles. At a major international conference last fall in Kyoto, Japan, the U.S. agreed to a 7 percent reduction in emissions of carbon dioxide and other "greenhouse gases" by the year 2010. Japan and European nations had already agreed to similar reductions, forcing U.S. automakers to improve fuel economy by approximately 10 percent if they want to compete successfully overseas.

WHAT ELSE IS NEW?

STABLE PRICES. You can expect car prices to remain flat or even decline a little this year.

SIMPLIFIED PRODUCT LINES. In order to hold down costs, carmakers are paring down their trim lines, the standard-equipment levels that distinguish a base model from, say, a GS or LS. Ford, for example, is offering just two trim lines on some of its cars. GM and Chrysler are moving in the same direction.

"Globalization" is another factor contributing to simplification. More and more, automakers are taming production costs by using a single platform—that is, a vehicle's mechanical underpinnings—outfitted with different features and details. Toyota, for example, uses the same platform worldwide for the Corolla, altering styling and features to suit national tastes. Ford takes globalization further, marketing the same product worldwide and changing little except the name. The Ford Contour, sold in North America, is known as the Mondeo in Europe.

FEWER BRAND-NEW MODELS OR COMPLETE REDESIGNS. The Volkswagen New Beetle, one of several newly designed small cars, has commanded considerable attention for its retro styling. (Under the skin, it's built on the new VW Golf platform.) Other new sedans include the Honda Accord and Volkswagen Passat, the large Chrysler Concorde and Dodge Intrepid, the medium-sized Oldsmobile Intrigue, the upscale Saab 9-5 (replacing the 9000), and the upscale Audi A6. Toyota's new Sienna offers a fine choice for minivan buyers.

Most of the action is with sport-utility vehicles. New players include the Dodge Durango and Lincoln Navigator. Other new entries include the Subaru Forester, Mercedes-Benz M-Class, Lexus RX300, and Toyota Land Cruiser. New pickup trucks for 1998 are the Ford Ranger, Mazda B-Series, and Nissan Frontier.

USING THIS BOOK

To present this comprehensive picture of the 1998 car market, CONSUMER REPORTS has pulled together the results of hundreds of tests and the findings of surveys that poll hundreds of thousands of car owners. For most people, buying a car takes time—gathering facts, making decisions, taking test drives. This book is designed to help you, wherever you are in that process.

The first chapter covers what's new in the 1998 automotive marketplace. It includes CONSUMER REPORTS' picks of the vehicles considered the best in various classes. The 1998 Car Finder lists the new models by type to give a snapshot of the whole car market. Highlighted are recommended models—those that have performed well in CONSUMER REPORTS' tests and are likely to be at least average in reliability.

Later chapters tell you how to buy or lease a car, what sort of safety and other equipment you can expect on modern cars, and ways to be smart about buying auto insurance.

The heart of the book is the car profiles—the collected results of CONSUMER REPORTS' surveys and tests for all the cars on the market. If you know which model you want, turn directly to its profile. The profiles are listed alphabetically by manufacturer and start on page 80.

The Ratings, on page 76, help you compare similar cars. You'll find, by type of vehicle, the overall results of CONSUMER REPORTS' extensive tests of performance, comfort, and convenience. After you know how a car scores, check its profile.

Finding a reliable car is often a big concern. The profiles include predictions on reliability for most 1998 vehicles. (CONSUMER REPORTS can do this because few car models change much from year to year, which gives a good idea of how the new models will perform.) See page 70.

New or redesigned for 1998

Audi A6
Cadillac Seville
Chevrolet Prizm
Chrysler 300M ('99)
Chrysler Concorde
Chrysler LHS ('99)
Dodge Durango
Dodge Intrepid
Ford Ranger
Honda Accord
Honda Passport
Isuzu Amigo
Isuzu Rodeo
Kia Sephia
Lexus GS300/GS400
Lexus LX470
Lexus RX300
Lincoln Town Car
Mazda 626
Mazda B-Series
Mazda Miata
Mercedes-Benz CLK
Mercedes-Benz M-Class
Mercury Cougar ('99)
Nissan Altima
Nissan Frontier
Oldsmobile Alero ('99)
Oldsmobile Intrigue
Pontiac Grand Am ('99)
Saab 9-3 (900)
Saab 9-5
Subaru Forester
Toyota Corolla
Toyota Land Cruiser
Toyota Sienna
Volkswagen New Beetle
Volkswagen Passat
Volvo C70
Volvo S/V70

BEST IN CLASS

The best vehicle for you depends on whether you need an economical car for commuting or a minivan or wagon that can haul lots of people, a load of camping gear, and, of course, the family dog. The list here covers the cars and trucks that CONSUMER REPORTS editors and auto-test engineers have selected as best-in-class.

FAMILY CARS. You have many choices in this crowded category, but the Toyota Camry, Volkswagen Passat, and Honda Accord excelled in our tests. Most Toyotas and Hondas are renowned for reliability. The VW has yet to prove itself.

UPSCALE SEDANS. If you want a luxurious car and are willing to spend $30,000 to $35,000, consider the Lexus ES300 or BMW 328i. Both offer very good reliability. The excellent Mercedes-Benz E320 combines strong acceleration with reasonable fuel economy, responsive handling, a serene ride, and fine reliability. It's the highest-scoring vehicle we've tested—but it costs $47,000.

THRIFTY RUNABOUTS. The Honda Civic is the best of the bunch in ride, fuel economy, and reliability. The Mazda Protegé ES is another good choice.

BEST CARS FOR FUN. Small coupes aren't as practical as sedans, but they can be fun to drive. In our tests, the Nissan 200SX SE-R and the Volkswagen Golf GTI outscored the competition.

MOVING THE TROOPS. Nothing beats a minivan when you have to transport lots of people or stuff. The new Toyota Sienna is our top recommended minivan, followed by the Dodge Caravan/Plymouth Voyager twins.

STRONG PICKUP. The Ford F-150, redesigned last year, is our clear choice among pickup trucks. It offers strong acceleration, fairly nimble handling, and average reliability.

SPORTING LIFE. The typical sport-utility vehicle delivers mediocre to poor fuel economy; there are also serious questions about safety for SUV passengers and for occupants of other cars in a crash (see "Getting there safely," page 57). Among larger SUVs, the Ford Explorer, Jeep Grand Cherokee, and Toyota 4Runner did the best in CONSUMER REPORTS' tests. Among smaller SUVs, our choices include the Subaru Forester, Toyota RAV4, and Honda CR-V.

The 1998 car finder

These lists sort this year's 187 vehicles by type. If a car fits more than one category, it's listed more than once. Models in **bold** are those we recommend, based on performance in our tests and reliability as reported by our readers. An * indicates a "promising" model—it tested well, but its reliability is not yet known.

Cars listed as coupes come only in a two-door version. The four-wheel-drive group includes full-time all-wheel and four-wheel systems. It doesn't include part-time systems (see page 46).

SMALL CARS

Acura Integra
Chevrolet Cavalier
Chevrolet Metro
Chevrolet Prizm
Dodge Neon
Ford Escort
Honda Civic
Hyundai Accent
Hyundai Elantra
Kia Sephia
Mazda Protegé
Mercury Tracer
Mitsubishi Mirage*
Nissan Sentra
Plymouth Neon
Pontiac Sunfire
Saturn
Subaru Impreza
Suzuki Esteem
Suzuki Swift
Toyota Corolla
Toyota Tercel
Volkswagen Golf
Volkswagen Jetta
Volkswagen New Beetle

HATCHBACKS

Acura Integra Coupe
BMW 318ti
Chevrolet Camaro
Chevrolet Metro
Honda Civic
Hyundai Accent
Hyundai Tiburon
Mercury Cougar
Mitsubishi Eclipse
Pontiac Firebird
Saab 9-3
Suzuki Swift
Toyota Celica
Volkswagen Golf
Volkswagen New Beetle

MEDIUM CARS UNDER $25,000

Buick Century
Buick Regal
Chevrolet Lumina
Chevrolet Malibu
Chrysler Cirrus
Dodge Stratus
Ford Contour
Ford Taurus
Honda Accord
Hyundai Sonata
Mazda 626
Mercury Mystique
Mercury Sable
Mitsubishi Galant
Nissan Altima
Nissan Maxima
Oldsmobile Alero
Oldsmobile Cutlass
Oldsmobile Intrigue*
Plymouth Breeze
Pontiac Grand Am
Pontiac Grand Prix
Subaru Legacy
Toyota Camry
Volkswagen Passat*

MEDIUM CARS OVER $25,000

Acura TL
Audi A4
Audi A6
BMW 3-Series
Cadillac Catera
Infiniti I30
Lexus ES300
Mazda Millenia
Mercedes-Benz C-Class
Mitsubishi Diamante
Oldsmobile Aurora
Saab 9-3
Saab 9-5
Volvo S70
Volvo S90

LARGE CARS UNDER $30,000

Buick LeSabre
Chrysler Concorde
Dodge Intrepid
Ford Crown Victoria
Mercury Grand Marquis
Oldsmobile 88
Pontiac Bonneville
Toyota Avalon

LARGE CARS OVER $30,000

Buick Park Avenue
Cadillac DeVille
Chrysler 300M
Chrysler LHS
Lincoln Town Car

LUXURY CARS

Acura RL
Audi A8
BMW 5-Series
BMW 7-Series
Cadillac Seville
Infiniti Q45
Jaguar XJ8
Lexus GS300/GS400
Lexus LS400
Lincoln Continental
Mercedes-Benz E-Class
Mercedes-Benz S-Class

SPORTS/SPORTY CARS UNDER $25,000

Acura Integra Coupe
BMW 318ti
Chevrolet Camaro
Ford Mustang
Honda Prelude
Hyundai Tiburon
Mazda MX-5 Miata
Mercury Cougar
Mitsubishi Eclipse
Nissan 200SX
Nissan 240SX
Pontiac Firebird
Saturn SC
Toyota Celica

SPORTS/SPORTY CARS OVER $25,000

BMW Z3
Chevrolet Corvette
Mercedes-Benz SLK
Mitsubishi 3000GT
Porsche Boxster
Toyota Supra

COUPES

Acura CL
Buick Riviera
Cadillac Eldorado
Chevrolet Monte Carlo
Chrysler Sebring
Dodge Avenger
Lexus SC300/SC400
Mercedes-Benz CLK
Volvo C70

CONVERTIBLES

BMW 323i/328i
BMW Z3
Chevrolet Camaro
Chevrolet Cavalier
Chevrolet Corvette
Chrysler Sebring JX
Ford Mustang
Mazda MX-5 Miata
Mercedes-Benz SLK
Mitsubishi Eclipse
Pontiac Firebird
Pontiac Sunfire
Porsche Boxster
Saab 9-3
Toyota Celica
Volkswagen Cabrio (Golf)

WAGONS

Audi A4 Avant
Audi A6 Avant
Ford Escort
Ford Taurus
Hyundai Elantra
Mercedes-Benz E-Class
Mercury Sable
Mercury Tracer
Saturn
Subaru Impreza
Subaru Legacy
Suzuki Esteem
Volkswagen Passat
Volvo V70
Volvo V90

MINIVANS

Chevrolet Astro
Chevrolet Venture
Chrysler Town & Country
Dodge Caravan
Dodge Grand Caravan
Ford Windstar
GMC Safari
Honda Odyssey
Isuzu Oasis
Mazda MPV
Mercury Villager
Nissan Quest
Oldsmobile Silhouette
Plymouth Grand Voyager
Plymouth Voyager
Pontiac Trans Sport
Toyota Sienna

SPORT-UTILITY VEHICLES

Acura SLX
Chevrolet Blazer
Chevrolet Suburban
Chevrolet Tahoe
Chevrolet Tracker
Dodge Durango
Ford Expedition
Ford Explorer
GMC Jimmy
GMC Suburban
GMC Yukon
Honda CR-V
Honda Passport
Infiniti QX4
Isuzu Amigo
Isuzu Rodeo
Isuzu Trooper
Jeep Cherokee
Jeep Grand Cherokee
Jeep Wrangler
Kia Sportage
Land Rover Discovery
Land Rover
Range Rover
Lexus LX470
Lexus RX300
Lincoln Navigator
Mercedes-Benz M-Class
Mercury Mountaineer
Mitsubishi Montero
Mitsubishi Montero Sport
Nissan Pathfinder
Oldsmobile Bravada
Subaru Forester
Suzuki Sidekick
Suzuki X90
Toyota 4Runner
Toyota Land Cruiser
Toyota RAV4

FULL-TIME FOUR-WHEEL DRIVE AVAILABLE

Acura SLX
Audi A4 Quattro
Audi A6 Quattro
Audi A8 4.2 Quattro
Chevrolet Astro
Chevrolet Suburban
Chevrolet Tahoe
Chrysler Town & Country
Dodge Durango
Dodge Grand Caravan
Ford Expedition
Ford Explorer
GMC Safari
GMC Suburban
GMC Yukon
Honda CR-V
Infiniti QX4
Isuzu Trooper
Jeep Cherokee
Jeep Grand Cherokee
Land Rover Discovery
Land Rover Range Rover
Lexus LX470
Lexus RX300
Lincoln Navigator
Mazda MPV
Mercedes-Benz E-Class
Mercedes-Benz M-Class
Mercury Mountaineer
Mitsubishi 3000GT VR-4
Mitsubishi Eclipse GSX
Mitsubishi Montero
Oldsmobile Bravada
Subaru Forester
Subaru Impreza
Subaru Legacy
Toyota Land Cruiser
Toyota RAV4
Volvo V70

PICKUP TRUCKS

Chevrolet C/K
Chevrolet S-10
Dodge Dakota
Dodge Ram
Ford F-Series
Ford Ranger
GMC Sierra
GMC Sonoma
Isuzu Hombre
Mazda B-Series
Nissan Frontier
Toyota T100
Toyota Tacoma

The CAR market

GUIDE TO THE MAKES

Worldwide, a relatively small number of large manufacturers dominates the automobile business. Here's a rundown of carmakers that market vehicles in the U.S. Models are noted as "recommended" or "promising" according to CONSUMER REPORTS' performance and reliability criteria (see page 75). Many of the makes are related—"twins" or "triplets" are made by the same company and are essentially similar, "cousins" are less similar. The term "rebadged" means that one automaker has put its name on another's vehicle to fill an empty niche in a product line. For a listing of related models, see page 23. Models are listed alphabetically.

BMW. This German company is one of the world's leading producers of high-quality sports sedans. Careful engineering makes the BMW a true "driver's car," with emphasis on good performance and precise handling, yet still maintaining high levels of comfort. All BMWs are rear-wheel-drive. Like other European makes sold here, BMW has invested a lot in crashworthiness and advanced safety features. Its plant in South Carolina makes the small Z3 roadster. Recommended models: 3-Series; 5-Series.

CHRYSLER CORP. The smallest of Detroit's Big Three was founded in 1925 as the successor to the Maxwell Motor Co. For most of its history, Chrysler has been a volatile company that has skirmished with bankruptcy more than once. Currently, Chrysler's finances look strong. The company more or less invented the front-wheel-drive minivan, whose sales skyrocketed in the 1980s. The Jeep division makes the company's best-known sport-utility vehicles. In addition to Jeep, Chrysler's car divisions include Chrysler, Dodge, and Plymouth.

Chrysler is the flagship name among the corporation's nameplates. The Chrysler brand offers the highest-end accoutrements with its cars—with prices to match—although most Chryslers are virtually identical under the skin to equivalent Dodge models.

Dodge is positioned slightly upmarket from Plymouth, with a broader product range and more offerings. It still aims primarily at the broad, bread-and-butter middle range of the market. You'll find the Dodge name on small, intermediate, and large sedans, as well as on a midsized coupe, on an SUV, and on minivans and pickups. Recommended models: Caravan; Dakota pickup.

Plymouth aims at the low-end buyer of Chrysler products. You won't find all the fancy trim lines among Plymouths that you'll find on their Dodge brethren. Similarly equipped, Plymouths are virtually identical to the Dodge versions of the same car. Recommended model: Voyager.

Jeep is the last descendant of the old American Motors Corp., which Chrysler absorbed in 1987. The Jeep brand remains vastly popular. Recommended model: Grand Cherokee.

FORD MOTOR CO. Henry Ford built his first car in 1896 and founded the Ford Motor Co. in 1903. Ford is the world's second-largest automobile producer, narrowing the sales gap between itself and General Motors considerably in recent years. A worldwide company with extensive European operations, Ford owns Jaguar and one-third of Mazda Motors. In the U.S., Ford has two passenger-car divisions: Lincoln-Mercury and Ford.

The Ford division aims at the broad middle market, and the most popular parts of its car lines are midsized and larger sedans. Since the 1920s, Ford's main rival has been Chevrolet. These days, about 45 percent of Ford's production is in trucks, thanks to the surging market for sport-utilities. Recommended models: Contour; Crown Victoria; Escort; Explorer; F-150 pickup.

Mercury aims a little higher in the market than the Ford Division. All Mercury vehicles are close copies of Ford products, but may have slightly plusher appointments. Recommended models: Grand Marquis; Mystique; Sable; Tracer; Villager.

Lincoln is Ford's luxury nameplate, although historically Lincolns have been big, plush freeway floaters rather than true luxury cars. The Town Car is frequently used as a limousine, since it's one of the largest, longest cars in mass production. The Navigator is Lincoln's upscale version of the Ford Expedition SUV. Recommended model: Town Car.

GENERAL MOTORS. Founded in 1908, GM remains the world's largest car and truck manufacturer. While Henry Ford tried to make one universal car that fit everyone, GM strove from the 1920s onward to make a car "for every purse and purpose." Even though it has lost market share in recent years, it still accounts for almost one-third of all passenger cars and light trucks sold in the United States. Over the last few years, GM has introduced lots of new models, hoping to spark sales in a product line that has been fairly humdrum. GM has six passenger-car divisions plus GMC, a truck division, which merged with Pontiac in 1996.

Buick sees itself as a premium American car company. Buicks are supposed to be a notch above Oldsmobiles and a notch below Cadillacs. Buick appeals, in GM's thinking, to affluent buyers who are not quite ready to step into a Cadillac. Recommended model: Park Avenue.

Cadillac, GM's luxury car division, for decades called itself "the standard of the world." By the 1980s it was clear that world standards were set by European and later Japanese luxury cars, but not by Cadillac. With the Catera, Cadillac has been trying to reposition itself as a direct competitor to Mercedes and BMW. Recommended model: DeVille.

Chevrolet has been part of General Motors since 1918. Chevrolets are GM's bread-and-butter cars, aimed at the broad lower-to-middle market. Traditionally, Chevrolet has competed directly against Ford, but like all of the domestics, it has also tried to position itself as an alternative to imports. Moderate pricing is still Chevrolet's long suit. The Chevrolet name appears on a full range of cars, trucks, vans, and sport-utility vehicles, as well as on what was for years America's only true sports car, the Corvette. Recommended models: Cavalier; Lumina; Malibu; Prizm.

GMC's consumer products, as opposed to commercial trucks, are virtual twins of Chevrolet trucks. Both GMC and Chevrolet light trucks are designed by GM's Truck and Bus division, built in the same plants, and labeled as one or the other.

Oldsmobile has been in existence for over a century. Recently, Oldsmobiles have been positioned to appeal to the buyers who normally shop imports, as Oldsmobile tries to shed its stodgy image with vehicles such as the Aurora and the Intrigue. Oldsmobile also offers an SUV, called the Bravada, which is similar to the Chevrolet Blazer/GMC Jimmy. Recommended model: Cutlass. Promising new model: Intrigue.

Pontiac aims at a sportier and younger-thinking crowd than the other GM divisions. Although its cars may differ only in small ways from other GM offerings, the substance of those differences is sporty suspension and styling, and bold colors. Recommended models: Bonneville; Grand Prix; Sunfire.

Saturn, founded in the 1980s, began selling cars widely in 1991. Saturns are aimed at young, educated people who might otherwise consider a Toyota Corolla or Honda Civic. Two-thirds of Saturn buyers are women. Among Saturn's unusual features are flexible plastic body panels that rebound rather than dent after a mild blow and are easy to replace. Saturn pioneered a low-pressure sales environment at the dealership and a "no-dicker sticker"—a non-negotiable selling price. Saturn dealers are consistently ranked very high in satisfaction surveys, including those done by CONSUMER REPORTS. Indeed, customers' loyalty to the brand is unmatched by any domestic nameplate. Recommended model: SC2.

HONDA. Honda was originally a motorcycle manufacturer. It started building cars in 1962, and it now ranks ninth in the world in auto sales. Honda started the Japanese luxury-car market in this country when it introduced an upscale brand line, Acura, in the late 1980s.

Honda's main strength has been good engineering and innovative design. In addition to its Accord and Civic sedans, and Prelude coupe, its line includes the Odyssey minivan and the CR-V, a small sport-utility vehicle, both built on a car, not a truck, chassis. Honda also sells a rebadged Isuzu Rodeo SUV as the Passport. The Accord has been one of the top-selling cars in the U.S. for a decade or more. (For a list of top-selling models, see above right.) Recommended models: Accord; CR-V; Civic; Odyssey; Prelude.

Acura proved that a Japanese car could crack the U.S. luxury-car market. It led the charge that was later followed by Toyota and Nissan with their Lexus and Infiniti lines. Acura's newer cars carry letter designations rather than model names. The replacement for the flagship Legend is called the RL. The TL is smaller than

Top-selling '97 vehicles

Vehicle	Sales
1. Ford F-Series pickup	746,111
2. Chevrolet C/K pickup	553,729
3. Toyota Camry	397,156
4. Honda Accord	384,609
5. Ford Explorer	383,852
6. Ford Taurus	357,162
7. Dodge Ram pickup	350,257
8. Honda Civic	315,546
9. Chevrolet Cavalier	302,161
10. Ford Ranger pickup	298,796

the RL. The CL is based on the pre-1998 Honda Accord coupe. The small Integra is a fancier and, depending on the model, higher-performance version of the Honda Civic. The Acura SLX sport-utility vehicle is a rebadged Isuzu Trooper. Recommended models: Integra; RL; TL.

HYUNDAI. This giant Korean heavy-industrial company began selling cars in the U.S. in 1986. Hyundai's sales formula has been low-priced cars with lots of content. An early reputation for shoddy quality has hurt the company's reputation. As its cars have improved, the price gap between Hyundais and Japanese competitors has narrowed.

ISUZU. Primarily a manufacturer of trucks, Isuzu has branched out into small cars from time to time. Right now it sells only SUVs, a GM-built compact pickup, and a Honda-built minivan, the Oasis, in the U.S. The noncommercial Isuzus include the Amigo, Rodeo, and Trooper. Overall, Isuzu has a tiny part of the U.S. market, and it shares its one North American manufacturing facility with Subaru. Recommended model: Oasis.

JAGUAR. Jaguar, owned by Ford, is one of the few English cars still sold in the U.S. Jaguar is a luxury nameplate that competes in price and prestige with the likes of Mercedes and BMW. Traditionally, Jaguar has had a poor reputation for reliability. Time will tell if Ford's ownership has any impact on the British marque's quality control.

KIA. Kia Motors, based in Seoul, South Korea, started as a bicycle-parts maker in 1944. Kia products include passenger cars, vans, and cargo trucks. The company previously built the Festiva and Aspire economy cars for Ford. Kia started selling its own vehicles in the U.S. in 1994, and says it will be nationwide by the end of this year. Its current model line includes the Sephia four-door sedan and the Sportage SUV.

LAND ROVER. This British company is now owned by BMW. It makes one of the costliest sport-utility vehicles, the Range Rover, as well as the smaller and cheaper four-wheel-drive Discovery. Land Rovers were the safari car of choice before SUVs became so trendy. They're still mostly designed more for off-road excursions than highway performance.

MAZDA. Mazda gained some fame as the only automaker ever to successfully market cars with the Wankel rotary engine. The RX-7 sports car was the only survivor of that interesting breed, but high prices and a decreasing demand for Japanese sports cars eventually forced the RX-7 off the market. Mazda sells a full range of respectable and good-performing sedans and trucks, along with the Miata, a relatively inexpensive, sporty two-seat roadster that debuted in 1989. A one-third ownership of Mazda Motors gives Ford effective control of that company. Recommended models: MX-5 Miata; Millenia; Protegé.

MERCEDES-BENZ. This company dates back to 1886, when two competitors, Daimler and Benz, built the world's first production cars. The two merged in 1926. The Mercedes name came about in 1900, when a successful car distributor in Nice, Emil Jellinek, agreed to handle Daimler's new models—if the cars were named after his 11-year-old daughter, Mercedes. Mercedes-Benz has always been a luxury-car marque. The focus is on superb engineering and solid design rather than on flamboyance. Safety has been a major design consideration for many years. The company produces a new series of SUVs—the six-cylinder ML320 and V8-powered ML430—in Alabama. Recommended models: C-Class; E-Class.

MITSUBISHI. Mitsubishi is part of a huge Japanese engineering company that started serious car production in 1959. Mitsubishi makes a range of products, from small cars, medium sedans, and sport coupes to SUVs. It has maintained ties with Chrysler for over 25 years, and for a long time it supplied the small Dodge and Plymouth Colt. Its U.S. facility makes Mitsubishi-nameplate cars such as the Galant and some Chrysler and Dodge cars. Recommended model: Galant. A promising redesign: Mirage.

NISSAN. Nissan, Japan's second-largest car company, competes closely with Toyota and Honda. Nissan's luxury-car division is Infiniti.

Nissan, which used to be called Datsun, earned high marks and a lot of attention when it introduced the sporty, affordable 240Z in the early 1970s. Nissan offers a full line of mostly well-designed and reliable cars and light trucks. Recommended models: 200SX; Altima; Maxima; Pathfinder; Quest; Sentra.

Infiniti markets two sedans and an SUV (a rebadged Nissan Pathfinder). Infinitis tend to be well-engineered and reliable. Recommended models: I30; Q45.

PORSCHE. This German company produced its first car in 1948. Called the 356, this rear-engine design was lightweight and aerodynamic. During the 1963 Geneva auto show, Porsche unveiled the 911, which, more than 30 years after its introduction, continues to be produced (a new 911 debuts for 1998). Never a mass-producer, Porsche has always been at the forefront of automotive technology. Innovations that eventually wound up on production cars were usually first tested on racetracks around the world.

SAAB. Saab, half-owned by General Motors, is Sweden's number-two automaker, behind Volvo. Saab has long been innovative. It used two-stroke engines in its cars well into the 1960s and offered front-wheel drive decades before it became popular. It was among the first small, inexpensive imports to offer unit-body construction and multivalve engines. Saab is one of the few carmakers that still builds turbocharged engines. The company has produced a more upscale product over the last 20 years. Modern Saabs appeal to the sports-sedan crowd.

SUBARU. Subaru, owned by Fuji Corp., is the only successful Japanese car manufacturer founded since World War II. Traditionally, Subaru competed near the low end of the market with relatively inexpensive, utilitarian cars. Subaru has gradually and successfully increased the overall quality of its offerings, and it's now the only carmaker to offer all-wheel drive on moderately priced sedans and station wagons. It introduced a new small SUV this year, the Forester. Recommended models: Forester; Impreza; Legacy.

SUZUKI. Suzuki, like Honda, was originally a motorcycle manufacturer. It started branching out into small trucks in the 1950s. In this country it has offered mostly small sport-utility vehicles and economy cars, including some sold by GM. The Chevrolet Tracker and Metro are rebadged Suzukis.

TOYOTA. Toyota, by far the largest Japanese car company, ranks third in the world in sales, behind GM and Ford. Toyota sales took off in the U.S. in the 1970s when the company offered inexpensive, reliable, fuel-efficient cars at the same time that soaring fuel prices made Detroit's overweight and inefficient models particularly unappealing. Toyota gradually added larger cars and finally the luxury Lexus name to its product range. Along with Volkswagen and Honda, it founded the earliest "transplants"—foreign-owned manufacturing facilities in the U.S. All Corollas and Camrys sold in the U.S. are assembled in North America. Recommended models: 4Runner; Avalon; Camry; Celica; RAV4; Sienna.

Lexus, Toyota's luxury nameplate, debuted in this country in 1989 and now offers a selection of four cars and two SUVs. Lexuses are justly famous for their smooth powertrains, near-total isolation of the passenger compartment from the road, superb ergonomics, and exceptional reliability. Recommended models: ES300; GS300/GS400; LS400; SC300/SC400.

VOLKSWAGEN. Volkswagen is the world's fourth largest auto manufacturer, although sales in the U.S. have fallen considerably from the heyday of the original Beetle. While poor quality has plagued VWs sold in the late 1980s and early 1990s, reliability seems to have improved of late. Overall, the Golf, Jetta, and Passat have proved capable and sensible cars. A new version of the Beetle debuted in 1998. Recommended models: Golf; Jetta. Promising redesign: Passat.

Audi, a German company, is owned by Volkswagen, and makes upmarket sports sedans and station wagons. Audi has always been an innovative company technically (most Audis offer a sophisticated all-wheel-drive option called Quattro). It is considered a leader in safety engineering. Recommended model: A4.

VOLVO. Volvo, Sweden's largest automaker, has a reputation for safety and stodginess with its famously boxy sedans and wagons. For the last decade or so, Volvos have been decidedly upscale family cars, sturdily constructed and roomy. Volvo started selling a front-wheel-drive car, the 850 (now called the S70), only in 1993. The 70-series line has been expanded for 1998 to include an all-wheel-drive station wagon, a coupe, and a convertible. The 960 (now called the S90) is the last rear-wheel-drive Volvo; a front-wheel-drive model will replace the S90 in 1999. Both the 70- and 90-series models are available as wagons, called V70 and V90. Recommended models: S70/V70; S90/V90.

Manufacturers' telephone numbers and web sites

MAKER	TELEPHONE NUMBER	WEB SITE
Acura	800 862-2672	www.acura.com
Audi	800 822-2834	www.audi.com
BMW	800 831-1117	www.bmwusa.com
Cadillac	800 458-8006	www.cadillac.com
Chevrolet	800 222-1020	www.chevrolet.com
Chrysler	800 992-1997	www.chrysler.com
Dodge	800 992-1997	www.chrysler.com
Ford	800 392-3673	www.ford.com
GMC	800 462-8782	www.gmc.com
Honda	310 783-2000	www.honda.com
Hyundai	800 633-5151	www.hmc.co.kr
Infiniti	800 662-6200	www.infinitimotors.com
Isuzu	562 949-0320	www.isuzu.com
Jaguar	800 544-4767	www.jaguarcars.com
Jeep	800 992-1997	www.chrysler.com
Kia	800 333-4542	www.kia.com
Lexus	800 872-5398	www.lexususa.com

MAKER	TELEPHONE NUMBER	WEB SITE
Lincoln	800 392-3673	www.lincolnvehicles.com
Mazda	800 222-5500	www.mazdausa.com
Mercedes-Benz	800 222-0100	www.mercedes-benz.com
Mercury	800 392-3673	www.mercuryvehicles.com
Mitsubishi	800 222-0037	www.mitsucars.com
Nissan	800 647-7261	www.nissan-usa.com
Oldsmobile	800 442-6537	www.oldsmobile.com
Plymouth	800 992-1997	www.chrysler.com
Pontiac	800 762-2737	www.pontiac.com
Porsche	800 767-7243	www.porsche-usa.com
Saab	800 955-9007	www.saabusa.com
Saturn	800 553-6000	www.saturn.com
Subaru	800 782-2783	www.subaru.com
Suzuki	714 996-7040	www.suzukiauto.com
Toyota	800 331-4331	www.toyota.com
Volkswagen	800 822-8987	www.vw.com
Volvo	800 458-1552	www.volvo.com

CAR TYPES

CONSUMER REPORTS defines car types and body styles as much of the industry does, although we've lumped various size categories of sedans into three—small, medium, and large. Types and styles are listed alphabetically.

CONVERTIBLES. These two-door passenger cars usually have a fabric top that folds down, but some sporty versions offer a removable or retractable hardtop. **Advantages:** A sporty appearance, usually good resale value, the utmost in ventilation, and very enjoyable to drive in warm, dry weather. **Disadvantages:** Bodies tend to twist and flex on rough roads. Interior noise is often high. If the convertible has rear seats, access with the top up can be a chore. Without power assistance, putting the top up and down or removing and mounting the roof may be tedious. Some have a flexible plastic rear window that may crease or become cloudy. Trunk room is more cramped than in an equivalent sedan. Convertibles are more expensive to buy, not as secure from robbery as a fixed-roof car, and are likely to be less safe in a rollover accident. As a result, they're costlier to insure than other types of cars.

COUPES. These two-door models often are the sportier incarnation of a four-door "family" sedan. **Advantages:** Coupes normally have a sporty appearance with a roof that slopes low toward the rear. The long doors give good access to the front seats. **Disadvantages:** Rear-seat access is usually a chore. Low roof often limits headroom in rear. Doors are often heavy, and difficult to open wide enough in tight parking spaces.

HATCHBACKS. These small or medium-sized cars have a trunk lid all of a piece with the back window. Trunk space is contiguous with passenger space. **Advantages:** A practical, versatile layout that maximizes cargo space and provides a large loading door through the rear. Usually cheaper than its four-door counterpart. **Disadvantages:** Interior noise levels may be higher than in a sedan, and the rear cargo area is not as secure as an enclosed, lockable trunk. If a rear wiper/washer/defroster isn't standard, it's a worthwhile option.

MEDIUM CARS. The largest automobile segment, medium-sized sedans make a good choice for a family. **Advantages:** They're usually roomy compared with a small car and should seat five in reasonable comfort. They're often more powerful and better riding than a small car. Some specialty "sports sedans" may handle especially well. **Disadvantages:** Some may seat only four people in comfort. Towing is usually limited to light loads.

LARGE CARS. Best for highway cruising, not winding country roads, these are usually long and wide, with a powerful engine and fully equipped interior. They make a good choice as a family sedan. **Advantages:** Roomy and plush compared with smaller vehicles, these cars have a long wheelbase that helps provide a smooth ride. They'll seat five with ease, sometimes six, and they're the best choice among sedans for towing heavy loads. Their weight and bulk may provide safety advantages. Large cars are relatively inexpensive to insure. **Disadvantages:** Handling is often not very agile, and their weight makes them clumsy. Fuel economy is mediocre to poor. They're hard to park in a tight spot.

LUXURY CARS. These medium to large cars are usually very high priced. They often include a full complement of equipment, including techno toys such as a satellite-positioning system. **Advantages:** Such cars usually, but not always, provide a luxurious ride—refined and unusually quiet, with precise handling, comfortable seats, effortless power, all the latest gadgets, and plush appointments. **Disadvantages:** Such a car may cost two or three times as much as a nonluxury car without being two or three times better. Some are more ostentatious than luxurious. Besides being costly to buy, they're costly to service and insure. Fuel economy may be poor.

MINIVANS. These vehicles offer large interiors but are usually no longer than a medium-sized car. They are the most practical, utilitarian choice for moving lots of people or cargo. **Advantages:** Many have a carlike ride and are easy to drive. There's plenty of room for up to seven passengers and plenty of cargo space, especially with the seats folded down or removed. Fuel economy is generally good, considering what they can carry. Some offer all-wheel drive. **Disadvantages:** Smaller vans can take lots of people, but not their luggage. Larger minivans can take both people and cargo, but cost more to buy and fuel up.

PICKUP TRUCKS. These vehicles were meant to haul cargo, not people, so it's not surprising that most do not provide a carlike ride or decent fuel economy. Pickups are sold in far more variations than sedans—with many engine variants, diverse bed lengths, and often several cab and door configurations. **Advantages:** Some are less expensive than a car. They're able to carry loads too high or bulky or dirty for enclosed vehicles. Four-wheel drive is usually available, and they're good for towing. Some extended-cab versions offer lockable cargo space and small seats behind the front seats. **Disadvantages:** Cargo is unsecured—and uncovered in the rain. Handling is often sluggish, the ride often uncomfortable. Rear-wheel-drive-only pickups are difficult to control in wet or snowy conditions. Passenger accommodations are minimal. Fuel economy is often poor, particularly with larger trucks. Reliability is often worse than average in four-wheel-drive versions.

SPORTS CARS AND SPORTY CARS. This category includes true sports cars—two-seaters—and sports-car wannabes, the coupes and hatchbacks whose performance, handling, and looks put them in contention. These cars are often impractical but usually fun to drive. **Advantages:** Most have good acceleration and braking, plus nimble handling. Fuel economy ranges from excellent to poor. **Disadvantages:** The ride is often stiff and jarring. The cabin is usually noisy and cramped. Luggage space may be close to zero. They're often expensive to buy, service, and insure.

SPORT-UTILITY VEHICLES (SUVS). Part truck, part minivan, part car, these are a popular alternative for those who dislike minivans and conventional station wagons. **Advantages:** SUVs give a high, commanding view of the road. All offer four-wheel-drive capability for traction and stability. They're good for hauling both people and cargo. The better ones have a carlike ride and are easy to maneuver in routine driving. A good choice for towing trailers. **Disadvantages:** Many SUVs are costly to buy and maintain. They're generally ponderous and clumsy in emergency-driving situations. SUVs are tippier than cars. Four-wheel drive may be a primitive part-time system. High step-up can make access difficult. Fuel economy is usually poor. Reliability may be a problem with some makes.

STATION WAGONS. These are usually four-door passenger cars with a long roof stretching to the rear of the car and a cargo area behind the rear seat that's contiguous with the passenger space. The rear opening is usually a tailgate with a window that opens either as one piece or as two. **Advantages:** A wagon's main appeal is its large, open cargo space. Some have accessory rear (third-row) seating, so the car can carry seven people in a pinch. A wagon usually rides and handles as well as its sedan counterpart. **Disadvantages:** Wagons tend to be a little noisier inside than a similar sedan. Compared to a minivan, their cargo space is quite limited. Items left in a wagon are vulnerable to theft, since there's no trunk in which to lock them out of sight. Accessory rear seating tends to be cramped and barely usable by an adult.

GUIDE TO RELATED MODELS

To make sure they're covering the maximum number of marketing niches without having to invest too much in manufacturing plants, many manufacturers sell essentially the same car under different nameplates, or sell another manufacturer's car under their own name. Knowing about the relationships can help you shop more wisely. If you can't get a good price from your local Mercury dealer, maybe there's a Ford dealer down the street selling virtually the same car for less.

Consumer Reports refers to models made by the same automaker as "twins" and "triplets" (essentially similar), and "cousins" (less similar). "Rebadged" means one automaker has put its name on another's vehicle.

Corporate twins usually come with slightly different equipment levels, aimed at different price points in the market. For instance, Chrysler, Dodge, and Plymouth share many cars and minivans, with the Plymouth shaded toward the low-price end, Dodge aiming at the middle, and Chrysler at the high end of the line. The Jeep brand has no relatives.

Most Ford models have a Mercury equivalent. There is usually substantial overlap, with virtually identical models available at any of the different franchises. Lincoln is Ford's luxury line. Ford also builds the Nissan-designed Mercury Villager/Nissan Quest minivan. The Ford Ranger is rebadged as the Mazda B-Series pickup.

Over at GM, Chevrolet is the low-priced brand, and from there GM wants you to graduate up to Oldsmobile, Buick, and then Cadillac. Pontiacs emphasize sportiness and tend to be priced a little higher than the Chevy version of the same car. The Chevrolet Metro and Prizm are a rebadged Suzuki Swift and Toyota Corolla, respectively. In the GM truck lines, GMC is the twin of Chevrolet. The Chevrolet Tracker SUV is a rebadged Suzuki Sidekick.

Lately, General Motors has been trying to create actual distinctions rather than just marketing and cosmetic differences among its many similar cars. Examples of distant cousinhood include the Buick Century, Buick Regal, Oldsmobile Intrigue, and Pontiac Grand Prix. They share the same platform and many parts, but their appearance, feel, and personality are distinct enough for them to seem like very different cars. The Chevrolet Malibu and Oldsmobile Cutlass are more closely related.

Honda rebadges the Isuzu Rodeo sport-utility vehicle as the Honda Passport and the Isuzu Trooper as the Acura SLX. Returning the favor, Isuzu sells the Honda Odyssey minivan as the Isuzu Oasis.

Among the European nameplates, Audi is the luxury division of Volkswagen. The Audi A4 and A6 are upscale cousins of the VW Passat.

Twins, triplets, and cousins

MODEL	RELATED MODEL OR MODELS
SMALL CARS	
Chevrolet Cavalier	Pontiac Sunfire
Chevrolet Metro	Suzuki Swift
Chevrolet Prizm	Toyota Corolla
Dodge Neon	Plymouth Neon
Ford Escort	Mercury Tracer
Mercury Tracer	Ford Escort
Plymouth Neon	Dodge Neon
Pontiac Sunfire	Chevrolet Cavalier
Suzuki Swift	Chevrolet Metro
Toyota Corolla	Chevrolet Prizm
SPORTY CARS	
Chevrolet Camaro	Pontiac Firebird
Pontiac Firebird	Chevrolet Camaro
MEDIUM CARS	
Audi A4, A6	Volkswagen Passat
Buick Century	Buick Regal, Oldsmobile Intrigue, Pontiac Grand Prix
Buick Regal	Buick Century, Oldsmobile Intrigue, Pontiac Grand Prix
Chevrolet Malibu	Oldsmobile Cutlass, Pontiac Grand Am
Chrysler Cirrus	Dodge Stratus, Plymouth Breeze
Dodge Stratus	Chrysler Cirrus, Plymouth Breeze
Ford Contour	Mercury Mystique
Ford Taurus	Mercury Sable
Infiniti I30	Nissan Maxima
Lexus ES300	Toyota Camry
Mercury Mystique	Ford Contour
Mercury Sable	Ford Taurus
Nissan Maxima	Infiniti I30
Oldsmobile Cutlass	Chevrolet Malibu, Pontiac Grand Am
Oldsmobile Intrigue	Buick Century, Buick Regal, Pontiac Grand Prix
Plymouth Breeze	Chrysler Cirrus, Dodge Stratus
Pontiac Grand Am	Chevrolet Malibu, Oldsmobile Cutlass
Pontiac Grand Prix	Buick Century, Buick Regal, Oldsmobile Intrigue
Toyota Camry	Lexus ES300
Volkswagen Passat	Audi A4, A6
LARGE CARS	
Chrysler Concorde, LHS, 300M	Dodge Intrepid
Dodge Intrepid	Chrysler Concorde, LHS, 300M
Ford Crown Victoria	Mercury Grand Marquis
Mercury Grand Marquis	Ford Crown Victoria
COUPES	
Chrysler Sebring	Dodge Avenger
Dodge Avenger	Chrysler Sebring

MODEL	RELATED MODEL OR MODELS
MINIVANS	
Chevrolet Astro	GMC Safari
Chevrolet Venture	Oldsmobile Silhouette, Pontiac Trans Sport
Chrysler Town & Country	Dodge Grand Caravan, Plymouth Grand Voyager
Dodge Caravan	Plymouth Voyager
Dodge Grand Caravan	Chrysler Town & Country, Plymouth Grand Voyager
GMC Safari	Chevrolet Astro
Honda Odyssey	Isuzu Oasis
Isuzu Oasis	Honda Odyssey
Mercury Villager	Nissan Quest
Nissan Quest	Mercury Villager
Oldsmobile Silhouette	Chevrolet Venture, Pontiac Trans Sport
Plymouth Grand Voyager	Chrysler Town & Country, Dodge Grand Caravan
Plymouth Voyager	Dodge Caravan
Pontiac Trans Sport	Chevrolet Venture, Oldsmobile Silhouette
SPORT-UTILITY VEHICLES	
Acura SLX	Isuzu Trooper
Chevrolet Blazer	GMC Jimmy, Oldsmobile Bravada
Chevrolet Suburban	GMC Suburban
Chevrolet Tahoe	GMC Yukon
Chevrolet Tracker	Suzuki Sidekick
Ford Expedition	Lincoln Navigator
Ford Explorer	Mercury Mountaineer
GMC Jimmy	Chevrolet Blazer, Oldsmobile Bravada
GMC Suburban	Chevrolet Suburban
GMC Yukon	Chevrolet Tahoe
Honda Passport	Isuzu Rodeo
Infiniti QX4	Nissan Pathfinder
Isuzu Rodeo	Honda Passport
Isuzu Trooper	Acura SLX
Lexus LX470	Toyota Land Cruiser
Lincoln Navigator	Ford Expedition
Mercury Mountaineer	Ford Explorer
Nissan Pathfinder	Infiniti QX4
Oldsmobile Bravada	Chevrolet Blazer, GMC Jimmy
Suzuki Sidekick	Chevrolet Tracker
Toyota Land Cruiser	Lexus LX470
PICKUP TRUCKS	
Chevrolet C/K	GMC Sierra
Chevrolet S-10	GMC Sonoma, Isuzu Hombre
Ford Ranger	Mazda B-Series
GMC Sierra	Chevrolet C/K
GMC Sonoma	Chevrolet S-10, Isuzu Hombre
Isuzu Hombre	Chevrolet S-10, GMC Sonoma
Mazda B-Series	Ford Ranger

BUY *or* LEASE

SHOPPING BASICS

Shopping for a new car can be intimidating. Probably one big reason why Saturn has consistently turned up near the top of our dealer-satisfaction surveys is its no-haggle policy. Saturns, however, have a high markup, at least $1,000 above what you might negotiate for an equivalent car.

You needn't be a skilled haggler to negotiate a good deal. You just have to shop around—the most basic tenet for getting the best price.

Another basic tenet is do your research. Decide on the vehicles and equipment you want, and find out what they cost the dealer.

Whether you buy or lease, here are some basics:

NARROW YOUR CHOICES. The profiles beginning on page 80 can help. Pay special attention to CONSUMER REPORTS' recommended models. We chose them because they performed competently in our tests and because they've proven at least reasonably reliable.

Some basically similar models from the same car company are available under more than one nameplate. If you can't find a Dodge Caravan at a good price, for example, check out the similar Plymouth Voyager. Besides the Chevrolet Cavalier, consider the Pontiac Sunfire. See page 23 for a guide on identifying such siblings.

CHECK OUT YOUR PICKS. Use the pages of this book, and pick up brochures at showrooms. All automakers and many dealers have an Internet web site where you can find specs and order literature.

TAKE SOME TEST DRIVES. On the road, see how the cars measure up. It's important that the driving position is comfortable and that the driver's seat is adjustable and accommodates everyone who will be driving the car. Be sure that you have a clear view in all directions and that there are no serious blind spots. Try the controls and the safety belt—they should be easy to use. Other factors to consider are whether or not it's difficult to get in and out of the rear seat, the roominess of the trunk, and how convenient the cargo area is to load. Drive the vehicle over good roads and bad to get a feel for the ride and noise level.

CONSIDER RENTING A VIABLE PROSPECT FOR A DAY OR TWO. For a relatively small investment, you might discover flaws, such as an uncomfortable seat or inconvenient controls, that a short test drive won't reveal. Some models may be hard to find in rental fleets, especially in rural areas, but it's worth a try.

DECIDE ON THE OPTIONS. For guidance, see "New equipment & designs," on page 43, and "Getting there safely," on page 57.

TALK TO YOUR INSURANCE AGENT. You may be surprised at the difference in premiums between seemingly comparable models. If you're thinking of leasing, ask about the cost of higher insurance coverage required under many lease contracts. For more on insurance, see page 36.

WHEN DEPRECIATION MATTERS

The value of a new car plummets the minute you drive it off the dealer's lot. The average car loses more than one-third of its value after three years and then depreciates more slowly.

The shape of the depreciation curve has several implications. It matters most if you buy or lease a new car every two or three years, since those first years are the most expensive years of the car's life. If you keep a car for most or all of its useful life, depreciation matters less. A used car is cheaper than a new one because someone else has paid for those most expensive years.

Because of depreciation, a good-performing, reliable two- or three-year-old car is often the best automotive value you'll find, particularly if you plan to own the car for a while.

Supply and demand in the used-car market help determine how quickly a car

TYPICAL DEPRECIATION CURVE

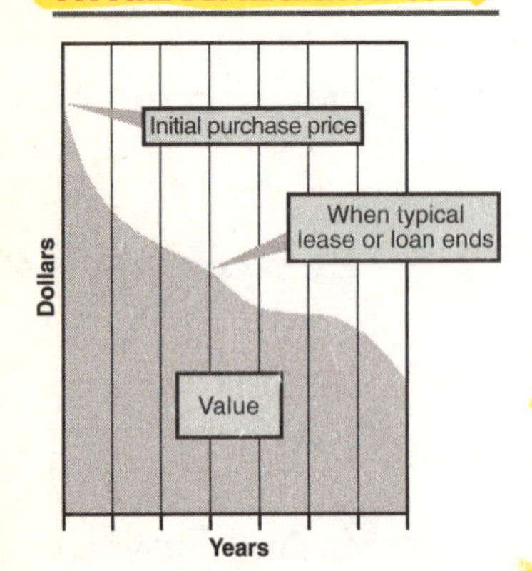

Average depreciation for vehicle type

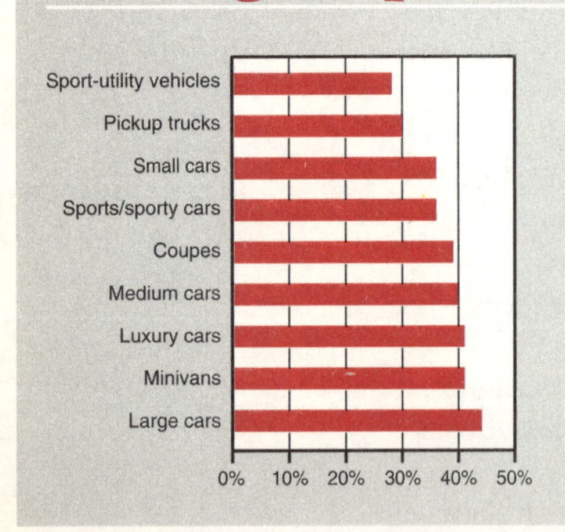

LOWEST DEPRECIATION AFTER 3 YEARS (20% OR LESS)

Chevrolet Suburban
GMC Suburban
Dodge Ram 1500
Chevrolet C/K 1500
GMC Sierra C/K 1500
Chevrolet Tahoe
GMC Yukon
Toyota Land Cruiser
Toyota 4Runner 4WD

HIGHEST DEPRECIATION AFTER 3 YEARS (50% OR MORE)

Infiniti Q45
Lincoln Continental
Lincoln Mark VIII
Mitsubishi Diamante

Source: CONSUMER REPORTS *comparison of 1995 list prices with late-1997 trade-in prices.*

loses value, so not all vehicles depreciate at the same rate. Certain types of vehicles hold their value better than other types, as the graph at the bottom of page 26 shows. As a group, sport-utility vehicles and pickups keep their value the best, and large cars are the biggest losers.

If you buy a car that holds its value well, it will be worth more when you sell it or trade it in. If you lease the vehicle, low depreciation may translate into lower monthly payments, other things being equal. Conversely, a model that depreciates quickly in its early years could be a good value to someone buying it used.

To help you factor depreciation into your buying decision, we give a prediction of depreciation for most models in the car profiles that begin on page 80.

CAR-SHOPPING ONLINE

Car shoppers who go online have a gigantic resource for research and even buying. You'll want to be selective about which sites you visit. You'll find hundreds of sites with specs, colors, prices, and names of nearby dealers. But you'll also run into all the usual Internet problems:

TOO MUCH INFORMATION. You can waste hours wandering around online.

NOT ENOUGH INFORMATION. Many sites are regional, incomplete, or amateurish. Others are clearly commercial. Carmakers and car dealers are unlikely to let you know the dealer's invoice price—you'll just get list prices. For tips on getting the best price, see page 28.

UNCERTAIN QUALITY OF INFORMATION. It may not be up-to-date. Search results are only as good as the information being searched. And you don't always know the biases of the presenter; sites that refer you to dealers typically get fees from the dealers, for instance. So in many ways, shopping online isn't so different from shopping elsewhere. You have to keep your wits about you. Here are the kinds of locales you'll find:

AUTOMAKER SITES. Every maker has one. Regard them as elaborate ads with links to dealers. You'll find lots of details about the cars, but only the manufacturer's suggested retail prices.

BUYING SERVICES. The four biggest—Auto-By-Tel, AutoVantage, Autoweb.com, and CarPoint—offer a firm quote that's faxed or e-mailed from them or a dealer in your area, freeing you from haggling. You get a "best offer" or "preferred price"—probably less than list, but not necessarily the best you could get if you shop around. Such sites provide other services and links, including information on dealer costs, financing, insurance, and used-car classifieds.

PRICE AND LEASING GUIDES. Familiar printed guides like Kelley Blue Book and Edmund's provide prices online. Intellichoice does, too, along with information on leasing. LeaseSource sells LeaseWizard software and includes an interactive way to evaluate lease deals.

SAFETY INFORMATION. The web sites of the National Highway Traffic Safety Administration (NHTSA) and the Insurance Institute for Highway Safety (IIHS) include crash-test results and other safety information. NHTSA's site provides recall information and a way to report safety problems.

CONSUMER REPORTS ONLINE. Site subscribers to *www.ConsumerReports.org* can find an interactive search engine, plus a used-car database. A listing of auto recalls is free.

HOW TO BUY A CAR

Falling in love with a car is a sure way to overpay. Look at several cars, and be ready to walk away from a deal that's not sweet enough.

HOW MUCH DID THE DEALER PAY?

Before you visit a showroom, determine how much room you have for negotiating. That means finding out the dealer's cost, or invoice price.

The Consumer Reports New Car Price Service offers more precise price information (see inside back cover). It provides a printout of sticker and invoice prices for the car and its factory options. And it spells out any factory "incentives," such as rebates or low-interest loans. The service can also provide the trade-in value of your current car.

Other price sources offer different levels of detail. Price guides at bookstores, newsstands, and libraries usually don't include incentives, and midyear price changes can quickly make such guides obsolete. Automobile clubs also offer prices, usually for a moderate fee. And prices are available on the Internet (see page 27).

BARGAINING ROOM

The difference between the sticker price and the dealer's wholesale cost is the room you have to bargain. Bargaining room differs from car to car, depending on the carmaker's selling strategy. The graph shows how it varies by vehicle type. Note that with rebates and other promotions, you can sometimes buy a car for less than the invoice price.

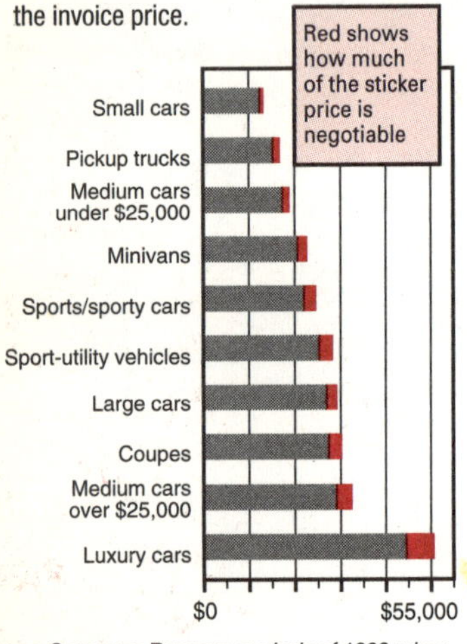

Source: CONSUMER REPORTS *analysis of 1998 prices.*

NO-NONSENSE NEGOTIATING

When you decide on a model, shop at three or four dealers. Some dealers may be more willing to operate on a smaller profit margin.

Don't let the salesperson coax you into naming a price or a monthly payment you can afford. State that you want the dealer's best price now, and that you'll be back only if that price is the lowest. Having the invoice price gives you a decided advantage. If your figures are challenged, ask to see the dealer's figures.

Don't put down a deposit, and resist pressure to buy immediately. A deal that's good today should be good tomorrow. Take notes to be sure you're pricing comparably equipped cars.

Keep the negotiations for the new car and your trade-in separate. Otherwise, the salesperson may quote an irresistible price on the new car but undervalue your trade, or vice versa.

WHAT'S A FAIR PRICE?

How much over invoice you can expect to pay depends on the demand for the model you want. Typically, you can buy models in ample supply for 4 to 8 percent over invoice. (Deduct any factory rebates from the invoice price.) But you may have to pay much more for high-demand models such as the Lincoln Navigator, Honda Accord, and Volkswagen New Beetle. Some leftover models at year's end—and even some current slow-moving models—may sell for less than invoice.

One way to gauge supply and demand is to shop around and see how many of the cars you're interested in are on the dealer's lot. Prices are another clue: When dealers are desperate to unload an unpopular model, price quotes tumble.

If you see a line on the sticker that says "ADM," or additional dealer markup, ignore it. Some dealers use this gimmick to inflate the price, typically by $500 or more. When our reporter asked a Chevrolet salesman in Seattle about ADM, he readily admitted that it's fantasy, but added that "every once in a while somebody pays it, no questions asked."

Another tricky item is the advertising charge that's imposed on some dealers by manufacturers' zone offices—and passed on to car buyers. This charge, typically $200 to $400, varies from region to region and model to model—and it doesn't show up in price guides. You can try to negotiate this, but don't get your hopes up. If the charge is exorbitant, consider a different make and model.

The destination charge is the cost of shipping the car from the factory to the dealer. It's a legitimate charge, and it's non-negotiable.

Don't buy an extended warranty, which adds coverage beyond the manufacturer's three or four years. It's not worth the money.

If a dealer complains about skimpy profits, don't feel too sorry. Dealers have other sources of income besides new-car sales: They make money on any financing or insurance they sell, on cars traded in, and on service, parts, and repairs. Most automakers also give their dealers a "holdback" of 2 or 3 percent of the sticker price for each vehicle sold.

TRADING IN

You can usually get a better price by advertising and selling your old car privately. But having strangers come to your home and drive your car is a hassle many people would rather avoid.

How good is the dealer?

When you buy a car, the dealer can have a major effect on how happy you are with the deal. According to responses to Consumer Reports' 1997 Annual Questionnaire, some dealers just do it better. And the best dealers aren't necessarily the ones who sell the costliest models, as Saturn's number-two position in the table shows. The table shows not only overall satisfaction with the brand, but also the range of satisfaction for the models within a brand. Average satisfaction and range of satisfaction are based on more than 110,000 new-car purchases. Circles show the averages of 1996 models with 100 or more responses. Data are adjusted for age, since older buyers tend to be more satisfied than younger ones.

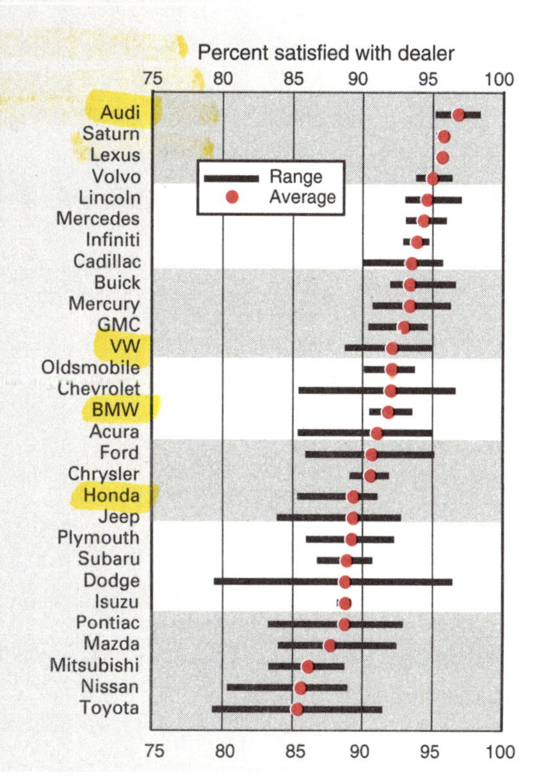

To get an idea of how much your old car is worth, whether from a dealer or in a private sale, you can use the Consumer Reports Used Car Price Service (see page 256) or other guides available at libraries, newsstands, and bookstores, and on the Internet. The monthly National Automobile Dealers Association Official Used Car Guide is widely used by the industry as well as by private sellers.

Beware of salespeople who refer to price guides with plain-paper covers and lowball prices. (They may display phony high-price guides when they deal with used-car buyers.) Be suspicious if a figure quoted by the salesperson differs widely from those in our price service or in other established price guides.

Before you shop for a new car, you can also visit several dealers and find out what they'd pay for your car in a straight cash sale. That should give you a realistic idea of the wholesale value of your car in your area.

If you're selling your old car privately, it may pay to make any needed repairs beforehand. Having the car "detailed"—polished, waxed, and cleaned up throughout—for $100 or so may also be a good investment.

FINANCING

By far the cheapest way to buy a car is to pay cash. But if you're financing your car, check the interest rates at banks and your credit union before you accept the dealer's financing. Ask about special promotions in which a manufacturer subsidizes interest rates on selected models. And refuse credit life insurance; it's costly protection you probably don't need.

Buy, borrow, or lease?

To get behind the wheel of a new car, most people either finance or lease. Spreading out the payments over time makes the cost bearable. In return, whether you lease or you borrow, you pay financing charges.

The table at right compares major out-of-pocket costs for three strategies:

1. You buy a $20,000 car outright and keep it for six years.
2. You take out a five-year loan for the car, and trade it in on an identical model after three years.
3. You lease the car for three years, then lease another car under identical terms for another three years.

The assumption for the strategies are spelled out below the table.

Financing comes out slightly better than leasing, but differences in the length of the loan or financing charges can tip the balance either way. Buying with cash is always cheapest.

Because of depreciation, anyone who jumps from one new car into another every three years will pay more than someone who wrings value out of a car by owning it most of its life.

ACQUISITION STRATEGIES COMPARED

	1. BUY AND KEEP	2. FINANCE AND TRADE	3. LEASE AND LEASE AGAIN
Money up front (initial cost, down payment, or lease start-up)	$20,000	$4,000	$2,082
Monthly payment	$0	$330 for 3 years, $315 for next 3	$307 for 6 years
Total cost minus value of car (if owned)			
After 3 years	$10,211	$12,202	$13,667
After 6 years	$17,666	$25,660	$28,845

Assumptions behind this table: Money up front does not include title, taxes, registration. Lease start-up assumes $1,000 down and $1,082 in other fees for each lease. Lease and loan have interest rate or equivalent of 8.75 percent. Total cost includes opportunity cost of 3.5 percent per year in forgone interest on money used for purchase, down payment, or lease start-up. Total cost for lease includes $350 end-of-lease fee. Depreciation is 40 percent after 3 years, 60 percent after 6. "Finance and trade" assumes first car used as $4,754.12 down payment on second car. To cover out-of-warranty repairs on car kept for 6 years, $1,000 added.

HOW TO LEASE A CAR

Leasing appeals to many because of the lure of low monthly payments, but it has no inherent advantage unless you can claim your payments as a tax deduction. If you get a new car every three or four years, your overall cost of ownership will be about the same whether you lease or buy—if you're sharp enough to spot the pitfalls in the contract. If you keep a car longer, leasing usually makes less sense.

Monthly lease payments are lower than car-loan payments because you pay only for the car's depreciation during the lease, plus interest and fees. Leasing can let you drive a car you can't afford to buy. But at the end of the lease, you're a pedestrian.

BEWARE OF BOOBY TRAPS. CONSUMER REPORTS' visits to dozens of new-car dealers found that most are actively pushing leasing. That's no surprise, since leasing offers far more opportunities for dealers to make money. For example, high surcharges for excess mileage or wear and tear could pose a nasty surprise for you at the end of the lease.

Comparing leasing costs can be difficult because you may not have access to needed information. Last summer and fall, one of our reporters visited 34 dealers in five states. Of those, 27 refused to disclose lease terms beyond the monthly payment.

As of January 1998, a standardized federal disclosure form requires dealers to spell out many items. You can find the form at the Federal Reserve Board's web site, along with information on shopping for a lease.

The form provides useful information—if the dealer provides it. (Legally, the dealer doesn't have to hand over the form until you're about to sign the contract.) In visits to five Los Angeles dealers soon after the disclosure rule took effect, our reporter was unable to extract a single completed disclosure form. One dealer offered a blank form; another professed to know nothing about the form at all.

Lease terms defined

WHAT THE DEALERS SAY	WHAT THEY MEAN
Acquisition or bank fee	A fee (average: $350) you pay to the dealer or bank to initiate the lease. Usually not negotiable.
Annual mileage allowance	You'll have to pay extra for any excess. The mileage limit is negotiable.
Gross capitalized cost	Price of the car that the lease is based on, plus all items and services in the lease. Negotiable.
Capitalized-cost reduction	Down payment. Negotiable.
Disposal or disposition fee	A fee you pay if you don't buy the car at end of lease. Sometimes negotiable.
Excess wear and tear	A fee you often pay for car damage at end of lease. Not negotiable—but have the dealer define this clearly in writing. Your "normal" may be his "excess."
GAP insurance	Guaranteed Auto Protection. Pays balance on the lease and early-termination penalties if the car is totaled or stolen. Often included, or negotiable.
Lease charge or money factor	Akin to the annual percentage rate on a loan. When multiplied by 2,400, it approximates the annual percentage rate. Not negotiable, but varies from lease to lease.
Purchase fee	A fee (average: $250) you pay if you buy the car at end of lease. Negotiable.
Purchase-option price	The price you pay to buy the car at end of lease. Negotiable.
Residual value	Car's estimated value at end of lease. Not negotiable.
Subvented lease	A lease that's subsidized, usually by the automaker. Not negotiable.

Legally, the dealer doesn't have to hand over the form until you're about to sign the contract, and dealers appear to be taking full advantage of that rule. One Toyota salesman said, "You'll get the form when we get a deposit." If you get that kind of response, we suggest you walk out.

NEGOTIATING A LEASE. Any car lease spells out a term (typically two to four years), an annual mileage allowance (typically 10,000 to 15,000 miles), and the amount of each monthly payment. Under the new federal disclosure rules, the lease must also quote the "residual value"—an estimate of what the car will be worth at the lease's end. Be prepared to live with the terms of the contract. Terminating early can set you back thousands of dollars.

Start negotiations with the price of the car. Find out the dealer-invoice price, and bargain as if you were buying the car. Then negotiate other lease items (see "Lease terms defined" on page 31).

Differences in the "money factor"—essentially a finance charge—may seem insignificant. The money factor offered by different lease companies on a three-year lease of a 1998 Chevrolet Lumina last winter typically ranged from 0.00310 to 0.00431. But when you convert those money factors to a roughly equivalent interest rate—multiply by 2,400—that translates to a low of 7.4 and a high of 10.3 percent.

Before you sign, make sure all provisions are accurately described and that any trade-in shows up as a deduction from the total amount you owe.

'SUBVENTED' LEASES. Automakers and some leasing companies target specific vehicles for cut-rate leases, often advertised nationally. These models can be a good deal.

LOOKING FOR VALUE: CAMRY VS. LEXUS

Over the years CONSUMER REPORTS has tested autos, more and more models have crowded into the top tiers of the Ratings. That's not surprising, since the car is a "mature" product whose engineering problems and dilemmas are well-known and have been solved more or less successfully many times over. In general, cars today are safer, perform better, and include as standard many items that were once high-priced options. In that way, most of today's cars represent good value.

The best values are models pretty close to the middle of the market: midsized, midpriced sedans costing around $20,000. That hotly competitive and big-selling segment encompasses many very good and even excellent cars, as you can see from checking the Ratings on page 76.

So if $20,000 or $25,000 can buy you an excellent, well-appointed car, what do you gain by spending $30,000 or $35,000? Or $45,000?

You could compare, say, the Honda Civic and the Mercedes E320, the cheapest and the most expensive cars that CONSUMER REPORTS rated best-in-class. But the Toyota Camry LE and its corporate cousin the Lexus ES300 present a particularly interesting case study because they're so similar. They share many parts, including the chassis. Both come with lots of standard equipment, including air conditioning, antilock brakes, cruise control, and power windows, locks, and mirrors.

Both cars have excelled in CONSUMER REPORTS' tests, particularly when the Camry is equipped with its optional V6 engine, something that's standard on the Lexus. Both handle well, though neither is particularly taut or sporty. Both have a quiet, supple ride. Inside the Camry, the cabin is well designed, the controls and displays are just about ideal, and the front seats are quite comfortable. The Lexus is even quieter. The front seats are a touch more accommodating, though the rear is a bit more cramped.

The Lexus ES300 starts at $30,790, but almost invariably comes with options that push the price past $34,000. The Camry LE V6 starts at $22,558. Equipping the Camry with options that make it more equivalent to the Lexus—keyless entry, alloy wheels, leather seats, traction control, side air bags—pushes its price to just over $25,000.

Here's what the extra $9,000 or so buys in a Lexus:

- A longer warranty, with roadside assistance.
- A slightly more comfortable car.
- Some luxury features not available on the Camry LE, like power seats, an automatic climate-control system, and a Nakamichi audio system.
- Better treatment by the dealer when you buy the car.
- The Lexus nameplate.

With a Lexus, you have a more valuable asset as it depreciates. But being more valuable, it will cost more to insure. The extra money buys nothing much in performance, safety, or reliability. Given the Camry's excellent reliability, the Lexus's more generous warranty is not the advantage it first seems. And if you choose a four-cylinder Camry LE and skip the extra options, you'll have a car nearly as good—a little slower, not as cushy or as whisper-quiet—for $20,640 instead of $34,535 for the Lexus.

WARRANTIES COMPARED

Not so many years ago, a new-car warranty lasted for 12 months or 12,000 miles, whichever came first, and that was all you could expect if anything went wrong with your new car. Automakers still use the whichever-comes-first ploy, but now at least the standard new-car warranty lasts three years or 36,000 miles. And these days a warranty tends to be quite comprehensive, covering everything but normal wear-and-tear items—tires, wipers, brake pads, filters, and such. Three of the German automakers (Audi, BMW, and Volkswagen) throw in free maintenance—including all the fluids and filters—for the first three years as well. A few makes, mostly luxury nameplates such as Acura, BMW, Cadillac, Lexus, and Mercedes, offer a basic warranty that runs for four years or 50,000 miles.

Except for emergencies, you must normally have warranty work performed at an authorized dealer for your make of car, although it doesn't have to be the dealer that sold you the car in the first place. You can still have routine maintenance such as oil changes performed by a local garage or other repair facility—or

Auto warranties compared

NAMEPLATE	BASIC WARRANTY	DRIVETRAIN	RUST-THROUGH	ROADSIDE AID
Acura	4 years/50,000 miles	4 years/50,000 miles	5 years/unlimited	4 years/50,000 miles
Audi	3 years/50,000 miles	3 years/50,000 miles	10 years/unlimited	3 years/unlimited
BMW	4 years/50,000 miles	4 years/50,000 miles	6 years/unlimited	4 years/50,000 miles
Buick	3 years/36,000 miles	3 years/36,000 miles	6 years/100,000 miles	3 years/36,000 miles
Cadillac	4 years/50,000 miles	4 years/50,000 miles	6 years/100,000 miles	4 years/50,000 miles
Chevrolet	3 years/36,000 miles	3 years/36,000 miles	6 years/100,000 miles	3 years/36,000 miles *
Chrysler	3 years/36,000 miles	3 years/36,000 miles	5 years/100,000 miles	3 years/36,000 miles
Dodge	3 years/36,000 miles	3 years/36,000 miles	5 years/100,000 miles	3 years/36,000 miles
Ford	3 years/36,000 miles	3 years/36,000 miles	5 years/unlimited	3 years/36,000 miles
GMC	3 years/36,000 miles	3 years/36,000 miles	6 years/100,000 miles	3 years/36,000 miles
Honda	3 years/36,000 miles	3 years/36,000 miles	5 years/unlimited	Limited
Hyundai	3 years/36,000 miles	5 years/60,000 miles	5 years/100,000 miles	3 years/36,000 miles
Infiniti	4 years/60,000 miles	6 years/70,000 miles	7 years/unlimited	4 years/unlimited
Isuzu	3 years/50,000 miles	5 years/60,000 miles	6 years/100,000 miles	5 years/60,000 miles
Jaguar	4 years/50,000 miles	4 years/50,000 miles	6 years/unlimited	4 years/50,000 miles
Jeep	3 years/36,000 miles	3 years/36,000 miles	5 years/100,000 miles	3 years/36,000 miles
Kia	3 years/36,000 miles	5 years/60,000 miles	5 years/100,000 miles	3 years/36,000 miles
Land Rover	4 years/50,000 miles	4 years/50,000 miles	6 years/unlimited	4 years/50,000 miles
Lexus	4 years/50,000 miles	6 years/70,000 miles	6 years/unlimited	4 years/unlimited
Lincoln	4 years/50,000 miles	4 years/50,000 miles	5 years/unlimited	4 years/50,000 miles
Mazda	3 years/50,000 miles	3 years/50,000 miles	5 years/unlimited	Varies
Mercedes-Benz	4 years/50,000 miles	4 years/50,000 miles	4 years/50,000 miles	Unlimited
Mercury	3 years/36,000 miles	3 years/36,000 miles	5 years/unlimited	3 years/36,000 miles
Mitsubishi	3 years/36,000 miles	5 years/60,000 miles	7 years/100,000 miles	Limited
Nissan	3 years/36,000 miles	5 years/60,000 miles	5 years/unlimited	Limited
Oldsmobile	3 years/36,000 miles	3 years/36,000 miles	6 years/100,000 miles	3 years/36,000 miles
Plymouth	3 years/36,000 miles	3 years/36,000 miles	5 years/100,000 miles	3 years/36,000 miles
Pontiac	3 years/36,000 miles	3 years/36,000 miles	6 years/100,000 miles	3 years/36,000 miles
Porsche	2 years/unlimited	2 years/unlimited	10 years/unlimited	2 years/unlimited
Saab	4 years/50,000 miles	4 years/50,000 miles	6 years/unlimited	4 years/50,000 miles
Saturn	3 years/36,000 miles	3 years/36,000 miles	6 years/100,000 miles	Limited
Subaru	3 years/36,000 miles	5 years/60,000 miles	5 years/unlimited	Limited
Suzuki	3 years/36,000 miles	3 years/36,000 miles	3 years/unlimited	Limited
Toyota	3 years/36,000 miles	5 years/60,000 miles	5 years/unlimited	Limited
Volkswagen	2 years/24,000 miles	10 years/100,000 miles	6 years/unlimited	2 years/unlimited
Volvo	4 years/50,000 miles	4 years/50,000 miles	8 years/unlimited	4 years/50,000 miles

** = Charge for this service.*

you can even do it yourself—without jeopardizing your warranty, as long as you keep service records and receipts and the work is done properly.

Warranties from some foreign automakers cover the drivetrain (the engine, transmission, and driveshaft) two or more years longer than the basic warranty does. In the last few years, "corrosion" warranties have become the norm. Surface rust isn't covered, but if a body panel rusts through, it's repaired or replaced free. That sounds generous, but in these days of factory-applied rustproofing and galvanized-steel body panels, the automakers aren't really taking much of a risk. Rust-through coverage usually lasts for five to ten years and for 100,000 or more miles.

Another common warranty feature that has grown popular in the past few years is roadside assistance. If you break down, lock yourself out, or run out of fuel, you can call an 800 number for help. Often, roadside assistance is comprehensive and free regardless of the trouble. The terms vary—check with the dealer or carmaker. In most cases, towing is free only if a warrantied part causes the breakdown. Towing may not be free if the car has been vandalized or was in a collision. If you're covered for towing another way—through an insurance policy or an auto club—then the warranty terms don't matter as much.

Under federal regulations, automakers must warrant all the emissions-related equipment—several dozen parts from the engine intake manifold all the way back to the tailpipe—for two years or 24,000 miles. Some emissions-related components, such as the catalytic converter and electronic emissions-control units, are covered for eight years or 80,000 miles. California requirements are more stringent still.

In most cases, an extended-service contract is nothing more than overpriced breakdown insurance. Coverage may not kick in until after the manufacturer's warranty expires. An extended-service contract might make sense for cars with a shoddy reliability record, but why buy a trouble-prone car?

SECRET WARRANTIES

If a design defect is serious enough to prompt a federally mandated recall, owners of the affected vehicles are notified by mail. But even if a defect doesn't trigger the recall machinery, manufacturers often decide to pay for repairing some particular defect on their own.

Of course, that free-repair policy doesn't do much good for the car's owners unless they know about it. In most states, owners often learn about these "secret warranties" only after persistent complaining to their dealer about the problem.

Another way you can find out about a secret warranty is to keep track of the manufacturer's technical service bulletins, which are regularly sent to dealers. Service bulletins are also available from the National Highway Traffic Safety Administration (800 424-9393, or on the web at *www.nhtsa.dot.gov*) and from private watchdog groups like the Center for Auto Safety (2001 S Street NW, Suite 410, Washington, D.C. 20009).

Consumer Reports has long believed that secret warranties are unfair. They give the impression that a dealer is being generous by fixing a problem free, when the truth is that the manufacturer has built a defective car that ought to be fixed. Besides that, secret warranties discriminate against the people who don't find out about them.

BUYING AUTO INSURANCE

It's a good time to shop for better insurance rates. Nearly all the major companies have begun reducing their premiums in some areas. The industry leader, State Farm Mutual Automobile Insurance Company, has led the way, cutting prices in 31 states and the District of Columbia in 1997, and in another 12 states so far in 1998. Most of the reductions have been modest, ranging from a few dollars to a few hundred dollars a year—not much to reverse the tripling in premiums of the last two decades.

Rates are still rising, however, in some states—and in parts of states where the overall average is lower—because repair, medical care, and legal costs continue to rise. And there has been no relief for most drivers in New Jersey, which continues to have the highest rates. According to one trade group, the Insurance Information Institute, rates will drop overall by an average of 1 percent in 1998, to $692 for the average policy.

Still, some of the cuts have been substantial: State Farm dropped its rates in Hawaii by 15 percent in January 1998, and the Hartford Financial Services Group, the 11th-largest auto insurer, lowered its rates in California by 30 percent in February. The bigger, more efficient companies have seen their claims fall most and have generally made the biggest cuts, analysts say, partly to hold or gain market share.

All this helps explain why you can find such a big spread in rates for identical coverage. A CONSUMER REPORTS study in seven big states found more than a fourfold difference in prices for identical coverage from different insurers. The study also found that buying from one of the bigger-name insurance companies is no guarantee you'll get the best rate. This section will describe some of the factors to consider when buying auto insurance, and how (and how not) to save yourself money.

These days, car buyers can use all the help they can get in choosing car insurance. Most states require all drivers to have it, assuring the insurance companies of a huge captive market. Companies have devised arcane ways to use that advantage to extract the highest premiums they can. Using customized computer databases, they can now evaluate each prospective policyholder and charge premiums presumably tailored to the risk they believe each driver poses.

The premium you pay depends on dozens of variables. Driving an expensive high-performance car, getting nabbed for moving violations, putting a lot of mileage on your car's odometer each year, and having a young driver at home will run up your insurance costs sharply.

But you should know, too, that the industry considers other personal variables when determining your premium, such as your marital status or credit history, what you do for a living, whether you own a home or rent, and, if you're not a U.S. citizen, your country of origin. Alter any detail, and the cost of your policy can change dramatically.

Consumers haven't been able to complain effectively about arbitrary or discriminatory factors because it's virtually impossible to tell how their rates are set. With hundreds of insurance companies writing policies offering a bewildering variety of coverage options, shopping for a policy has become such a confusing ordeal that many people don't bother.

KNOW THE COVERAGE YOU NEED

Don't waste money on coverage you can do without. Remember, insurance is intended to protect you from serious losses. You can cut your premiums substantially by raising your policy's deductibles. Many insurers raise rates after a claim, so you won't want to file for a loss you can afford to pay yourself. Here are the coverage choices you will face when you buy an auto policy, and our advice on how you can save money:

BODILY-INJURY LIABILITY. In an accident where you are found to have been at fault, this pays for the medical treatments, rehabilitation, or funeral costs incurred by another driver, the other driver's passengers, passengers in your car, and pedestrians. It also pays legal costs and settlements for non-monetary losses (pain and suffering). Coverage limits can be as low as your state requires and as high as $500,000 per person and $1 million per accident.

If you have a home, bank accounts, and a reasonably well-paying job, buy at least $100,000 per person, $300,000 per accident. Buy less only if you have little income or few assets to protect. If a court ruled you owed more, you might have to dip into your other assets, so it may make sense to have supplemental coverage through an umbrella policy. This insurance pays for losses beyond what's protected by an auto or homeowner's policy. A $1 million policy costs about $200 a year.

PROPERTY-DAMAGE LIABILITY. This covers repair or replacement of other people's vehicles or property that someone insured on your policy damages in an accident. Each state requires drivers to have property-damage liability coverage up to certain specified limits, typically $15,000 per accident.

You can buy up to $100,000 worth of this coverage. In many parts of the country, the minimums don't come close to covering potential losses. Here, too, an umbrella policy would provide the extra margin of safety you need.

COLLISION AND COMPREHENSIVE. Collision pays for the repair of your car or replacement of its market value, regardless of who was at fault. Comprehensive pays for replacement or repairs after your car has been damaged as a result of events such as fire, flood, and windstorm, or theft.

Most insurers sell this coverage (with deductibles) in increments of $250, typically up to a $1000 deductible. Buy this if your car is less than four years old or worth more than about $4000. The bigger the deductible you're willing to live with, the cheaper the coverage. We recommend a minimum collision deductible of $500.

MEDICAL PAYMENTS. Also called "med pay," this pays physicians and hospital bills, rehabilitation costs, and some funeral expenses for you and your passengers. It also pays limited compensation for services needed during convalescence. Coverage is optional, and you can buy it in increments of $1000 or $5000, up to $25,000. There is no deductible.

Your health plan, if you have one, probably covers you and your household already. If you aren't covered elsewhere, or if you have high health-insurance copayments and deductibles, you may want to buy more to cover what your health insurance won't.

PERSONAL-INJURY PROTECTION (PIP). PIP is a broader form of medical-payments coverage that covers medical and funeral costs for you and members of your household. It also pays a portion of lost wages and the costs of in-home assistance. It is mandatory in some states with no-fault auto insurance, and optional in many others. Basic coverage is required, usually with upper limits set at $50,000. In some states, PIP coverage includes a deductible.

If you already have good health, life, and disability insurance, and if your state doesn't require you to have PIP, don't buy it. Otherwise, buy only the statutory minimum.

UNINSURED- AND UNDERINSURED-MOTORIST COVERAGE. This pays you and members of your household for medical costs, rehabilitation, funeral costs, and losses from pain and suffering resulting from an accident caused by a hit-and-run driver, or by a driver who lacks sufficient insurance or who has no insurance at all. Mandatory in many states. Limits are similar to those of bodily-injury liability, and most state laws will not allow you to purchase more of this coverage than the liability coverage you carry.

This coverage is essential, especially in densely populated states where lots of people drive uninsured. Buy at least $100,000 per person and $300,000 per accident, where such limits are offered.

GLASS BREAKAGE. This covers replacement of cracked glass to your car, regardless of how it occurred. Coverage usually adds 15 to 20 percent to the cost of your comprehensive coverage; there is no deductible. Unless you live in an area with dirt roads and lots of errant rocks or car break-ins, this insurance is not worth buying if it costs more than a few dollars a year.

RENTAL REIMBURSEMENT AND TOWING. This covers towing your wrecked car and the payment for a car rental while your auto is being fixed after an accident or after being stolen. Rental coverage costs just $15 to $25 a year but typically pays about $15 per day for up to 30 days. Towing coverage typically pays up to $50 per tow and costs about $5 per car per year. Buy rental if you have only one car and no alternative transportation. You won't be able to collect on towing unless your car is undrivable following an accident where you were at fault or damaged other than through a collision.

UNINSURED-MOTORIST PROPERTY DAMAGE. This coverage pays for damage to your property by someone without insurance, or without enough insurance to reimburse your costs. The coverage limit is typically not more than $25,000. Where offered, buy this only if you don't have collision coverage.

OTHER FACTORS THAT WILL AFFECT YOUR COST

With car insurance, policies are tailored to specific drivers, and costs vary widely. The insurance company that gave the best deal to your retired parents won't necessarily be the cheapest for you.

Buying a policy from a big-name company is no guarantee that you'll get a favorable rate. You should take a close look at some of the less widely known companies in your state (big and small companies are subject to the specific rules where they operate).

Among the big insurers, companies that rely on their own exclusive sales reps and those known in industry parlance as "direct writers" (so-called because they sell policies directly to the public without having to pay independent agents' commissions) are worth checking out. Prominent among these are Colonial Penn Franklin, GEICO, State Farm, and United Services Automobile Association (USAA), which insures only military personnel and veterans.

If you're insuring a teenage driver, you're likely to pay a markedly higher premium no matter which insurer you ultimately choose. That's because insurers consider young drivers to pose a higher risk. Insurance premiums are also steeper for city drivers than for their suburban counterparts.

Insurers contend that the much larger premiums urban drivers pay simply reflect the greater risk the companies incur. Theft and accident rates are higher in cities, as are the amounts insurers say they must pay to settle claims. But these actuarial facts may be masking some discriminatory practices. Some insurance companies require their agents to "size up" prospective customers before they will agree to issue a policy. If the agents don't like the way you look or how you speak, they may turn you down. Other insurers have simply closed their offices in some urban communities.

With fewer companies competing to sell policies to city dwellers, the insurance coverage that states require is going to be more expensive—if it's available at all. In many inner-city districts of New York, for example, car owners are forced into the so-called "Auto Insurance Plan"—a risk pool that the state requires all car insurance companies doing business within its borders to join. Because these plans must insure drivers who cannot otherwise buy coverage, the policies are exorbitantly expensive. Their transgression is not being "high-risk" drivers—most have clean records—but living in what the industry apparently considers a "high-risk" community.

SMART WAYS TO SAVE

You could be wasting hundreds of dollars a year, or more, by failing to compare how your insurance carrier's premiums stack up against the competition's. You should also reevaluate regularly the level of coverage you need. A study by the insurance industry found that fully one-third of all drivers admitted that it had been at least six years since they last shopped for a new policy. Another 20 percent said they never shopped at all.

Ask about rate reductions for which you may qualify. You can realize big savings by taking advantage of discounts available to most drivers, but you do have to ask; agents don't always volunteer this information. According to one estimate, U.S. consumers may be paying insurance companies over $300 million more than they need to each year by failing to ask about discounts. Here are ones you should look into:

COMBINE POLICIES WITH ONE CARRIER. Most owners with two or more cars know that it makes sense to insure all their autos on a single policy. But you can also get a multi-vehicle discount if you insure a trailer or recreational vehicle on the same policy as your car. Similarly, auto insurers that also offer homeowner's and life insurance will shave your car premium if you buy other coverage from them. Don't switch carriers, however, unless the rates for the other policies are competitive.

BUY A CAR THAT COSTS LESS TO INSURE. Expensive high-performance cars may be fun to drive, but they're costly to repair. Premiums to insure a BMW, Porsche, or Mercedes run two to three times higher than those for a more plebeian Ford or Dodge. Some cars souped up with customized engines and suspensions may be uninsurable through standard policies.

And consider that certain vehicles are stolen more than others. The Honda Accord, Chevrolet pickups, and several other domestic sedans are consistently among the most stolen vehicles. For a complete list of the top-10 stolen vehicles, see page 53.

EQUIP YOUR NEW CAR WITH SAFETY GEAR. Air bags for both driver and passenger reduce the risk of serious injury—and costly medical bills—in an accident, and they may qualify you for a discount on most policies. An approved alarm system or other devices that deter thefts can get you a savings of 5 to 10 percent. Some insurers no longer offer discounts for cars that have antilock brakes, citing evidence that equipment that prevents skidding in emergency stops is not measurably reducing accidents. CONSUMER REPORTS disagrees; we believe these brakes can help prevent accidents when used properly, and we recommend them.

KEEP YOUR DRIVING RECORD CLEAN. No claims or tickets for 36 months will qualify you for a reduced premium. Drivers over age 50 who have a clean record can also claim a rate reduction. Insurers in many states will give policyholders who pass an authorized defensive driving course a discount typically 5 to 15 percent off their liability coverage for up to three years.

USE PUBLIC TRANSIT OR A CARPOOL TO GET TO WORK. Drivers who hold their driving below 7500 miles a year generally qualify for a discount.

TELL YOUR TEEN TO CRACK THE BOOKS. Insurers will usually provide a discount if the teenage driver in your home maintains a good academic record—on top of any break they give for passing an approved drivers' education course. Another discount may apply if your child goes off to college more than 100 miles from home and doesn't take a car along.

ASSIGN YOUR TEEN TO ONLY ONE CAR. If you own more than one vehicle (and your insurance company allows it), add the teenager to your policy as the occasional driver of your least expensive auto—and make sure he or she drives only that car. If your teenager owns a car, you shouldn't insure it under a separate policy because the chances are that he or she would have to purchase coverage from your state's costly high-risk pool.

HOW NOT TO CUT COSTS

Don't withhold information from your insurer that may increase your premium. If you misrepresent material facts about where your car is garaged, who is using it, or how it's being used—and suffer a sizable claim—your insurer will likely find out and could refuse to pay, decide not to renew your policy, or both. Don't file for claims you can easily absorb yourself. With many companies, a single sizable claim can result in a breathtaking hike in your rates.

BE WARY OF COLLISION REPAIR

Eager to hold the line on accident-repair costs, more insurers are directing claimants to "preferred" auto body shops. This "managed care" for cars can be convenient, but it could cost you.

Nearly three-quarters of all insurers have adopted some form of this cost-cutting approach, which they call "direct repair programs." Most companies make the program voluntary, and consumers may find it easy to use the body shop the insurer suggests: Simply drop the car off, and it's fixed with no haggling over the cost or waiting for a claims adjuster to prepare a report.

Just how the car is fixed is another matter. Interviews with insurers, body-shop owners, car manufacturers, and appraisers led us to conclude that by their very agreement to hold their collision-repair costs to a minimum, body shops put themselves under pressure to cut corners. Some succumb by taping around exterior parts like door handles rather than removing them when they paint. This leaves areas where paint can chip, allowing rust to form. Others use plastic filler rather than replacing a damaged body panel. Some even replace deployed air bags with salvaged ones.

One big area where body shops hold down costs is by using generic—or even salvage—parts rather than new parts from your car's original manufacturer. For example, the hood of a Mazda 626 costs a body shop about $450 when bought from Mazda Corp.; a substitute hood may cost less than half as much.

Obviously, the original equipment manufacturers—OEMs, as they're known in the trade—object to the use of substitute auto parts because they want to sell more of their own parts. Still, they do have some evidence to support their assertions that generic parts don't fit as well, aren't as sturdy, and are more prone to rust.

You can usually have the car fixed at a shop of your choosing; most policies still afford you the right to negotiate with the insurer over how your car is repaired. If you do choose to go with a shop the insurance company suggests, look carefully at the estimate. If you see "LKQ" parts, that means substitute parts that are supposed

Insurance information

For more information on automobile insurance, contact the state office that oversees the industry where you live. Most states publish shopping guides with rate comparisons, unless the list indicates NG (no guide).

Alabama	334 269-3550
Alaska	907 269-7900
Arizona	602 912-8444
Arkansas (NG)	800 852-5494
California	800 927-4357
Colorado	303 894-7499
Connecticut	860 297-3867
Delaware	800 282-8611
Florida	850 922-3132
Georgia (NG)	404 656-2070
Hawaii	808 587-1234
Idaho (NG)	800 721-3272
Illinois (NG)	217 782-4515
Indiana (NG)	800 622-4461
Iowa (NG)	515 281-5705
Kansas (NG)	800 432-2484
Kentucky	502 564-3630
Louisiana	800 259-5301
Maine	207 624-8475
Maryland	800 492-6116
Massachusetts	617 521-7777
Michigan	517 373-9273
Minnesota	800 657-3602
Mississippi (NG)	601 359-3569
Missouri	800 726-7390
Montana	800 332-6148
Nebraska	402 471-2201
Nevada	800 992-0900
New Hampshire (NG)	800 852-3416
New Jersey	800 446-7467
New Mexico (NG)	800 947-4722
New York	800 342-3736
North Carolina (NG)	800 662-7777
North Dakota	800 247-0560
Ohio	800 686-1526
Oklahoma (NG)	800 522-0071
Oregon	503 947-7984
Pennsylvania	717 787-2317
Rhode Island	401 222-2223
South Carolina	800 768-3467
South Dakota (NG)	605 773-3563
Tennessee (NG)	800 342-4029
Texas	800 252-3439
Utah	800 439-3805
Vermont	802 828-3301
Virginia	800 552-7945
Washington	800 562-6900
Washington, D.C. (NG)	202 727-8000
West Virginia	800 642-9004
Wisconsin	800 236-5414
Wyoming	800 438-5768

to be of "like kind and quality," not OEM parts. Finally, when the repair work is complete, it may be worthwhile to have an appraiser check your car for any reduction in its value. Your policy should allow you to collect for any diminution.

SAVINGS IN THE FUTURE

Putting a lid on escalating auto insurance costs will require consumers to be more willing to comparison shop. It will also take efforts by the insurance industry and government.

Insurers should make their pricing policies more transparent. The industry feeds consumer mistrust and, worse, may discriminate unfairly when it relies on suspect criteria to set premiums. The most recent manifestation of this disturbing trend is the reliance by many insurers on consumers' credit records as an indicator of their insurance risk. The industry has yet to demonstrate a convincing link between past credit problems and increased driver risk.

Insurers should also crack down more aggressively on fraud; suspicious injury claims alone may add $130 to the cost of insuring every car in the U.S., according to an estimate by the RAND Corporation's Institute for Civil Justice. Until recently, insurers had been so lax in challenging suspect claims that several states, including California, Florida, New Jersey, and New York, passed laws requiring them to do so. Some bigger companies, such as State Farm, Allstate, and Nationwide, have shaken off their torpor and are stepping up fraud investigations. More insurers should join them.

For its part, government needs to pass sensible no-fault insurance legislation in the 37 states that still don't have it, and improve it in most of the states that do. Under no-fault, accident victims are compensated by their own insurance company for injuries they suffer in an accident, instead of having to resort to an expensive lawsuit to assess responsibility.

CONSUMER REPORTS believes that no-fault insurance is the most equitable and efficient way to compensate accident victims—but not the way it is currently implemented in many jurisdictions. As no-fault now works in some states, claimants can bring a court case only if their losses due to injury exceed a certain dollar amount. But setting a minimum dollar threshold encourages victims and their physicians to exaggerate the injuries' cost.

The no-fault system in Michigan may be a model worth emulating. All motorists must carry sufficient basic insurance to cover all but the most severe losses. But accident victims can still get their day in court if they can demonstrate that their injuries exceed a minimum threshold of severity, such as the loss of a limb, disfigurement, or other permanent impairment of bodily function. The Michigan no-fault system has effectively held down costs while still allowing people with grave injuries access to justice. Fairness and good value for auto-insurance protection is the right combination for everyone.

C H A P T E R F O U R

EQUIPPING *a car*

NEW EQUIPMENT & DESIGNS

As styling grows more similar and cars run more capably and reliably, equipment can make some cars stand out from the pack. For those who haven't driven a new car lately, here's a guide to items that add to safety, comfort, and convenience.

FEATURES THAT ADD TO SAFETY. Cars are getting more and better safety equipment every year. All passenger cars now offer standard or optional **antilock brakes.** All come with **dual air bags** and of course **safety belts,** the most important piece of safety equipment. **Pretensioners,** which instantly take up belt slack in a collision, are becoming more common.

Here are some newer safety items:

Stability control, currently found on a few luxury models from BMW, Cadillac, Lexus, and Mercedes-Benz, uses the ABS computer and various sensors to help keep the car on course while cornering on slick pavement. These systems work by selectively applying the brakes to one or more wheels. We consider them a major advance.

Most 1998 models have **reduced-power front air bags.** Advanced systems found on some BMWs sense whether the passenger seat is occupied and if the occupant is wearing a belt. The air bags deploy at different speeds, or not at all, according to conditions. **Side-impact air bags** are growing more common. Most are designed to protect only the torso. BMW has a system that protects the head as well. Volvo and Mercedes are due to follow soon with similar systems. The

Audi A8 is the first car to have side-impact air bags for rear-seat passengers.

Many cars' head restraints are too low to prevent whiplash injuries. Saab has just introduced a clever **active head restraint.** It's a simple mechanical lever system in the seatback that automatically moves the head restraint up and forward as you are thrown back against the seat.

An **integrated child seat,** available with some sedans and many minivans, can be a boon since it comes properly installed and is always available. When folded, though, some can make a stiff backrest for an adult.

Automatic headlights, found on many Ford, GM, and Lexus vehicles and the Toyota Corolla, turn on automatically at dusk, in case you forget to turn them on yourself. They go off a short time after you remove the key. Daytime running lights go on with the ignition.

For more on safety, see page 57.

COMFORT, CONVENIENCE FEATURES. Features that add to comfort and convenience could also be considered safety features if they make the driver more comfortable and alert, or improve visibility. That's why we've long recommended **air conditioning,** for instance. These days, air conditioning, **power windows and mirrors,** and a **stereo sound system** are almost universal. If you buy a car without such things, you may find it hard to sell later on.

A **power driver's seat** provides a height adjustment often not available with a non-powered seat. A **powered sliding door,** found on GM minivans, works from inside the van or from the key fob. **Retained power for accessories** such as the radio and power windows gives you a few minutes' grace after you switch off the engine—until you open the door (the Ford and GM system) or remove the key (the Audi system).

A **sun-visor extension,** a broad plastic leaf that slides out of the visor end, can be very handy to block sun the visor is too short to catch. Some cars have dual visors that let you shade the side window and windshield at the same time. Others, including the Audi A4, Mercedes-Benz E-Class, and Volkswagen Passat, use a small third visor or darkened glass above the mirror to block sun there.

Japanese cars have long been known for thoughtful touches like **coin holders, map pockets,** and **vanity mirrors.** Now all carmakers have learned that building in items like **overhead bins** can add greatly to a car's appeal, often at very little cost to the manufacturer.

The Ford Windstar has a small **wide-angle mirror** that pulls down from the ceiling to let you keep an eye on children in the rear seats. **Heated side mirrors,** found on many cars, defrost the outside mirrors, usually when you turn on the rear defroster—very useful in the Northern states.

With an **automatic climate system,** you set the temperature, and the system does the rest. At present, the best-designed systems are found on Fords, GM vehicles, Infinitis, Nissans, and Volvos. **Dual-zone climate controls,** found on some minivans and midpriced sedans and on many high-priced sedans, let passengers regulate the temperature independently of the driver.

Heated seats are welcome in cold weather, particularly in cars with leather upholstery. Some Audis and BMWs have a heated steering wheel as well.

A **fold-down rear seatback,** offered in many small and midsized cars, expands the cargo space so you can tote long or bulky items. Best are split folding seatbacks, which enable you to fold down one side while leaving a habitable rear seat.

SOME DESIGNS THAT DON'T MAKE IT. When Consumer Reports tests cars, it assesses how the controls are laid out and other elements of a car's design, and calls out things that would be annoying to live with. For instance, we've long faulted Honda for putting small horn buttons on the steering-wheel spokes, a practice Honda finally abandoned in the 1998 Accord. Here are other designs we hope will be abandoned soon:

On many vehicles, **the clock and radio dials** share space. If you can see the radio-frequency numbers you can't see the clock, and vice versa. On cars like the Buick Century and Regal, poorly designed **auxiliary radio controls** let you hit the buttons as you turn the wheel, so you inadvertently change radio stations or volume.

Poorly designed **cruise controls** can also be a nuisance. Perhaps the worst: Mercedes-Benz's design. It's a lever on the steering column, close to the turn-signal lever. You can easily set a cruise speed when you wish to signal a turn. Runner up: a design on many GM vehicles that crams the cruise controls onto a single lever with the controls for the wipers and turn signal.

Cosmetic running boards, found on the Mercury Mountaineer and Infiniti QX4 and many other SUVs, not only don't help you get in or out, they inevitably smear road grime on your pants. Many sedans have large, curving, **intrusive trunk hinges** that can crush items placed in the trunk when you shut the lid.

HOW OPTIONS ARE SOLD. Options vary by trim line—the model version designated GL, DL, and so on. They often come as part of a package, called a "preferred equipment group" or "quick-order package." Sometimes it's hard to buy an option a la carte without accepting a package of unrelated goodies. For instance, the $325 powered driver's seat that improves driving position and visibility on a Ford Windstar GL is available only if you first order a $3,075 package that includes tinted glass, an auxiliary air conditioner, an overhead console, a roof rack, and other gear.

Most of the cars on a dealer's lot come with one or another of those packages, installed at the factory. Don't confuse manufacturer's equipment with dealer "packs"—extra-cost add-ons put there by the dealer, not the factory. They include dealer-installed rustproofing, pinstripes, extra-dark window tinting, and paint and upholstery preservatives. They're not worth the money.

Worthy options

Consider these if they're available and fit your needs.

- Antilock brake system
- Side air bags
- Traction control
- Adjustable steering column
- Driver's seat with adjustable height
- All-wheel drive
- Remote keyless entry
- Central locking system
- Power mirrors
- Heated mirrors
- Air conditioning
- Integrated child seat
- Daytime running lights

GETTING TRACTION

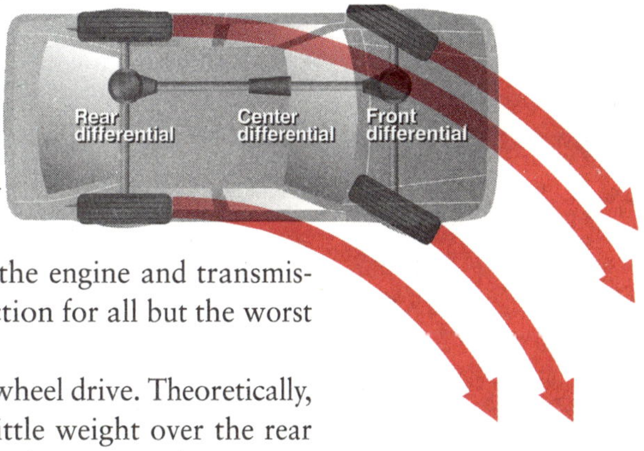

In a corner, the outside wheels travel farther than the inside ones. The differentials on a four-wheel-drive vehicle let all the wheels turn at different speeds to prevent damage to the tires and driveline.

Most cars today have front-wheel drive. The weight of the engine and transmission over the front driving wheels provides sufficient traction for all but the worst road conditions.

Some luxury and high-performance models have rear-wheel drive. Theoretically, this design allows more responsive handling. But with little weight over the rear driving wheels, such a car can lose traction more easily in slippery conditions.

Whether your car has front- or rear-wheel drive, features such as a limited-slip differential or traction control can help reduce wheel spin on slippery surfaces. But for the ultimate in traction, either because you have to get through blizzard conditions or rugged terrain, or simply because you want added peace of mind, nothing beats four-wheel drive.

THE BASICS. Technically, the greatest challenge to traction arises from the simple physical fact shown in the diagram above: When a car rounds a curve, each of its four wheels follows a different arc, so each must travel at a different speed.

The mechanism that lets the drive wheels turn at different speeds is the differential, a gear assembly that distributes the engine's power between the left and right drive wheels. Without the differential, the inside wheels would turn too quickly and scrub across the pavement in turns. Conventional cars have one differential on their drive axle. Four-wheel-drive models have two or three.

Choosing a four-wheel-drive system

PART-TIME FOUR-WHEEL DRIVE

Found in: Many pickup trucks and sport-utility vehicles (SUVs). You select the mode with a lever or switch. All allow you to "shift on the fly"—engage four-wheel drive without stopping.

Pros:

- Effective in deep snow and mud.
- Has a low range for off-road.

Cons:

- Not suitable for use on dry pavement.
- You must engage and disengage four-wheel drive as conditions dictate.

Examples: Pickup trucks: All Chevrolets, Dodges, Fords, GMCs, Mazdas, Nissans, Toyotas. SUVs: Chevrolet Blazer; Dodge Durango; GMC Jimmy; Honda Passport; Isuzu Amigo, Rodeo; Jeep Cherokee, Wrangler; Mitsubishi Montero Sport; Nissan Pathfinder; all Suzukis; Toyota 4Runner.

SELECTABLE FULL-TIME FOUR-WHEEL DRIVE

Found in: Some SUVs. You select the mode with a lever or switch.

Pros:

- Effective in deep snow and mud.
- Center differential allows use of four-wheel drive on dry pavement.
- You can lock the center differential for added traction in poor conditions.
- Has a low range for off-road.

Cons:

- With most, you must lock or unlock the center differential manually.
- Vehicle may be in two-wheel drive when four-wheel drive is needed.

Examples: Chevrolet Tahoe, Suburban; Dodge Durango; GMC Yukon, Suburban; Jeep Cherokee, Grand Cherokee; Mitsubishi Montero. With auto-locking center differential: Acura SLX; Ford Expedition; Infiniti QX4; Isuzu Trooper; Lincoln Navigator.

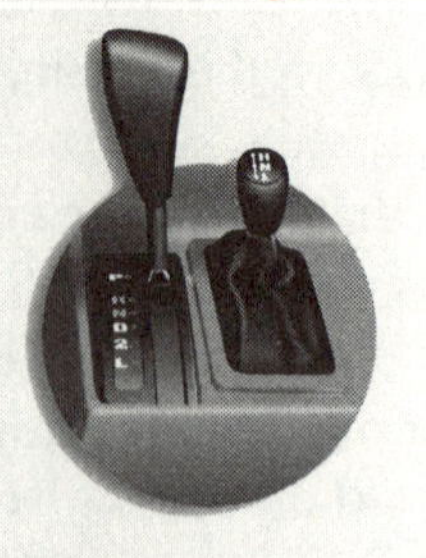

PERMANENT FOUR-WHEEL DRIVE

Found in: Some SUVs. Like a selectable full-time system, but without a two-wheel-drive mode. The center differential or equivalent usually locks and unlocks automatically.

Pros:

- Effective in deep snow and mud.
- Stays in four-wheel drive at all times.
- Automatically locks the center differential for added traction in poor conditions.
- Has a low range for off-road.

Cons:

- May cost more than all other systems.

Examples: Ford Explorer V6; Jeep Grand Cherokee; Land Rover Discovery (has a manual center differential) and Range Rover; Lexus LX470; Mercedes-Benz ML320; Mercury Mountaineer V6; Toyota Land Cruiser.

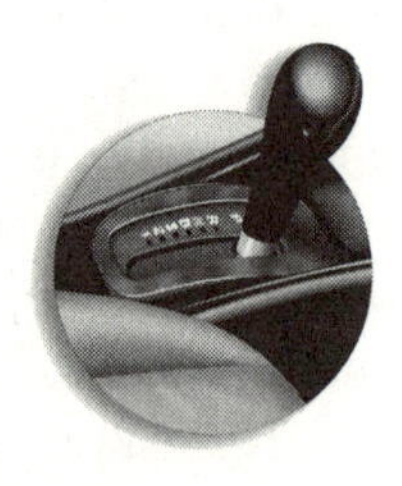

ALL-WHEEL DRIVE

Found in: Some cars, minivans, and SUVs. Four-wheel drive is engaged permanently, and the center differential locks and unlocks automatically.

Pros:

- Simplest to use; you needn't make any decisions.
- Transfers power instantly to wheels with the best grip.

Cons:

- Lacks a low range, so unsuited for true off-roading.

Examples: Cars: Audi Quattro; Mercedes-Benz E320; Mitsubishi Eclipse, 3000GT; all Subarus; Volvo V70. Minivans: Chevrolet Astro; Chrysler Town & Country; Dodge Grand Caravan; GMC Safari; Mazda MPV (also has a two-wheel-drive mode). SUVs: Ford Explorer V8; Honda CR-V; Lexus RX300; Mercury Mountaineer V8; Oldsmobile Bravada; Subaru Forester; Toyota RAV4.

Vital as it is, the differential has a serious drawback: Since power from the engine follows the path of least resistance, the differential tends to divert power to the wheel that has less grip. That's why you can find yourself spinning one wheel helplessly while the other wheel remains stationary.

TRACTION AIDS. A limited-slip differential uses a type of clutch to limit the power to a slipping wheel. It's at its best when you're driving straight, not in turns. If the surface is slick under both drive wheels, it's no help; both will slip.

Traction control came along with antilock-brake-system technology. ABS is electronically controlled by an onboard computer, which can brake each wheel separately if need be. On a slick road, the traction-control system limits wheel spin by braking the wheel that's slipping. It works well whether you're cornering or going straight.

Traction control benefits cars with front-wheel drive, though they have good traction to start with. But it's most effective in cars with rear-wheel drive. Two types are available:

Low-speed traction control uses just the antilock brakes. It's good for getting started, but it quits above 25 mph or so, to preserve the brake linings. It's optional in the Dodge Intrepid, Toyota Camry, and Volvo S70 and V70.

All-speed traction control is far more effective because it uses the engine-control computer as well as the ABS. Besides braking a wheel, it can reduce the engine power or shift to a higher gear to reduce wheel spin. It's standard or optional in cars from BMW, Cadillac, Infiniti, Jaguar, Lexus, Mercedes-Benz, and, yes, Saturn.

Stability control uses the ABS computer as well as motion sensors to keep the car from "yawing," or sliding sideways. It generally works by braking one or more wheels in short bursts. So far, it's found only in a few costly models such as the BMW 7-Series, Cadillac DeVille and Seville, Lexus GS300/GS400, LS400, and Mercedes E-Class and S-Class.

FOUR-WHEEL DRIVE. Four-wheel drive gives optimum traction in slippery conditions, and it's a must for driving off-road. There are two basic types, part-time and full-time, and several subtypes, which vary in convenience and utility.

All four-wheel drives have a front and a rear differential. The systems that give the best traction also use a center differential to modulate power between the front and rear wheels.

In addition, most four-wheel drives have a "low range," with very low gearing. It's for the worst conditions—deep mud or snow, steep inclines, or when crawling over boulders.

Part-time four-wheel drive grips as well as any four-wheel-drive system, but you can use it only on loose or slick surfaces. Engaging it with a separate shift lever or a switch on the dash "locks" the front and rear axles so they turn at the same speed. That's great for traction—but with the axles yoked, one or more tires scrub during cornering. That can damage the tires and driveline on dry roads, though it's not a problem in mud or snow.

Full-time four-wheel drive, unlike part-time, can be used all the time.

A selectable full-time four-wheel-drive system is especially versatile. It offers you a choice of three modes: two-wheel drive, part-time four-wheel drive, and full-time four-wheel drive.

CONSUMER REPORTS recommends leaving the system in full-time four-wheel drive at all times. That stabilizes handling, and our tests show no fuel penalty.

In that mode, the center differential or equivalent mechanism ordinarily lets the front and rear wheels turn independently when you're cornering. In difficult conditions, the center differential can lock, providing traction as good as that of part-time four-wheel drive. The best systems do that automatically. A few make you press a button or shift a lever.

A permanent four-wheel-drive system is the best of both worlds. It stays in four-wheel drive at all times. When conditions get especially tough, the center differential locks automatically.

Both the selectable and full-time systems provide a low range for heavy-duty or off-road use.

All-wheel drive, used in some sedans, wagons, minivans, sports cars, and sport-utility vehicles, is convenient. Most of the power ordinarily goes to two wheels. As those wheels start to slip, more power automatically goes to the other two wheels.

All-wheel drive is much like full-time four-wheel drive, except it has no low-range gear. That makes it unsuitable for serious off-road use. Also, vehicles with all-wheel drive generally have insufficient ground clearance for truly rough terrain.

AUTOSOUND SYSTEMS

Factory-installed sound systems range from the adequate to the sublime, with the latter often costing many hundreds of dollars more than a basic system. An aftermarket radio/tape/CD player and speaker system, installed by an autosound specialist, might cost less, have exactly the features you want, and sound better than what the manufacturer offers. In fact, if you're shopping for a new car, you can sometimes "delete" the standard audio system and subtract its price from the total cost of the car, a price reduction that could defray some of the cost of a superior aftermarket system.

In an audio dealer's showroom, you can try out a radio, cassette, or CD player, but playing the wall-mounted display won't give you a clue as to how the system will sound in your car. That's determined primarily by the way the speakers you choose are installed and how they interact with the car. Music played inside a car will be acoustically different from music played in the dealer's showroom or in your home. The passenger compartment, considerably smaller than a typical living room, causes variations in loudness across the music spectrum that are quite different from what occurs in most rooms. In the car, music competes with wind, road, and engine noise.

Autosound systems come in various configurations. AM/FM radios are standard, combined with either a cassette tape deck or a CD player. Units that combine all three are rare. CD changers, usually mounted in the trunk, can be added on to an existing radio/cassette player. The latest offerings from the auto manufacturers and aftermarket companies are minidisc players.

RADIO/TAPE PLAYERS

RECEPTION. FM radio waves bounce off buildings, hills, and even other cars. When the same radio signal arrives at the car antenna at different times, especially prevalent in a moving car, you may hear increased noise or garble known as multipath distortion. Multipath can also cause bursts of noise as you drive along. You can often reorient an audio system's antenna to correct the problem at home, but you can't do that on the road. Some receivers—especially models that use two separate antennas—are much better than others at coping with multipath distortion, but there is no clear correlation between multipath resistance and price.

POWER. The more amplifier power, the louder the sound the system can produce. A receiver's power output is stated in watts. Wattage numbers have become a major marketing point, but manufacturers' claims do call for skepticism. With home audio, federal law prohibits advertisers from overstating their power. That's not the case with car audio, where manufacturers sometimes inflate their figures by adding the power levels of both channels instead of stating them individually.

For a system that has two speakers, an actual power level of 10 to 20 watts per channel, easy to accomplish without sophisticated circuitry, should provide all the power you need to flood the car with sound. For four-speaker systems, 10 to 20 watts per speaker should be fine.

TUNING. Digital tuning is standard with radio/cassette players, including 10 or more presets, the programmable buttons you can set to your favorite stations. Separate bass and treble controls are the norm. Some players even offer a built-in equalizer.

Station seek finds the next station up or down the dial. Some models let you limit reception to strong stations.

Station scan lets you hop automatically along the entire radio band from one station to another, pausing briefly at each. You stop the scan when you hear what you like.

Preset scan finds only the stations you've programmed with the preset buttons.

Auto-preset sets the tuning buttons to the strongest signals it finds on the dial, a help when you travel in unfamiliar areas.

TAPE PLAYING. Cassette players can jump forward or backward to successive selections on the tape at the press of a button. Tape scan plays the first few seconds of each selection, helpful in finding a particular selection while driving. Most tape players offer some form of noise suppression. Dolby noise reduction greatly reduces background noise and hiss, but you may not realize its full benefits amid the noise of the highway. Dolby circuitry is common, usually only the "B" type. It can play Dolby "C" and "S" tapes without much degradation.

MOUNTING CHOICES. Radio/tape players usually fit what's called a DIN (Deutsche Industrie Normenausschus) mounting: an opening approximately two by seven inches in the dash. A few cars require the smaller ISO (International Standards Organization) mounting, which uses screw holes for a special bracket. Some other car models call for a special bracket to accommodate an aftermarket radio/tape player.

Adapters and kits are available for installing almost any radio/tape player in almost any car. But a model designed to fit your car's specific type of mounting generally makes a neater and more secure installation. One way to be sure the radio/cassette player fits is to have it installed by the audio dealer. Installers are usually familiar with most car-and-stereo combinations and know which additional parts may be needed.

DETERRING THEFT. A conventional car alarm isn't an effective deterrent in preventing equipment theft, according to many experts. Consequently, audio manufacturers have developed various antitheft tactics. One is to make the receiver removable. Some DIN-mounted models slide out from a box in the dash with the flick of a handle. The obvious drawback: You have to lug around a car radio or hide it in the trunk.

A neater solution that's becoming more common: a removable faceplate. The face contains all the switches and displays. It's coded in a way that prevents substitution of another face. Without the face, the receiver is useless to a thief.

Some models have an electronic security system that requires you to enter a three- or four-digit code to activate the stereo when it's reconnected. If you forget or lose the code, you're out of luck.

CD PLAYERS

Compact-disc players reproduce uniformly excellent sound quality, although the intrusions of road noise and the distorting effects of a car's interior apply to CDs much as they do to radio and tape sound.

If you're prepared to start from scratch, consider a receiver with a CD player built in. But if you don't want to scrap an existing system just to add CD capability, you do have some alternatives:

DASH-MOUNT PLAYERS. Some cars have an unfilled DIN slot in the dashboard, which may masquerade as a small bin in the dash. You can buy a CD player that occupies that space and is permanently wired to the receiver. Some car stereos have a rear jack for that purpose. If your car radio has CD controls on its faceplate but no CD player, then it should accept a CD player.

CD CHANGERS. If you don't want to fuss with discs and plastic boxes while driving, a multiple-disc changer might appeal to you. A changer can play hours of music without your having to lift a finger. You usually mount the changer, which is about the size of a hardcover book, in the trunk. It is controlled by the receiver, if the receiver has that capability, or by a small controller on the dash.

PORTABLE CD PLAYERS. Portable CD players can pipe their sound through existing auto sound systems. If the car's receiver has a front CD input jack, you can plug the CD player into the receiver with an inexpensive audio cord that has stereo mini-phone plugs at each end.

Without a CD jack, you have two options. You can use a cassette adapter—available at audio stores—that plays a CD through the tape player. Such devices add some background noise and slight inaccuracy in frequency response. Or you may be able to buy a modulator that connects the CD player's output to your radio's antenna jack. To hear a CD, you tune to a predetermined FM frequency.

To conserve a portable CD player's batteries, you can plug it into a car's cigarette-lighter socket with an adapter. If the shocks of the road turn out to be too harsh, consider a shock-absorbing mounting cradle, standard with some portables and available for most others.

LOUDSPEAKERS

Speakers alone can improve a car's audio system greatly, since speakers affect sound quality more directly than other components do. Some points to consider:

ACCURACY. A very accurate speaker produces sounds that correspond closely to the electrical signals from the radio or tape player. Speakers should reproduce low-frequency notes with minimal distortion. Because the rumble of background noise tends to drown out low notes, car speakers need a boost in the lowest bass frequencies to make those frequencies audible. But since car speakers are often much smaller than those in a home audio system, they may strain to deliver loud, distortion-free bass.

POWER REQUIREMENT. The more powerful the amplifier, the louder the sound that's potentially available from a given pair of speakers. In addition, the more efficient the speakers, the louder the sound they'll produce from a given amplifier. Speaker efficiency is no measure of sound quality. But efficiency is an important consideration in a car, where a basic receiver may put out only 10 to 20 watts.

Some speakers demand lots of amplifier power, 30 watts or more per channel. Such speakers can't produce very loud sound unless you match them with a very high-powered receiver or an external amplifier. If you're planning to keep your present receiver and you're not sure how powerful it is, choose speakers that need relatively little power.

INSTALLING. Simply replacing the original speakers with aftermarket speakers of the same size is usually a straightforward job. But installing speakers where there were none before demands skill. If you have a choice, mount the speakers on the package shelf behind the back seats. That location takes advantage of the large trunk enclosure to produce the strongest bass. In hatchbacks and wagons, you'll have to settle for door or kick-panel mounting. With a door mount, the speakers should be placed as high as possible for best performance at high frequencies.

To accommodate do-it-yourselfers, speakers typically come with instructions for installation. Some instructions are clear, some not so clear. To ease installation, most cars have cutouts, holes in the car's panels shaped to accept the speakers, generally covered by a layer of upholstery. Mounting speakers larger than the factory cutouts requires cutting metal, quite an involved job. Speakers usually come with templates to guide the cutting operation. They generally include mounting hardware, although a few models come without speaker wire.

Because most installations involve some cutting of the car's interior, letting the auto sound dealer install the speakers may be a prudent investment. If you have any reservations about the job, leave it to a professional.

BUYING ADVICE

If you just want to improve the system in your present car, start with the speakers. Better speakers may improve the sound enough to make the purchase of a new radio/tape player unnecessary.

Car audio systems tend to perform very well in important categories such as FM reception and tape accuracy. While AM fidelity is not as good as FM, a car's AM tuner is generally better designed than the one found in a home stereo receiver.

Make sure you have the option of returning or exchanging the system if it doesn't perform satisfactorily in your locale.

Whether or not you plan to do the installation yourself, do your homework before you shop. Check the available space where you plan to place your speakers, and measure the clearance behind or below the mounting panel. If you have any problems making these measurements, get some advice. A well-informed salesperson should be able to determine which models will fit your car.

Try for larger, oval speakers if your car can accommodate them. As a class, they offer slightly better accuracy and bass capability than circular speakers. It's reasonable to expect good performance with oval speakers once the receiver's tone controls have been adjusted. Therefore, your choice of oval speakers may depend primarily on power requirements and price. If your car has room for only smaller, circular speakers, try to audition them before buying.

AUTO ALARMS

An unprotected car is an easy mark for a professional thief. Car thieves want to work quickly and furtively, so the main goals of car alarms and other security devices are to scare thieves away or slow them down so much that they'll give up the attempt.

Experts emphasize "layered" protection: presenting a thief with a series of challenges. The first layer is common sense: Remove the ignition key; close windows; lock doors; and park in well-lit and well-frequented areas.

The second layer consists of visible or audible deterrents—a steering wheel lock, a siren that sounds when the car is nudged or a door opened. Even just a car-alarm decal can work as a bluff.

A third layer includes devices that disable the starter, ignition, or fuel system. These may deter even a practiced criminal. The more sophisticated security systems combine elements of all three.

Of all these security devices, alarm systems predominate. Some are "factory installed" or "port installed" by the manufacturer. Or the dealer may arrange for installation at a local auto-security shop or car-alarm dealer, where most alarm systems are sold. You can take the car to such a shop yourself, of course. Most systems are professionally installed. A number of alarm manufacturers also sell systems intended for installation by ambitious do-it-yourselfers. If you've installed electronic car equipment before, you have some inkling of what you're in for. But if you've never drilled through sheet metal or poked around under the dashboard, installing an alarm could be frustrating, time-consuming, and even damaging to the car.

In CONSUMER REPORTS' experience, the simplest, cheapest, do-it-yourself alarm systems aren't very good. They lack most of the features we judge necessary. More sophisticated models require installing more hardware and connecting more wires, which can prove a real challenge to the nonprofessional.

But it may even be hard to find a pro who does the job right. Many professional installations are sloppy or incorrect. Signs of a bad job include clumsily routed wiring that is not concealed, wires that are twisted and merely taped together, or an installation where the alarm system's control box is placed just under the driver's side of the dashboard, where it's easy for a thief to reach. A sloppy installation or improper adjustment can cause a system to malfunction or result in false alarms. But even with a perfectly functioning system, nuisance alarms are inevitable.

The more forms of resistance an alarm system puts up, the more likely it is to foil a break-in. Here are some of the common features you'll find.

REMOTE CONTROL. This keychain device arms and disarms the system—and lets you lock or unlock the car from up to 100 feet away. Some can close windows, open the trunk, or even start the car. The remote controls for some systems have too short an operating range. Having a long range can be handy, for example, if you want to control the system from your living room. A long range also lets you control the alarm's panic feature at a safe distance from the car. Many of the claimed distances are overly optimistic, according to CONSUMER REPORTS' tests. If you are putting an alarm in a second vehicle, make sure you can program one remote for both systems instead of carrying two remote controls.

ACTIVE OR PASSIVE ARMING. You set an alarm (arm it, in alarm-speak) either actively or passively. Active arming uses a small remote control you carry with you. You press a button on the remote and receive a confirming chirp telling you the system is armed.

With passive arming, you don't have to use the remote. After you close the trunk or last door, a passive system typically activates itself 30 seconds or so later. When you return to the car, you must use the remote control to disarm the system before entering.

VALET/EMERGENCY OVERRIDE. This switch lets you turn off the system. The valet is handy when you're having the car serviced or parked, or if you're cleaning your car. The emergency override lets you disarm the system if you've lost or damaged the remote.

SIGNAL OPTIONS. Each time any of these systems arms or disarms, its siren chirps to confirm the operation; parking lights usually flash as well. Some systems let you silence chirps with the remote, use a light sensor to suppress the chirps at night, or let you program silence.

SIREN. This is a system's major attention-getter, so it should sound long enough and loud enough to attract attention but not so long that a false alarm seriously disturbs the peace. Several cycles of a minute or two each should be adequate. You don't want a siren that simply blares continuously until the car battery dies.

ENGINE DISABLER. This prevents an important component like the starter or fuel pump from operating. By itself, it won't prevent a break-in or vandalism. But a thief won't be able to drive off once inside.

Disablers come integrated with many alarm systems, but you can also install disabling switches independent of, or in the absence of, any alarm system.

INTRUSION SENSORS. These detect disturbances early, possibly before a thief has even opened a door. Shock sensors detect a sharp blow to the vehicle's body; motion detectors react to jacking, swaying, or bouncing motions; glass-breakage sensors respond if someone tampers with or breaks any of the car's glass. If a sensor is too sensitive, it can trigger false alarms. Most systems have a screw or a stem for adjusting sensitivity. Others can be adjusted using the system's remote control.

IGNORING NUISANCE ALARMS. Some systems temporarily bypass a sensor that sets them off repeatedly during a certain period of time. If the same sensor remains quiet for, say, 60 minutes after its last triggering, it goes back on duty. The ability to bypass an open or faulty sensor while leaving the rest of the system intact is a desirable feature.

DOOR, HOOD, AND TRUNK PROTECTION. Some alarms monitor the doors, trunk, and hood by detecting changes in a car's electrical usage. Those alarms will

The most stolen vehicles

1. Honda Accord
2. Oldsmobile Cutlass/Supreme
3. Toyota Camry
4. Honda Civic
5. Ford Mustang
6. Chevrolet C/K pickup
7. Toyota Corolla
8. Cadillac DeVille
9. Chevrolet Caprice
10. Jeep Cherokee

Source: 1996 list from National Insurance Crime Bureau.

sound, for example, if someone opens a door and the dome light goes on. If the car lacks courtesy lights under the hood or in the trunk, or if the alarm system lacks electrical sensing, the system should come with a set of pin switches (similar to the light switch sensors in the door jambs) to protect the hood and trunk. Some alarm systems automatically lock power doors when they are armed.

PANIC ALARM. This allows you to trigger the alarm with the remote control if you see someone trying to break into the car or if you see someone suspicious approaching while you're in the car.

ALARM ALTERNATIVES

CLUB AND SHIELD. Bar locks like The Club look sturdy, but a thief can easily cut through the steering wheel to remove them. The Shield is a barrier designed to protect parts of the steering wheel so they can't be cut. Equally important, it's also supposed to keep the driver's air bag from being stolen. Despite claims of toughness, CONSUMER REPORTS could saw through The Shield and the steering wheel in about a minute.

STEERING-COLUMN CUFF. Many older General Motors cars (and other vehicles with the ignition linkage high on the steering column) can be stolen by breaking the housing to expose the ignition switch's actuators. Steel collars can forestall that kind of attack by shrouding the steering column.

TRACKING SYSTEMS. The Lojack system is one of several aftermarket tracking devices installed in the car. If your car is stolen, you simply inform local authorities who can (you hope) home in on your vehicle. The more time that elapses between the theft and your reporting to police, the harder it can be to recover the car.

BUYING ADVICE

In order to get a full-featured alarm that's easy to use, you'll have to buy a professionally installed model.

Keeping your car safe from thieves

Auto theft was down nationwide in 1997. The hottest vehicles to steal, according to the Insurance Institute for Highway Safety, were the Toyota Land Cruiser and the Mitsubishi Montero, both midsized SUVs.

Today's car thieves want vehicles to export or to use for parts, says the IIHS's Kim Hazelbaker. A promising deterrent, he says, is technology that deactivates the engine when the key is removed.

In CONSUMER REPORTS' 1997 Annual Questionnaire, one in seven readers reported that someone stole, tried to steal, or broke into their car in the past five years. Of these, 20 percent had their car stolen. Owners of car alarms and wheel-locking devices were less likely to have their car stolen (by 6 percentage points and 4 percentage points, respectively, when other variables were controlled for). Alarms also limited losses from car burglaries (not surprisingly, wheel-locking devices did not). This reader data may not be projectable to the population as a whole.

Use what you have. About one of five readers with any security device failed to activate it at the time of the incident; many of them had their car stolen.

And lock up. Relatively few readers who reported an incident said they left keys in the ignition, but almost half who did said their car was stolen.

Lastly, keep valuables out of sight, including purses and shopping bags.

Choose the installer with care. Inspect the work area, ask for references, and be sure to get written price quotes.

Spend time with the installers, discussing where each component will go. Find out where they intend to put the control box and valet switch. Make it clear that you want wires soldered together or held with solderless connectors, not just twisted and taped. You probably won't be able to check all the installation details yourself. But make sure that all the alarm system's features work before you pay for the job.

An alarm's ease of use wouldn't seem to have much bearing on how well it protects your car. But if a system is a nuisance, you might stop using it, which defeats the purpose of a security system and wastes your investment.

An alarm system might qualify you for a small discount on the comprehensive part of your auto-insurance premium. Check with your insurance company.

CHAPTER FIVE

SAFETY & RELIABILITY

GETTING THERE SAFELY

The biggest push in auto safety these days is to raise drivers' awareness of wearing seatbelts. Unfortunately, the U.S. still lags behind many countries in this area: Only sixty-eight percent of Americans buckle up. Through state and federal measures, officials hope to increase that to 85 percent in the next two years, and 90 percent by 2005—a rate that Canada and other countries have already achieved. That, and efforts to curb drunk driving, are designed to reduce America's motor-vehicle fatality rate over the next decade by 35 percent, from 1.7 to 1.1 deaths per 100 million vehicle-miles (the latest rate is for 1996, the most recent year available). The death rate hasn't dropped since 1993.

Another issue of increasing concern is the incompatibility between cars and sport-utility vehicles or pickups. When cars collide with these heavier, higher riding vehicles, the death rate for the car occupants is four times that for the occupants of the SUVs or pickups, on average—and up to 47 times greater when the lightest cars are involved. Those findings, by the Insurance Institute for Highway Safety (IIHS), a nonprofit group funded by the insurance industry, have prompted the IIHS to call for a redesign of SUVs and pickups. Concern over SUV rollovers is also an important issue.

Of course, cars are safer now than ever. (Remember family excursions in the early 1960s, when the baby sat on a grownup's lap in the front seat, and the other kids crawled around in back?) But even good drivers need to know about their car and the best safety features, review their driving habits—and watch out for everybody else on the road.

More cars this year offer a safety-belt design that features a pretensioner. This works better than conventional designs by taking up slack in the belt in the event of a crash, so you're not thrust forward.

After safety belts, air bags and antilock brakes are the most important safety equipment. Now, almost all passenger vehicles come with driver and front-passenger air bags, and most 1998 models have air bags that inflate less "aggressively" than older models. (Air bags have saved 2,844 lives in the past decade, but they've also killed some 90 people, most of whom were not wearing safety belts and were too close to an air bag when it deployed in low-speed crashes. Children and short adults were most at risk.) Air bags on some BMWs sense whether the passenger seat is occupied and if the occupant is wearing a belt; accordingly, they deploy at different speeds or not at all.

Consumer Reports also recommends side air bags, which should become more available as demand grows. BMW 5-Series and 7-Series cars also have tube-shaped air bags that provide head protection. Ford, Mercedes, and Volvo plan to offer similar systems. We hope the technology will keep trickling down.

A device Consumer Reports doesn't recommend—except for pickup trucks or convertibles without a back seat—is the new air-bag on/off switch. Some 1998 trucks and two-seaters have this device; cars can also be retrofitted with one if you apply to the National Highway Traffic Safety Administration (NHTSA). With a switch, it's too easy to forget to turn the air bag back on when there's no baby in the front seat.

A century of safety facts

1890s First U.S. autos are manufactured.

1895 The only two autos in Ohio crash; one driver dies, becoming one of the first known motor-vehicle fatalities.

1902 Savannah, San Francisco, and Cincinnati adopt 8-mph speed limit.

1903 First mass-produced Fords.

1908 Model T Ford introduced for $950; within two decades, 15 million will be sold.

1909 Thirty-four states adopt speed limit of 25 mph.

1913 An estimated 4,200 people are killed in car accidents. For the next 19 years, the death toll increases by more than 1,000 a year.

1914 *The New York Times* estimates that there is one car for every 100 Americans.

1922 Auto fatalities this year reach 14,859, or 21.9 per 100 million vehicle-miles (the rate has since dropped to 1.7).

1924 Herbert Hoover convenes first national conference on street and highway safety.

1928 Higher horsepower is the big trend.

1935 *Reader's Digest* publishes a powerful essay, "And Sudden Death," which underscores driving dangers.

1936 Cord

1936 In its first year, Consumers Union decries auto shoddiness: "Manufacturers have deliberately cheapened their cars so that they will not last too long."

1938 There are 25 million motorists in the U.S.

1942-1946 Because of World War II, autos are not made for domestic use. The national speed limit, 40 mph, is reduced to 35 mph to conserve fuel and tires.

1952 Officials discover that the U.S. armed services have lost more men to auto accidents than combat.

1954 The American Medical Association recommends that automakers install safety belts.

1955 Standard safety features include tubeless tires, sealed-beam headlights,

Antilock brakes are now widely available, and we strongly recommend them. They allow a car to stop sooner on wet pavement, and to stop straight instead of after spinning around (if you're going to crash, it's better to hit an object with the front of your vehicle than the side). They also let you steer when you brake hard, so you can get around an obstacle that you'd hit if your wheels were locked up. Research hasn't shown that antilock brakes save lives, but there is evidence that many people don't know how the brake pedal feels and sounds when the antilock braking system is activated. In a vacant parking lot, practice hitting the brakes as hard as you can, keeping the pedal down, and steering around imaginary objects so you won't panic and let up on the brakes in an emergency.

Crash tests can't guarantee a car's safety—there are too many variables in real crashes. They do give an idea of how the car's body and safety equipment will hold up. Use the safety judgments in the profiles section to study your prospective car's performance in head-on crashes, side-impact crashes, and offset crashes. All things being equal, the smaller car in a collision is at greater risk.

The head-on data are from a test performed as part of the federal government's New Car Assessment Program. Cars are crashed into a flat, rigid barrier at 35 mph. The tests show only what would happen if the vehicle in question collided with a similar vehicle, not one that's lighter or heavier. And the findings apply only to belted drivers and passengers. Still, avoid poor-performing cars.

The new side-impact test simulates a crash in which a car traveling at 17 mph is hit from the side at 34 mph. A less severe side-impact standard applies to 1997 cars and 1999 SUVs; data are not yet available on many models.

1955 Chevrolet

better handling, and sometimes fewer projections and hard surfaces. Still, no manufacturer has made "the slightest gesture toward the installation of safety belts, even as an extra cost option," CONSUMER REPORTS says.

1956 Twenty-six of 39 brands of safety belt fail CONSUMER REPORTS' durability test.

1957 Ford cars, advertised to the safety-conscious, sell poorly, prompting the expression, "Ford sold safety while Chevy sold cars."

Safety belts are optional in most new cars.

1961 Only 3 percent of the nation's cars have safety belts.

1965 Ralph Nader's book "Unsafe at Any Speed: The Designed-In Dangers of the American Automobile" launches Nader as the nation's best-known consumer advocate.

1960 Corvette

1974 National speed limit of 55 mph is enacted.

1984-1987 Safety-belt use increases from 14 percent to 42 percent as a result of laws in 31 states. In all states, minimum drinking age is 21.

1987 Federal law allows states to increase speed limit on rural interstate highways to 65 mph.

1990-1992 Safety-belt use increases from 49 percent to 62 percent.

1995 States are allowed to raise speed limits.

1996 Motor-vehicle fatalities total 41,907, or 1.7 per 100 million vehicle-miles. Another 3.5 million are injured.

1997 Air bags are required in all cars.

1998 States adopt zero-alcohol-tolerance laws for drivers under 21. Federal legislation is pending that would push more states to adopt laws presuming impairment for any adult with a blood-alcohol level of 0.08; in many states, the standard is 0.10.

1998 BMW

Sources: "Styling vs. Safety," by Joel W. Eastman; "Test and Protest: The Influence of Consumers Union," by Norman Isaac Silber; federal statistics.

Safety overview

The death rate has declined considerably over the years . . .

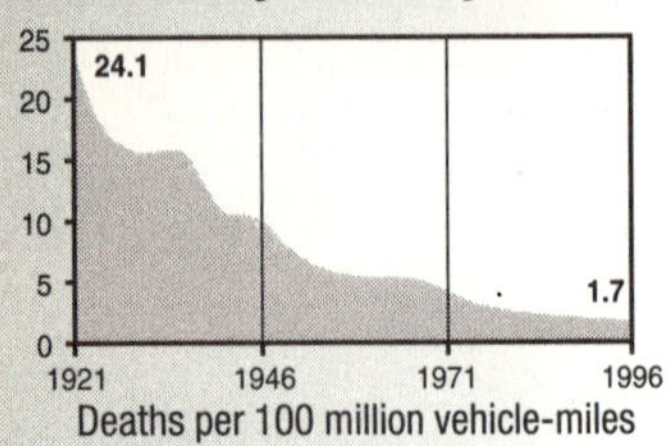

Deaths per 100 million vehicle-miles

. . . but in 1996, nearly half of those involved in fatal car crashes weren't wearing safety belts . . .

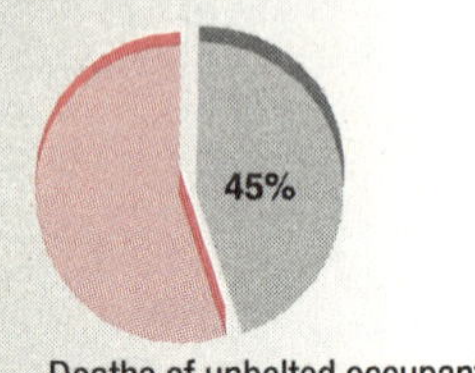

Deaths of unbelted occupants

. . . and alcohol was involved in about 4 of 10 fatal crashes.

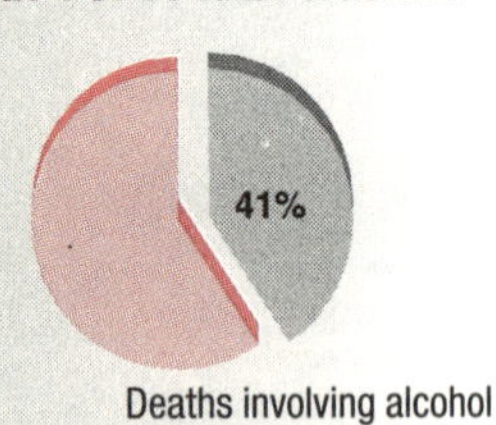

Deaths involving alcohol

An offset test, which the government doesn't require, is conducted by the IIHS and simulates cars colliding head-to-head but off-center at 40 mph. Only the left corner of the car absorbs the impact.

Lastly, consider the color of your car: Those that match the terrain and sky—brown, green, or blue—make your car less visible. Bright colors stand out better, CONSUMER REPORTS engineers say.

THE MOST COMMON DRIVING SINS

Law-enforcement officials have seen motorists make the same mistakes time and time again. The gravest, of course, are not wearing a safety belt and driving while intoxicated. Here are other ways to avoid accidents:

BUCKLE UP KIDS IN THE REAR SEAT. Children up to 20 pounds and up to one year old should be restrained in an infant carrier and face the rear. Kids up to 40 pounds should use a forward-facing seat. We recommend a high-backed booster seat for children 40 pounds and more; use a booster seat until the child's torso is long enough so the shoulder strap doesn't cut across the neck.

When adults buckle up, safety-belt use among their children 12 and under is 94 percent; when adults don't, child safety-belt use plummets to 30 percent, federal officials say.

SLOW DOWN. No one is obligated to drive as fast as the speed limit in heavy traffic, when it's raining or dark, or when the terrain is unfamiliar. "People seem to think it's all right because the speed is posted," says Steve Kohler of the California Highway Patrol. In 1996, speeding, which includes observing the posted limit but going too fast for conditions, was a factor in 30 percent of fatal crashes, according to NHTSA.

KNOW YOUR ABILITIES. Beginning at about age 55, your night vision, peripheral vision, and reaction time are not as sharp as they used to be, says Mary Sweitzer, Pennsylvania's coordinator for the American Association of Retired Persons' 55 Alive driving course. (Many states and the District of Columbia give insurance discounts to drivers 55 and older who take the course; call 800 261-7271 between 9 a.m. and 9 p.m. Eastern time on weekdays.) To compensate, don't drive at night if you're uncomfortable. Increase the distance between your car and the car in front of you. Try to arrange appointments so you're not on the road during rush hours.

The same advice applies to new drivers. Increasingly, states are adopting licensing rules for young drivers that allow them to drive at night or with teenage passengers only after they gain experience on the road.

PLAN AHEAD. What would you do if someone swerved into your lane? Always plan for emergencies. When you're stopped in traffic, give yourself enough room to swing around the car in front if you need to. If you spot what seems to be a drunk driver ahead of you, don't try to pass; you're safer behind. If you suspect a drunk driver is behind you, turn right at the nearest intersection so the car can pass.

AVOID DISTRACTIONS. People can get in trouble when they try to drive and talk on the car phone, attend to children, or look for coins for tolls.

SIT PROPERLY. When you're sitting correctly and comfortably, you're better able to concentrate on the road and react appropriately.

PREVENT ROAD RAGE. Change lanes when you can to allow other drivers to merge. Let others pass you. If someone thwarts your efforts to pass, don't be obnoxious.

ACKNOWLEDGE YOUR MISTAKES. "I wish someone would come up with a sign," says Major Ken Howes of the Florida Highway Patrol. Waving or pretending to slap yourself on the forehead are ideas from an online survey by the AAA Foundation for Traffic Safety.

SAFER CARS AND ROADS

Federal and state officials should do the following to make driving safer:

- Adopt primary safety-belt-use laws, which would allow law-enforcement officers to pull over drivers for not wearing safety belts. In most states, an officer can cite an unbelted motorist only after pulling over the person for another offense.
- Approve an offset-crash standard for passenger vehicles.
- Set a rollover standard for SUVs. Federal officials last year granted our petition to create an emergency handling test. Over the years, our tests showed that some models had a propensity to tip up in emergency-avoidance maneuvers. Of the SUVs involved in fatal crashes, 37 percent rolled over—more than other vehicles.
- Categorize SUVs and minivans as passenger cars, not light trucks, for emissions, safety, and fuel-economy standards. This would require SUVs and minivans to get better fuel economy (and thus be lighter) and SUVs to have lower bumpers, among other things that would make them less dangerous to other vehicles in crashes.
- Collect more data. NHTSA collects detailed reports on all fatalities, but on only 5,000 of the millions of nonfatal, tow-away crashes each year. More analysis could yield injury rates, rollover rates, and other information on individual models.

THE SPECIAL PROBLEMS OF SPORT-UTILITY VEHICLES

For better or worse, sport-utility vehicles are still the fastest-growing segment of the auto market. Ten years ago, only 23 SUV models were available, and their sales were about 6.3 percent of the total market. For 1998, you can choose from among 38 models, from basic runabout to luxury land yacht, and sales are expected to top 17 percent.

"Conventional" SUVs—models like the Chevrolet Blazer, Dodge Durango, Ford Explorer, and Toyota 4Runner—occupy the middle ground, with prices in the mid-$20s to mid-$30s. Most are built like trucks—heavy and high off the ground, with their body bolted to a full frame. In a crash, their bulk and high stance can cause devastating injuries to a passenger car's occupants. And their high center of gravity makes them more prone to roll over.

A new category of small SUVs includes the Honda CR-V and Toyota RAV4—and as of 1998, the Subaru Forester. They're derived from passenger cars with "unit body" construction: The body, rather than a frame, provides structural rigidity. These car-based SUVs are lighter, and perhaps less lethal in a crash.

They also ride more like cars than trucks, and they use fuel more sparingly.

But they lack the towing capacity of the truck-based models, and the low-range gearing and ground clearance needed for extreme off-road use. Prices range from the mid-teens to the mid-$20s.

A University of Michigan study conducted for the National Highway Traffic Safety Administration and released in February analyzed fatal accidents occurring between 1991 and 1994. It found that when a sport-utility vehicle struck the driver's side of a car, the car's driver was 30 times more likely to die than the SUV's driver. In a similar car-to-car collision, the driver of the struck car was only 6½ times more likely to die than the driver of the striking car. Currently, such SUV-into-car crashes are so infrequent that they account for only 4 percent of passenger-car fatalities. But as more SUVs are sold, that percentage is sure to increase.

The damage SUVs can inflict on other vehicles is sobering—but then, a selfish thought can't help but intrude. You may wonder: Should I buy an SUV for my own safety and that of my passengers, no matter what? Not necessarily.

Clearly, in a crash between a car and a typical SUV, you're safer in the SUV. A midsized SUV weighs about 4,000 pounds; a midsized car, about 3,000 pounds. Most SUVs are also higher off the ground. And their high bumpers, attached to a rigid truck frame, act like a battering ram, overriding a car's crumple zone and mangling its passenger compartment.

But what happens when an SUV hits a concrete abutment or a tree? Accident data are lacking, but you might guess that the SUV's rigid construction would be a drawback. And in fact, SUVs have done a bit worse, overall, than cars in 35-mph government barrier crash tests. What's more, in the offset-crash tests conducted by the Insurance Institute for Highway Safety, none of the tested SUVs received the IIHS's highest rating of "good."

The overall death rate is a little lower for SUVs than for cars. But that may not mean much. Kennerly Digges, director of biomechanics for the federally funded National Crash Analysis Center, reported in a recent study that once an SUV is in an accident, its occupants are just as likely to die as the people in a car. The reason, he suggests, is that SUVs roll over about four times as often as cars, offsetting their lower death rates in other types of crashes. Digges adds that a rollover can be especially deadly if you're unbelted.

Small SUVs like the Subaru Forester, Toyota RAV4, and Honda CR-V not only are lighter and lower, they have crumple zones, designed to absorb energy in a crash with another vehicle. Because these models were introduced within the past couple of years, no on-the-road safety data are available for them.

This year, Mercedes-Benz introduced a large SUV with bumpers that are compatible with those of cars. The ML-series, made in Alabama, has a suspension and drivetrain that nestle above the frame—which, unlike other truck frames, is designed to crumple in a crash.

The U.S. auto industry argues that more research is needed before major changes are made to SUVs and other light trucks. Andrew Card, president of the American Automobile Manufacturers Association, starkly cautions, "We must ensure that any changes in design . . . do not inadvertently decrease the safety of the occupants." But Mercedes argues that its SUV already provides good off-road capability without compromising its occupants' safety.

SUVs and minivans are designed primarily to carry people. CONSUMER REPORTS thinks they should meet all the safety and fuel-economy standards that apply to passenger cars. If they did, they'd have to become lighter, and SUVs would have to have lower bumpers. Until that happens, here are some steps you can take to be safer on the road:

- When you shop for a car or light truck, choose one that handles and brakes safely and that has done well in crash tests. Those scores are listed in the Profiles.
- Make sure your next vehicle is new enough to have dual air bags. In addition, all 1997 and 1998 cars must meet tougher side-impact standards. (Some earlier models met those standards voluntarily.)
- Whatever vehicle you're in, always buckle up.

CHILD SAFETY SEATS

Automobile accidents remain the leading cause of death for children under age five in the United States. The National Highway Traffic Safety Administration (NHTSA) estimates that some 700 children die in car crashes each year; another 80,000 are injured.

Parents who don't use a safety seat must shoulder some of the blame for many of those deaths and injuries. Despite laws in every state that require infants and small children to ride in a safety seat, only about 65 percent actually do, according to NHTSA.

Other parents unwittingly contribute to death and injury statistics by failing to install and use the safety seat properly. That's not necessarily their fault. Serious incompatibilities exist between some child seats and some cars—the child seat is too large for the car, the car's belts are too short, its buckle end is too long, or the place you need to mount the seat is too narrow. Nor are safety seats easy to install properly, even if they do fit.

Faulty safety seats may also contribute to the toll. Our crash tests of child safety seats in 1995 and 1996 turned up 4 models of 28 tested that failed under one condition or another in our crash tests. (Three of those have since been recalled or had repair kits made available for them.)

THE BASIC DESIGNS

Choosing the right safety seat goes a long way toward making your child safer and more comfortable. And the more convenient the seat is to use, the more likely it is to be used every time your child is in the car. Here are the main types of seats sold:

INFANT SEATS. These double as a baby carrier. They consist of a carrier and a V-shaped harness that loops through a buckle. A few come with a base that is installed with the vehicle's safety belt and remains in the car. The carrier snaps into and out of the base. Some are part of a multifunctional system where the seat can be used as a carrier, an infant safety seat, or snapped into a stroller base. Infant seats are installed facing rearward in a semireclined position that helps support the baby's head, neck, and back.

Seats made through August 1996 are labeled for use by babies up to 20 pounds. Seats manufactured after that may be labeled for use by babies up to 22 pounds, the weight of a typical one-year-old. In judging fit, remember that the baby's head must be completely contained within the carrier. Price range: $30 to $70.

CONVERTIBLE SEATS. These are designed for both babies and small children. For babies up to at least one year (regardless of weight), convertible seats should be installed in the rear-facing position. After the child outgrows that position after age one, the seat is installed facing forward. A convertible seat may not recline enough or provide a very good fit for a very young baby. Harness designs vary. Price range: $50 to $210.

BOOSTER SEATS. These are for children who are too big for a convertible seat but too small to use a vehicle's safety belts. There are two basic designs: high-back and no-back. Both can come with a removable shield on the harness. Boosters used with the shield are suitable only for younger children who may not remain seated unless confined. Boosters without the shield are used by older kids to raise the child high enough to use the vehicle's safety belts; that's best with children old enough to understand the importance of staying seated and buckled up. But you'll need a car with a shoulder harness in the back seat. Price range: $18 to $115.

BUILT-IN SEATS. Most automotive manufacturers, including Chrysler, Ford, GM, Mitsubishi, Saab, Toyota, and Volvo, offer an optional safety seat (or in some minivans, two seats) built into the vehicle's rear seat. Built-ins are suitable for children over one year. They avoid the problems associated with safety-seat installation. They can't dislodge from the vehicle seat in a crash, and they place the child farther away from the front seat, reducing the risk of head injury. Built-in seats may lack head support for a sleeping child, but those in some cars solve the problem by being able to recline. Other possible disadvantages are that a folded seat sometimes makes an uncomfortable back rest, and there is an inherent lack of flexibility in not being able to transport the seat to another vehicle. Dealer prices range from $100 to $225.

HARNESS DESIGNS

Convertible seats offer different harness designs:

5-POINT HARNESS. This type of restraint uses three or five straps—two at the sides to secure the shoulders and hips, or two at the sides and two across the legs, with a buckle at the crotch that ties them together. It provides the best protection against head injury for all children, and the best fit for small infants, and is easy to buckle and unbuckle. Straps can get in the way when you put the child in the seat, however.

T-SHIELD. This type uses a plastic, T-shaped yoke that buckles into the seat at the crotch, connected to a pair of harness straps. It provides good protection and is easy to move out of the way when seating the child. It's usually easy to buckle and unbuckle. But a small infant's head may not clear the shield.

OVERHEAD SHIELD. This type has a padded, traylike shield that swings down over the child's head. It's generally easy to use. Some shields are adjustable to fit a smaller child or to accommodate bulky winter clothing. But shields don't protect against head injury as well as other designs. A small infant's head may not clear the shield. And the shield may block your view of the buckle.

TETHER STRAP. This type uses a strap to secure the top of a child seat to the car's rear shelf or cargo area. It provides effective protection against head injury by reducing seat movement in the event of a collision. We tested two seats—the *Fisher Price Safe Embrace* ($140) and the *Britax Roundabout* ($200)—in the forward-facing position, and the tether strap helped both earn an excellent rating. The

Britax can also be used in the rear-facing position as well. Without the strap, their performance was only fair. (Both also performed well without the strap in the rear-facing position.) Tether anchor kits can be purchased from your car dealer, though not always easily. Check with your dealer before you purchase either seat.

INSTALLATION PROBLEMS

Correctly installing a safety seat involves following different steps, depending on the belt designs. Consult your car's owner's manual and instructions that come with the safety seat for specific directions. The best place to install a child safety seat is in the rear seat. Also, before purchasing a child safety seat, insist that the retailer let you try to install it in your car so you know it can be installed properly.

WITH LAP-ONLY BELTS. The center rear is regarded as the safest spot in a vehicle, and for that reason it is the preferred location for mounting a safety seat. In most cars, the center rear has a lap belt only. However, more and more cars are being equipped with lap-and-shoulder belt combinations. Lap-only belts are generally the easiest to anchor a child seat tightly. Most are tightened by pulling on the free end of the belt webbing. Even so, the belt may loosen if the buckle rests at an angle on the child-seat frame or belt slot. Check by pulling forward on the child seat after the belt is tightened. If the belt loosens, check the child-seat instructions, as well as the vehicle's owner's manual, for possible solutions, or move the restraint to another position on the seat.

WITH LAP-AND-SHOULDER BELTS. Shoulder belts are now required in back outboard as well as front outboard seats. There are two basic kinds of lap-and-shoulder belts. One allows the lap belt to be locked; the other doesn't. Some locking belts have a latch plate that allows the webbing to move through it in only one direction when you tighten the belt. To release the webbing, you tilt the latch plate. That design usually makes it easy to secure a safety seat.

Many belts have a free-sliding latch plate that does not incorporate a locking mechanism in the latch. The belt stays loose during normal driving but locks in a sudden stop, using a mechanism called an emergency locking retractor (ELR). This type of belt will not hold a child restraint tightly without a locking clip. Install the child seat as instructed by the manufacturer, and clamp the lap-and-shoulder portions together at the latch plate with the locking clip. The lap belt will now stay tightly secured. All child seats are sold with these locking clips, along with instructions on how to install them.

Most shoulder belts on late-model cars can switch the retractor so the webbing locks firmly every inch or so as it retracts to keep a child seat firmly anchored. To activate the locking feature, you pull the shoulder belt all the way out until it clicks, and then let it rewind. Listen for clicks signaling that the webbing is ratcheting back in. If your vehicle has switchable retractors, a label on the belt will usually tell you about it. Details can be found in the vehicle owner's manual.

OTHER COMPATIBILITY PROBLEMS

In many cars, belts come out of the seat cushion from one to several inches in front of the base of the seatback. This configuration improves lap-belt fit for adults and older children but makes it difficult or impossible to mount some safety seats. Whether or not you can tightly secure a seat with such belts depends on the child-restraint belt path and the shape of the seat cushion.

In some cars, seat cushions may be deeply dished out or narrower than your child seat, and belts may be as much as 10 inches forward of the seatback, with buckles on a long, stiff stalk. All of these features make child-seat installation difficult, if not impossible.

WHEN CHILDREN HAVE OUTGROWN CHILD SAFETY SEATS

Lap-and-shoulder belts rarely fit a child who has just outgrown a child seat. Ideally, the lap belt should go over the upper thighs, and the shoulder portion should cross the collarbone and follow a straight line to the buckle. Until the child is tall enough, the shoulder belt might go across the face or throat, and the lap belt might ride up around the waist. Such poor fit increases the risk of injury. A booster seat can bridge the gap.

If the shoulder belt rubs against the neck, a soft cloth or collar between the belt and the neck will make it more comfortable. You can buy aftermarket devices to deflect the shoulder belt away from the neck, for use by both older children and small adults.

General Motors has introduced a "comfort guide" in some of its models (recommended for ages six to ten), which allows a child to use the shoulder belt by keeping it away from the face and neck. It's available in rear seats only.

The front seat is a less safe place than the rear seat, regardless of the seat-belt arrangement. Children should always ride in the rear, even when they are large enough to use the vehicle's safety belt.

Never tuck the shoulder belt under the arm. In a crash the belt may crush the child's ribs and increase the chance of "submarining"—sliding under the belt—which can cause severe abdominal and spinal injuries.

A rear-facing child seat should never be mounted in the front seat, where an air bag can strike it. A front-facing child seat is less dangerous in the front seat, but still much safer in the rear seat. Children belong in the rear. If you must use a front-facing safety seat in the front, slide the seat all the way back.

EMERGENCY EQUIPMENT

Every car needs some sort of auxiliary warning device in case of a breakdown. You may find yourself stranded in the middle of the night far away from home. Something as minor as a shard of glass can disable a car without warning. If you don't have a cellular phone on board and you can't call for help, you'll need to carry other equipment to keep a brief delay from becoming a major interruption.

WARNING DEVICES

TRIANGLE REFLECTORS. Compared with emergency flares or warning lights, triangles have several advantages: They're reusable and they don't require electrical power. You can place them hundreds of feet from the car. And they can sit in the trunk for years without losing their effectiveness. You should have at least three triangles.

To be effective at night, a triangle must be placed perpendicular to the traffic flow. Turn it more than a few degrees from that position and its visibility drops off sharply.

FUSÉE FLARES. Like triangle reflectors, flares can be placed as far from the car as necessary, and they don't require electric power. These powder-filled tubes produce a small, bright red flame when they're struck like a match.

Though widely used, flares have a number of drawbacks: They don't command attention as well as triangles, except in fog. Their light isn't very conspicuous at a distance and could be mistaken for a taillight. Their light may not last until help arrives. They produce gagging fumes and smoke and pose a fire hazard near dry brush or combustible materials. And they decay; they should be replaced about every three years for maximum effectiveness, according to one manufacturer.

FLASHING LIGHTS. These lights, which typically mount magnetically on the car roof, resemble the flasher on an emergency vehicle. They draw power from the car's cigarette-lighter socket, so they won't work in every emergency. Up close, the flashes emanating from these lights may seem bright enough. But from a couple of hundred feet away, even the better lights we have tested were no more visible than the car's own emergency flashers.

FLASHLIGHTS. Add a couple of blinking bulbs to a flashlight, put a word like "hazard" on the package, and you have a product that might seem to pass as a roadside emergency signal. Don't be taken in. We have tried several popular brands: They provided virtually no light from a distance. A flashlight can be invaluable in an emergency, but not to warn motorists.

OTHER EMERGENCY GEAR TO HAVE ON HAND

The following list, by no means exhaustive, should serve as a rough guide to other items you should carry. All the equipment is readily available at auto-parts shops, hardware stores, and pharmacies.

FIRST-AID KIT. No driver should be without one. Include any special medication you need, such as a bee-sting kit. Small kits sold at pharmacies for home use are often better stocked than those targeted for use in a car. Cost: about $15. The American Red Cross also sells a well-stocked first-aid kit for about $30. Contact your local Red Cross chapter for ordering information.

BOOSTER CABLES. If the battery conks out, booster cables enable a passing motorist to give you a jump start. If you drive in a cold climate, we recommend a hefty four- or six-gauge set of cables. For added reach, get a 16-foot version.

SPARE CHANGE. For telephone calls.

WHITE TOWEL. A towel or even a pillowcase can protect clothing if you have to crawl under the car, and it can serve as a warning flag.

BASIC TOOLS. You may not be handy with tools, but a passing Good

Samaritan might be. Keep these tools in a small pouch or tackle box in the trunk: pliers, screwdrivers (both flat and Phillips head), open-end wrenches, adjustable wrench, electrical tape and duct tape, a spool of piano wire, a wire hanger, and a pocketknife.

EXTRA FUSES. A blown fuse can disable taillights or even prevent the car from running. Keep a few replacement fuses of assorted amperages in the glove compartment. Check the car's owner's manual for the size of fuses you need and the location of the fuse box.

FIRE EXTINGUISHER. You may never need to use a fire extinguisher, but you may want to keep one onboard for an added sense of security. Be sure you buy one with an Underwriters Laboratories rating of at least 1A;10B,C. (Those letters and numbers, standard coding on fire extinguishers, denote a unit that can handle small fires of all types.)

FINDING A RELIABLE CAR

CONSUMER REPORTS has been reporting on automobile reliability for more than 40 years. Findings are based on the real-life experiences of hundreds of thousands of readers who each year report the past year's car troubles on CONSUMER REPORTS' Annual Questionnaire.

From those reports, we know that, overall, the reliability of vehicles has improved sharply over the past 15 years. Problems in American cars have shown the greatest improvement, but Japanese and European makes have improved, too. Sport-utility vehicles and pickup trucks used to be particularly troublesome, but the reliability of those types of vehicles has improved dramatically since 1980.

In the most recent survey (1997), readers reported on troubles with 575,000 cars, minivans, pickup trucks, and sport-utility vehicles. CONSUMER REPORTS asks

Reliability compared

On average, cars with a Japanese nameplate are more reliable than European makes, which are more reliable than American makes. The differences are narrowing, particularly in newer models. On average, some manufacturers are more reliable than others, as the "Maker vs. Maker" graph shows. Some makes—Subaru and Isuzu, for instance—have greatly improved their cars in recent model years.

U.S. VS. EUROPE VS. JAPAN

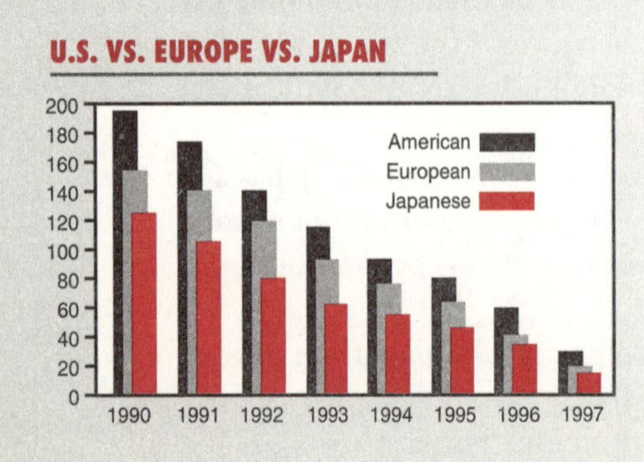

MAKER VS. MAKER

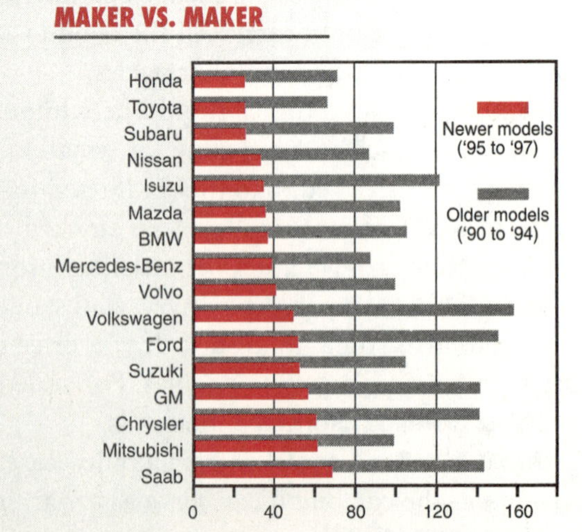

for "serious" problems only—ones that are expensive to repair, put the car out of commission for a time, or cause safety problems.

We sort the reports by model year, developing a snapshot of each model's history. When that history is combined with CONSUMER REPORTS auto engineers' knowledge of automotive design—which models are new, which are carryovers from previous years—we're able to develop predictions about this year's models as well. (Each year, most "new" models aren't substantially changed from the previous year—complete redesigns of autos involve too large an investment of money and time for a car company to do it every year. Most companies redesign their models on three-, four-, or five-year cycles. In some models, the "new" is supplied by minor changes, often purely cosmetic.)

News from this year's survey:

- New cars continue to improve. One-year-old vehicles suffered 25 problems per 100 cars this year, compared with 31 and 28 in the last two surveys.
- The most trouble-free 1997 car overall was the Acura Integra, with only 3 problems reported per 100 cars.
- The most trouble-free 1997 car from Detroit was the Chrysler Concorde, with 15 problems per 100 cars. It also topped the list for 1996 Detroit models. That surprised us, since the 1993 and 1994 versions of the Concorde were among the most troublesome cars. The Concorde was redesigned for the 1998 model year, and time will tell how reliable that design will be.
- The reliability of new sport-utility vehicles and trucks has improved substantially, with an overall problem rate for 1997 models equal to that of cars and minivans. The most reliable 1997 SUV was the Toyota RAV4, with 8 problems per 100 cars.
- The worst, most troublesome 1997 models overall were the redesigned GM minivans—the Chevrolet Venture, Oldsmobile Silhouette, and Pontiac Trans Sport triplets, which had a problem rate of 71 per 100 cars.

USING THE RELIABILITY INFORMATION

CONSUMER REPORTS presents reliability information in three ways in this book:

THE RELIABILITY HISTORY CHARTS. Found on the Profile page for each car, these detail the relevant history (problem rates in 16 trouble areas) from the past model years of the current design. Some models have a consistent track record; even if the model has been redesigned, the reliability records remain essentially unchanged. If a model is new or has been substantially redesigned, the chart is marked "No data new model." If we don't get enough survey responses, the chart is marked "Not enough data to rate." We standardize the data to minimize the effects of varying mileage.

PREDICTED RELIABILITY. Derived from the three most recent, relevant years of reliability data, these judgments can be found in each vehicle's test-judgments table. On a five-point scale, from much worse than average to much better than average, they show our predictions about reliability for this year's models. Over the years, we've found that past experience is a good indicator of future reliability.

THE RELIABILITY COMPARISONS. These graphs zoom in on the relevant cumulative three-year records for model-by-model comparisons by car type. They're on pages 70 to 71.

Reliability

Predictions for the 1998 models

Hundreds of thousands of real-life reader experiences help us predict how reliable the 1998 cars will be. We're able to do that because cars are not redesigned every year and most of the 1998 models are mechanically similar—or identical—to earlier models.

These graphs tell at a glance which new vehicles are most and least likely to be reliable. To create these graphs, CONSUMER REPORTS uses the same analysis that gives the reliability predictions used in the profiles that start on page 80. Vehicles are listed by type. If you're not sure of a car's type, check the profiles.

We give results only for models for which there were sufficient survey responses to make a judgment. The zero line in each graph is the average trouble rate of all 1995 to 1997 vehicles in our most recent reader survey. Cars with identical scores and cars that are "twins" or "triplets"—essentially similar models released under two or more names—are listed alphabetically. Each bar is based on data on the 1997, 1996, and 1995 models if the design was the same. Three-year data are also used for newly redesigned models if the old version was exceptionally reliable. If a model is marked with an asterisk (*), the index is based on one model year only, because the model is new, or recently redesigned, or there weren't enough data for other years.

Subaru Impreza

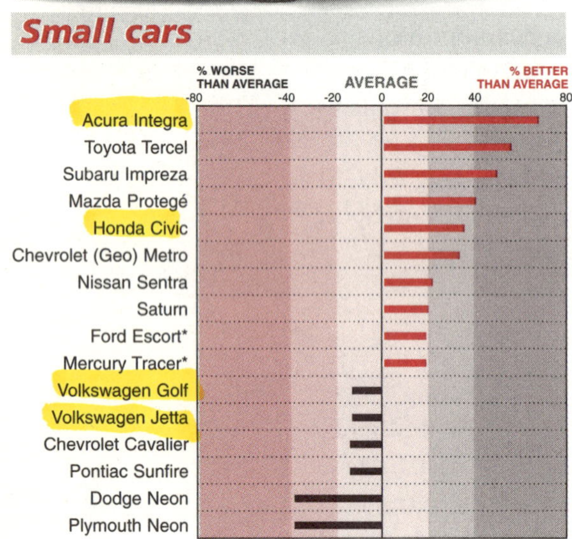

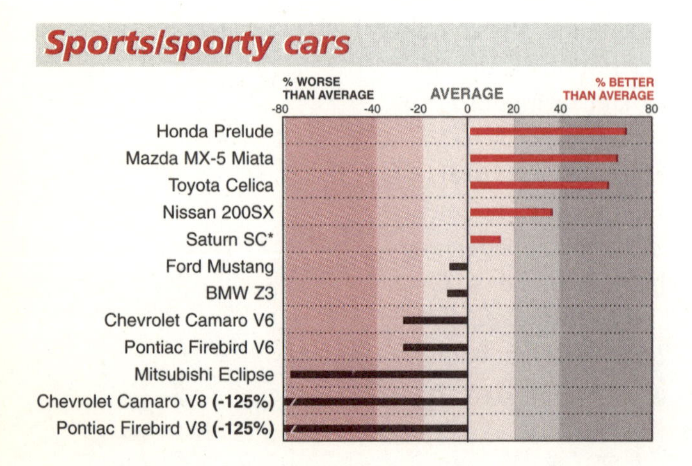

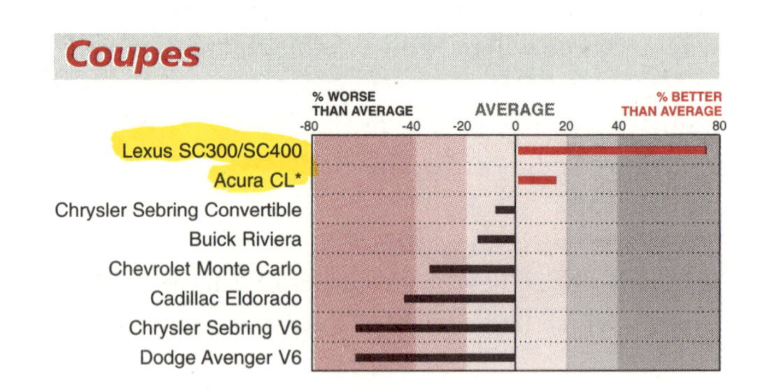

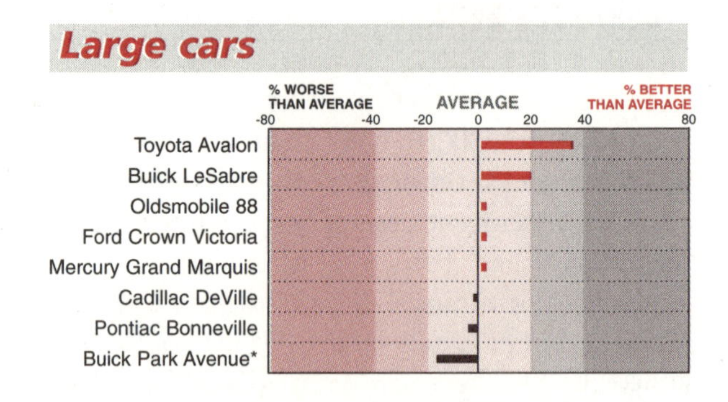

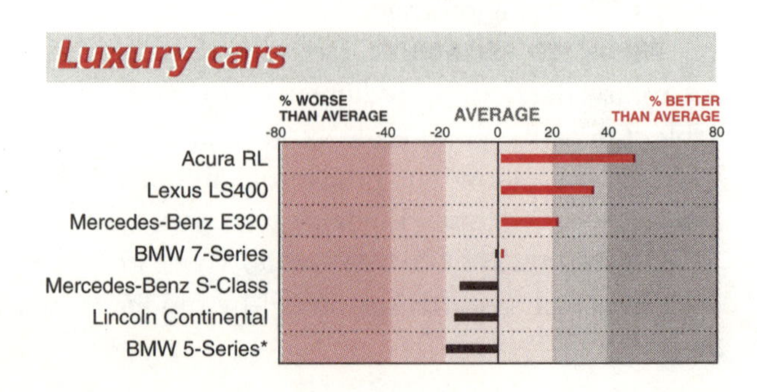

Nissan Maxima

Medium cars

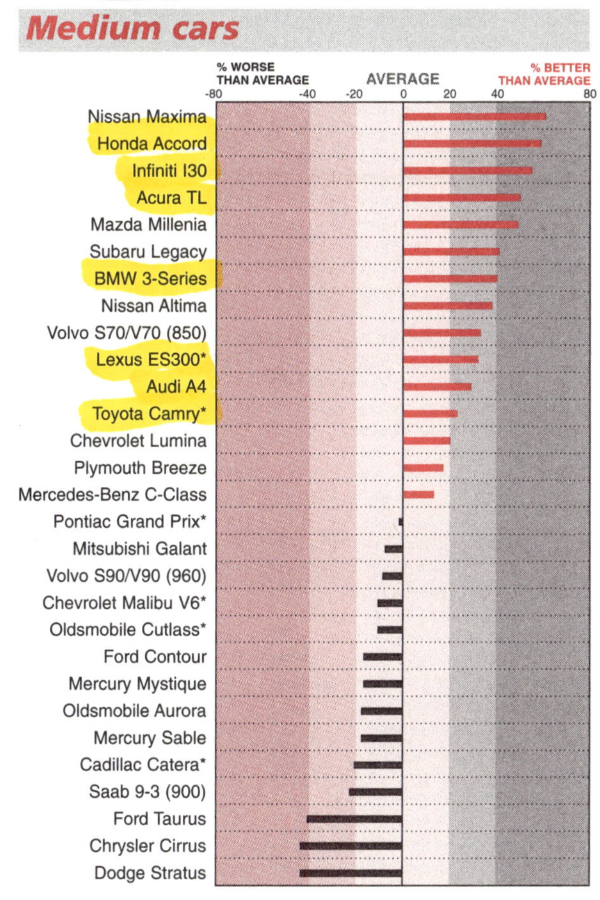

Pickup trucks

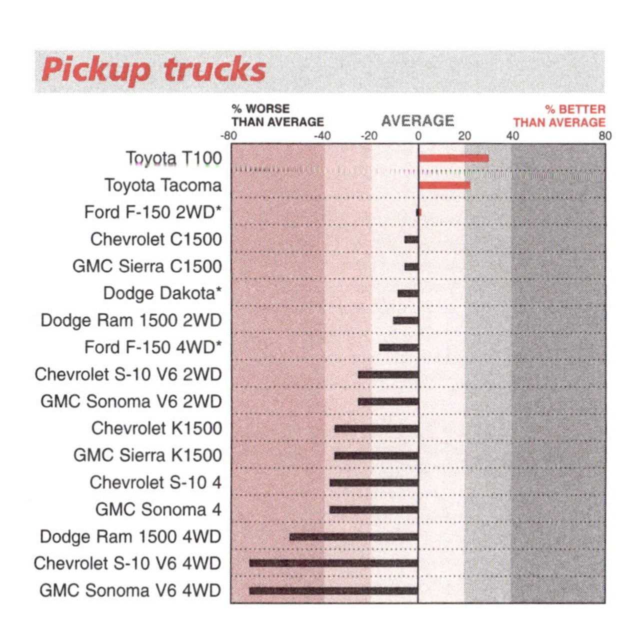

Sport-utility vehicles

% WORSE THAN AVERAGE
AVERAGE
% BETTER THAN AVERAGE
-80 -40 -20 0 20 40 80

Isuzu Trooper
Toyota RAV4
Toyota 4Runner 2WD
Oldsmobile Bravada
Honda CR-V*
Mitsubishi Montero*
Chevrolet (Geo) Tracker
Suzuki Sidekick
Toyota 4Runner 4WD
Ford Explorer
Mercury Mountaineer*
Ford Expedition 2WD*
Nissan Pathfinder 4WD
Jeep Wrangler*
Jeep Grand Cherokee
Jeep Cherokee
Chevrolet Tahoe
GMC Yukon
Ford Expedition 4WD*
Chevrolet Suburban
GMC Suburban
Chevrolet Blazer
GMC Jimmy

Honda Odyssey

Minivans

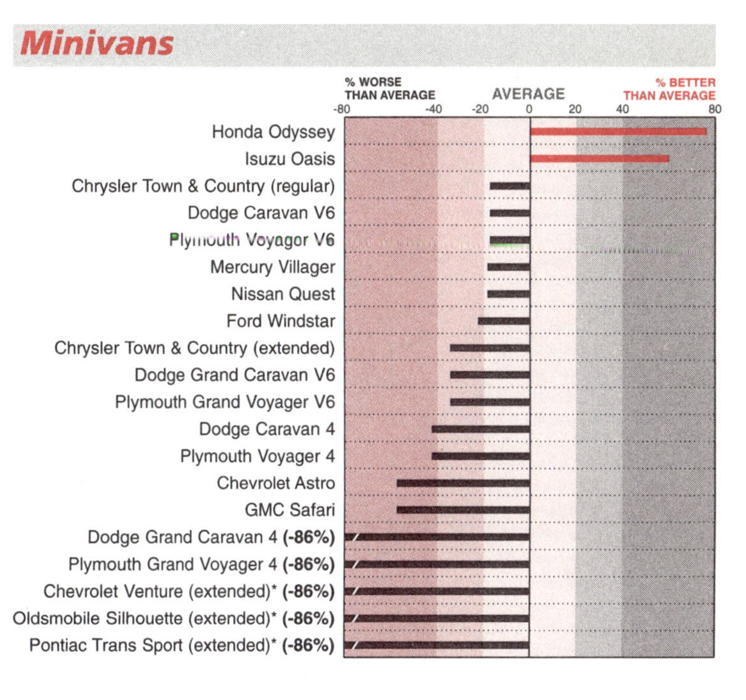

The PROFILES

BEHIND THE TESTS

CONSUMER REPORTS tests and reports on autos throughout the year. We buy a variety of cars, minivans, sport-utility vehicles, and pickup trucks, focusing on new designs and the models most in demand. CONSUMER REPORTS' auto engineers keep track of new-car introductions and redesigns before planning which new models to choose and which older existing models warrant a retest.

Once the test roster is decided, our staff acquires the cars—about 40 vehicles per year. We shop around and bargain for the best price, just as you do. Car dealers are not told that our shoppers are from CONSUMER REPORTS until we actually take delivery of the car. All our test scores and formal evaluations are based on the vehicles we buy.

As soon as a new car arrives, CONSUMER REPORTS' technicians make a thorough inspection using a 50-item checklist. We make sure fluid levels, wheel alignment, and other items meet manufacturer's specifications. We fix minor problems, but if there's a major defect, the dealer makes the repair.

CONSUMER REPORTS' auto-test staffers break in each car with several thousand miles of everyday driving. Then the engineers put the cars through formal tests at our 327-acre facility in East Haddam, Conn., and on surrounding public roads—revealing characteristics about driving comfort, handling, acceleration, and braking that you can't learn during a test drive at a car dealership. The evaluations concentrate on safety, performance, comfort, convenience, and fuel economy.

Safety is a central theme in all the tests. One aspect of safety is a car's ability to protect its occupants in a crash. CONSUMER REPORTS analyzes and interprets crash-

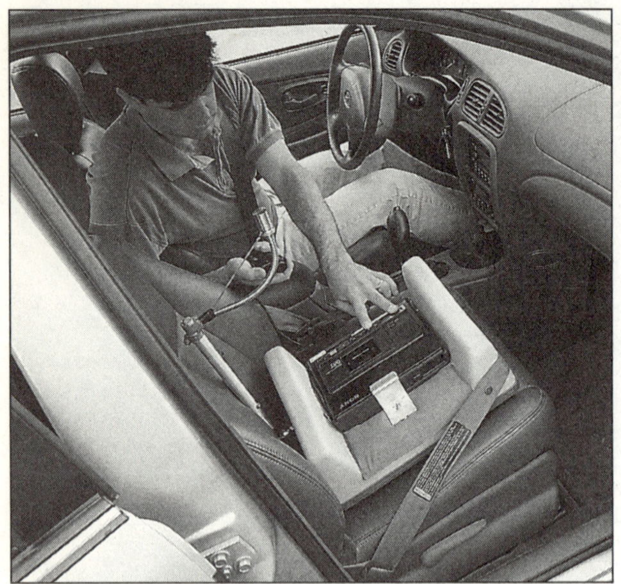

Quietness judgments come from ears and instruments.

test results and notes the availability of safety equipment.

Perhaps more important than crash-test results is a car's ability to avoid a crash in the first place. Indications of that emerge in our testing. Good acceleration is important, because it lets you merge into traffic safely, for instance. A car that handles well communicates information about the road surface, and lets you swerve around obstacles without undue drama. Braking tests tell how short and straight the car can stop.

Ergonomics—how well a car's interior fits the human form—plays a safety role as well. You should be able to reach and use the controls without taking your eyes off the road. And you should be able to find a comfortable position behind the wheel, to avoid fatigue that could compromise your alertness.

When Consumer Reports tests one vehicle, the results often apply to other models as well. Many models are sold under more than one nameplate. (See page 23 for a guide to identical or closely related models.)

TESTING A VEHICLE'S HANDLING. Our avoidance maneuver consists of an abrupt swerve to the left, another swerve to the right, and a final turn left to resume course. Consumer Reports tests at progressively higher speeds, swerving around traffic cones, until the vehicle can't get through without knocking over a cone.

JUDGING A VEHICLE'S RIDE. To find out how a vehicle rides with a full load of passengers and luggage, we use sections of inner tube, each filled with 25 pounds of sand. Some sandbags go on the seats and some in the trunk, up to the maximum weight recommended by the manufacturer.

For ride tests, sandbags give a car a full load.

HOW QUIET IS THE INTERIOR? Test drivers form their own opinions about how quiet each car is. Consumer Reports also uses digital tape decks to make recordings of the interior sound, which our audio engineers analyze.

BUMPER STRENGTH. A heavy hydraulic ram, our bumper-basher, hits each test car front and rear at 3 and 5 mph. Some cars withstand such hits; others sustain hundreds of dollars in damage.

CARGO CAPACITY. To gauge cargo volume for minivans, wagons, and sport-utility vehicles, Consumer Reports uses an adjustable pipe-frame "box." We expand the box as far as it will go until it will just fit through the rear opening and allow the liftgate to close.

OFF-ROAD DRIVING. Consumer Reports' off-road course is littered with stumps, mud, boulders, and other obstacles. We use the course to evaluate the off-road capabilities of sport-utility vehicles, even though most SUVs never traverse anything rougher than a gravel driveway.

BRAKING TESTS. Antilock brake systems show their superiority particularly well in tests on a special section of CONSUMER REPORTS' test track. In this test, the asphalt under one side of the car is much slicker than the asphalt under the other side. Cars with ABS usually stop dead straight here, while those without ABS often veer sharply to one side or spin out. CONSUMER REPORTS also tests the brakes on dry pavement.

Another component of brake tests is fade, which simulates how well the brakes retain their braking ability during a descent from a mountain, for instance.

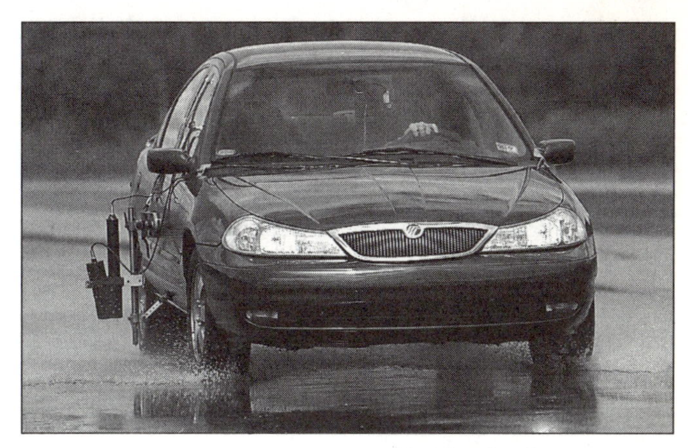

Testing brake systems at the track.

A GUIDE TO THE PROFILES

The profiles of the 1998 cars and trucks are in two sections. The first and larger section covers the vehicles for which CONSUMER REPORTS' tests still apply. Because most cars don't change significantly from year to year, the previous test judgments remain valid for most of this year's models.

The second section summarizes new models, models redesigned since CONSUMER REPORTS' last tests, and models that haven't been tested recently. Though complete test results for those models are unavailable, we can still tell you something about them and where they fit in the universe of automobiles.

Throughout the profiles, NA means data are not available—the model has changed, information is outdated, or the data were unusable or not applicable.

RECOMMENDED, PROMISING. A model recommended by CONSUMER REPORTS performed well in its class and has proven at least reasonably reliable. For vehicles not tested in the new model year, the manufacturers' specs were assessed to determine how close each vehicle is to the previously tested model, and CONSUMER REPORTS has used the latest survey results to predict how well the vehicle will hold up. The lack of a Recommended label doesn't necessarily indicate a poor performer. The model's reliability may have been below par. With a new model, we may not know how it will perform. A new or redesigned model that performed well in its class, but whose reliability CONSUMER REPORTS can't yet predict, is given a Promising label.

BODY STYLES AND PRICES. For each model, available body styles and trim lines are covered, and a range of list (base sticker) prices, without options. CONSUMER REPORTS gives estimates (marked E) where prices were not available. Prices do not include the destination charge, which ranges from $250 to $600 or so. Models often sell at well below sticker price. For more information on negotiating the lowest price at the dealership, see page 28. Four-wheel drive is available in various forms; see page 45 for more information. Throughout the profiles, "FWD," "2WD," "4WD," and "AWD" are front-, two-, four-, and all-wheel drive, respectively.

RELIABILITY. Most car profiles include a judgment of predicted reliability, plus a chart detailing the past reliability of major components such as engine, transmis-

Ratings
Performance results

Consumer Reports bases its Ratings of cars and trucks on expert evaluations and dozens of tests performed over several months of driving each vehicle.

The models are evaluated against other, similar vehicles. Scores for different types are weighted differently. That's particularly true when factoring in cargo capacity and handling. Some models have been tested in more than one version.

Vehicles that haven't been tested recently do not appear here. Scores, from poor to excellent, are based on performance, comfort, convenience, safety equipment, and fuel economy.

The scoring system Consumer Reports uses was revised slightly for 1998, to give extra credit to cars with side air bags and a three-point belt in the center rear seat. Reliability is not part of the score.

✔ means the model is recommended: It performed competently in our tests, and we predict that its reliability will be at least average.
🡅 means this new model is promising: It performed well, but we cannot yet predict its reliability.
The engine or transmission is noted for the model tested if there's a choice and if it makes a difference in the overall Rating.

Small cars with automatic transmission

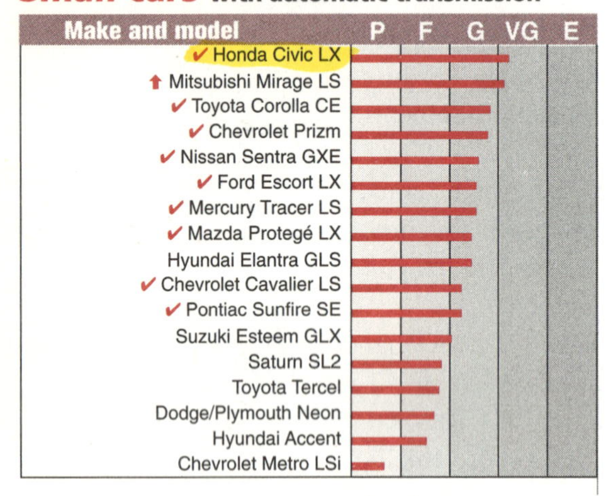

Medium cars under $25,000

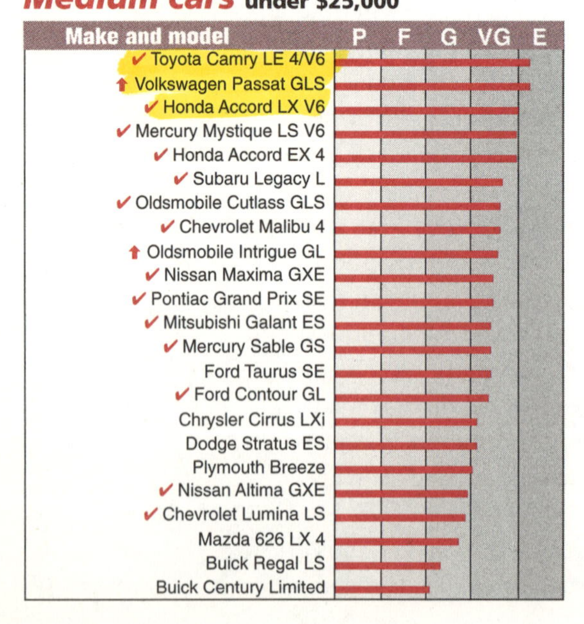

Medium cars over $25,000

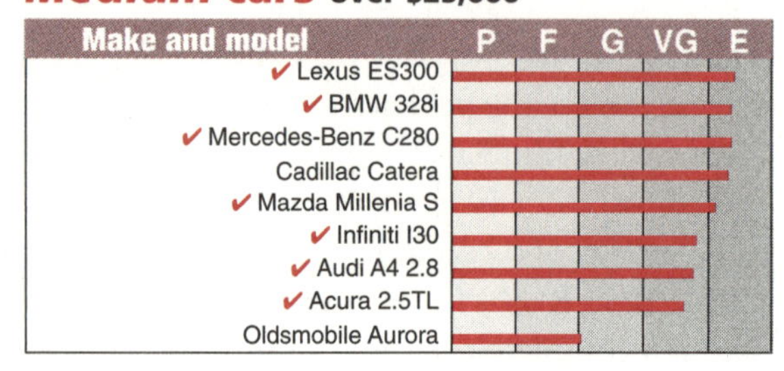

Coupes

Make and model | P F G VG E

Chrysler Sebring LXi
Dodge Avenger ES
Chrysler Sebring Convertible JXi
Chevrolet Monte Carlo Z34
Buick Riviera

Honda Civic

Small coupes with manual transmission

Make and model | P F G VG E

✔ Nissan 200SX SE-R
✔ Volkswagen Golf GTI 4
✔ Acura Integra LS
✔ Honda Civic EX Coupe
Hyundai Tiburon FX
✔ Saturn SC2
✔ Chevrolet Cavalier Z24
✔ Pontiac Sunfire GT
Dodge/Plymouth Neon

Large cars

Make and model	P	F	G	VG	E
✔ Toyota Avalon XL					
✔ Buick Park Avenue Ultra					
✔ Cadillac DeVille					
✔ Lincoln Town Car Executive					
Chrysler Concorde LXi					
Dodge Intrepid					
✔ Ford Crown Victoria					
✔ Mercury Grand Marquis GS					
Buick LeSabre Custom					

Luxury cars

Make and model	P	F	G	VG	E
✔ Mercedes-Benz E320					
✔ BMW 528i					
✔ Acura RL					
Lincoln Continental					

Volvo V70

Station wagons

Make and model	P	F	G	VG	E
✔ Volvo V70 GLT					
✔ Subaru Legacy GT					
Ford Taurus SE					
✔ Mercury Sable LS					
✔ Subaru Legacy Outback					
✔ Subaru Impreza Outback Sport					
✔ Ford Escort SE					
✔ Mercury Tracer LS					

Minivans

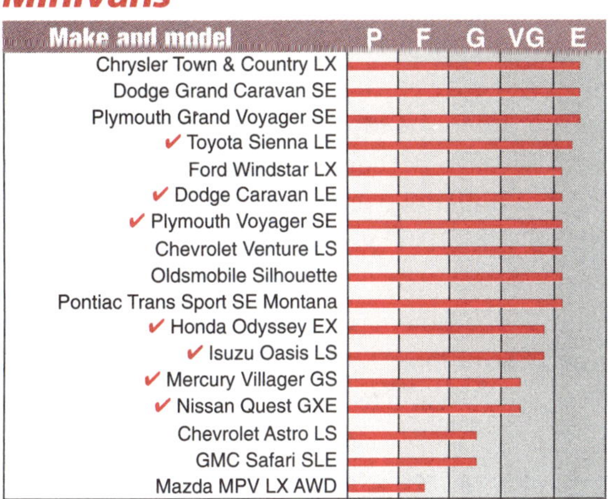

Small sport-utility vehicles

Make and model	P	F	G	VG	E
✔ Subaru Forester S					
✔ Toyota RAV4					
✔ Honda CR-V EX					
Jeep Cherokee Sport 6					
Suzuki Sidekick Sport					
Chevrolet Tracker					
Jeep Wrangler Sahara 6					

Toyota 4Runner

Sport-utility vehicles

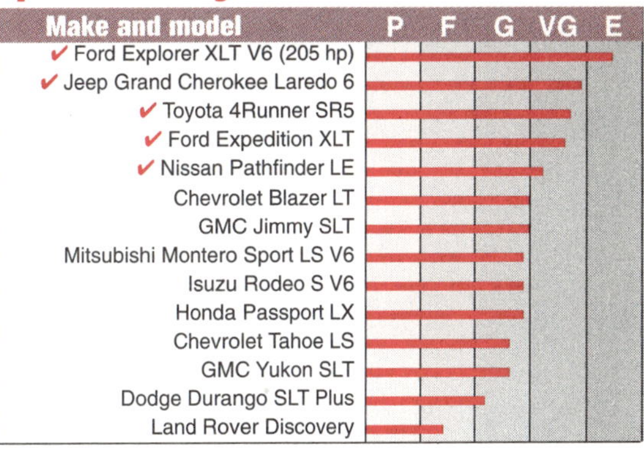

Compact pickup trucks extended cab

Make and model	P	F	G	VG	E
✔ Dodge Dakota SLT V6					
Chevrolet S-10 V6					
GMC Sonoma SLE V6					

Large pickup trucks extended cab

Make and model	P	F	G	VG	E
✔ Ford F-150 XLT					
Chevrolet C1500 Silverado					
GMC Sierra C1500 SLE					
Dodge Ram 1500 Laramie SLT					

Ford F-150

sion, brakes, and so forth. These data are derived from annual surveys of CONSUMER REPORTS subscribers, covering experiences with hundreds of thousands of vehicles. For over 40-odd years CONSUMER REPORTS has assessed reliability by asking readers about their cars. A vehicle's past experience is a good indicator of future reliability.

For these profiles, we've used reliability data from our 1997 annual survey of subscribers. CONSUMER REPORTS asked respondents to identify problems they considered serious in their 1990-1997 models. We standardized the data to minimize the effect of varying mileage. If a model has been redesigned, only years relevant to the 1998 model are shown.

In the chart, the scores for the individual trouble spots represent the percentage of respondents who reported a serious problem in that area. Interpretation of the results depends partly on the car's age. The 1997 models reported on were less than six months old, with an average of only about 3,000 miles; a score of ○ or worse is a sign of trouble in a car that new. A score of ○ is not necessarily cause for alarm in older models, but a score of ◒ or ● is a bad omen.

KEY FOR TROUBLE SPOTS

Percentage of readers reporting problems
- ◉ 2.0% or less
- ◓ 2.0% to 5.0%
- ○ 5.0% to 9.3%
- ◒ 9.3% to 14.8%
- ● More than 14.8%
- * Insufficient data
- ■ Car lacked this feature

SAFETY INFORMATION

No equipment or series of tests can guarantee a vehicle is safe. But they can give you important directions for choosing what to buy. Results are given only for models whose design and safety restraints are similar to the 1998 models.

Except for the Toyota T100 pickup, all 1998 models have **dual air bags.** More and more cars have **side air bags** as well. Standard **ABS** means all four wheels have an antilock braking system. **Traction control** helps a car keep its grip in slippery driving conditions; see page 45 for more on how it works.

Safety belts are the most important piece of safety equipment in the car. All vehicles have three-point lap-and-shoulder belts for the two front seats; all sedans, minivans, and SUVs also provide them for at least two rear passengers. Safety-belt **pretensioners** instantly take up slack in the belt upon impact. CONSUMER REPORTS also notes models that have a three-point belt in the **center** of the **rear** seat.

Front and **side crash** judgments (for driver and passenger side) are from CONSUMER REPORTS' interpretation of results from the National Highway Traffic Safety Administration (NHTSA) crash tests. These simulate a head-on crash at 35 mph and a crash in which a car traveling 17 mph is hit from the side at 34 mph. **Offset crash** results are based on 40-mph off-center collision tests run by the Insurance Institute for Highway Safety (IIHS), an insurance-industry organization. **Injury claim rate** gives an idea of how often occupants have been injured in accidents based on data gathered by the Highways Loss Data Institute, part of the IIHS. The judgments are our interpretation of the data for each model, compared with all vehicles (**overall**) and with cars of that type (**for type**).

Throughout, "optional" means the equipment is available at extra cost; "varies" means that availability varies by trim line; "NA" means the information is not available—the vehicle wasn't tested, wasn't tested recently, or data were unusable or not applicable.

TEST JUDGMENTS. Test judgments are a reflection of the evaluations of

KEY FOR CRASH-PROTECTION JUDGMENTS

- ◉ Probably no injury or a minor injury
- ◓ Moderate injury likely
- ○ Certain injury, possibly severe
- ◒ Severe or fatal injury highly likely
- ● Severe or fatal injury virtually certain

KEY FOR INJURY CLAIM RATES

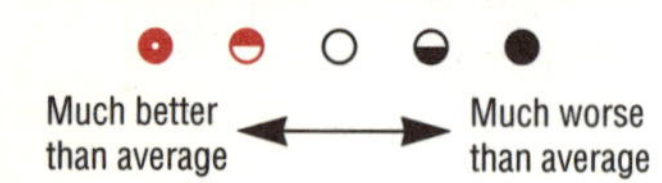

CONSUMER REPORTS' engineers, who have driven recent versions of the vehicles for thousands of miles over several months at our test track and on public roads. (See "Behind the tests," on page 73.)

PREDICTED RELIABILITY. Predicted reliability is a judgment based on CONSUMER REPORTS latest information on reliability.

PREDICTED DEPRECIATION. Predicted depreciation is based on the difference between a model's original sticker price and its resale value after three years. The average depreciation for all vehicles was 36 percent, but the figures range widely, depending on the model and the type of vehicle. As a group, sport-utility vehicles and pickups have the lowest depreciation rate.

KEY FOR TEST JUDGMENTS

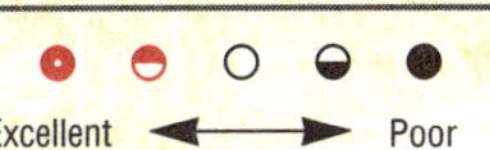

KEY FOR PREDICTED RELIABILITY & DEPRECIATION

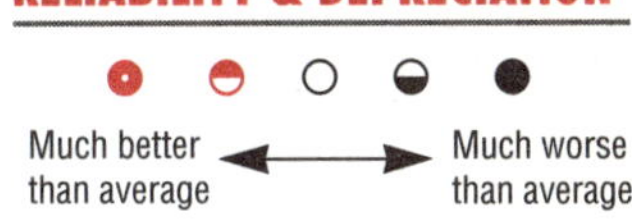

TEST DATA

Most of these measurements were made by CONSUMER REPORTS' engineers. All acceleration runs except for the 45- to 65-mph passing test are from a standstill, with the engine idling.

The fuel-economy figures include U.S. Environmental Protection Agency estimates for city and highway. All other fuel-economy figures are measured by CONSUMER REPORTS, using a precision electronic flow meter spliced into the fuel line, and are rounded to the nearest mile per gallon. Cruising range is derived from the fuel economy recorded on a 150-mile trip. The amount and cost of fuel used in 15,000 miles are calculated from equal portions of city driving, expressway driving, and the 150-mile trip, using $1.20 per gallon for regular, $1.30 for mid-grade, and $1.40 for premium. The cost is rounded to the nearest $5.

Braking figures are from 60 mph, with no wheels locked. Pedal-effort measurements are derived from 10 moderate (one-half g) stops at one-third-mile intervals. The difference in pedal effort between the 1st and 10th stops indicates the amount of brake fade.

SPECIFICATIONS. The number of passengers is as specified by the manufacturer and includes the front, middle (if any), and rear seat. It does not take seat comfort into account.

Most dimensions are from manufacturers' specs, as are engine data. For tested cars, the turning circle (the bumper clearance needed to make a U-turn) and curb weight are measured by CONSUMER REPORTS. Maximum load includes occupants and luggage.

For cars for which CONSUMER REPORTS has test information, interior room figures come from our measurements. Headroom is the clearance above a 5-foot, 9-inch tester's head. Front legroom is the distance from the heel of the accelerator foot to the seatback. Rear fore-and-aft room is the horizontal distance from the rear seatback to the back of the front seatback, with front legroom set at 40 inches. If a vehicle has a middle seat, its fore-and-aft room is measured the same way.

Luggage capacity indicates the number of Pullman cases plus weekend cases we could fit in the luggage area. A "Pullman" case is basically a large, hard-sided suitcase that measures 24 to 36 inches across. Cargo volume (for vans, wagons, SUVs) is the volume of a pipe-frame "box" that is expanded until it just fits the cargo area through the rear opening. For pickup trucks, CONSUMER REPORTS gives no cargo volume because there's no set height.

Small car

Acura Integra

The Integra is an upscale relative of the Honda Civic. The standard 140-hp Four accelerates more than adequately. The five-speed manual transmission shifts crisply. Handling is quite nimble. The sportier GS-R version comes with a 170-hp VTEC engine. The GS-R rides stiffly, while the lower trim lines offer a more comfortable ride. Antilock brakes are standard except in the RS version, where they're unavailable. The front seats are firm—maybe too firm for some—and the cushions are low.

Body styles and prices

	Price range	Trim lines
2-door hatchback	$16,200 - $21,300	RS, LS, GS, GS-R
4-door	$20,000 - $21,600	LS, GS, GS-R

Safety information

Safety belt pretensioners .... No
Center rear safety belt .... Lap
Dual air bags .... Standard
Side air bags .... Not offered
Antilock brakes .... Standard (not offered on RS)
Traction control .... Not offered
Gov't front-crash test, driver/front passenger .... ◓/○
Gov't side-crash test, driver/rear passenger .... NA/NA
IIHS offset crash test .... NA
Injury claim rate compared with all cars/type .... ○/◉

Reliability history

TROUBLE SPOTS	Acura Integra 90	91	92	93	94	95	96	97
Engine	◓	◓	◓	◉	◉	◉	◉	◉
Cooling	◓	○	◓	◓	◉	◉	◉	◉
Fuel	◉	◉	◉	◉	◉	◉	◉	◉
Ignition	◓	◓	○	◓	◉	◉	◉	◉
Auto. transmission	◓	◉	◉	◉	◓	◉	◉	*
Man. transmission	◉	◉	◉	◉	◉	◉	◉	*
Clutch	○	◓	○	◓	◉	◉	◉	*
Electrical	○	○	○	◓	◓	◓	◓	◉
Air conditioning	○	◓	◓	○	◓	◉	◉	◉
Suspension	○	◉	◓	◉	◉	◉	◉	◉
Brakes	◒	○	◒	○	○	◓	◉	◉
Exhaust	●	◒	●	◒	◉	◉	◉	◉
Body rust	◓	◓	◉	◉	◉	◉	◉	◉
Paint/trim	○	◓	◓	◓	◓	◓	◉	◓
Body integrity	◒	○	○	○	○	○	◓	◉
Body hardware	○	○	○	◓	○	◓	◓	◉

Test judgments

Performance

Acceleration .... ◓
Transmission .... ◉
Routine handling .... ◓
Emergency handling .... ○
Braking .... ○

Comfort

Ride, normal load .... ○
Ride, full load .... ○
Noise .... ○
Driving position .... ◓
Front-seat comfort .... ◓
Rear-seat comfort .... ●
Climate-control system .... ◉

Convenience

Access .... ○
Controls and displays .... ○
Trunk .... ◒

Other

Fuel economy .... ◉
Predicted reliability .... ◉
Predicted depreciation .... ○

Test data

Acceleration

0-30 mph, sec. 3.4
0-60 mph, sec. 9.3
Quarter mile, sec. 17.1
Quarter mile, mph 83
45-65 mph, sec. 6.2

Fuel economy (regular)

EPA city/highway, mpg 25/31
CU's overall mileage, mpg 31
CU's city/highway, mpg 23/40
CU's 150-mile trip, mpg 34
Fuel refill capacity, gal. 13.2
Cruising range, mi. 415
Annual fuel: gal./cost .... 490/$585

Braking from 60 mph

Dry pavement, ft. 143
Wet pavement, ft. 158
Pedal effort, 1st stop, lb. 20
Pedal effort, 10th stop, lb. 25

Specifications

Drive wheels

Front

Seating

Passengers, front/rear 2/3

Dimensions and weight

Length, in. 172
Width, in. 67
Wheelbase, in. 101
Turning circle, ft. 39
Curb weight, lb. 2635
Percent weight, front/rear 62/38
Max. load, lb. 700

Interior room

Front shoulder room, in. 51.5
Front leg room, in. 41.5
Front head room, in. 2.0
Rear shoulder room, in. 46.5
Rear fore-aft room, in. 25.0
Rear head room, in. 0.5
Door top to ground, in. 47.5
Luggage capacity .... 3+2

Engines available

1.8-liter 4 (140 or 170 hp)

Transmissions available

5-speed manual
4-speed automatic

Tested model

1997 LS 2-door hatchback, 1.8-liter Four, 5-speed manual

Tires as tested

Michelin XGT H4, size P195/60R14

Luxury car

Acura RL

Acura's flagship sedan is quiet, spacious, and refined, though rather bland overall. For 1998 Acura made heated side mirrors standard and added a lap-and-shoulder safety belt for the center rear seat. The RL rides comfortably and quietly, even when its V6 is revved. Fit and finish are flawless. However, the RL still lacks separate climate controls for the driver and front passenger, power head restraints, and side air bags. Overall, the RL is a notch below competitors from Mercedes and BMW in performance, handling, comfort, and fuel economy.

Body styles and prices

	Price range	Trim lines
4-door	\$41,200 - \$44,000	Base, Premium

Safety information

Safety belt pretensioners	Front
Center rear safety belt	3-point
Dual air bags	Standard
Side air bags	Not offered
Antilock brakes	Standard
Traction control	Optional
Gov't front-crash test, driver/front passenger	NA/NA
Gov't side-crash test, driver/rear passenger	NA/NA
IIHS offset crash test	NA
Injury claim rate compared with all cars/type	NA/NA

Reliability history

TROUBLE SPOTS — Acura 3.5RL (90 91 92 93 94 95 96 97)

Engine; Cooling; Fuel; Ignition; Auto. transmission; Man. transmission; Clutch; Electrical; Air conditioning; Suspension; Brakes; Exhaust; Body rust; Paint/trim; Body integrity; Body hardware

97: Insufficient data

Test judgments

Performance
- Acceleration
- Transmission
- Routine handling
- Emergency handling
- Braking

Comfort
- Ride, normal load
- Ride, full load
- Noise
- Driving position
- Front-seat comfort
- Rear-seat comfort
- Climate-control system

Convenience
- Access
- Controls and displays
- Trunk

Other
- Fuel economy
- Predicted reliability
- Predicted depreciation ..... NA

Test data

Acceleration

0-30 mph, sec.	3.4
0-60 mph, sec.	8.5
Quarter mile, sec.	16.7
Quarter mile, mph	86
45-65 mph, sec.	5.2

Fuel economy (premium)

EPA city/highway, mpg	19/25
CU's overall mileage, mpg	20
CU's city/highway, mpg	14/30
CU's 150-mile trip, mpg	21
Fuel refill capacity, gal.	18.0
Cruising range, mi.	355
Annual fuel: gal./cost	770/\$1080

Braking from 60 mph

Dry pavement, ft.	133
Wet pavement, ft.	159
Pedal effort, 1st stop, lb.	20
Pedal effort, 10th stop, lb.	25

Specifications

Drive wheels
Front

Seating

Passengers, front/rear	2/3

Dimensions and weight

Length, in.	195
Width, in.	71
Wheelbase, in.	115
Turning circle, ft.	39
Curb weight, lb.	3670
Percent weight, front/rear	60/40
Max. load, lb.	850

Interior room

Front shoulder room, in.	57.0
Front leg room, in.	43.0
Front head room, in.	2.5
Rear shoulder room, in.	55.5
Rear fore-aft room, in.	29.5
Rear head room, in.	3.0
Door top to ground, in.	50.5
Luggage capacity	5+0

Engines available
3.5-liter V6 (210 hp)

Transmissions available
4-speed automatic

Tested model
1996 4-door, 3.5-liter V6, 4-speed automatic

Tires as tested
Michelin Energy MXV4, size P215/60R16

Medium car over $25,000

Acura TL

This upscale midsized sedan competes with the Infiniti I30, Lexus ES300, Mazda Millenia, and other "near luxury" models. Fit and finish are excellent—typical of most Acura/Honda products—but the overall driving experience is unexceptional. While the TL handles soundly and delivers a quiet ride that's firm but supple, it also leans considerably during cornering. The front seats provide comfortable support. The rear seat easily holds two, but three's a crowd. The 2.5TL version has a smooth, strong 176-hp, 2.5-liter five-cylinder engine. The plusher 3.2TL comes with a refined 200-hp, 3.2-liter V6. A new TL is due in the fall.

Body styles and prices

	Price range	Trim lines
4-door	$30,700 - $33,150	2.5TL, 3.2TL

Safety information

Safety belt pretensioners .... No
Center rear safety belt .... Lap
Dual air bags .... Standard
Side air bags .... Not offered
Antilock brakes .... Standard
Traction control .... Optional on 3.2TL
Gov't front-crash test, driver/front passenger .... ◓/◓
Gov't side-crash test, driver/rear passenger .... NA/NA
IIHS offset crash test .... NA
Injury claim rate compared with all cars/type .... ○/◒

Reliability history

TROUBLE SPOTS	Acura TL 90	91	92	93	94	95	96	97
Engine							●	●
Cooling							●	●
Fuel							●	●
Ignition							●	●
Auto. transmission							●	●
Man. transmission								
Clutch								
Electrical							◓	●
Air conditioning							●	●
Suspension							●	●
Brakes							◓	●
Exhaust							●	●
Body rust							●	●
Paint/trim							◓	●
Body integrity							◓	◓
Body hardware							◓	◓

Test judgments

Performance
Acceleration .... ◓
Transmission .... ◓
Routine handling .... ◓
Emergency handling .... ○
Braking .... ◓

Comfort
Ride, normal load .... ◓
Ride, full load .... ◓
Noise .... ◓
Driving position .... ◓
Front-seat comfort .... ◓
Rear-seat comfort .... ◓
Climate-control system .... ●

Convenience
Access .... ◓
Controls and displays .... ◓
Trunk .... ○

Other
Fuel economy .... ○
Predicted reliability .... ●
Predicted depreciation .... NA

Test data

Acceleration
0-30 mph, sec. 3.8
0-60 mph, sec. 9.7
Quarter mile, sec. 17.6
Quarter mile, mph 81
45-65 mph, sec. 6.1

Fuel economy (premium)
EPA city/highway, mpg 20/25
CU's overall mileage, mpg 23
CU's city/highway, mpg 16/34
CU's 150-mile trip, mpg 26
Fuel refill capacity, gal. 17.2
Cruising range, mi. 410
Annual fuel: gal./cost .... 660/$920

Braking from 60 mph
Dry pavement, ft. 133
Wet pavement, ft. 152
Pedal effort, 1st stop, lb. 20
Pedal effort, 10th stop, lb. 25

Specifications

Drive wheels
Front

Seating
Passengers,front/rear 2/3

Dimensions and weight
Length, in. 192
Width, in. 70
Wheelbase, in. 112
Turning circle, ft. 39
Curb weight, lb. 3280
Percent weight, front/rear 59/41
Max. load, lb. 850

Interior room
Front shoulder room, in. 55.0
Front leg room, in. 43.0
Front head room, in. 3.0
Rear shoulder room, in. 53.5
Rear fore-aft room, in. 28.5
Rear head room, in. 2.5
Door top to ground, in. 50.0
Luggage capacity .... 5+1

Engines available
2.5-liter 5 (176 hp)
3.2-liter V6 (200 hp)

Transmissions available
4-speed automatic

Tested model
1996 2.5TL 4-door, 2.5-liter Five, 4-speed automatic

Tires as tested
Bridgestone Potenza RE92, size 205/60R15

Medium car over $25,000

Audi A4

The A4 is a German sedan that rides firmly and handles precisely and nimbly. The 2.8-liter V6 version is a solid competitor in the "near luxury" class. The less-costly 1.8T version, with a 150-hp turbocharged Four, is smooth, economical, and also comes well equipped. The automatic climate control system is first rate. Since we tested the A4, it has gained more power. The optional five-speed automatic transmission has a Tiptronic feature that allows easy manual shifts with a flick of the lever. The seat and driving position are nearly ideal, but the rear is cramped. A wagon version, called the A4 Avant, is new for 1998. Side air bags are standard. Audi's all-wheel-drive Quattro feature is a worthwhile option.

Body styles and prices

	Price range	Trim lines
4-door	$23,790 - $28,390	1.8T, 2.8
4-door wagon	$30,465	Avant

Safety information

Safety belt pretensioners	Front
Center rear safety belt	Lap
Dual air bags	Standard
Side air bags	Standard
Antilock brakes	Standard
Traction control	Standard
Gov't front-crash test, driver/front passenger	●/●
Gov't side-crash test, driver/rear passenger	NA/NA
IIHS offset crash test	NA
Injury claim rate compared with all cars/type	NA/NA

Reliability history

TROUBLE SPOTS	Audi A4 90	91	92	93	94	95	96	97
Engine							●	●
Cooling							●	●
Fuel							●	●
Ignition							●	●
Auto. transmission							○	*
Man. transmission							●	*
Clutch							●	*
Electrical							◒	◓
Air conditioning							●	●
Suspension							◓	●
Brakes							◓	●
Exhaust							●	●
Body rust							●	●
Paint/trim							●	●
Body integrity							◓	●
Body hardware							○	◓

Test judgments

Performance

Acceleration	◓
Transmission	○
Routine handling	●
Emergency handling	◓
Braking	◓

Comfort

Ride, normal load	○
Ride, full load	◓
Noise	◓
Driving position	●
Front-seat comfort	●
Rear-seat comfort	◒
Climate-control system	●

Convenience

Access	◓
Controls and displays	○
Trunk	◓

Other

Fuel economy	◒
Predicted reliability	◓
Predicted depreciation	NA

Test data

Acceleration

0-30 mph, sec.	3.4
0-60 mph, sec.	9.8
Quarter mile, sec.	17.5
Quarter mile, mph	82
45-65 mph, sec.	6.5

Fuel economy (premium)

EPA city/highway, mpg	18/28
CU's overall mileage, mpg	22
CU's city/highway, mpg	13/37
CU's 150-mile trip, mpg	27
Fuel refill capacity, gal.	16.4
Cruising range, mi.	405
Annual fuel: gal./cost	695/$975

Braking from 60 mph

Dry pavement, ft.	130
Wet pavement, ft.	149
Pedal effort, 1st stop, lb.	20
Pedal effort, 10th stop, lb.	20

Specifications

Drive wheels

Front or all

Seating

Passengers, front/rear	2/3

Dimensions and weight

Length, in.	178
Width, in.	68
Wheelbase, in.	103
Turning circle, ft.	37
Curb weight, lb.	3220
Percent weight, front/rear	63/37
Max. load, lb.	1212

Interior room

Front shoulder room, in.	54.0
Front leg room, in.	43.5
Front head room, in.	3.5
Rear shoulder room, in.	52.0
Rear fore-aft room, in.	26.0
Rear head room, in.	2.5
Door top to ground, in.	50.0
Luggage capacity	5+0

Engines available

1.8-liter 4 turbo (150 hp)
2.8-liter V6 (190 hp)

Transmissions available

5-speed manual
5-speed automatic

Tested model

1996 4-door, 2.8-liter V6, 5-speed automatic

Tires as tested

Goodyear Eagle RS-A, size 205/55R16

Medium car over $25,000

BMW 3-Series

The new 323i convertible and 323iS coupe, powered by a 2.5-liter Six, replaced the four-cylinder 318i convertible and 318iS coupe for 1998. All models get standard side air bags in front. The rear-drive 3-Series focuses on sporty driving characteristics rather than roomy accommodations. This agile car handles crisply and corners neatly, with tenacious tire grip. The 328's 2.8-liter Six accelerates briskly, and the brakes work well. The ride is firm but compliant and quiet, and all-speed traction control effectively limits rear-wheel spin. The 3-Series will be redesigned for the 1999 model year.

Body styles and prices

	Price range	Trim lines
2-door	$28,700 - $39,700	323iS, 328iS, M3
4-door	$26,150 - $39,700	318i, 328i, M3
Convertible	$34,700 - $45,900	323iC, 328iC, M3

Safety information

Safety belt pretensioners ....Front
Center rear safety belt ....Lap
Dual air bags ....Standard
Side air bags ....Standard
Antilock brakes..Standard
Traction control ....Standard
Gov't front-crash test, driver/front passenger ....◓/◓
Gov't side-crash test, driver/rear passenger ....NA/NA
IIHS offset crash test ....NA
Injury claim rate compared with all cars/type ....○/◒

Reliability history

TROUBLE SPOTS	90	91	92	93	94	95	96	97
Engine	Insufficient data	●	○	◓	◉	◉	◉	◉
Cooling		◒	◒	○	◓	◉	◉	◉
Fuel		◒	○	○	◓	◓	◓	◉
Ignition		○	○	◓	◓	◉	◓	◉
Auto. transmission		*	◓	◓	◉	◉	◉	*
Man. transmission		◓	◓	◓	◉	◓	◉	*
Clutch		◉	◓	○	◉	◓	◉	*
Electrical		●	●	◒	◒	○	○	◉
Air conditioning		◒	◒	◓	◓	◉	◉	◉
Suspension		○	○	◓	◉	◉	◉	◉
Brakes		●	○	◒	◓	◓	◓	◉
Exhaust		○	◓	◓	◉	◉	◉	◉
Body rust		◓	◉	◉	◉	◉	◉	◉
Paint/trim		◓	◓	◓	◉	◉	◉	◉
Body integrity		○	○	○	○	◓	○	◉
Body hardware		●	●	◒	◒	○	○	◉

Test judgments

Performance
Acceleration ....◓
Transmission ....◉
Routine handling ....◉
Emergency handling ....◓
Braking ....◓

Comfort
Ride, normal load ....◓
Ride, full load ....◓
Noise ....◓
Driving position ....◓
Front-seat comfort ....◉
Rear-seat comfort ....○
Climate-control system ....◉

Convenience
Access ....◓
Controls and displays ....◉
Trunk ....◒

Other
Fuel economy ....○
Predicted reliability ....◓
Predicted depreciation ....○

Test data

Acceleration
0-30 mph, sec. 2.9
0-60 mph, sec. 7.6
Quarter mile, sec. 16.0
Quarter mile, mph 89
45-65 mph, sec. 5.0

Fuel economy (premium)
EPA city/highway, mpg 18/26
CU's overall mileage, mpg 24
CU's city/highway, mpg.......16/36
CU's 150-mile trip, mpg 28
Fuel refill capacity, gal. 16.4
Cruising range, mi. 430
Annual fuel: gal./cost ......635/$885

Braking from 60 mph
Dry pavement, ft. 133
Wet pavement, ft. 150
Pedal effort, 1st stop, lb. 15
Pedal effort, 10th stop, lb. 15

Specifications

Drive wheels
Rear

Seating
Passengers,front/rear...............2/3

Dimensions and weight
Length, in. 175
Width, in. 67
Wheelbase, in. 106
Turning circle, ft. 36
Curb weight, lb. 3225
Percent weight, front/rear 51/49
Max. load, lb. 970

Interior room
Front shoulder room, in. 53.5
Front leg room, in. 42.0
Front head room, in. 3.5
Rear shoulder room, in. 53.0
Rear fore-aft room, in. 28.0
Rear head room, in. 2.5
Door top to ground, in. 49.5
Luggage capacity ....3+2

Engines available
1.9-liter 4 (138 hp), 2.5-liter 6 (168 hp), 2.8-liter 6 (190 hp) 3.2-liter 6 (240 hp)

Transmissions available
5-speed manual, 4-speed automatic

Tested model
1997 328i 4-door, 2.8-liter Six, 4-speed automatic

Tires as tested
Michelin Energy MXV4, size 205/60R15

Luxury car

BMW 5-Series

The 5-Series embodies pure precision: These superbly designed rear-wheel-drive luxury sports sedans handle nimbly and responsively. The 5-Series comes in six- and eight-cylinder versions, and offers both manual and automatic transmissions. The ride is supple and quiet, with extremely comfortable, supportive seats. The cabin and trunk are a bit tight, but adequate, and the finish is meticulous. The brakes are exceptional, and the standard all-speed traction-control system effectively reduces wheel spin. Side-impact and head-level air bags are standard up front and—new for 1998—chest-level side air bags are optional in the rear.

Body styles and prices

	Price range	Trim lines
4-door	$38,900 - $53,300	528i, 540i

Safety information

Safety belt pretensioners	Front
Center rear safety belt	3-point
Dual air bags	Standard
Side air bags	Standard
Antilock brakes	Standard
Traction control	Standard
Gov't front-crash test, driver/front passenger	NA/NA
Gov't side-crash test, driver/rear passenger	NA/NA
IIHS offset crash test	Good
Injury claim rate compared with all cars/type	NA/NA

Reliability history

TROUBLE SPOTS	BMW 5-Series 90	91	92	93	94	95	96	97
Engine								●
Cooling								●
Fuel								●
Ignition								●
Auto. transmission								●
Man. transmission								*
Clutch								*
Electrical								○
Air conditioning								●
Suspension								●
Brakes								●
Exhaust								●
Body rust								●
Paint/trim								●
Body integrity								○
Body hardware								○

Test judgments

Performance

Acceleration	◓
Transmission	●
Routine handling	●
Emergency handling	◓
Braking	◓

Comfort

Ride, normal load	◓
Ride, full load	◓
Noise	●
Driving position	●
Front-seat comfort	●
Rear-seat comfort	◓
Climate-control system	◓

Convenience

Access	◓
Controls and displays	◓
Trunk	○

Other

Fuel economy	◒
Predicted reliability	○
Predicted depreciation	○

Test data

Acceleration

0-30 mph, sec.	3.1
0-60 mph, sec.	8.2
Quarter mile, sec.	16.5
Quarter mile, mph	87
45-65 mph, sec.	5.4

Fuel economy (premium)

EPA city/highway, mpg	18/26
CU's overall mileage, mpg	20
CU's city/highway, mpg	13/34
CU's 150-mile trip, mpg	22
Fuel refill capacity, gal.	18.5
Cruising range, mi.	380
Annual fuel: gal./cost	755/$1055

Braking from 60 mph

Dry pavement, ft.	129
Wet pavement, ft.	148
Pedal effort, 1st stop, lb.	15
Pedal effort, 10th stop, lb.	15

Specifications

Drive wheels

Rear

Seating

Passengers,front/rear	2/3

Dimensions and weight

Length, in.	188
Width, in.	71
Wheelbase, in.	111
Turning circle, ft.	38
Curb weight, lb.	3585
Percent weight, front/rear	51/49
Max. load, lb.	1015

Interior room

Front shoulder room, in.	57.0
Front leg room, in.	43.0
Front head room, in.	3.5
Rear shoulder room, in.	55.0
Rear fore-aft room, in.	29.0
Rear head room, in.	3.5
Door top to ground, in.	51.0
Luggage capacity	4+1

Engines available

2.8-liter 6 (190 hp)
4.4-liter V8 (282 hp)

Transmissions available

5-speed manual, 6-speed manual
4-speed auto., 5-speed auto.

Tested model

1997 528i 4-door, 2.8-liter Six, 4-speed automatic

Tires as tested

Continental ContiTouring Contact, size 225/60R15

Medium car under $25,000

Buick Century

Even though the Century was redesigned for 1997, it still feels like a throwback to an earlier era. The ride is quiet and smooth, at least at low speeds, but bumpy roads easily upset its composure. Handling is unresponsive and ungainly. Braking is inferior. The only engine is a 160-hp, 3.1-liter V6. Power is adequate, and the transmission shifts smoothly. The front bench seat is roomy—the car nominally seats six—but the soft seats offer little support. Rear seats are soft, as in the front, but they too lack support. The trunk is spacious.

Body styles and prices

	Price range	Trim lines
4-door	$18,215 - $19,575	Custom, Limited

Safety information

Safety belt pretensioners	No
Center rear safety belt	Lap
Dual air bags	Standard
Side air bags	Not offered
Antilock brakes	Standard
Traction control	Not offered
Gov't front-crash test, driver/front passenger	NA/NA
Gov't side-crash test, driver/rear passenger	○/○
IIHS offset crash test	NA
Injury claim rate compared with all cars/type	NA/NA

Reliability history

TROUBLE SPOTS	90 91 92 93 94 95 96 97
Engine	
Cooling	
Fuel	
Ignition	NOT
Auto. transmission	
Man. transmission	ENOUGH
Clutch	
Electrical	
Air conditioning	DATA
Suspension	
Brakes	TO
Exhaust	
Body rust	RATE
Paint/trim	
Body integrity	
Body hardware	

Test judgments

Performance

Acceleration	◓
Transmission	◓
Routine handling	○
Emergency handling	◒
Braking	◒

Comfort

Ride, normal load	○
Ride, full load	○
Noise	●
Driving position	◓
Front-seat comfort	○
Rear-seat comfort	○
Climate-control system	●

Convenience

Access	◓
Controls and displays	○
Trunk	◓

Other

Fuel economy	○
Predicted reliability	NA
Predicted depreciation	NA

Test data

Acceleration

0-30 mph, sec.	3.3
0-60 mph, sec.	9.4
Quarter mile, sec.	17.2
Quarter mile, mph	82
45-65 mph, sec.	6.2

Fuel economy (regular)

EPA city/highway, mpg	20/29
CU's overall mileage, mpg	22
CU's city/highway, mpg	14/38
CU's 150-mile trip, mpg	27
Fuel refill capacity, gal.	17.0
Cruising range, mi.	435
Annual fuel: gal./cost	685/$820

Braking from 60 mph

Dry pavement, ft.	149
Wet pavement, ft.	183
Pedal effort, 1st stop, lb.	15
Pedal effort, 10th stop, lb.	25

Specifications

Drive wheels

Front

Seating

Passengers,front/rear	3/3

Dimensions and weight

Length, in.	195
Width, in.	73
Wheelbase, in.	109
Turning circle, ft.	40
Curb weight, lb.	3350
Percent weight, front/rear	64/36
Max. load, lb.	1075

Interior room

Front shoulder room, in.	58.0
Front leg room, in.	44.0
Front head room, in.	5.0
Rear shoulder room, in.	57.0
Rear fore-aft room, in.	30.0
Rear head room, in.	2.0
Door top to ground, in.	50.5
Luggage capacity	5+1

Engines available

3.1-liter V6 (160 hp)

Transmissions available

4-speed automatic

Tested model

1997 Limited 4-door, 3.1-liter V6, 4-speed automatic

Tires as tested

General Ameri*G4S, size P205/70R15

Large car under $30,000

Buick LeSabre

The LeSabre remains a large, quiet-riding, softly sprung freeway cruiser. The 205-hp, 3.8-liter V6 provides lively performance and fairly good fuel economy. But the steering feels vague and slow, and the car leans sharply and wallows through turns. Rough roads upset its composure, and braking is subpar. The front seats feel soft but lack support, so they become fatiguing on long trips. Three adults fit comfortably in the back, however. The gauges are small, and the controls are dated.

Body styles and prices

	Price range	Trim lines
4-door	$22,465 - $25,790	Custom, Limited

Safety information

Safety belt pretensioners	No
Center rear safety belt	Lap
Dual air bags	Standard
Side air bags	Not offered
Antilock brakes	Standard
Traction control	Optional
Gov't front-crash test, driver/front passenger	◓/◓
Gov't side-crash test, driver/rear passenger	○/○
IIHS offset crash test	NA
Injury claim rate compared with all cars/type	◉/◉

Reliability history

TROUBLE SPOTS	Buick LeSabre 90	91	92	93	94	95	96	97
Engine	◓	◓	◓	◓	◓	◓	◉	◉
Cooling	◒	○	◒	○	◓	◉	◉	◉
Fuel	○	○	◓	◓	◓	◓	◓	◉
Ignition	●	●	◒	◒	○	◓	◓	◉
Auto. transmission	◓	◓	◓	○	◓	◓	◓	◉
Man. transmission								
Clutch								
Electrical	◒	◒	◒	◒	○	○	○	◓
Air conditioning	◒	◒	◒	○	◓	○	◉	◓
Suspension	◓	○	○	◓	◓	◓	◓	◉
Brakes	●	●	●	●	○	○	◓	◓
Exhaust	◓	◉	◓	○	◉	◉	◓	◉
Body rust	○	○	◓	◉	◉	◉	◉	◉
Paint/trim	◒	○	◒	○	◓	◓	◉	◉
Body integrity	○	○	◒	◒	○	○	○	◓
Body hardware	○	◒	◒	◒	◒	○	○	◓

Test judgments

Performance

Acceleration	◓
Transmission	◉
Routine handling	◒
Emergency handling	◒
Braking	◒

Comfort

Ride, normal load	◓
Ride, full load	○
Noise	◉
Driving position	○
Front-seat comfort	○
Rear-seat comfort	◓
Climate-control system	◉

Convenience

Access	◓
Controls and displays	○
Trunk	◓

Other

Fuel economy	◒
Predicted reliability	○
Predicted depreciation	○

Test data

Acceleration

0-30 mph, sec.	3.6
0-60 mph, sec.	9.0
Quarter mile, sec.	16.9
Quarter mile, mph	86
45-65 mph, sec.	6.2

Fuel economy (regular)

EPA city/highway, mpg	19/30
CU's overall mileage, mpg	20
CU's city/highway, mpg	12/38
CU's 150-mile trip, mpg	25
Fuel refill capacity, gal.	18.0
Cruising range, mi.	420
Annual fuel: gal./cost	740/$890

Braking from 60 mph

Dry pavement, ft.	155
Wet pavement, ft.	184
Pedal effort, 1st stop, lb.	15
Pedal effort, 10th stop, lb.	30

Specifications

Drive wheels

Front

Seating

Passengers, front/rear	3/3

Dimensions and weight

Length, in.	200
Width, in.	75
Wheelbase, in.	111
Turning circle, ft.	42
Curb weight, lb.	3450
Percent weight, front/rear	65/35
Max. load, lb.	1076

Interior room

Front shoulder room, in.	59.5
Front leg room, in.	42.5
Front head room, in.	6.5
Rear shoulder room, in.	59.5
Rear fore-aft room, in.	32.0
Rear head room, in.	4.5
Door top to ground, in.	50.5
Luggage capacity	5+1

Engines available

3.8-liter V6 (205 hp)

Transmissions available

4-speed automatic

Tested model

1996 Custom 4-door, 3.8-liter V6, 4-speed automatic

Tires as tested

General Ameri Tech ST, size P205/70R15

Large car over $30,000

Buick Park Avenue

This is Buick's top-of-the-line sedan. It has the flavor of traditional large American freeway cruisers without their historically poor handling and floaty ride. The base model has a 205-hp V6, and the Ultra gets a very responsive 240-hp supercharged version of the same engine. Acceleration is effortless, and very quick with the Ultra, though the engine lacks the refinement of the Northstar V8 engine found in Cadillacs. Handling is pretty good for a car this large, and with the optional Gran Touring suspension option the car corners responsively and holds body lean in check. The Park Avenue has a roomy and quiet interior. The seats are comfortable front and rear. Cabin amenities are extensive and well executed, and the automatic climate system works well, but the cabin appointments may lack the ambience of a true luxury car.

Body styles and prices

	Price range	Trim lines
4-door	$30,675 - $35,550	Base, Ultra

Safety information

Safety belt pretensioners	No
Center rear safety belt	Lap
Dual air bags	Standard
Side air bags	Not offered
Antilock brakes	Standard
Traction control	Optional
Gov't front-crash test, driver/front passenger	NA/NA
Gov't side-crash test, driver/rear passenger	NA/NA
IIHS offset crash test	NA
Injury claim rate compared with all cars/type	NA/NA

Reliability history

TROUBLE SPOTS	Buick Electra, Park Ave. & Ultra 90	91	92	93	94	95	96	97
Engine								●
Cooling								●
Fuel								●
Ignition								●
Auto. transmission								●
Man. transmission								
Clutch								
Electrical								○
Air conditioning								◐
Suspension								●
Brakes								◐
Exhaust								●
Body rust								●
Paint/trim								◐
Body integrity								◐
Body hardware								○

Test judgments

Performance

Acceleration	●
Transmission	●
Routine handling	◐
Emergency handling	○
Braking	◐

Comfort

Ride, normal load	◐
Ride, full load	◐
Noise	●
Driving position	◐
Front-seat comfort	◐
Rear-seat comfort	◐
Climate-control system	●

Convenience

Access	◐
Controls and displays	◐
Trunk	●

Other

Fuel economy	○
Predicted reliability	○
Predicted depreciation	NA

Test data

Acceleration

0-30 mph, sec.	3.0
0-60 mph, sec.	7.5
Quarter mile, sec.	15.8
Quarter mile, mph	92
45-65 mph, sec.	4.9

Fuel economy (premium)

EPA city/highway, mpg	18/27
CU's overall mileage, mpg	21
CU's city/highway, mpg	13/36
CU's 150-mile trip, mpg	26
Fuel refill capacity, gal.	18.5
Cruising range, mi.	450
Annual fuel: gal./cost	715/$1000

Braking from 60 mph

Dry pavement, ft.	139
Wet pavement, ft.	159
Pedal effort, 1st stop, lb.	20
Pedal effort, 10th stop, lb.	25

Specifications

Drive wheels

Front

Seating

Passengers, front/rear	3/3

Dimensions and weight

Length, in.	207
Width, in.	75
Wheelbase, in.	114
Turning circle, ft.	43
Curb weight, lb.	3880
Percent weight, front/rear	62/38
Max. load, lb.	950

Interior room

Front shoulder room, in.	59.5
Front leg room, in.	42.5
Front head room, in.	6.0
Rear shoulder room, in.	58.5
Rear fore-aft room, in.	31.5
Rear head room, in.	3.0
Door top to ground, in.	51.0
Luggage capacity	6+2

Engines available

3.8-liter V6 (205 hp)
3.8-liter V6 supercharged (240 hp)

Transmissions available

4-speed automatic

Tested model

1998 Ultra 4-door, 3.8-liter supercharged V6, 4-speed automatic

Tires as tested

Goodyear Eagle LS, size P225/60R16

Medium car under $25,000

Buick Regal

This car has a few virtues but many drawbacks. It rides well at low speeds, its V6 accelerates well, and the automatic transmission is very smooth. The cabin is quiet. However, the ride is so-so, the engine is a bit unrefined, and the rubbery steering conveys little road feel. (The Gran Touring suspension option improves the ride and handling somewhat.) The climate system's dash vents are too low and blow air on your elbows. The seats feel soft at first but grow less comfortable as time passes. The rear seatback has a small port for passing through long narrow objects like skis.

Body styles and prices

	Price range	Trim lines
4-door	$20,945 - $23,690	LS, GS

Reliability history

TROUBLE SPOTS	90 91 92 93 94 95 96 97
Engine	
Cooling	
Fuel	
Ignition	
Auto. transmission	NO
Man. transmission	
Clutch	DATA
Electrical	
Air conditioning	NEW
Suspension	
Brakes	MODEL
Exhaust	
Body rust	
Paint/trim	
Body integrity	
Body hardware	

Safety information

Safety belt pretensioners ....No
Center rear safety belt ....Lap
Dual air bags ....Standard
Side air bags....Not offered
Antilock brakes....Standard
Traction control ....Standard
Gov't front-crash test, driver/front passenger....NA/NA
Gov't side-crash test, driver/rear passenger....○/○
IIHS offset crash test ....NA
Injury claim rate compared with all cars/type....NA/NA

Test judgments

Performance
Acceleration .... ◓
Transmission .... ●
Routine handling .... ○
Emergency handling .... ◒
Braking .... ○

Comfort
Ride, normal load .... ◓
Ride, full load .... ◓
Noise .... ◓
Driving position .... ◓
Front-seat comfort .... ◓
Rear-seat comfort .... ◓
Climate-control system .... ●

Convenience
Access .... ◓
Controls and displays .... ○
Trunk .... ○

Other
Fuel economy .... ○
Predicted reliability ....New
Predicted depreciation ....NA

Test data

Acceleration
0-30 mph, sec. 3.3
0-60 mph, sec. 9.2
Quarter mile, sec. 17.0
Quarter mile, mph 84
45-65 mph, sec. 6.0

Fuel economy (regular)
EPA city/highway, mpg 19/30
CU's overall mileage, mpg 21
CU's city/highway, mpg....12/38
CU's 150-mile trip, mpg 26
Fuel refill capacity, gal. 17.0
Cruising range, mi. 410
Annual fuel: gal./cost ....725/$870

Braking from 60 mph
Dry pavement, ft. 137
Wet pavement, ft. 178
Pedal effort, 1st stop, lb. 20
Pedal effort, 10th stop, lb. 30

Specifications

Drive wheels
Front

Seating
Passengers,front/rear....2/3

Dimensions and weight
Length, in. 196
Width, in. 73
Wheelbase, in. 109
Turning circle, ft. 40
Curb weight, lb. 3325
Percent weight, front/rear 63/37
Max. load, lb. 926

Interior room
Front shoulder room, in. 58.0
Front leg room, in. 43.0
Front head room, in. 5.0
Rear shoulder room, in. 56.5
Rear fore-aft room, in. 29.0
Rear head room, in. 2.5
Door top to ground, in. 50.5
Luggage capacity ....5+1

Engines available
3.8-liter V6 (195 hp)
3.8-liter V6 supercharged (240 hp)

Transmissions available
4-speed automatic

Tested model
1998 LS 4-door, 3.8-liter V6, 4-speed automatic

Tires as tested
Firestone FR680, size P215/70R15

Coupe

Buick Riviera

This large, heavy coupe shares the Oldsmobile Aurora's platform. But instead of the Aurora's refined Northstar V8, it gets a supercharged 3.8-liter V6. The 240-hp engine is as powerful as the Olds V8, but is a little crude. The ride is pleasant on expressways but ponderous on country roads. The body leans a lot in turns. Tall drivers need more head room, and short drivers must sit too close to the wheel. We also found rear-seat access difficult and rear head room skimpy. The displays are awkward, and some controls are hard to reach. The Riviera's future is uncertain.

Body styles and prices

	Price range	Trim lines
2-door	$32,500	—

Safety information

Safety belt pretensioners	No
Center rear safety belt	Lap
Dual air bags	Standard
Side air bags	Not offered
Antilock brakes	Standard
Traction control	Optional
Gov't front-crash test, driver/front passenger	NA/NA
Gov't side-crash test, driver/rear passenger	NA/NA
IIHS offset crash test	NA
Injury claim rate compared with all cars/type	◓/◓

Reliability history

TROUBLE SPOTS	Buick Riviera 90	91	92	93	94	95	96	97
Engine						○	◉	Insufficient data
Cooling						◓	◓	
Fuel						◓	◉	
Ignition						◓	◓	
Auto. transmission						◓	◓	
Man. transmission								
Clutch								
Electrical						●	●	
Air conditioning						○	◓	
Suspension						◓	◓	
Brakes						○	◓	
Exhaust						◉	◓	
Body rust						◉	◉	
Paint/trim						◓	◉	
Body integrity						◒	◒	
Body hardware						●	○	

Test judgments

Performance

Acceleration	◓
Transmission	◉
Routine handling	○
Emergency handling	○
Braking	◓

Comfort

Ride, normal load	◓
Ride, full load	◓
Noise	◉
Driving position	○
Front-seat comfort	◓
Rear-seat comfort	○
Climate-control system	◓

Convenience

Access	○
Controls and displays	○
Trunk	◓

Other

Fuel economy	●
Predicted reliability	○
Predicted depreciation	◒

Test data

Acceleration

0-30 mph, sec.	2.9
0-60 mph, sec.	7.9
Quarter mile, sec.	16.1
Quarter mile, mph	88
45-65 mph, sec.	5.1

Fuel economy (premium)

EPA city/highway, mpg	18/27
CU's overall mileage, mpg	17
CU's city/highway, mpg	10/33
CU's 150-mile trip, mpg	21
Fuel refill capacity, gal.	18.5
Cruising range, mi.	395
Annual fuel: gal./cost	870/$1215

Braking from 60 mph

Dry pavement, ft.	133
Wet pavement, ft.	147
Pedal effort, 1st stop, lb.	15
Pedal effort, 10th stop, lb.	30

Specifications

Drive wheels

Front

Seating

Passengers,front/rear	2/3

Dimensions and weight

Length, in.	207
Width, in.	75
Wheelbase, in.	114
Turning circle, ft.	42
Curb weight, lb.	3770
Percent weight, front/rear	62/38
Max. load, lb.	926

Interior room

Front shoulder room, in.	58.0
Front leg room, in.	42.5
Front head room, in.	2.5
Rear shoulder room, in.	52.5
Rear fore-aft room, in.	29.5
Rear head room, in.	2.0
Door top to ground, in.	50.0
Luggage capacity	5+3

Engines available

3.8-liter V6 supercharged (240 hp)

Transmissions available

4-speed automatic

Tested model

1995 2-door, 3.8-liter supercharged V6, 4-speed automatic

Tires as tested

Goodyear Eagle GA Touring, size P225/60R16

Medium car over $25,000

Cadillac Catera

The midsized Catera yields nothing in performance to competing German and Japanese sports sedans; in fact, it's more fun to drive than most of its competitors. The Catera handles with agility and grace. Its V6 accelerates briskly. The ride is firm, supple, and well controlled. An effective traction-control system is standard. A roomy interior offers niceties such as seat heaters front and rear. The front seats are large and supportive, and three adults have no problem sharing the rear seat. 1998 brings a lap-and-shoulder safety belt to the center rear seat. Reliability was worse than average in the first year.

Body styles and prices

	Price range	Trim lines
4-door	$29,995 - $33,610	Base, Leather

Safety information

Safety belt pretensioners	Front
Center rear safety belt	3-point
Dual air bags	Standard
Side air bags	Not offered
Antilock brakes	Standard
Traction control	Standard
Gov't front-crash test, driver/front passenger	NA/NA
Gov't side-crash test, driver/rear passenger	NA/NA
IIHS offset crash test	NA
Injury claim rate compared with all cars/type	NA/NA

Reliability history

TROUBLE SPOTS	Cadillac Catera 90	91	92	93	94	95	96	97
Engine								●
Cooling								●
Fuel								●
Ignition								●
Auto. transmission								●
Man. transmission								
Clutch								
Electrical								○
Air conditioning								●
Suspension								●
Brakes								◐
Exhaust								●
Body rust								●
Paint/trim								○
Body integrity								○
Body hardware								◐

Test judgments

Performance	
Acceleration	◐
Transmission	●
Routine handling	●
Emergency handling	◐
Braking	●
Comfort	
Ride, normal load	◐
Ride, full load	◐
Noise	◐
Driving position	◐
Front-seat comfort	●
Rear-seat comfort	◐
Climate-control system	●
Convenience	
Access	◐
Controls and displays	◐
Trunk	○
Other	
Fuel economy	◓
Predicted reliability	◓
Predicted depreciation	NA

Test data

Acceleration

0-30 mph, sec.	3.4
0-60 mph, sec.	9.2
Quarter mile, sec.	17.0
Quarter mile, mph	83
45-65 mph, sec.	5.5

Fuel economy (premium)

EPA city/highway, mpg	18/24
CU's overall mileage, mpg	20
CU's city/highway, mpg	12/32
CU's 150-mile trip, mpg	24
Fuel refill capacity, gal.	18.0
Cruising range, mi.	405
Annual fuel: gal./cost	775/$1085

Braking from 60 mph

Dry pavement, ft.	126
Wet pavement, ft.	142
Pedal effort, 1st stop, lb.	15
Pedal effort, 10th stop, lb.	15

Specifications

Drive wheels

Rear

Seating

Passengers, front/rear	2/3

Dimensions and weight

Length, in.	194
Width, in.	70
Wheelbase, in.	107
Turning circle, ft.	37
Curb weight, lb.	3805
Percent weight, front/rear	54/46
Max. load, lb.	890

Interior room

Front shoulder room, in.	55.5
Front leg room, in.	41.0
Front head room, in.	5.0
Rear shoulder room, in.	55.5
Rear fore-aft room, in.	30.5
Rear head room, in.	3.5
Door top to ground, in.	51.0
Luggage capacity	4+2

Engines available

3.0-liter V6 (200 hp)

Transmissions available

4-speed automatic

Tested model

1997 4-door, 3.0-liter V6, 4-speed automatic

Tires as tested

Goodyear Eagle RS-A, size P225/55R16

Large car over $30,000

Cadillac DeVille

Cadillac's best-selling model is a big, roomy, and plush four-door. The more expensive Concours comes with individual front seats and a 300-hp, 4.6-liter Northstar V8. The plain DeVille gets a bench front seat and a slightly less powerful version of the same engine. The muscular, refined V8 provides smooth and powerful acceleration. The ride is compliant most of the time but large bumps make the body move about buoyantly. Handling is good for a car this large, and the steering is reasonably responsive, though you are always aware of the car's sheer bulk. You have to reach around the steering wheel to get at the climate system's controls, but the system works well. All DeVilles offer stability control—a sophisticated device that helps prevent sideways skids—as part of the antilock brake system. Side air bags for the front seats are standard.

Body styles and prices

	Price range	Trim lines
4-door	$37,695 - $42,295	Base, d'Elegance, Concours

Safety information

Safety belt pretensioners	No
Center rear safety belt	Lap
Dual air bags	Standard
Side air bags	Standard
Antilock brakes	Standard
Traction control	Standard
Gov't front-crash test, driver/front passenger	◓/◓
Gov't side-crash test, driver/rear passenger	◓/◓
IIHS offset crash test	NA
Injury claim rate compared with all cars/type	⊙/⊙

Reliability history

TROUBLE SPOTS	Cadillac DeVille, Concours (FWD) 90	91	92	93	94	95	96	97
Engine					◓	◓	◓	⊙
Cooling					⊙	⊙	⊙	⊙
Fuel					◓	◓	◓	◓
Ignition					◓	◓	◓	⊙
Auto. transmission					◓	⊙	◓	◓
Man. transmission								
Clutch								
Electrical					◒	◒	○	○
Air conditioning					○	◓	◓	◓
Suspension					○	○	◓	⊙
Brakes					○	○	◓	◓
Exhaust					⊙	⊙	⊙	⊙
Body rust					⊙	⊙	⊙	⊙
Paint/trim					◓	◓	◓	◓
Body integrity					◓	○	○	○
Body hardware					●	◒	○	○

Test judgments

Performance

Acceleration	◓
Transmission	⊙
Routine handling	○
Emergency handling	○
Braking	○

Comfort

Ride, normal load	◓
Ride, full load	◓
Noise	⊙
Driving position	◓
Front-seat comfort	◓
Rear-seat comfort	◓
Climate-control system	⊙

Convenience

Access	◓
Controls and displays	○
Trunk	⊙

Other

Fuel economy	◒
Predicted reliability	○
Predicted depreciation	◒

Test data

Acceleration

0-30 mph, sec.	3.8
0-60 mph, sec.	9.3
Quarter mile, sec.	17.0
Quarter mile, mph	91
45-65 mph, sec.	4.7

Fuel economy (premium)

EPA city/highway, mpg	17/26
CU's overall mileage, mpg	20
CU's city/highway, mpg	12/32
CU's 150-mile trip, mpg	25
Fuel refill capacity, gal.	20.0
Cruising range, mi.	465
Annual fuel: gal./cost	765/$1075

Braking from 60 mph

Dry pavement, ft.	146
Wet pavement, ft.	154
Pedal effort, 1st stop, lb.	20
Pedal effort, 10th stop, lb.	20

Specifications

Drive wheels

Front

Seating

Passengers,front/rear	3/3

Dimensions and weight

Length, in.	210
Width, in.	77
Wheelbase, in.	114
Turning circle, ft.	44
Curb weight, lb.	4020
Percent weight, front/rear	62/38
Max. load, lb.	1100

Interior room

Front shoulder room, in.	62.0
Front leg room, in.	42.0
Front head room, in.	4.5
Rear shoulder room, in.	61.5
Rear fore-aft room, in.	33.0
Rear head room, in.	4.0
Door top to ground, in.	50.5
Luggage capacity	6+2

Engines available

4.6-liter V8 (275 or 300 hp)

Transmissions available

4-speed automatic

Tested model

1998 Base 4-door, 4.6-liter V8, 4-speed automatic

Tires as tested

Michelin XW4, size P225/60R16

Minivan

Chevrolet Astro

The rear-wheel-drive Astro and similar GMC Safari can haul lots of cargo or tow a heavy trailer. They also offer optional all-wheel drive—handy for slippery roads and snowy climes. But these medium-sized vans feel far more like a truck than a car. They handle ponderously, and ride uncomfortably—especially when fully loaded. Some controls are inconveniently located. The wheel wells and engine compartment rob foot room in front. Optional Dutch (upper and lower) rear doors aid loading but are cumbersome to manage. Reliability has been notably poor.

Body styles and prices

	Price range	Trim lines
Minivan 2WD	$20,074 - $23,849	Base, LS, LT
Minivan AWD	$22,374 - $25,593	Base, LS, LT

Safety information

Safety belt pretensioners	No
Center rear safety belt	Lap
Dual air bags	Standard
Side air bags	Not offered
Antilock brakes	Standard
Traction control	Not offered
Gov't front-crash test, driver/front passenger	○/○
Gov't side-crash test, driver/rear passenger	NA/NA
IIHS offset crash test	Poor
Injury claim rate compared with all cars/type	◓/◓

Reliability history

TROUBLE SPOTS	Chevrolet Astro 90	91	92	93	94	95	96	97
Engine	○	○	○	○	◓	◓	◉	◉
Cooling	◒	◓	◓	◓	◓	◉	◓	◉
Fuel	◓	◓	◓	○	○	○	◓	○
Ignition	◒	◒	◒	●	○	◓	◓	◓
Auto. transmission	○	○	◓	○	◓	◓	◓	◓
Man. transmission								
Clutch								
Electrical	●	●	◒	●	●	○	○	◓
Air conditioning	◒	◒	○	○	◒	◓	◓	◓
Suspension	◒	◒	◒	◒	○	○	◓	◓
Brakes	●	●	●	●	●	◒	○	◉
Exhaust	◒	◒	○	◒	◓	◉	◓	◉
Body rust	◓	◓	◓	◉	◓	◉	◉	◉
Paint/trim	●	●	◒	◒	○	◓	◓	◓
Body integrity	●	●	●	●	●	●	●	◒
Body hardware	●	●	●	●	●	◒	●	◒

Test judgments

Performance

Acceleration	○
Transmission	◉
Routine handling	◒
Emergency handling	◒
Braking	◒

Comfort

Ride, normal load	○
Ride, full load	○
Noise	○
Driving position	○
Front-seat comfort	◓
Middle-seat comfort	◓
Rear-seat comfort	◓
Climate-control system	◉

Convenience

Access	○
Controls and displays	◓
Cargo area	◉

Other

Fuel economy	●
Predicted reliability	●
Predicted depreciation	○

Test data

Acceleration

0-30 mph, sec.	3.4
0-60 mph, sec.	10.2
Quarter mile, sec.	17.8
Quarter mile, mph	77
45-65 mph, sec.	6.8

Fuel economy (regular)

EPA city/highway, mpg	16/20
CU's overall mileage, mpg	15
CU's city/highway, mpg	10/24
CU's 150-mile trip, mpg	18
Fuel refill capacity, gal.	25.0
Cruising range, mi.	400
Annual fuel: gal./cost	1000/$1200

Braking from 60 mph

Dry pavement, ft.	158
Wet pavement, ft.	184
Pedal effort, 1st stop, lb.	20
Pedal effort, 10th stop, lb.	25

Specifications

Drive wheels

Rear or all

Seating

Passengers,front/mid/rear......2/3/3

Dimensions and weight

Length, in.	190
Width, in.	78
Wheelbase, in.	111
Turning circle, ft.	45
Curb weight, lb.	4520
Percent weight, front/rear	53/47
Max. load, lb.	1425

Interior room

Front shoulder room, in.	64.5
Front leg room, in.	41.0
Front head room, in.	4.0
Middle shoulder room, in.	67.5
Middle fore-aft room, in.	33.5
Middle head room, in.	4.0
Rear shoulder room, in.	66.5
Rear fore-aft room, in.	28.5
Rear head room, in.	3.0
Door top to ground, in.	68.0
Cargo volume, cu.ft.	98.0

Engines available

4.3-liter V6 (190 hp)

Transmissions available

4-speed automatic

Tested model

1996 GMC Safari SLE Minivan 2WD, 4.3-liter V6, 4-speed automatic

Tires as tested

Goodyear Eagle GA, size P215/75R15

Sport-utility vehicle

Chevrolet Blazer

The 1998 Blazer and similar GMC Jimmy and Olds Bravada finally have dual air bags. This year also brought a new dashboard and revised front styling, but the biggest improvement was in the brakes, which used to be distinctly subpar but are now OK. Ride and handling are both so-so. A wide turning circle makes for clumsy maneuvering around town. The engine accelerates powerfully but sounds coarse. The Jimmy's and Blazer's optional four-wheel-drive system is part-time only. The Bravada has a type of full-time four-wheel drive. The rear seat is a bit skimpy, but the split seatback folds down easily to form a generous cargo hold. Reliability has been poor. The Bravada has held up better.

Body styles and prices

	Price range	Trim lines
2-door wagon 2WD	$21,663 - $24,714	Base, LS
2-door wagon 4WD	$23,651 - $26,836	Base, LS, ZR2
4-door wagon 2WD	$23,188 - $28,904	Base, LS, LT
4-door wagon 4WD	$25,176 - $30,512	Base, LS, LT

Safety information

Safety belt pretensioners	No
Center rear safety belt	Lap
Dual air bags	Standard
Side air bags	Not offered
Antilock brakes	Standard
Traction control	Not offered
Gov't front-crash test, driver/front passenger	◓/◓
Gov't side-crash test, driver/rear passenger	NA/NA
IIHS offset crash test	Poor
Injury claim rate compared with all cars/type	NA/NA

Reliability history

TROUBLE SPOTS	Chevrolet Blazer 90	91	92	93	94	95	96	97
Engine						○	○	◉
Cooling						◉	◉	◉
Fuel						◒	○	◓
Ignition						○	◓	◉
Auto. transmission						◓	◓	◉
Man. transmission						*	*	*
Clutch						*	*	*
Electrical						◒	○	◓
Air conditioning						◓	◓	◉
Suspension						◓	◓	◉
Brakes						●	○	◓
Exhaust						◉	◉	◉
Body rust						◉	◉	◉
Paint/trim						○	◓	◉
Body integrity						●	○	○
Body hardware						●	○	◓

Test judgments

Performance

Acceleration	○
Transmission	◓
Routine handling	○
Emergency handling	●
Braking	○

Comfort

Ride, normal load	○
Ride, full load	○
Noise	◓
Driving position	◓
Front-seat comfort	◓
Rear-seat comfort	○
Climate-control system	◉

Convenience

Access	◓
Controls and displays	◓
Cargo area	◓

Other

Fuel economy	●
Predicted reliability	●
Predicted depreciation	○

Test data

Acceleration

0-30 mph, sec.	3.4
0-60 mph, sec.	10.4
Quarter mile, sec.	17.9
Quarter mile, mph	77
45-65 mph, sec.	7.0

Fuel economy (regular)

EPA city/highway, mpg	16/20
CU's overall mileage, mpg	15
CU's city/highway, mpg	10/25
CU's 150-mile trip, mpg	19
Fuel refill capacity, gal.	18.0
Cruising range, mi.	310
Annual fuel: gal./cost	975/$1170

Braking from 60 mph

Dry pavement, ft.	144
Wet pavement, ft.	163
Pedal effort, 1st stop, lb.	20
Pedal effort, 10th stop, lb.	25

Specifications

Drive wheels

Rear or part-time 4WD

Seating

Passengers,front/rear	3/3

Dimensions and weight

Length, in.	183
Width, in.	68
Wheelbase, in.	107
Turning circle, ft.	46
Curb weight, lb.	4225
Percent weight, front/rear	55/45
Max. load, lb.	1040

Interior room

Front shoulder room, in.	56.5
Front leg room, in.	42.5
Front head room, in.	4.5
Rear shoulder room, in.	57.0
Rear fore-aft room, in.	30.0
Rear head room, in.	4.0
Door top to ground, in.	60.5
Cargo volume, cu.ft.	40.0

Engines available

4.3-liter V6 (190 hp)

Transmissions available

5-speed manual
4-speed automatic

Tested model

1998 LT 4-door wagon 4WD, 4.3-liter V6, 4-speed automatic

Tires as tested

Michelin XW4, size P235/70R15

Pickup truck

Chevrolet C/K 1500

The Chevrolet and similar GMC Sierra C/K 1500 pickups received dual air bags last year. These trucks are pleasant enough to drive on good roads, and the cabin is quiet. The automatic transmission shifts smoothly. But braking is mediocre, and the steering feels sluggish. Front seats are soft but unsupportive. An optional third door on the passenger's side makes loading people or cargo easier. Reliability of the four-wheel-drive version has been worse than average; the two-wheel-drive version has been average. A redesign is due for 1999.

Body styles and prices

	Price range	Trim lines
Reg. cab 2WD	$15,456 - $22,145	W/T, Cheyenne, Silverado
Reg. cab 4WD	$18,640 - $25,303	W/T, Cheyenne, Silverado
Ext. cab 2WD	$18,433 - $21,977	W/T, Cheyenne, Silverado
Ext. cab 4WD	$21,234 - $25,294	W/T, Cheyenne, Silverado

Safety information

Safety belt pretensioners	No
Center rear safety belt	Lap
Dual air bags	Standard
Side air bags	Not offered
Antilock brakes	Standard
Traction control	Not offered
Gov't front-crash test, driver/front passenger	◓/○
Gov't side-crash test, driver/rear passenger	NA/NA
IIHS offset crash test	NA*
Injury claim rate compared with all cars/type	⊙/⊙

Reliability history

TROUBLE SPOTS	Chevrolet C1500 Pickup 90	91	92	93	94	95	96	97
Engine	○	◓	◓	◓	◓	◓	◓	⊙
Cooling	○	○	◓	◓	◓	⊙	◓	⊙
Fuel	◓	◓	◓	◓	◓	⊙	◓	◓
Ignition	◒	◒	◒	○	◓	◓	◓	⊙
Auto. transmission	○	○	◒	◓	◓	⊙	◓	⊙
Man. transmission	◓	○	◓	*	*	◓	*	*
Clutch	◒	●	◒	*	*	◒	*	*
Electrical	◒	◒	◒	○	○	○	◓	◓
Air conditioning	○	◒	○	◓	○	◓	◓	⊙
Suspension	○	○	○	◓	◓	◓	○	○
Brakes	◒	◒	○	○	○	◓	○	⊙
Exhaust	●	●	◒	○	◓	⊙	◓	⊙
Body rust	◓	⊙	⊙	⊙	⊙	⊙	⊙	⊙
Paint/trim	●	◒	◒	○	◓	◓	◓	⊙
Body integrity	○	○	○	○	○	○	○	○
Body hardware	○	◒	◒	○	○	○	◒	○

Test judgments

Performance

Acceleration	◓
Transmission	⊙
Routine handling	○
Emergency handling	◒
Braking	◒

Comfort

Ride, normal load	◒
Ride, full load	○
Noise	◓
Driving position	○
Front-seat comfort	○
Rear-seat comfort	●
Climate-control system	⊙

Convenience

Access	◓
Controls and displays	◓
Cargo area	◓

Other

Fuel economy	●
Predicted reliability	○
Predicted depreciation	◓

Test data

Acceleration

0-30 mph, sec.	3.5
0-60 mph, sec.	9.6
Quarter mile, sec.	17.3
Quarter mile, mph	81
45-65 mph, sec.	6.2

Fuel economy (regular)

EPA city/highway, mpg	15/20
CU's overall mileage, mpg	15
CU's city/highway, mpg	10/24
CU's 150-mile trip, mpg	18
Fuel refill capacity, gal.	25.0
Cruising range, mi.	400
Annual fuel: gal./cost	1000/$1200

Braking from 60 mph

Dry pavement, ft.	149
Wet pavement, ft.	175
Pedal effort, 1st stop, lb.	15
Pedal effort, 10th stop, lb.	30

Specifications

Drive wheels

Rear or part-time 4WD

Seating

Passengers, front/rear ... 3/3

Dimensions and weight

Length, in.	218
Width, in.	77
Wheelbase, in.	142
Turning circle, ft.	50
Curb weight, lb.	4605
Percent weight, front/rear	58/42
Max. load, lb.	1595

Interior room

Front shoulder room, in.	65.0
Front leg room, in.	40.5
Front head room, in.	5.0
Rear shoulder room, in.	59.5
Rear fore-aft room, in.	22.5
Rear head room, in.	2.5
Door top to ground, in.	64.5

Engines available

4.3-liter V6 (200 hp), 5.0-liter V8 (230 hp), 5.7-liter V8 (255 hp) 6.5-liter V8 turbodiesel (190 hp)

Transmissions available

5-speed manual, 4-speed automatic

Tested model

1996 Silverado Extended cab 2WD, 5.0-liter V8, 4-speed automatic

Tires as tested

Uniroyal Tiger Paw, size P235/75R15

Small car

Chevrolet Cavalier

The Cavalier aims at the broad middle market while its cousin, the Pontiac Sunfire, emphasizes sporty styling. The standard 115-hp, 2.2-liter Four sounds raucous when revved, but it accelerates adequately. The optional 150-hp, 2.4-liter Four is noticeably gutsier. Rough roads make the body bounce. The standard five-speed manual transmission feels sloppy and imprecise. The optional four-speed automatic is the best choice. The front seats feel comfortable on short trips, but are fatiguing on long journeys. The rear seat is barely adequate. A new 150-hp Z24 convertible joins the range for 1998.

Body styles and prices

	Price range	Trim lines
2-door	$11,610 - $15,710	Base, RS, Z24
4-door	$11,810 - $14,250	Base, LS
Convertible	$19,410	Z24

Safety information

Safety belt pretensioners	No
Center rear safety belt	Lap
Dual air bags	Standard
Side air bags	Not offered
Antilock brakes	Standard
Traction control	Standard with 4-speed automatic
Gov't front-crash test, driver/front passenger	◓/◓
Gov't side-crash test, driver/rear passenger	●/○
IIHS offset crash test	Poor
Injury claim rate compared with all cars/type	◒/◓

Reliability history

TROUBLE SPOTS	Chevrolet Cavalier 90	91	92	93	94	95	96	97
Engine						○	◓	◉
Cooling						◓	◓	◉
Fuel						◓	◓	◉
Ignition						◓	◓	◓
Auto. transmission						◓	◓	◉
Man. transmission						*	◓	◓
Clutch						*	○	◉
Electrical						◒	◒	◓
Air conditioning						◉	◉	◉
Suspension						◓	◓	◓
Brakes						◒	○	◓
Exhaust						◓	◓	◉
Body rust						◉	◉	◉
Paint/trim						◓	◓	◉
Body integrity						◒	●	○
Body hardware						◒	○	◓

Test judgments

Performance	
Acceleration	○
Transmission	◉
Routine handling	◓
Emergency handling	○
Braking	○
Comfort	
Ride, normal load	○
Ride, full load	◒
Noise	○
Driving position	○
Front-seat comfort	○
Rear-seat comfort	○
Climate-control system	◉
Convenience	
Access	○
Controls and displays	◉
Trunk	○
Other	
Fuel economy	◓
Predicted reliability	○
Predicted depreciation	○

Test data

Acceleration	
0-30 mph, sec.	3.8
0-60 mph, sec.	11.1
Quarter mile, sec.	18.3
Quarter mile, mph	76
45-65 mph, sec.	6.7
Fuel economy (regular)	
EPA city/highway, mpg	23/31
CU's overall mileage, mpg	26
CU's city/highway, mpg	16/43
CU's 150-mile trip, mpg	31
Fuel refill capacity, gal.	15.2
Cruising range, mi.	440
Annual fuel: gal./cost	585/$700
Braking from 60 mph	
Dry pavement, ft.	144
Wet pavement, ft.	172
Pedal effort, 1st stop, lb.	20
Pedal effort, 10th stop, lb.	25

Specifications

Drive wheels	
Front	
Seating	
Passengers, front/rear	2/3
Dimensions and weight	
Length, in.	180
Width, in.	67
Wheelbase, in.	104
Turning circle, ft.	38
Curb weight, lb.	2795
Percent weight, front/rear	65/35
Max. load, lb.	880
Interior room	
Front shoulder room, in.	54.5
Front leg room, in.	41.5
Front head room, in.	4.5
Rear shoulder room, in.	53.5
Rear fore-aft room, in.	28.0
Rear head room, in.	2.0
Door top to ground, in.	50.5
Luggage capacity	4+1

Engines available
2.2-liter 4 (115 hp)
2.4-liter 4 (150 hp)

Transmissions available
5-speed manual, 3-speed automatic, 4-speed automatic

Tested model
1997 LS 4-door, 2.2-liter Four, 4-speed automatic

Tires as tested
BF Goodrich Touring T/A, size P195/65R15

Medium car under $25,000

Chevrolet Lumina

The midsized Lumina is essentially unchanged for 1998. It does most things adequately but unexceptionally. Its ride and handling are mediocre. The standard 3.1-liter V6 accelerates soundly, and the four-speed automatic shifts smoothly. The optional 3.8-liter V6 produces 40 hp more. Overall, the cabin remains quiet at cruising speeds. Controls and displays are generally well designed, but the seats are thinly padded. The front bench seat is tight for three adults; the rear seat is low, short, and uncomfortable.

Body styles and prices

	Price range	Trim lines
4-door	$17,245 - $19,745	Base, LS, LTZ

Safety information

Safety belt pretensioners	No
Center rear safety belt	Lap
Dual air bags	Standard
Side air bags	Not offered
Antilock brakes	Standard (optional on Base)
Traction control	Not offered
Gov't front-crash test, driver/front passenger	◓/●
Gov't side-crash test, driver/rear passenger	◓/○
IIHS offset crash test	Good
Injury claim rate compared with all cars/type	◓/●

Reliability history

TROUBLE SPOTS	Chevrolet Lumina 90	91	92	93	94	95	96	97
Engine						◓	●	●
Cooling						●	●	●
Fuel						●	◓	●
Ignition						◓	◓	●
Auto. transmission						◓	◓	●
Man. transmission								
Clutch								
Electrical						○	◓	◓
Air conditioning						◓	●	●
Suspension						◓	◓	●
Brakes						◒	◓	●
Exhaust						●	●	●
Body rust						●	●	●
Paint/trim						◓	◓	◓
Body integrity						○	○	◓
Body hardware						◒	○	◓

Test judgments

Performance

Acceleration	◓
Transmission	●
Routine handling	○
Emergency handling	○
Braking	○

Comfort

Ride, normal load	○
Ride, full load	○
Noise	◓
Driving position	◓
Front-seat comfort	○
Rear-seat comfort	○
Climate-control system	●

Convenience

Access	◓
Controls and displays	◓
Trunk	◓

Other

Fuel economy	○
Predicted reliability	◓
Predicted depreciation	○

Test data

Acceleration

0-30 mph, sec.	3.4
0-60 mph, sec.	9.8
Quarter mile, sec.	17.4
Quarter mile, mph	81
45-65 mph, sec.	6.5

Fuel economy (regular)

EPA city/highway, mpg	20/29
CU's overall mileage, mpg	22
CU's city/highway, mpg	14/36
CU's 150-mile trip, mpg	26
Fuel refill capacity, gal.	16.6
Cruising range, mi.	410
Annual fuel: gal./cost	695/$835

Braking from 60 mph

Dry pavement, ft.	139
Wet pavement, ft.	165
Pedal effort, 1st stop, lb.	20
Pedal effort, 10th stop, lb.	25

Specifications

Drive wheels

Front

Seating

Passengers,front/rear	3/3

Dimensions and weight

Length, in.	201
Width, in.	73
Wheelbase, in.	108
Turning circle, ft.	44
Curb weight, lb.	3350
Percent weight, front/rear	64/36
Max. load, lb.	1060

Interior room

Front shoulder room, in.	58.5
Front leg room, in.	42.5
Front head room, in.	4.5
Rear shoulder room, in.	57.0
Rear fore-aft room, in.	30.0
Rear head room, in.	2.0
Door top to ground, in.	51.0
Luggage capacity	5+1

Engines available

3.1-liter V6 (160 hp)
3.8-liter V6 (200 hp)

Transmissions available

4-speed automatic

Tested model

1997 LS 4-door, 3.1-liter V6, 4-speed automatic

Tires as tested

Goodyear Eagle GA, size P225/60R16

Medium car under $25,000

Chevrolet Malibu

RECOMMENDED

The midsized Malibu, along with the similar Oldsmobile Cutlass, was new for 1997. It's positioned as a lower-priced alternative to a Honda Accord or Toyota Camry. But it's a little less refined than those two. The Malibu handles soundly. The ride is firm and generally well controlled. The base four-cylinder engine is quick enough, but coarse and noisy. The optional 3.1-liter V6 is a better choice. The standard automatic transmission shifts very smoothly. The interior is roomy, the seats are fairly comfortable, and the controls are logically laid out. The trunk is large, and the rear seat-back folds down to expand it further.

Body styles and prices

	Price range	Trim lines
4-door	$15,670 - $18,470	Base, LS

Safety information

- Safety belt pretensioners .... No
- Center rear safety belt .... Lap
- Dual air bags .... Standard
- Side air bags .... Not offered
- Antilock brakes .... Standard
- Traction control .... Not offered
- Gov't front-crash test, driver/front passenger .... ◒/◒
- Gov't side-crash test, driver/rear passenger .... ●/○
- IIHS offset crash test .... NA
- Injury claim rate compared with all cars/type .... NA/NA

Reliability history

TROUBLE SPOTS	90	91	92	93	94	95	96	97
	Chevrolet Malibu V6							
Engine								◉
Cooling								◉
Fuel								◉
Ignition								◉
Auto. transmission								◉
Man. transmission								
Clutch								
Electrical								○
Air conditioning								◒
Suspension								◒
Brakes								○
Exhaust								◉
Body rust								◉
Paint/trim								◒
Body integrity								○
Body hardware								◉

Test judgments

Performance
- Acceleration .... ◒
- Transmission .... ◉
- Routine handling .... ◒
- Emergency handling .... ○
- Braking .... ◒

Comfort
- Ride, normal load .... ◒
- Ride, full load .... ◒
- Noise .... ○
- Driving position .... ◒
- Front-seat comfort .... ◒
- Rear-seat comfort .... ◒
- Climate-control system .... ◉

Convenience
- Access .... ◒
- Controls and displays .... ◉
- Trunk .... ◒

Other
- Fuel economy .... ○
- Predicted reliability .... ○
- Predicted depreciation .... NA

Test data

Acceleration
- 0-30 mph, sec. 3.3
- 0-60 mph, sec. 9.4
- Quarter mile, sec. 17.2
- Quarter mile, mph 82
- 45-65 mph, sec. 5.9

Fuel economy (regular)
- EPA city/highway, mpg 23/32
- CU's overall mileage, mpg 24
  - CU's city/highway, mpg 16/41
  - CU's 150-mile trip, mpg 28
- Fuel refill capacity, gal. 15.0
- Cruising range, mi. 400
- Annual fuel: gal./cost .... 615/$740

Braking from 60 mph
- Dry pavement, ft. 135
- Wet pavement, ft. 154
- Pedal effort, 1st stop, lb. 15
- Pedal effort, 10th stop, lb. 20

Specifications

Drive wheels
Front

Seating
- Passengers, front/rear 2/3

Dimensions and weight
- Length, in. 190
- Width, in. 69
- Wheelbase, in. 107
- Turning circle, ft. 39
- Curb weight, lb. 3040
- Percent weight, front/rear 64/36
- Max. load, lb. 917

Interior room
- Front shoulder room, in. 55.5
- Front leg room, in. 42.5
- Front head room, in. 4.5
- Rear shoulder room, in. 54.5
- Rear fore-aft room, in. 30.0
- Rear head room, in. 2.0
- Door top to ground, in. 51.0
- Luggage capacity .... 5+1

Engines available
2.4-liter 4 (150 hp)
3.1-liter V6 (150 hp)

Transmissions available
4-speed automatic

Tested model
1997 Base 4-door, 2.4-liter Four, 4-speed automatic

Tires as tested
Firestone Affinity (Touring T2), size P215/60R15

Small car

Chevrolet Metro

This sedan, formerly called the Geo Metro, is a close copy of the Suzuki Swift hatchback—one of the smallest, lightest cars on the road. For 1998, the Geo name was dropped, but few changes were made to the car. The four-cylinder engine gained 9 hp. The Metro isn't great for nipping through city traffic, and it's even worse on long trips. The ride is choppy and noisy. The base three-cylinder engine is underpowered and not all that thrifty; several other slightly larger small cars match the Metro's fuel economy. The optional Four isn't much better.

Body styles and prices

	Price range	Trim lines
2-door hatchback	$8,655 - $9,455	Base, LSi
4-door	$10,055	LSi

Safety information

Safety belt pretensioners .... No
Center rear safety belt .... NA
Dual air bags .... Standard
Side air bags .... Not offered
Antilock brakes .... Optional
Traction control .... Not offered
Gov't front-crash test, driver/front passenger .... ◓/◓
Gov't side-crash test, driver/rear passenger .... NA/NA
IIHS offset crash test .... NA
Injury claim rate compared with all cars/type .... ●/◒

Reliability history

TROUBLE SPOTS	Geo Metro 90	91	92	93	94	95	96	97
Engine	○	○	○	◓	◓	◉	◉	Insufficient data
Cooling	◓	◓	◓	◉	◉	◉	◉	
Fuel	○	◓	◓	◉	◉	◓	◉	
Ignition	○	○	◒	◓	◓	◉	◓	
Auto. transmission	*	*	◓	*	*	*	*	
Man. transmission	◓	○	◓	◉	◉	◉	*	
Clutch	◓	◓	◓	◓	◉	◉	*	
Electrical	○	○	◒	◒	○	◒	○	
Air conditioning	●	●	◓	○	○	●	○	
Suspension	○	◓	◓	◓	◓	◓	◉	
Brakes	●	◒	◒	○	○	◓	◉	
Exhaust	●	●	●	◒	◓	◉	◉	
Body rust	○	○	◓	◉	◉	◉	◉	
Paint/trim	◒	○	◓	◓	◉	◓	◓	
Body integrity	●	●	●	○	○	○	◓	
Body hardware	●	●	●	●	◒	◒	○	

Test judgments

Performance
Acceleration .... ◒
Transmission .... ○
Routine handling .... ○
Emergency handling .... ○
Braking .... ○

Comfort
Ride, normal load .... ◒
Ride, full load .... ◒
Noise .... ◒
Driving position .... ○
Front-seat comfort .... ○
Rear-seat comfort .... ◒
Climate-control system .... ◓

Convenience
Access .... ○
Controls and displays .... ◓
Trunk .... ◒

Other
Fuel economy .... ◓
Predicted reliability .... ◓
Predicted depreciation .... ○

Test data

Acceleration
0-30 mph, sec. 5.0
0-60 mph, sec. 15.3
Quarter mile, sec. 20.4
Quarter mile, mph 68
45-65 mph, sec. 10.0

Fuel economy (regular)
EPA city/highway, mpg 30/34
CU's overall mileage, mpg 29
CU's city/highway, mpg 19/42
CU's 150-mile trip, mpg 35
Fuel refill capacity, gal. 10.3
Cruising range, mi. 335
Annual fuel: gal./cost .... 520/$625

Braking from 60 mph
Dry pavement, ft. 151
Wet pavement, ft. 172
Pedal effort, 1st stop, lb. 25
Pedal effort, 10th stop, lb. 35

Specifications

Drive wheels
Front

Seating
Passengers, front/rear 2/2

Dimensions and weight
Length, in. 164
Width, in. 63
Wheelbase, in. 93
Turning circle, ft. 35
Curb weight, lb. 2065
Percent weight, front/rear 61/39
Max. load, lb. 688

Interior room
Front shoulder room, in. 49.5
Front leg room, in. 40.5
Front head room, in. 5.0
Rear shoulder room, in. 47.0
Rear fore-aft room, in. 27.0
Rear head room, in. 2.0
Door top to ground, in. 49.5
Luggage capacity .... 4+0

Engines available
1.0-liter 3 (55 hp)
1.3-liter 4 (79 hp)

Transmissions available
5-speed manual
3-speed automatic

Tested model
1995 LSi 4-door 4-door, 1.3-liter Four, 3-speed automatic

Tires as tested
Goodyear Invicta GL, size P155/80R13

Coupe

Chevrolet Monte Carlo

This coupe version of Chevrolet's Lumina handles sloppily, and it leaps and bounds on rough roads. The Z34 model retains its name despite getting a 3.8-liter V6 for 1998. This version's "performance" suspension doesn't live up to its name: It's too stiff on small bumps and too soft over big ones. The LS version rides better. The cabin has plenty of room up front, but the cloth seats feel lumpy and lack support. The rear seat barely accommodates two tall people, and access to the rear is a chore.

Body styles and prices

	Price range	Trim lines
2-door	$17,795 - $20,295	LS, Z34

Safety information

Safety belt pretensioners .... No
Center rear safety belt .... Lap
Dual air bags .... Standard
Side air bags .... Not offered
Antilock brakes .... Standard
Traction control .... Not offered
Gov't front-crash test, driver/front passenger .... ◓/◓
Gov't side-crash test, driver/rear passenger .... NA/NA
IIHS offset crash test .... NA
Injury claim rate compared with all cars/type .... ◓/○

Reliability history

TROUBLE SPOTS	Chevrolet Monte Carlo 90	91	92	93	94	95	96	97
Engine						○	○	Insufficient data
Cooling						◓	◉	
Fuel						◉	○	
Ignition						◓	○	
Auto. transmission						◓	◓	
Man. transmission								
Clutch								
Electrical						◒	○	
Air conditioning						◓	◓	
Suspension						◓	◓	
Brakes						●	○	
Exhaust						◉	◉	
Body rust						◉	◉	
Paint/trim						○	○	
Body integrity						◒	◒	
Body hardware						●	○	

Test judgments

Performance
Acceleration .... ◓
Transmission .... ◉
Routine handling .... ◓
Emergency handling .... ○
Braking .... ○

Comfort
Ride, normal load .... ○
Ride, full load .... ○
Noise .... ◓
Driving position .... ◓
Front-seat comfort .... ○
Rear-seat comfort .... ◒
Climate-control system .... ◉

Convenience
Access .... ○
Controls and displays .... ◉
Trunk .... ◓

Other
Fuel economy .... ●
Predicted reliability .... ◒
Predicted depreciation .... ○

Test data

Acceleration
0-30 mph, sec. 3.1
0-60 mph, sec. 8.5
Quarter mile, sec. 16.5
Quarter mile, mph 86
45-65 mph, sec. 5.4

Fuel economy (regular)
EPA city/highway, mpg 19/30
CU's overall mileage, mpg 18
CU's city/highway, mpg 11/34
CU's 150-mile trip, mpg 23
Fuel refill capacity, gal. 16.6
Cruising range, mi. 365
Annual fuel: gal./cost .... 825/$990

Braking from 60 mph
Dry pavement, ft. 139
Wet pavement, ft. 165
Pedal effort, 1st stop, lb. 30
Pedal effort, 10th stop, lb. 35

Specifications

Drive wheels
Front

Seating
Passengers, front/rear 3/3

Dimensions and weight
Length, in. 201
Width, in. 72
Wheelbase, in. 108
Turning circle, ft. 43
Curb weight, lb. 3450
Percent weight, front/rear 65/35
Max. load, lb. 908

Interior room
Front shoulder room, in. 57.5
Front leg room, in. 41.5
Front head room, in. 3.5
Rear shoulder room, in. 56.5
Rear fore-aft room, in. 28.5
Rear head room, in. 2.0
Door top to ground, in. 49.0
Luggage capacity .... 5+1

Engines available
3.1-liter V6 (160 hp)
3.8-liter V6 (200 hp)

Transmissions available
4-speed automatic

Tested model
1995 Z34 2-door, 3.4-liter V6, 4-speed automatic

Tires as tested
Goodyear Eagle RS-A, size P225/60R16

Small car

Chevrolet Prizm

RECOMMENDED

Formerly called the Geo Prizm, this car is a close cousin of the Toyota Corolla. They were redesigned for 1998, and differ only in body styling, interior trim, and the placement of some controls. These are among the first low-priced cars to get side-impact air bags. The Prizm rides quite comfortably and quietly and gets good fuel economy. The four-cylinder engine accelerates briskly. The front seats are firm and supportive, but the nontilting steering wheel in the base version is too low. Base versions and some high-trim LSi models made before April 1998 lacked a front stabilizer bar, which rendered handling subpar in rapid maneuvers. Models made since all have that bar, whose presence is noted on the window sticker. The Toyota Corolla is often priced higher than the Prizm, but the Corolla has a more sensible control layout.

Body styles and prices

	Price range	Trim lines
4-door	$12,043 - $14,614	Base, LSi

Safety information

Safety belt pretensioners	Front
Center rear safety belt	3-point
Dual air bags	Standard
Side air bags	Optional
Antilock brakes	Optional
Traction control	Not offered
Gov't front-crash test, driver/front passenger	◓/◓
Gov't side-crash test, driver/rear passenger	○/○
IIHS offset crash test	Acceptable
Injury claim rate compared with all cars/type	NA/NA

Reliability history

TROUBLE SPOTS	90 91 92 93 94 95 96 97
Engine	
Cooling	
Fuel	
Ignition	
Auto. transmission	NO
Man. transmission	
Clutch	DATA
Electrical	
Air conditioning	NEW
Suspension	
Brakes	MODEL
Exhaust	
Body rust	
Paint/trim	
Body integrity	
Body hardware	

Test judgments

Performance

Acceleration	○
Transmission	◓
Routine handling	○
Emergency handling	○
Braking	○

Comfort

Ride, normal load	◓
Ride, full load	○
Noise	◓
Driving position	○
Front-seat comfort	◓
Rear-seat comfort	◒
Climate-control system	●

Convenience

Access	○
Controls and displays	●
Trunk	◒

Other

Fuel economy	●
Predicted reliability	●
Predicted depreciation	NA

Test data

Acceleration

0-30 mph, sec.	3.8
0-60 mph, sec.	10.7
Quarter mile, sec.	18.0
Quarter mile, mph	79
45-65 mph, sec.	6.0

Fuel economy (regular)

EPA city/highway, mpg	28/36
CU's overall mileage, mpg	31
CU's city/highway, mpg	21/46
CU's 150-mile trip, mpg	36
Fuel refill capacity, gal.	13.2
Cruising range, mi.	450
Annual fuel: gal./cost	485/$580

Braking from 60 mph

Dry pavement, ft.	152
Wet pavement, ft.	168
Pedal effort, 1st stop, lb.	20
Pedal effort, 10th stop, lb.	25

Specifications

Drive wheels

Front

Seating

Passengers,front/rear	2/3

Dimensions and weight

Length, in.	175
Width, in.	67
Wheelbase, in.	97
Turning circle, ft.	34
Curb weight, lb.	2480
Percent weight, front/rear	61/39
Max. load, lb.	850

Interior room

Front shoulder room, in.	52.5
Front leg room, in.	40.5
Front head room, in.	4.0
Rear shoulder room, in.	52.0
Rear fore-aft room, in.	26.5
Rear head room, in.	2.0
Door top to ground, in.	48.0
Luggage capacity	4+1

Engines available

1.8-liter 4 (120 hp)

Transmissions available

5-speed manual
3-speed automatic
4-speed automatic

Tested model

1998 Base 4-door, 1.8-liter Four, 4-speed automatic

Tires as tested

Firestone FR680, size P175/65R14

Pickup truck

Chevrolet S-Series

The compact S-Series and similar GMC Sonoma pickups finally get a passenger-side air bag (with a deactivation switch) for 1998. Both trucks ride stiffly and lean a lot in corners. The steering feels vague and heavy, and the rear wheels hop on washboard roads. On the plus side, the cabin is commendably quiet, and the 4.3-liter V6 feels sprightly. On extended-cab versions, an optional third door aids loading and unloading. Reliability has been a problem, particularly with four-wheel-drive models.

Body styles and prices

	Price range	Trim lines
Regular cab 2WD	$11,898 - $12,868	Base, LS
Regular cab 4WD	$16,273 - $17,738	Base, LS
Extended cab 2WD	$12,041 - $14,748	Base, LS
Extended cab 4WD	$16,603 - $19,073	Base, LS

Safety information

Safety belt pretensioners ....No
Center rear safety belt ....NA
Dual air bags ....Standard
Side air bags....Not offered
Antilock brakes....Standard
Traction control ....Not offered
Gov't front-crash test, driver/front passenger ....◓/◓
Gov't side-crash test, driver/rear passenger ....NA/NA
IIHS offset crash test ....NA
Injury claim rate compared with all cars/type....NA/NA

Reliability history

TROUBLE SPOTS	Chevrolet S-10 Pickup V6 (2WD) 90	91	92	93	94	95	96	97
Engine					◓	◓	○	◉
Cooling					◓	◉	◓	◉
Fuel					○	○	○	◉
Ignition					○	○	◓	◉
Auto. transmission					◓	◉	◓	◉
Man. transmission					*	◓	*	*
Clutch					*	◓	*	*
Electrical					◒	◒	◓	◓
Air conditioning					○	◓	◓	◉
Suspension					○	◓	◓	◉
Brakes					●	◒	○	◉
Exhaust					◓	◉	◉	◉
Body rust					◉	◉	◉	◉
Paint/trim					○	○	◓	◓
Body integrity					○	◒	◒	○
Body hardware					◒	◒	○	○

Test judgments

Performance
Acceleration ....◓
Transmission ....◉
Routine handling ....○
Emergency handling ....○
Braking ....◒

Comfort
Ride, normal load ....◒
Ride, full load ....◒
Noise ....◓
Driving position ....◓
Front-seat comfort ....○
Rear-seat comfort ....●
Climate-control system ....◉

Convenience
Access ....○
Controls and displays ....◓
Cargo area ....○

Other
Fuel economy ....●
Predicted reliability ....◒
Predicted depreciation ....○

Test data

Acceleration
0-30 mph, sec. 3.3
0-60 mph, sec. 9.2
Quarter mile, sec. 17.2
Quarter mile, mph 82
45-65 mph, sec. 6.0

Fuel economy (regular)
EPA city/highway, mpg 17/22
CU's overall mileage, mpg 17
CU's city/highway, mpg....11/30
CU's 150-mile trip, mpg 20
Fuel refill capacity, gal. 20.0
Cruising range, mi. 405
Annual fuel: gal./cost ....865/$1035

Braking from 60 mph
Dry pavement, ft. 156
Wet pavement, ft. 178
Pedal effort, 1st stop, lb. 20
Pedal effort, 10th stop, lb. 25

Specifications

Drive wheels
Rear or part-time 4WD

Seating
Passengers,front/rear....3/2

Dimensions and weight
Length, in. 204
Width, in. 68
Wheelbase, in. 123
Turning circle, ft. 43
Curb weight, lb. 3560
Percent weight, front/rear 61/39
Max. load, lb. 1042

Interior room
Front shoulder room, in. 57.0
Front leg room, in. 42.0
Front head room, in. 4.5
Rear shoulder room, in. 18.5
Rear fore-aft room, in. 46.0
Rear head room, in. 2.0
Door top to ground, in. 58.5

Engines available
2.2-liter 4 (120 hp)
4.3-liter V6 (175, 180, or 190 hp)

Transmissions available
5-speed manual, 4-speed automatic

Tested model
1995 GMC Sonoma Extended cab 2WD, 4.3-liter V6, 4-speed automatic

Tires as tested
Uniroyal Tiger Paw, size P205/75R15

Sport-utility vehicle

Chevrolet Tahoe

The Tahoe and its twin, the GMC Yukon, slot between Chevrolet's enormous Suburban and compact Blazer. The cargo bay is almost as roomy as a minivan's. For 1998, selectable full-time four-wheel drive has been added as an option. The Tahoe rides relatively well for a truck. The spacious cabin is generally quiet. The steering feels a little vague, but it's responsive, and the 5.7-liter V8 provides plenty of torque for towing. The transmission shifts smoothly. On the downside, fuel economy is dismal, and the brakes are mediocre.

Body styles and prices

	Price range	Trim lines
2-door wagon 2WD	$23,585 - $29,304	Base, LS, LT
2-door wagon 4WD	$26,185 - $31,904	Base, LS, LT
4-door wagon 2WD	$29,385 - $30,735	LS, LT
4-door wagon 4WD	$31,985 - $33,335	LS, LT

Safety information

Safety belt pretensioners ....No
Center rear safety belt ....Lap
Dual air bags ....Standard
Side air bags....Not offered
Antilock brakes....Standard
Traction control ....Not offered
Gov't front-crash test, driver/front passenger ..../
Gov't side-crash test, driver/rear passenger ....NA/NA
IIHS offset crash test ....NA
Injury claim rate compared with all cars/type..../

Reliability history

TROUBLE SPOTS	90	91	92	93	94	95	96	97
Engine								
Cooling								
Fuel								
Ignition								
Auto. transmission								
Man. transmission						*		
Clutch						*		
Electrical								
Air conditioning								
Suspension								
Brakes								
Exhaust								
Body rust								
Paint/trim								
Body integrity								
Body hardware								

Chevrolet Tahoe

Test judgments

Performance
Acceleration ....
Transmission ....
Routine handling ....
Emergency handling ....
Braking ....

Comfort
Ride, normal load ....
Ride, full load ....
Noise ....
Driving position ....
Front-seat comfort ....
Rear-seat comfort ....
Climate-control system ....

Convenience
Access ....
Controls and displays ....
Cargo area ....

Other
Fuel economy ....
Predicted reliability ....
Predicted depreciation ....

Test data

Acceleration
0-30 mph, sec. 3.3
0-60 mph, sec. 9.7
Quarter mile, sec. 17.4
Quarter mile, mph 79
45-65 mph, sec. 6.2

Fuel economy (regular)
EPA city/highway, mpg 15/19
CU's overall mileage, mpg 13
CU's city/highway, mpg....8/21
CU's 150-mile trip, mpg 16
Fuel refill capacity, gal. 30.0
Cruising range, mi. 450
Annual fuel: gal./cost ..1160/$1390

Braking from 60 mph
Dry pavement, ft. 158
Wet pavement, ft. 187
Pedal effort, 1st stop, lb. 20
Pedal effort, 10th stop, lb. 25

Specifications

Drive wheels
Rear or selectable 4WD

Seating
Passengers,front/rear....3/3

Dimensions and weight
Length, in. 199
Width, in. 76
Wheelbase, in. 118
Turning circle, ft. 45
Curb weight, lb. 5335
Percent weight, front/rear 52/48
Max. load, lb. 1465

Interior room
Front shoulder room, in. 65.0
Front leg room, in. 41.5
Front head room, in. 5.0
Rear shoulder room, in. 65.0
Rear fore-aft room, in. 30.0
Rear head room, in. 4.5
Door top to ground, in. 66.5
Cargo volume, cu.ft. 66.0

Engines available
5.7-liter V8 (255 hp)
6.5-liter V8 turbodiesel (180 hp)

Transmissions available
4-speed automatic

Tested model
1996 LS 4-door wagon 4WD, 5.7-liter V8, 4-speed automatic

Tires as tested
BF Goodrich Radial Long Trail T/A, size P245/75R16

Sport-utility vehicle

Chevrolet Tracker

Previously called the Geo Tracker, this small SUV is similar to the Suzuki Sidekick. The Geo name has been dropped. The Tracker's handling remains ungainly and imprecise. The ride is punishing on any road, and the cabin is noisy. Fold-and-stow rear seats help switch the Tracker from people-carrying to cargo-carrying duties. The two-door Tracker version has a soft top. Overall, the Tracker is a dated design with mediocre crashworthiness. A newly redesigned Tracker is due for 1999.

Body styles and prices

	Price range	Trim lines
4-door wagon 2WD	$14,860	—
4-door wagon 4WD	$15,605	—
Convertible 2WD	$13,655	—
Convertible 4WD	$14,655	—

Safety information

Safety belt pretensioners	No
Center rear safety belt	NA
Dual air bags	Standard
Side air bags	Not offered
Antilock brakes	Optional
Traction control	Not offered
Gov't front-crash test, driver/front passenger	◒/○
Gov't side-crash test, driver/rear passenger	NA/NA
IIHS offset crash test	NA
Injury claim rate compared with all cars/type	●/●

Reliability history

TROUBLE SPOTS	Geo Tracker 90	91	92	93	94	95	96	97
Engine	○	◓	⊙	◓	◓	⊙	◓	Insufficient data
Cooling	◓	◓	◓	◓	◓	⊙	⊙	
Fuel	◒	◓	◓	⊙	◓	◓	⊙	
Ignition	○	○	○	○	○	○	⊙	
Auto. transmission	*	*	*	*	*	⊙	◓	
Man. transmission	*	*	*	*	⊙	◓	⊙	
Clutch	*	*	*	*	◓	◓	⊙	
Electrical	◒	◒	◒	○	○	○	○	
Air conditioning	*	*	*	○	◓	◓	◓	
Suspension	◓	⊙	○	◓	⊙	⊙	⊙	
Brakes	●	●	●	○	○	◓	○	
Exhaust	●	●	◒	○	⊙	⊙	⊙	
Body rust	◒	◓	⊙	◓	⊙	◓	⊙	
Paint/trim	○	◓	○	⊙	⊙	◓	◓	
Body integrity	◒	◒	◒	◒	●	◒	○	
Body hardware	●	◒	●	○	◒	◒	○	

Test judgments

Performance

Acceleration	◒
Transmission	◓
Routine handling	○
Emergency handling	◒
Braking	○

Comfort

Ride, normal load	◒
Ride, full load	◒
Noise	◒
Driving position	○
Front-seat comfort	○
Rear-seat comfort	○
Climate-control system	◒

Convenience

Access	◓
Controls and displays	○
Cargo area	◒

Other

Fuel economy	○
Predicted reliability	○
Predicted depreciation	◒

Test data

Acceleration

0-30 mph, sec.	4.6
0-60 mph, sec.	13.5
Quarter mile, sec.	19.5
Quarter mile, mph	71
45-65 mph, sec.	8.5

Fuel economy (regular)

EPA city/highway, mpg	23/26
CU's overall mileage, mpg	24
CU's city/highway, mpg	17/33
CU's 150-mile trip, mpg	29
Fuel refill capacity, gal.	14.5
Cruising range, mi.	395
Annual fuel: gal./cost	615/$740

Braking from 60 mph

Dry pavement, ft.	143
Wet pavement, ft.	155
Pedal effort, 1st stop, lb.	25
Pedal effort, 10th stop, lb.	30

Specifications

Drive wheels

Rear or part-time 4WD

Seating

Passengers,front/rear 2/2

Dimensions and weight

Length, in.	159
Width, in.	64
Wheelbase, in.	98
Turning circle, ft.	38
Curb weight, lb.	2780
Percent weight, front/rear	52/48
Max. load, lb.	749

Interior room

Front shoulder room, in.	51.5
Front leg room, in.	42.0
Front head room, in.	6.0
Rear shoulder room, in.	51.0
Rear fore-aft room, in.	26.5
Rear head room, in.	4.5
Door top to ground, in.	60.0
Cargo volume, cu.ft.	24.0

Engines available

1.6-liter 4 (95 hp)

Transmissions available

5-speed manual
3-speed automatic
4-speed automatic

Tested model

1996 LSi 4-door wagon 4WD, 1.6-liter Four, 5-speed manual

Tires as tested

Goodyear Wrangler RT/S, size P205/75R15

Minivan

Chevrolet Venture

The Venture is similar to the Pontiac Trans Sport and Oldsmobile Silhouette. All three offer a useful, left-side sliding door and a powered right-side door. The front seats are comfortable, but middle-row and third-row seats are too low. These are among the few minivans that offer a three-seat middle row. The Trans Sport did especially poorly in an offset frontal crash test conducted by the Insurance Institute for Highway Safety. We assume the Venture and Silhouette would have fared similarly. First-year reliability has been extremely poor.

Body styles and prices

	Price range	Trim lines
Minivan regular	$19,925 - $23,000	Base, LS
Minivan extended	$21,414 - $24,037	Base, LS

Safety information

Safety belt pretensioners .... No
Center rear safety belt .... Lap
Dual air bags .... Standard
Side air bags .... Not offered
Antilock brakes .... Standard
Traction control .... Optional
Gov't front-crash test, driver/front passenger .... ◒/○
Gov't side-crash test, driver/rear passenger .... NA/NA
IIHS offset crash test .... Poor
Injury claim rate compared with all cars/type .... NA/NA

Reliability history

TROUBLE SPOTS	Chevrolet Venture (ext.) 90	91	92	93	94	95	96	97
Engine								◉
Cooling								◉
Fuel								◒
Ignition								◒
Auto. transmission								◉
Man. transmission								
Clutch								
Electrical								○
Air conditioning								◒
Suspension								◒
Brakes								◒
Exhaust								◒
Body rust								◉
Paint/trim								○
Body integrity								◓
Body hardware								●

Test judgments

Performance
Acceleration .... ◒
Transmission .... ◉
Routine handling .... ○
Emergency handling .... ○
Braking .... ○

Comfort
Ride, normal load .... ◒
Ride, full load .... ◒
Noise .... ◒
Driving position .... ◒
Front-seat comfort .... ◒
Middle-seat comfort .... ○
Rear-seat comfort .... ○
Climate-control system .... ◉

Convenience
Access .... ◒
Controls and displays .... ◒
Cargo area .... ◒

Other
Fuel economy .... ◓
Predicted reliability .... ●
Predicted depreciation .... NA

Test data

Acceleration
0-30 mph, sec. 3.5
0-60 mph, sec. 10.0
Quarter mile, sec. 17.5
Quarter mile, mph 81
45-65 mph, sec. 6.6

Fuel economy (regular)
EPA city/highway, mpg 18/25
CU's overall mileage, mpg 19
CU's city/highway, mpg 12/33
CU's 150-mile trip, mpg 24
Fuel refill capacity, gal. 25.0
Cruising range, mi. 565
Annual fuel: gal./cost .... 785/$940

Braking from 60 mph
Dry pavement, ft. 147
Wet pavement, ft. 176
Pedal effort, 1st stop, lb. 15
Pedal effort, 10th stop, lb. 25

Specifications

Drive wheels
Front

Seating
Passengers, front/mid/rear 2/2/3

Dimensions and weight
Length, in. 201
Width, in. 72
Wheelbase, in. 120
Turning circle, ft. 42
Curb weight, lb. 3890
Percent weight, front/rear 59/41
Max. load, lb. 1475

Interior room
Front shoulder room, in. 60.0
Front leg room, in. 41.0
Front head room, in. 6.0
Middle shoulder room, in. 61.5
Middle fore-aft room, in. 30.0
Middle head room, in. 5.5
Rear shoulder room, in. 60.0
Rear fore-aft room, in. 29.5
Rear head room, in. 5.0
Door top to ground, in. 62.0
Cargo volume, cu.ft. 76.0

Engines available
3.4-liter V6 (180 hp)

Transmissions available
4-speed automatic

Tested model
1997 LS Minivan extended, 3.4-liter V6, 4-speed automatic

Tires as tested
Firestone FR680, size P215/70R15

Medium car under $25,000

Chrysler Cirrus

The Cirrus and similar Dodge Stratus and Plymouth Breeze offer a well-designed interior with a relatively roomy rear seat. But ride is not this car's long suit. Handling is sound, but not as nimble as that of the Ford Contour and Mercury Mystique. The Cirrus's standard V6 provides lively acceleration. The four-speed automatic transmission shifts smoothly but doesn't always downshift quickly enough. The front seats are fairly comfortable. And roomy though it is, the rear can easily seat two adults but not three. Reliability has remained poor for the Cirrus/Stratus pair; reliability for the Breeze is average.

Body styles and prices

	Price range	Trim lines
4-door	$19,460	LXi

Safety information

- Safety belt pretensioners .... No
- Center rear safety belt .... Lap
- Dual air bags .... Standard
- Side air bags .... Not offered
- Antilock brakes .... Standard
- Traction control .... Not offered
- Gov't front-crash test, driver/front passenger .... ○/◓
- Gov't side-crash test, driver/rear passenger .... ○/◒
- IIHS offset crash test .... Poor
- Injury claim rate compared with all cars/type .... ○/◓

Reliability history

TROUBLE SPOTS	Chrysler Cirrus 90	91	92	93	94	95	96	97
Engine						◓	◓	⊙
Cooling						⊙	⊙	⊙
Fuel						◓	◓	⊙
Ignition						◓	◓	◓
Auto. transmission						◓	◓	⊙
Man. transmission								
Clutch								
Electrical						◒	○	◓
Air conditioning						◒	◓	⊙
Suspension						◒	○	⊙
Brakes						●	○	⊙
Exhaust						⊙	⊙	⊙
Body rust						⊙	⊙	⊙
Paint/trim						●	◓	⊙
Body integrity						●	◒	◓
Body hardware						◒	○	◓

Test judgments

Performance
- Acceleration .... ◓
- Transmission .... ◓
- Routine handling .... ◓
- Emergency handling .... ◓
- Braking .... ○

Comfort
- Ride, normal load .... ○
- Ride, full load .... ○
- Noise .... ◓
- Driving position .... ◓
- Front-seat comfort .... ◓
- Rear-seat comfort .... ○
- Climate-control system .... ⊙

Convenience
- Access .... ◓
- Controls and displays .... ⊙
- Trunk .... ◓

Other
- Fuel economy .... ○
- Predicted reliability .... ●
- Predicted depreciation .... ○

Test data

Acceleration
- 0-30 mph, sec. 3.5
- 0-60 mph, sec. 10.0
- Quarter mile, sec. 17.6
- Quarter mile, mph 80
- 45-65 mph, sec. 6.4

Fuel economy (regular)
- EPA city/highway, mpg 19/28
- CU's overall mileage, mpg 22
- CU's city/highway, mpg 13/36
- CU's 150-mile trip, mpg 28
- Fuel refill capacity, gal. 16.0
- Cruising range, mi. 410
- Annual fuel: gal./cost .... 695/$835

Braking from 60 mph
- Dry pavement, ft. 144
- Wet pavement, ft. 181
- Pedal effort, 1st stop, lb. 15
- Pedal effort, 10th stop, lb. 25

Specifications

Drive wheels
Front

Seating
- Passengers,front/rear 2/3

Dimensions and weight
- Length, in. 186
- Width, in. 72
- Wheelbase, in. 108
- Turning circle, ft. 39
- Curb weight, lb. 3170
- Percent weight, front/rear 64/36
- Max. load, lb. 865

Interior room
- Front shoulder room, in. 55.0
- Front leg room, in. 42.0
- Front head room, in. 4.0
- Rear shoulder room, in. 54.5
- Rear fore-aft room, in. 31.0
- Rear head room, in. 1.5
- Door top to ground, in. 49.0
- Luggage capacity .... 5+0

Engines available
2.5-liter V6 (168 hp)

Transmissions available
4-speed automatic

Tested model
1997 LXi V6 4-door, 2.5-liter V6, 4-speed automatic

Tires as tested
Michelin Energy MXV4, size P195/65R15

Large car under $30,000

Chrysler Concorde

The Chrysler Concorde was redesigned for 1998 along with the similar Dodge Intrepid. Flamboyant styling overlays a basically middling car. It handles fairly nimbly for such a large car. The ride is supple and controlled, with something of the feel of a European sedan. The 3.2-liter V6 lacks refinement but is better than the standard 2.7-liter V6. Road noise is a constant companion. The column shifter is too hard to manipulate. A console shifter is available with the five-passenger version. The interior is roomy. The leather seats in the LXi are more supportive than the cloth upholstery. The low roof and curvy roof pillars make access a chore. The trunk is very large. Fit and finish on our sample was worryingly poor. First year reliability of Chryslers has often been subpar.

Body styles and prices

	Price range	Trim lines
4-door	$21,305 - $24,740	LX, LXi

Safety information

Safety belt pretensioners	No
Center rear safety belt	Lap
Dual air bags	Standard
Side air bags	Not offered
Antilock brakes	Standard (optional on LX)
Traction control	Optional
Gov't front-crash test, driver/front passenger	NA/NA
Gov't side-crash test, driver/rear passenger	NA/NA
IIHS offset crash test	NA
Injury claim rate compared with all cars/type	NA/NA

Reliability history

TROUBLE SPOTS	90 91 92 93 94 95 96 97
Engine	
Cooling	
Fuel	
Ignition	
Auto. transmission	NO
Man. transmission	
Clutch	DATA
Electrical	
Air conditioning	NEW
Suspension	
Brakes	MODEL
Exhaust	
Body rust	
Paint/trim	
Body integrity	
Body hardware	

Test judgments

Performance

Acceleration	◓
Transmission	○
Routine handling	◓
Emergency handling	○
Braking	○

Comfort

Ride, normal load	◓
Ride, full load	◓
Noise	◓
Driving position	◓
Front-seat comfort	◓
Rear-seat comfort	◓
Climate-control system	●

Convenience

Access	○
Controls and displays	◓
Trunk	●

Other

Fuel economy	○
Predicted reliability	New
Predicted depreciation	NA

Test data

Acceleration

0-30 mph, sec.	3.5
0-60 mph, sec.	9.5
Quarter mile, sec.	17.2
Quarter mile, mph	84
45-65 mph, sec.	5.9

Fuel economy (regular)

EPA city/highway, mpg	19/29
CU's overall mileage, mpg	21
CU's city/highway, mpg	14/36
CU's 150-mile trip, mpg	26
Fuel refill capacity, gal.	17.0
Cruising range, mi.	415
Annual fuel: gal./cost	695/$835

Braking from 60 mph

Dry pavement, ft.	140
Wet pavement, ft.	158
Pedal effort, 1st stop, lb.	30
Pedal effort, 10th stop, lb.	35

Specifications

Drive wheels

Front

Seating

Passengers, front/rear	3/3

Dimensions and weight

Length, in.	209
Width, in.	74
Wheelbase, in.	113
Turning circle, ft.	41
Curb weight, lb.	3535
Percent weight, front/rear	64/36
Max. load, lb.	1015

Interior room

Front shoulder room, in.	58.5
Front leg room, in.	42.0
Front head room, in.	4.0
Rear shoulder room, in.	57.0
Rear fore-aft room, in.	34.0
Rear head room, in.	2.0
Door top to ground, in.	49.0
Luggage capacity	7+0

Engines available

2.7-liter V6 (200 hp)
3.2-liter V6 (225 hp)

Transmissions available

4-speed automatic

Tested model

1998 LXi 4-door, 3.2-liter V6, 4-speed automatic

Tires as tested

Goodyear Eagle GA Touring, size P225/60R16

Coupe

Chrysler Sebring

This sporty coupe and its cousin, the Dodge Avenger, are built in Illinois by Mitsubishi. We prefer it equipped with the 163-hp, 2.5-liter Mitsubishi V6 rather than the noisy Chrysler 140-hp, 2.0-liter Four. Handling is competent. The chassis absorbs large bumps well, but small pavement flaws transmit firm kicks. The front seats provide quite good support, though the rear seat is tight for three adults. Some minor controls are poorly placed, but the gauges are clear. The trunk is large, and the rear seatbacks can be folded. Reliability has been disappointing.

Body styles and prices

	Price range	Trim lines
2-door	$16,840 - $21,015	LX, LXi

Safety information

- Safety belt pretensioners .... No
- Center rear safety belt .... NA
- Dual air bags .... Standard
- Side air bags .... Not offered
- Antilock brakes .... Standard (optional on LX)
- Traction control .... Not offered
- Gov't front-crash test, driver/front passenger .... ⊙/⊙
- Gov't side-crash test, driver/rear passenger .... NA/NA
- IIHS offset crash test .... NA
- Injury claim rate compared with all cars/type .... ○/◒

Reliability history

TROUBLE SPOTS (Chrysler Sebring V6)	90	91	92	93	94	95	96	97
Engine						◓	⊙	Insufficient data
Cooling						⊙	⊙	
Fuel						○	◓	
Ignition						◒	○	
Auto. transmission						○	◓	
Man. transmission						*		
Clutch						*		
Electrical						◒	◒	
Air conditioning						⊙	◓	
Suspension						◓	◓	
Brakes						●	○	
Exhaust						⊙	◓	
Body rust						◓	⊙	
Paint/trim						◒	○	
Body integrity						●	●	
Body hardware						●	●	

Test judgments

Performance

- Acceleration .... ○
- Transmission .... ◓
- Routine handling .... ◓
- Emergency handling .... ◓
- Braking .... ◓

Comfort

- Ride, normal load .... ○
- Ride, full load .... ○
- Noise .... ○
- Driving position .... ◓
- Front-seat comfort .... ◓
- Rear-seat comfort .... ◒
- Climate-control system .... ○

Convenience

- Access .... ○
- Controls and displays .... ◓
- Trunk .... ◓

Other

- Fuel economy .... ○
- Predicted reliability .... ●
- Predicted depreciation .... ○

Test data

Acceleration

- 0-30 mph, sec. 3.5
- 0-60 mph, sec. 10.0
- Quarter mile, sec. 17.6
- Quarter mile, mph 80
- 45-65 mph, sec. 6.6

Fuel economy (regular)

- EPA city/highway, mpg 19/28
- CU's overall mileage, mpg 22
- CU's city/highway, mpg 15/35
- CU's 150-mile trip, mpg 26
- Fuel refill capacity, gal. 16.9
- Cruising range, mi. 390
- Annual fuel: gal./cost .... 675/$805

Braking from 60 mph

- Dry pavement, ft. 129
- Wet pavement, ft. 157
- Pedal effort, 1st stop, lb. 10
- Pedal effort, 10th stop, lb. 20

Specifications

Drive wheels

Front

Seating

- Passengers, front/rear 2/3

Dimensions and weight

- Length, in. 190
- Width, in. 70
- Wheelbase, in. 104
- Turning circle, ft. 43
- Curb weight, lb. 3175
- Percent weight, front/rear 64/36
- Max. load, lb. 827

Interior room

- Front shoulder room, in. 53.0
- Front leg room, in. 41.5
- Front head room, in. 3.0
- Rear shoulder room, in. 53.5
- Rear fore-aft room, in. 27.5
- Rear head room, in. 2.5
- Door top to ground, in. 46.5
- Luggage capacity .... 5+0

Engines available

2.0-liter 4 (140 hp)
2.5-liter V6 (163 hp)

Transmissions available

5-speed manual
4-speed automatic

Tested model

1995 Dodge Avenger ES 2-door, 2.5-liter V6, 4-speed automatic

Tires as tested

Goodyear Eagle GT+4, size P205/55R16

Coupe

Chrysler Sebring Convertible

Although this convertible shares its name with the Chrysler Sebring coupe, its underpinnings have more in common with the Chrysler Cirrus. Good points include front safety belts that retract into the seatback, and a glass rear window with a defroster. The V6 is a better choice than the Four. As a convertible, the Sebring is stylish and fun, and the soft top goes up and down easily and quickly. But as a car, it's distinctly mediocre. The ride is jittery, and rough pavement makes this car shake like a wet dog. It handles predictably but not crisply.

Body styles and prices

	Price range	Trim lines
Convertible	$20,575 - $25,840	JX, JXi, Limited

Safety information

- Safety belt pretensioners ... No
- Center rear safety belt ... NA
- Dual air bags ... Standard
- Side air bags ... Not offered
- Antilock brakes ... Standard (optional on JX)
- Traction control ... Optional with ABS
- Gov't front-crash test, driver/front passenger ... ◒/◒ (very good/very good)
- Gov't side-crash test, driver/rear passenger ... NA/NA
- IIHS offset crash test ... NA
- Injury claim rate compared with all cars/type ... NA/NA

Reliability history

TROUBLE SPOTS	Chrysler Sebring Convertible 90	91	92	93	94	95	96	97
Engine							⦿	⦿
Cooling							⦿	⦿
Fuel							⦿	⦿
Ignition							◒	⦿
Auto. transmission							◒	⦿
Man. transmission								
Clutch								
Electrical							◓	○
Air conditioning							⦿	⦿
Suspension							◒	⦿
Brakes							○	⦿
Exhaust							⦿	⦿
Body rust							⦿	⦿
Paint/trim							◒	◒
Body integrity							◓	○
Body hardware							◓	◒

Test judgments

Performance
- Acceleration ... ○
- Transmission ... ◒
- Routine handling ... ◒
- Emergency handling ... ○
- Braking ... ○

Comfort
- Ride, normal load ... ○
- Ride, full load ... ○
- Noise ... ○
- Driving position ... ◒
- Front-seat comfort ... ◒
- Rear-seat comfort ... ◓
- Climate-control system ... ⦿

Convenience
- Access ... ○
- Controls and displays ... ⦿
- Trunk ... ◓

Other
- Fuel economy ... ○
- Predicted reliability ... ○
- Predicted depreciation ... NA

Test data

Acceleration
- 0-30 mph, sec. ... 3.6
- 0-60 mph, sec. ... 10.3
- Quarter mile, sec. ... 17.8
- Quarter mile, mph ... 79
- 45-65 mph, sec. ... 6.5

Fuel economy (regular)
- EPA city/highway, mpg ... 19/29
- CU's overall mileage, mpg ... 21
- CU's city/highway, mpg ... 13/34
- CU's 150-mile trip, mpg ... 25
- Fuel refill capacity, gal. ... 16.0
- Cruising range, mi ... 370
- Annual fuel: gal./cost ... 725/$870

Braking from 60 mph
- Dry pavement, ft. ... 141
- Wet pavement, ft. ... 170
- Pedal effort, 1st stop, lb. ... 20
- Pedal effort, 10th stop, lb. ... 30

Specifications

Drive wheels
Front

Seating
- Passengers, front/rear ... 2/2

Dimensions and weight
- Length, in. ... 193
- Width, in. ... 70
- Wheelbase, in. ... 106
- Turning circle, ft. ... 42
- Curb weight, lb. ... 3445
- Percent weight, front/rear ... 62/38
- Max. load, lb. ... 715

Interior room
- Front shoulder room, in. ... 54.5
- Front leg room, in. ... 41.5
- Front head room, in. ... 5.0
- Rear shoulder room, in. ... 43.5
- Rear fore-aft room, in. ... 27.0
- Rear head room, in. ... 2.0
- Door top to ground, in. ... 48.5
- Luggage capacity ... 3+1

Engines available
2.4-liter 4 (150 hp)
2.5-liter V6 (168 hp)

Transmissions available
4-speed automatic

Tested model
1997 JXi Convertible, 2.5-liter V6, 4-speed automatic

Tires as tested
Michelin XGT 4, size P215/55R16

Minivan

Chrysler Town & Country

The extended-length version of the Town & Country is similar to the Dodge Grand Caravan and Plymouth Grand Voyager. They ride quietly, handle quite nimbly, and convert easily from people-carrier to cargo-hauler. A second, left-side sliding door is standard in the Town & Country, and a very useful feature. Both the 3.3-liter and the 3.8-liter V6s accelerate well. The automatic transmission shifts smoothly. The front seats provide good support. While the middle and rear seats are easy to remove, they're very heavy. Reliability has been spotty.

Body styles and prices

	Price range	Trim lines
Minivan reg. 2WD	$26,680	SX
Minivan ext. 2WD	$27,135 - $31,885	LX, LXi
Minivan ext. AWD	$30,135 - $34,260	LX, LXi

Safety information

Safety belt pretensioners .... No
Center rear safety belt .... Lap
Dual air bags .... Standard
Side air bags .... Not offered
Antilock brakes .... Standard
Traction control .... Standard
Gov't front-crash test, driver/front passenger .... ○/◒
Gov't side-crash test, driver/rear passenger .... NA/NA
IIHS offset crash test .... Marginal
Injury claim rate compared with all cars/type .... ●/●

Reliability history

TROUBLE SPOTS	Chrysler Town & Country (ext.) 90	91	92	93	94	95	96	97
Engine							●	●
Cooling							◓	●
Fuel							○	●
Ignition							●	●
Auto. transmission							◓	●
Man. transmission								
Clutch								
Electrical							◒	○
Air conditioning							◓	●
Suspension							◓	●
Brakes							◒	◓
Exhaust							●	●
Body rust							●	●
Paint/trim							◓	◓
Body integrity							◒	○
Body hardware							◒	○

Test judgments

Performance
Acceleration .... ○
Transmission .... ●
Routine handling .... ○
Emergency handling .... ○
Braking .... ◓

Comfort
Ride, normal load .... ◓
Ride, full load .... ◓
Noise .... ◓
Driving position .... ◓
Front-seat comfort .... ◓
Middle-seat comfort .... ◓
Rear-seat comfort .... ◓
Climate-control system .... ●

Convenience
Access .... ◓
Controls and displays .... ●
Cargo area .... ◓

Other
Fuel economy .... ◒
Predicted reliability .... ◒
Predicted depreciation .... ○

Test data

Acceleration
0-30 mph, sec. 3.7
0-60 mph, sec. 11.2
Quarter mile, sec. 18.4
Quarter mile, mph 75
45-65 mph, sec. 7.2

Fuel economy (regular)
EPA city/highway, mpg 18/24
CU's overall mileage, mpg 18
CU's city/highway, mpg 11/31
CU's 150-mile trip, mpg 23
Fuel refill capacity, gal. 20.0
Cruising range, mi. 420
Annual fuel: gal./cost .... 825/$990

Braking from 60 mph
Dry pavement, ft. 139
Wet pavement, ft. 168
Pedal effort, 1st stop, lb. 20
Pedal effort, 10th stop, lb. 25

Specifications

Drive wheels
Front or all

Seating
Passengers, front/mid/rear 2/2/3

Dimensions and weight
Length, in. 200
Width, in. 77
Wheelbase, in. 119
Turning circle, ft. 41
Curb weight, lb. 4050
Percent weight, front/rear 58/42
Max. load, lb. 1150

Interior room
Front shoulder room, in. 62.5
Front leg room, in. 41.0
Front head room, in. 5.5
Middle shoulder room, in. 64.0
Middle fore-aft room, in. 29.5
Middle head room, in. 5.0
Rear shoulder room, in. 61.0
Rear fore-aft room, in. 30.0
Rear head room, in. 3.0
Door top to ground, in. 60.5
Cargo volume, cu.ft. 76.0

Engines available
3.3-liter V6 (158 hp)
3.8-liter V6 (180 hp)

Transmissions available
4-speed automatic

Tested model
1997 Plymouth Grand Voyager SE Minivan, 3.3-liter V6, 4-speed automatic

Tires as tested
Goodyear Conquest, size P215/65R15

Coupe

Dodge Avenger

This sporty coupe and its Chrysler Sebring counterpart were designed by Chrysler and are built in Illinois by Mitsubishi. We prefer it equipped with the 163-hp, 2.5-liter Mitsubishi-built V6 rather than the noisy Chrysler 140-hp, 2.0-liter Four. Handling is competent. The chassis absorbs big bumps well, but pavement flaws transmit firm kicks. The front seats provide quite good support, but the rear is a tight fit for three. Some minor controls are poorly placed, but the gauges are clear. The trunk is large, and the rear seatbacks can fold. Reliability has been disappointing.

Body styles and prices

	Price range	Trim lines
2-door	$15,185 - $17,460	Base, ES

Safety information

Safety belt pretensioners .... No
Center rear safety belt .... NA
Dual air bags .... Standard
Side air bags .... Not offered
Antilock brakes .... Standard (optional on Base)
Traction control .... Not offered
Gov't front-crash test, driver/front passenger .... ◉/◉
Gov't side-crash test, driver/rear passenger .... NA/NA
IIHS offset crash test .... NA
Injury claim rate compared with all cars/type .... ○/◒

Reliability history

TROUBLE SPOTS	90	91	92	93	94	95	96	97
Engine						◓	◉	Insufficient data
Cooling						◉	◉	
Fuel						○	◓	
Ignition						◒	○	
Auto. transmission						○	◓	
Man. transmission						*		
Clutch						*		
Electrical						◒	◒	
Air conditioning						◉	◓	
Suspension						◓	◓	
Brakes						●	○	
Exhaust						◉	◓	
Body rust						◓	◉	
Paint/trim						◒	○	
Body integrity						●	●	
Body hardware						●	●	

Dodge Avenger V6

Test judgments

Performance
Acceleration .... ○
Transmission .... ◓
Routine handling .... ◓
Emergency handling .... ◓
Braking .... ◓

Comfort
Ride, normal load .... ○
Ride, full load .... ○
Noise .... ○
Driving position .... ◓
Front-seat comfort .... ◓
Rear-seat comfort .... ◒
Climate-control system .... ○

Convenience
Access .... ○
Controls and displays .... ◓
Trunk .... ◓

Other
Fuel economy .... ○
Predicted reliability .... ●
Predicted depreciation .... ○

Test data

Acceleration
0-30 mph, sec. 3.5
0-60 mph, sec. 10.0
Quarter mile, sec. 17.6
Quarter mile, mph 80
45-65 mph, sec. 6.6

Fuel economy (regular)
EPA city/highway, mpg 19/28
CU's overall mileage, mpg 22
CU's city/highway, mpg 15/35
CU's 150-mile trip, mpg 26
Fuel refill capacity, gal. 16.9
Cruising range, mi. 390
Annual fuel: gal./cost .... 675/$805

Braking from 60 mph
Dry pavement, ft. 129
Wet pavement, ft. 157
Pedal effort, 1st stop, lb. 10
Pedal effort, 10th stop, lb. 20

Specifications

Drive wheels
Front

Seating
Passengers, front/rear 2/3

Dimensions and weight
Length, in. 190
Width, in. 69
Wheelbase, in. 104
Turning circle, ft. 43
Curb weight, lb. 3175
Percent weight, front/rear 64/36
Max. load, lb. 827

Interior room
Front shoulder room, in. 53.0
Front leg room, in. 41.5
Front head room, in. 3.0
Rear shoulder room, in. 53.5
Rear fore-aft room, in. 27.5
Rear head room, in. 2.5
Door top to ground, in. 46.5
Luggage capacity .... 5+0

Engines available
2.0-liter 4 (140 hp)
2.5-liter V6 (163 hp)

Transmissions available
5-speed manual
4-speed automatic

Tested model
1995 ES V6 2-door, 2.5-liter V6, 4-speed automatic

Tires as tested
Goodyear Eagle GT+4, size P205/55R16

Minivan

Dodge Caravan

The Dodge Caravan/Plymouth Voyager twins perform well overall. They ride quietly and handle more nimbly than some sedans. A handy, left-side sliding door is available. Low-speed traction control is optional. The 3.3-liter V6 is the engine of choice. The front seats provide good support. Reaching the rearmost seat takes agility. While the middle and rear seats are easy to unhitch, they're very heavy. Reliability has been spotty.

Body styles and prices

	Price range	Trim lines
Minivan	$17,415 - $25,030	Base, SE, LE

Safety information

Safety belt pretensioners .... No
Center rear safety belt .... Lap
Dual air bags .... Standard
Side air bags .... Not offered
Antilock brakes .... Standard (optional on Base)
Traction control .... Optional on LE
Gov't front-crash test, driver/front passenger .... ○/○
Gov't side-crash test, driver/rear passenger .... NA/NA
IIHS offset crash test .... NA
Injury claim rate compared with all cars/type .... ◓/○

Reliability history

TROUBLE SPOTS	Dodge Caravan V6 90	91	92	93	94	95	96	97
Engine							◓	◉
Cooling							◉	◉
Fuel							○	◉
Ignition							◉	◉
Auto. transmission							◓	◉
Man. transmission								
Clutch								
Electrical							○	◓
Air conditioning							◓	◉
Suspension							◓	◉
Brakes							◒	◓
Exhaust							◉	◉
Body rust							◉	◉
Paint/trim							◓	◉
Body integrity							○	○
Body hardware							◒	○

Test judgments

Performance
Acceleration .... ○
Transmission .... ◉
Routine handling .... ◓
Emergency handling .... ○
Braking .... ○

Comfort
Ride, normal load .... ◓
Ride, full load .... ◓
Noise .... ◓
Driving position .... ◓
Front-seat comfort .... ◓
Middle-seat comfort .... ◓
Rear-seat comfort .... ◓
Climate-control system .... ◉

Convenience
Access .... ◓
Controls and displays .... ◉
Cargo area .... ◓

Other
Fuel economy .... ●
Predicted reliability .... ○
Predicted depreciation .... ◒

Test data

Acceleration
0-30 mph, sec. 3.6
0-60 mph, sec. 11.0
Quarter mile, sec. 18.3
Quarter mile, mph 76
45-65 mph, sec. 7.4

Fuel economy (regular)
EPA city/highway, mpg 18/24
CU's overall mileage, mpg 19
CU's city/highway, mpg 12/30
CU's 150-mile trip, mpg 22
Fuel refill capacity, gal. 20.0
Cruising range, mi. 420
Annual fuel: gal./cost .... 810/$970

Braking from 60 mph
Dry pavement, ft. 144
Wet pavement, ft. 155
Pedal effort, 1st stop, lb. 20
Pedal effort, 10th stop, lb. 30

Specifications

Drive wheels
Front

Seating
Passengers, front/mid/rear 2/2/3

Dimensions and weight
Length, in. 186
Width, in. 76
Wheelbase, in. 113
Turning circle, ft. 40
Curb weight, lb. 3985
Percent weight, front/rear 59/41
Max. load, lb. 1150

Interior room
Front shoulder room, in. 62.5
Front leg room, in. 41.0
Front head room, in. 5.5
Middle shoulder room, in. 64.0
Middle fore-aft room, in. 28.0
Middle head room, in. 5.0
Rear shoulder room, in. 61.5
Rear fore-aft room, in. 26.5
Rear head room, in. 3.0
Door top to ground, in. 60.0
Cargo volume, cu.ft. 64.0

Engines available
2.4-liter 4 (150 hp), 3.0-liter V6 (150 hp), 3.3-liter V6 (158 hp) 3.8-liter V6 (180 hp)

Transmissions available
3-speed automatic
4-speed automatic

Tested model
1996 LE Minivan, 3.3-liter V6, 4-speed automatic

Tires as tested
Michelin XW4, size P215/65R15

Pickup truck

Dodge Dakota

The Dakota was redesigned and vastly improved for 1997. It handles nimbly for a truck. The Dakota feels stable and predictable during hard cornering. The standard 3.9-liter V6 accelerates adequately, but it drinks fuel like a V8. The optional automatic transmission shifts smoothly but not always promptly. The ride is jarring, especially if there's no load in the bed. The skimpy rear bench in extended-cab versions supposedly seats three, but leg room is scant. First-year reliability has been average.

Body styles and prices

	Price range	Trim lines
Regular cab 2WD	$12,975 - $14,960	Base, Sport, SLT, R/T
Regular cab 4WD	$16,955 - $19,120	Base, Sport, SLT
Extended cab 2WD	$16,170 - $17,110	Base, Sport, SLT, R/T
Extended cab 4WD	$19,755 - $20,875	Base, Sport, SLT

Safety information

Safety belt pretensioners ..... No
Center rear safety belt ..... Lap
Dual air bags ..... Standard
Side air bags ..... Not offered
Antilock brakes ..... Optional
Traction control ..... Not offered
Gov't front-crash test, driver/front passenger ..... ◓/◓
Gov't side-crash test, driver/rear passenger ..... NA/NA
IIHS offset crash test ..... NA
Injury claim rate compared with all cars/type ..... NA/NA

Reliability history

TROUBLE SPOTS	Dodge Dakota Pickup (2WD) 90	91	92	93	94	95	96	97
Engine								◉
Cooling								◉
Fuel								◉
Ignition								◉
Auto. transmission								◓
Man. transmission								*
Clutch								*
Electrical								◓
Air conditioning								◉
Suspension								◉
Brakes								◉
Exhaust								◉
Body rust								◉
Paint/trim								◉
Body integrity								○
Body hardware								◓

Test judgments

Performance
Acceleration ..... ○
Transmission ..... ◓
Routine handling ..... ◓
Emergency handling ..... ○
Braking ..... ◒

Comfort
Ride, normal load ..... ◒
Ride, full load ..... ◒
Noise ..... ◓
Driving position ..... ◓
Front-seat comfort ..... ◓
Rear-seat comfort ..... ●
Climate-control system ..... ◉

Convenience
Access ..... ◓
Controls and displays ..... ◉
Cargo area ..... ○

Other
Fuel economy ..... ●
Predicted reliability ..... ○
Predicted depreciation ..... NA

Test data

Acceleration
0-30 mph, sec. 3.9
0-60 mph, sec. 11.2
Quarter mile, sec. 18.5
Quarter mile, mph 76
45-65 mph, sec. 7.4

Fuel economy (regular)
EPA city/highway, mpg 16/21
CU's overall mileage, mpg 16
CU's city/highway, mpg 10/26
CU's 150-mile trip, mpg 21
Fuel refill capacity, gal. 22.0
Cruising range, mi. 425
Annual fuel: gal./cost ..... 935/$1125

Braking from 60 mph
Dry pavement, ft. 143
Wet pavement, ft. 233
Pedal effort, 1st stop, lb. 20
Pedal effort, 10th stop, lb. 25

Specifications

Drive wheels
Rear or part-time 4WD

Seating
Passengers, front/rear 3/3

Dimensions and weight
Length, in. 215
Width, in. 72
Wheelbase, in. 131
Turning circle, ft. 44
Curb weight, lb. 3840
Percent weight, front/rear 60/40
Max. load, lb. 1320

Interior room
Front shoulder room, in. 57.5
Front leg room, in. 42.0
Front head room, in. 5.5
Rear shoulder room, in. 52.0
Rear fore-aft room, in. 22.5
Rear head room, in. 4.0
Door top to ground, in. 60.0

Engines available
2.5-liter 4 (120 hp), 3.9-liter V6 (175 hp), 5.2-liter V8 (230 hp) 5.9-liter V8 (250 hp)

Transmissions available
5-speed manual, 4-speed automatic

Tested model
1997 SLT Regular cab 2WD, 3.9-liter V6, 4-speed automatic

Tires as tested
Goodyear Invicta GL, size P215/75R15

Sport-utility vehicle

Dodge Durango

The Durango is new for 1998. It's based on the Dodge Dakota pickup truck (an old-school SUV concept). The result is a fairly compact SUV that manages to have three rows of seats; it's smaller than large SUVs like the Ford Expedition and Chevy Suburban, which also offer three rows of seats. The ride is stiff, choppy, and trucklike. The 5.2-liter V8 guzzles gasoline but doesn't give the heavy Durango the oomph it needs. The brakes are mediocre as well. The front seats are reasonably comfortable, though the seatbacks are a bit lumpy. The rearmost bench is hard to access and is low, flat, and too firm. Selectable full-time four-wheel drive is optional.

Body styles and prices

	Price range	Trim lines
4-door wagon 4WD	$25,950 - $29,085	Base, SLT, SLT Plus

Safety information

Safety belt pretensioners ....No
Center rear safety belt ....Lap
Dual air bags ....Standard
Side air bags ....Not offered
Antilock brakes ....Optional
Traction control ....Not offered
Gov't front-crash test, driver/front passenger ....NA/NA
Gov't side-crash test, driver/rear passenger ....NA/NA
IIHS offset crash test ....NA
Injury claim rate compared with all cars/type ....NA/NA

Reliability history

TROUBLE SPOTS	90 91 92 93 94 95 96 97
Engine	
Cooling	
Fuel	
Ignition	
Auto. transmission	NO
Man. transmission	
Clutch	DATA
Electrical	
Air conditioning	NEW
Suspension	
Brakes	MODEL
Exhaust	
Body rust	
Paint/trim	
Body integrity	
Body hardware	

Test judgments

Performance
Acceleration .... ◓
Transmission .... ◓
Routine handling .... ○
Emergency handling .... ◒
Braking .... ◒

Comfort
Ride, normal load .... ○
Ride, full load .... ○
Noise .... ○
Driving position .... ◓
Front-seat comfort .... ◓
Middle-seat comfort .... ○
Rear-seat comfort .... ●
Climate-control system .... ●

Convenience
Access .... ○
Controls and displays .... ◓
Cargo area .... ◓

Other
Fuel economy .... ●
Predicted reliability ....New
Predicted depreciation ....NA

Test data

Acceleration
0-30 mph, sec. 3.3
0-60 mph, sec. 9.5
Quarter mile, sec. 17.4
Quarter mile, mph 79
45-65 mph, sec. 5.8

Fuel economy (regular)
EPA city/highway, mpg 13/17
CU's overall mileage, mpg 13
CU's city/highway, mpg....................8/21
CU's 150-mile trip, mpg 16
Fuel refill capacity, gal. 25.0
Cruising range, mi. 365
Annual fuel: gal./cost ..1150/$1380

Braking from 60 mph
Dry pavement, ft. 155
Wet pavement, ft. 195
Pedal effort, 1st stop, lb. 20
Pedal effort, 10th stop, lb. 30

Specifications

Drive wheels
Part-time or selectable 4WD

Seating
Passengers,front/mid/rear......3/3/2

Dimensions and weight
Length, in. 193
Width, in. 72
Wheelbase, in. 116
Turning circle, ft. 41
Curb weight, lb. 4710
Percent weight, front/rear 57/43
Max. load, lb. 1690

Interior room
Front shoulder room, in. 57.0
Front leg room, in. 43.5
Front head room, in. 5.0
Middle shoulder room, in. 57.0
Middle fore-aft room, in. 30.0
Middle head room, in. 7.0
Rear shoulder room, in. 56.5
Rear fore-aft room, in. 27.5
Rear head room, in. 4.0
Door top to ground, in. 63.0
Cargo volume, cu.ft. 39.5

Engines available
3.9-liter V6 (175 hp), 5.2-liter V8 (230 hp), 5.9-liter V8 (250 hp)

Transmissions available
4-speed automatic

Tested model
1998 SLT Plus 4-door wagon 4WD, 5.2-liter V8, 4-speed automatic

Tires as tested
Goodyear Wrangler RT/S, size P235/75R15

Minivan

Dodge Grand Caravan

This long-wheelbase version of the Dodge Caravan rides quietly and handles nimbly. (The Chrysler Town & Country and Plymouth Grand Voyager are similar.) The 3.3-liter and the 3.8-liter V6s both accelerate adequately. The front seats are fairly comfortable, but some of our testers found the padding a little lumpy. Tall drivers may find leg room a little tight. The middle and rear seats are very heavy, but they're easy to unhitch. A second, left-side sliding door is a handy option. Reliability has been spotty.

Body styles and prices

	Price range	Trim lines
Minivan 2WD	$20,125 - $27,180	Base, SE, LE, ES
Minivan AWD	$26,580 - $30,210	SE, LE, ES

Safety information

Safety belt pretensioners .... No
Center rear safety belt .... NA
Dual air bags .... Standard
Side air bags .... Not offered
Antilock brakes .... Standard (optional on Base)
Traction control .... Optional on LE
Gov't front-crash test, driver/front passenger .... ○/◒
Gov't side-crash test, driver/rear passenger .... NA/NA
IIHS offset crash test .... Marginal
Injury claim rate compared with all cars/type .... ◉/◉

Reliability history

TROUBLE SPOTS	90	91	92	93	94	95	96	97
	Dodge Grand Caravan V6							
Engine							◉	◉
Cooling							◓	◉
Fuel							○	◉
Ignition							◉	◉
Auto. transmission							◓	◉
Man. transmission								
Clutch								
Electrical							◒	○
Air conditioning							◓	◉
Suspension							◓	◉
Brakes							◒	◓
Exhaust							◉	◉
Body rust							◉	◉
Paint/trim							◓	◓
Body integrity							◒	○
Body hardware							◒	○

Test judgments

Performance
Acceleration .... ○
Transmission .... ◉
Routine handling .... ○
Emergency handling .... ○
Braking .... ◓

Comfort
Ride, normal load .... ◓
Ride, full load .... ◓
Noise .... ◓
Driving position .... ◓
Front-seat comfort .... ◓
Middle-seat comfort .... ◓
Rear-seat comfort .... ◓
Climate-control system .... ◉

Convenience
Access .... ◓
Controls and displays .... ◉
Cargo area .... ◓

Other
Fuel economy .... ◒
Predicted reliability .... ◒
Predicted depreciation .... ◒

Test data

Acceleration
0-30 mph, sec. 3.7
0-60 mph, sec. 11.2
Quarter mile, sec. 18.4
Quarter mile, mph 75
45-65 mph, sec. 7.2

Fuel economy (regular)
EPA city/highway, mpg 18/24
CU's overall mileage, mpg 18
CU's city/highway, mpg 11/31
CU's 150-mile trip, mpg 23
Fuel refill capacity, gal. 20.0
Cruising range, mi. 420
Annual fuel: gal./cost ...... 825/$990

Braking from 60 mph
Dry pavement, ft. 139
Wet pavement, ft. 168
Pedal effort, 1st stop, lb. 20
Pedal effort, 10th stop, lb. 25

Specifications

Drive wheels
Front or all

Seating
Passengers, front/mid/rear 2/2/3

Dimensions and weight
Length, in. 200
Width, in. 77
Wheelbase, in. 119
Turning circle, ft. 41
Curb weight, lb. 4050
Percent weight, front/rear 58/42
Max. load, lb. 1150

Interior room
Front shoulder room, in. 62.5
Front leg room, in. 41.0
Front head room, in. 5.5
Middle shoulder room, in. 64.0
Middle fore-aft room, in. 29.5
Middle head room, in. 5.0
Rear shoulder room, in. 61.0
Rear fore-aft room, in. 30.0
Rear head room, in. 3.0
Door top to ground, in. 60.5
Cargo volume, cu.ft. 76.0

Engines available
2.4-liter 4 (150 hp), 3.0-liter V6 (150 hp), 3.3-liter V6 (158 hp) 3.8-liter V6 (180 hp)

Transmissions available
3-speed auto., 4-speed auto.

Tested model
1997 Plymouth Grand Voyager SE Minivan, 3.3-liter V6, 4-speed auto.

Tires as tested
Goodyear Conquest, size P215/65R15

Large car under $30,000

Dodge Intrepid

The Dodge Intrepid and its stablemate, the Chrysler Concorde, were redesigned for 1998. The Intrepid is a large and stylish car with overall middling performance. The 2.7-liter V6 engine is noisy and transmits some vibration into the cabin. It also feels rather lame at low revs. Handling is nimble and competent. The ride is steady and absorbent. The interior is roomy but the cloth seats could provide better support. The low roof and slanted roof pillars make getting in or out a chore. One feature we find annoying is that the driver's door lock doesn't control the other doors, so you can't lock or unlock the car with the turn of the key. Chrysler products are often plagued with problems their first year, so we would proceed with caution.

Body styles and prices

	Price range	Trim lines
4-door	$19,925 - $22,020	Base, ES

Safety information

Safety belt pretensioners	No
Center rear safety belt	Lap
Dual air bags	Standard
Side air bags	Not offered
Antilock brakes	Optional
Traction control	Optional
Gov't front-crash test, driver/front passenger	NA/NA
Gov't side-crash test, driver/rear passenger	NA/NA
IIHS offset crash test	NA
Injury claim rate compared with all cars/type	NA/NA

Reliability history

TROUBLE SPOTS	90	91	92	93	94	95	96	97
Engine								
Cooling								
Fuel								
Ignition								
Auto. transmission								
Man. transmission								
Clutch								
Electrical								
Air conditioning								
Suspension								
Brakes								
Exhaust								
Body rust								
Paint/trim								
Body integrity								
Body hardware								

NO DATA NEW MODEL

Test judgments

Performance

Acceleration	◒
Transmission	◒
Routine handling	◒
Emergency handling	○
Braking	○

Comfort

Ride, normal load	◒
Ride, full load	◒
Noise	○
Driving position	◒
Front-seat comfort	○
Rear-seat comfort	◒
Climate-control system	●

Convenience

Access	○
Controls and displays	◒
Trunk	◒

Other

Fuel economy	○
Predicted reliability	New
Predicted depreciation	NA

Test data

Acceleration

0-30 mph, sec.	3.5
0-60 mph, sec.	9.4
Quarter mile, sec.	17.1
Quarter mile, mph	84
45-65 mph, sec.	5.8

Fuel economy (regular)

EPA city/highway, mpg	21/30
CU's overall mileage, mpg	22
CU's city/highway, mpg	14/38
CU's 150-mile trip, mpg	28
Fuel refill capacity, gal.	17.0
Cruising range, mi.	440
Annual fuel: gal./cost	670/$805

Braking from 60 mph

Dry pavement, ft.	141
Wet pavement, ft.	159
Pedal effort, 1st stop, lb.	30
Pedal effort, 10th stop, lb.	35

Specifications

Drive wheels

Front

Seating

Passengers,front/rear	3/3

Dimensions and weight

Length, in.	204
Width, in.	75
Wheelbase, in.	113
Turning circle, ft.	40
Curb weight, lb.	3455
Percent weight, front/rear	64/36
Max. load, lb.	865

Interior room

Front shoulder room, in.	58.5
Front leg room, in.	43.0
Front head room, in.	4.5
Rear shoulder room, in.	57.0
Rear fore-aft room, in.	32.5
Rear head room, in.	2.5
Door top to ground, in.	49.0
Luggage capacity	6+1

Engines available

2.7-liter V6 (200 hp)
3.2-liter V6 (225 hp)

Transmissions available

4-speed automatic

Tested model

1998 4-door, 2.7-liter V6, 4-speed automatic

Tires as tested

Goodyear Eagle GA Touring, size P225/60R16

Small car

Dodge Neon

The Dodge and Plymouth Neon twins remain basically unchanged for 1998. A sporty Dodge Neon R/T is due sometime in 1998. The Neon has a relatively roomy interior. The stronger of the two four-cylinder engines is fairly sprightly when it's mated to the five-speed manual transmission, though it sounds harsh. The three-speed automatic transmission robs lots of power from the engine, and fuel economy is unimpressive for a small car. Handling is predictable, but the ride is harsh and jittery. The coupe version corners nimbly and responsively. Reliability has been subpar.

Body styles and prices

	Price range	Trim lines
2-door	$11,200 - $13,595	Base, Highline, R/T
4-door	$11,300 - $11,555	Base, Highline

Safety information

Safety belt pretensioners .... No
Center rear safety belt .... Lap
Dual air bags .... Standard
Side air bags .... Not offered
Antilock brakes .... Optional
Traction control .... Not offered
Gov't front-crash test, driver/front passenger .... ○/◓
Gov't side-crash test, driver/rear passenger .... ◒/○
IIHS offset crash test .... Poor
Injury claim rate compared with all cars/type .... ◒/○

Reliability history

TROUBLE SPOTS	90	91	92	93	94	95	96	97
						Dodge Neon		
Engine						○	◓	⊙
Cooling						⊙	◓	⊙
Fuel						○	◓	⊙
Ignition						○	◓	⊙
Auto. transmission						◓	◓	⊙
Man. transmission						◓	⊙	*
Clutch						⊙	⊙	*
Electrical						◒	◒	⊙
Air conditioning						○	◓	◓
Suspension						◓	◓	⊙
Brakes						●	○	⊙
Exhaust						◓	⊙	⊙
Body rust						⊙	⊙	⊙
Paint/trim						○	◓	⊙
Body integrity						●	◒	○
Body hardware						◒	◒	⊙

Test judgments

Performance
Acceleration .... ○
Transmission .... ○
Routine handling .... ◓
Emergency handling .... ◓
Braking .... ○

Comfort
Ride, normal load .... ◒
Ride, full load .... ●
Noise .... ○
Driving position .... ◓
Front-seat comfort .... ◓
Rear-seat comfort .... ◒
Climate-control system .... ⊙

Convenience
Access .... ○
Controls and displays .... ⊙
Trunk .... ◒

Other
Fuel economy .... ○
Predicted reliability .... ◒
Predicted depreciation .... ○

Test data

Acceleration
0-30 mph, sec. 4.6
0-60 mph, sec. 11.7
Quarter mile, sec. 18.8
Quarter mile, mph 78
45-65 mph, sec. 8.1

Fuel economy (regular)
EPA city/highway, mpg 24/33
CU's overall mileage, mpg 26
CU's city/highway, mpg 17/39
CU's 150-mile trip, mpg 31
Fuel refill capacity, gal. 12.5
Cruising range, mi. 355
Annual fuel: gal./cost .... 585/$705

Braking from 60 mph
Dry pavement, ft. 148
Wet pavement, ft. 152
Pedal effort, 1st stop, lb. 15
Pedal effort, 10th stop, lb. 20

Specifications

Drive wheels
Front

Seating
Passengers,front/rear 2/3

Dimensions and weight
Length, in. 172
Width, in. 68
Wheelbase, in. 104
Turning circle, ft. 38
Curb weight, lb. 2600
Percent weight, front/rear 64/36
Max. load, lb. 865

Interior room
Front shoulder room, in. 53.5
Front leg room, in. 41.5
Front head room, in. 5.0
Rear shoulder room, in. 52.0
Rear fore-aft room, in. 29.0
Rear head room, in. 2.0
Door top to ground, in. 49.5
Luggage capacity .... 3+2

Engines available
2.0-liter 4 (132 hp)
2.0-liter 4 (150 hp)

Transmissions available
5-speed manual
3-speed automatic

Tested model
1996 Highline 4-door, 2.0-liter Four, 3-speed automatic

Tires as tested
Goodyear Eagle GA, size P185/65R14

Pickup truck

Dodge Ram 1500

Dual air bags finally arrive for 1998, along with a four-door Quad Cab version in some extended-cab models. The Ram's bulk takes a toll on acceleration and fuel economy. Handling is ponderous but predictable. The front seats are comfortable except for insufficient lower-back support. Even the regular-cab models have generous storage room behind the reclining seatbacks. Reliability of the four-wheel-drive version has been much worse than average; the two-wheel-drive version has been average.

Body styles and prices

	Price range	Trim lines
Regular cab 2WD	$14,530 - $16,590	WS, ST, Laramie SLT
Regular cab 4WD	$19,860 - $20,200	WS, ST, Laramie SLT
Ext. cab 2WD or 4WD	$19,020 - $22,580	ST, Laramie SLT
4-door ext. cab 2WD	$19,770 - $20,055	ST, Laramie SLT
4-door ext. cab 4WD	$23,000 - $23,330	ST, Laramie SLT

Safety information

Safety belt pretensioners ....No
Center rear safety belt ....Lap
Dual air bags ....Standard
Side air bags ....Not offered
Antilock brakes..Optional
Traction control ....Not offered
Gov't front-crash test, driver/front passenger ....◓/◓
Gov't side-crash test, driver/rear passenger ....NA/NA
IIHS offset crash test ....NA
Injury claim rate compared with all cars/type ....◒/◉

Reliability history

TROUBLE SPOTS	Dodge Ram Pickup (2WD) 90	91	92	93	94	95	96	97
Engine					◓	◓	◓	◉
Cooling					◓	◉	◉	◉
Fuel					○	◓	◓	◉
Ignition					○	◓	◉	◉
Auto. transmission					○	◓	◓	◓
Man. transmission					*	*	*	*
Clutch					*	*	*	*
Electrical					◒	○	○	◓
Air conditioning					◓	◓	◓	◉
Suspension					◒	◒	○	◓
Brakes					○	◒	○	◓
Exhaust					◓	◓	◉	◉
Body rust					◓	◉	◉	◉
Paint/trim					○	◓	◓	◓
Body integrity					○	○	○	◓
Body hardware					◒	◓	◓	◉

Test judgments

Performance
Acceleration ....○
Transmission ....◓
Routine handling ....○
Emergency handling ....◒
Braking ....○

Comfort
Ride, normal load ....◒
Ride, full load ....○
Noise ....◓
Driving position ....◓
Front-seat comfort ....◓
Rear-seat comfort ....●
Climate-control system ....◓

Convenience
Access ....○
Controls and displays ....◓
Cargo area ....◓

Other
Fuel economy ....●
Predicted reliability ....○
Predicted depreciation ....◉

Test data

Acceleration
0-30 mph, sec. 3.7
0-60 mph, sec. 10.3
Quarter mile, sec. 17.8
Quarter mile, mph 79
45-65 mph, sec. 6.8

Fuel economy (regular)
EPA city/highway, mpg 13/18
CU's overall mileage, mpg 13
CU's city/highway, mpg.........8/22
CU's 150-mile trip, mpg 16
Fuel refill capacity, gal. 26.0
Cruising range, mi. 395
Annual fuel: gal./cost ..1120/$1340

Braking from 60 mph
Dry pavement, ft. 149
Wet pavement, ft. 191
Pedal effort, 1st stop, lb. 25
Pedal effort, 10th stop, lb. 35

Specifications

Drive wheels
Rear or part-time 4WD

Seating
Passengers,front/rear................3/3

Dimensions and weight
Length, in. 224
Width, in. 79
Wheelbase, in. 139
Turning circle, ft. 48
Curb weight, lb. 4785
Percent weight, front/rear 57/43
Max. load, lb. 1615

Interior room
Front shoulder room, in. 66.0
Front leg room, in. 41.5
Front head room, in. 5.5
Rear shoulder room, in. 67.5
Rear fore-aft room, in. 23.5
Rear head room, in. 4.0
Door top to ground, in. 67.0

Engines available
3.9-liter V6 (175 hp), 5.2-liter V8 (230 hp), 5.9-liter V8 (250 hp)

Transmissions available
5-speed manual, 4-speed auto.

Tested model
1996 Laramie SLT Extended cab 2WD, 5.2-liter V8, 4-speed automatic

Tires as tested
Goodyear Wrangler AP, size P245/75R16

Medium car under $25,000

Dodge Stratus

The Stratus and similar Plymouth Breeze and Chrysler Cirrus offer a roomy and nicely designed interior. The ride, though, is a bit nervous and jiggly. Handling is competent, but not as nimble as it might be. The optional V6 provides lively acceleration. The four-speed automatic transmission shifts smoothly but doesn't always downshift promptly. The available four-cylinder engines are noisy. The front seats are fairly comfortable. And roomy though it is, the rear can easily seat two adults but not three. Reliability has remained poor for the Stratus/Cirrus pair; reliability for the Breeze is average.

Body styles and prices

	Price range	Trim lines
4-door	$14,840 - $17,665	Base, ES

Safety information

Safety belt pretensioners	No
Center rear safety belt	Lap
Dual air bags	Standard
Side air bags	Not offered
Antilock brakes	Optional
Traction control	Not offered
Gov't front-crash test, driver/front passenger	○/◓
Gov't side-crash test, driver/rear passenger	○/◒
IIHS offset crash test	Poor
Injury claim rate compared with all cars/type	○/◓

Reliability history

TROUBLE SPOTS	90	91	92	93	94	95	96	97
Engine						◓	◓	◉
Cooling						◉	◉	◉
Fuel						◓	◓	◉
Ignition						◓	◓	◓
Auto. transmission						◓	◓	◉
Man. transmission						*	*	*
Clutch						*	*	*
Electrical						◒	○	◓
Air conditioning						◒	◓	◉
Suspension						◒	○	◉
Brakes						●	○	◉
Exhaust						◉	◉	◉
Body rust						◉	◉	◉
Paint/trim						●	◓	◉
Body integrity						●	◒	◓
Body hardware						◒	○	◓

(Dodge Stratus)

Test judgments

Performance

Acceleration	○
Transmission	◓
Routine handling	◓
Emergency handling	○
Braking	○

Comfort

Ride, normal load	○
Ride, full load	○
Noise	○
Driving position	◓
Front-seat comfort	◓
Rear-seat comfort	◓
Climate-control system	◓

Convenience

Access	◓
Controls and displays	◉
Trunk	◓

Other

Fuel economy	◒
Predicted reliability	●
Predicted depreciation	○

Test data

Acceleration

0-30 mph, sec.	3.8
0-60 mph, sec.	10.9
Quarter mile, sec.	18.2
Quarter mile, mph	78
45-65 mph, sec.	7.2

Fuel economy (regular)

EPA city/highway, mpg	21/30
CU's overall mileage, mpg	20
CU's city/highway, mpg	12/36
CU's 150-mile trip, mpg	26
Fuel refill capacity, gal.	16.0
Cruising range, mi.	385
Annual fuel: gal./cost	735/$885

Braking from 60 mph

Dry pavement, ft.	150
Wet pavement, ft.	162
Pedal effort, 1st stop, lb.	20
Pedal effort, 10th stop, lb.	30

Specifications

Drive wheels

Front

Seating

Passengers, front/rear	2/3

Dimensions and weight

Length, in.	186
Width, in.	71
Wheelbase, in.	108
Turning circle, ft.	39
Curb weight, lb.	3085
Percent weight, front/rear	63/37
Max. load, lb.	865

Interior room

Front shoulder room, in.	55.0
Front leg room, in.	41.5
Front head room, in.	4.0
Rear shoulder room, in.	55.0
Rear fore-aft room, in.	30.5
Rear head room, in.	2.0
Door top to ground, in.	49.0
Luggage capacity	5+0

Engines available

2.0-liter 4 (132 hp)
2.4-liter 4 (150 hp)
2.5-liter V6 (168 hp)

Transmissions available

5-speed manual
4-speed automatic

Tested model

1995 Base 4-door, 2.4-liter Four, 4-speed automatic

Tires as tested

Michelin XW4, size P195/70R14

Medium car under $25,000

Ford Contour

The Contour and similar Mercury Mystique have the driving feel of European cars: nimble handling with a firm, supple ride. They were freshened a year ago and received a few minor improvements. A sportier 195-hp version called the Contour SVT joined the lineup. Handling is especially good in high-trim versions, although the lower-trim car delivers a better ride. Engine choices include a 2.0-liter Four or a smooth, powerful 2.5-liter V6—the one to choose if it fits your budget. The automatic transmission works well with either engine. The front seats are comfortable; the rear is cramped.

Body styles and prices

	Price range	Trim lines
4-door	$14,460 - $22,405	LX, SE, SVT

Safety information

Safety belt pretensioners	No
Center rear safety belt	3-point
Dual air bags	Standard
Side air bags	Not offered
Antilock brakes	Optional
Traction control	Not offered
Gov't front-crash test, driver/front passenger	●/◓
Gov't side-crash test, driver/rear passenger	○/◓
IIHS offset crash test	Poor
Injury claim rate compared with all cars/type	○/○

Reliability history

TROUBLE SPOTS	Ford Contour 90	91	92	93	94	95	96	97
Engine						◓	●	●
Cooling						◓	●	●
Fuel						◒	○	◓
Ignition						◓	◓	◓
Auto. transmission						○	●	●
Man. transmission						●	●	*
Clutch						●	●	*
Electrical						◒	○	○
Air conditioning						◓	●	●
Suspension						○	◓	◓
Brakes						◒	◓	◓
Exhaust						●	●	●
Body rust						●	●	●
Paint/trim						○	◓	●
Body integrity						◒	○	○
Body hardware						◒	◒	○

Test judgments

Performance

Acceleration	○
Transmission	◓
Routine handling	◓
Emergency handling	◓
Braking	◓

Comfort

Ride, normal load	◓
Ride, full load	◓
Noise	○
Driving position	◓
Front-seat comfort	◓
Rear-seat comfort	○
Climate-control system	●

Convenience

Access	◓
Controls and displays	◓
Trunk	○

Other

Fuel economy	○
Predicted reliability	○
Predicted depreciation	◒

Test data

Acceleration

0-30 mph, sec.	4.0
0-60 mph, sec.	11.1
Quarter mile, sec.	18.4
Quarter mile, mph	77
45-65 mph, sec.	7.0

Fuel economy (regular)

EPA city/highway, mpg	24/32
CU's overall mileage, mpg	24
CU's city/highway, mpg	14/42
CU's 150-mile trip, mpg	29
Fuel refill capacity, gal.	14.5
Cruising range, mi.	390
Annual fuel: gal./cost	635/$765

Braking from 60 mph

Dry pavement, ft.	138
Wet pavement, ft.	167
Pedal effort, 1st stop, lb.	20
Pedal effort, 10th stop, lb.	25

Specifications

Drive wheels

Front

Seating

Passengers, front/rear	2/3

Dimensions and weight

Length, in.	185
Width, in.	69
Wheelbase, in.	107
Turning circle, ft.	38
Curb weight, lb.	2895
Percent weight, front/rear	64/36
Max. load, lb.	880

Interior room

Front shoulder room, in.	54.0
Front leg room, in.	41.0
Front head room, in.	4.0
Rear shoulder room, in.	53.0
Rear fore-aft room, in.	28.5
Rear head room, in.	2.0
Door top to ground, in.	51.0
Luggage capacity	5+1

Engines available

2.0-liter 4 (125 hp)
2.5-liter V6 (170 or 195 hp)

Transmissions available

5-speed manual
4-speed automatic

Tested model

1996 GL 4-door, 2.0-liter Four, 4-speed automatic

Tires as tested

Goodyear Eagle GA, size P185/70R14

Large car under $30,000

Ford Crown Victoria

The Grand Marquis and the similar Ford Crown Victoria embody the hallmarks of the classic American freeway cruisers, without suffering from that species' traditional ailments. They are almost the last of the full-frame, rear-drive American V8s. 1998 brought a restyled front and rear and improvements to the suspension. If you want a big, quiet, comfortable-riding large sedan for the least money, look no further. Handling is not bad for a car this large, although the steering is a bit light. Braking and emergency-handling are fairly good. Although the powertrain lacks refinement and good fuel economy, readily available power is there for the asking. Traction control effectively keeps the car on course on slippery roads. The front seat feels soft but could use more support. The rear seat is less accommodating than you would expect in a car this large, but the trunk is cavernous.

Body styles and prices

	Price range	Trim lines
4-door	$20,935 - $23,135	Base, LX

Safety information

Safety belt pretensioners	No
Center rear safety belt	Lap
Dual air bags	Standard
Side air bags	Not offered
Antilock brakes	Optional
Traction control	Optional
Gov't front-crash test, driver/front passenger	⦿/⦿
Gov't side-crash test, driver/rear passenger	◓/◓
IIHS offset crash test	NA
Injury claim rate compared with all cars/type	⦿/◓

Reliability history

TROUBLE SPOTS	Ford Crown Victoria, LTD Crown Victoria 90	91	92	93	94	95	96	97
Engine	○	○	◓	⦿	⦿	⦿	⦿	⦿
Cooling	◒	○	⦿	⦿	⦿	⦿	⦿	⦿
Fuel	○	○	○	◓	◓	◓	◓	⦿
Ignition	◒	◒	●	◒	◓	◓	◓	⦿
Auto. transmission	○	○	◒	●	●	○	◓	⦿
Man. transmission								
Clutch								
Electrical	●	●	◒	◒	○	◒	○	◓
Air conditioning	●	◒	◒	◓	◓	◓	⦿	⦿
Suspension	○	○	◓	◓	◓	◓	○	⦿
Brakes	●	●	●	●	◒	◒	○	◓
Exhaust	●	●	◒	⦿	⦿	⦿	⦿	⦿
Body rust	○	○	⦿	⦿	⦿	⦿	⦿	⦿
Paint/trim	◒	○	○	◓	◓	◓	◓	◓
Body integrity	○	○	○	○	○	○	○	◓
Body hardware	●	●	●	◒	○	○	○	◓

Test judgments

Performance

Acceleration	◓
Transmission	◓
Routine handling	○
Emergency handling	○
Braking	◓

Comfort

Ride, normal load	◓
Ride, full load	⦿
Noise	⦿
Driving position	◓
Front-seat comfort	○
Rear-seat comfort	○
Climate-control system	⦿

Convenience

Access	◓
Controls and displays	◓
Trunk	◓

Other

Fuel economy	◒
Predicted reliability	○
Predicted depreciation	◒

Test data

Acceleration

0-30 mph, sec.	3.3
0-60 mph, sec.	9.2
Quarter mile, sec.	17.0
Quarter mile, mph	83
45-65 mph, sec.	6.2

Fuel economy (regular)

EPA city/highway, mpg	17/24
CU's overall mileage, mpg	19
CU's city/highway, mpg	12/32
CU's 150-mile trip, mpg	23
Fuel refill capacity, gal.	19.0
Cruising range, mi.	400
Annual fuel: gal./cost	805/$965

Braking from 60 mph

Dry pavement, ft.	143
Wet pavement, ft.	149
Pedal effort, 1st stop, lb.	20
Pedal effort, 10th stop, lb.	25

Specifications

Drive wheels

Rear

Seating

Passengers, front/rear	3/3

Dimensions and weight

Length, in.	212
Width, in.	78
Wheelbase, in.	115
Turning circle, ft.	44
Curb weight, lb.	3985
Percent weight, front/rear	56/44
Max. load, lb.	1100

Interior room

Front shoulder room, in.	61.0
Front leg room, in.	42.0
Front head room, in.	5.0
Rear shoulder room, in.	60.0
Rear fore-aft room, in.	29.5
Rear head room, in.	4.0
Door top to ground, in.	52.0
Luggage capacity	6+2

Engines available

4.6-liter V8 (200 or 215 hp)

Transmissions available

4-speed automatic

Tested model

1998 Mercury Grand Marquis GS 4-door, 4.6-liter V8, 4-speed automatic

Tires as tested

Michelin Symmetry, size P225/60R16

Small car

Ford Escort

The Escort and similar Mercury Tracer were partly redesigned—and greatly improved—for 1997, and they're virtually unchanged for 1998. The Escort corners fairly nimbly. The ride feels choppy but remains composed in bumpy turns. The cabin is a little noisy. The transmission shifts smoothly enough but makes the engine labor annoyingly at times. Leg room is a little tight for tall drivers. The front seats are small but supportive; the rear seat is cramped. The wagon version offers respectable cargo space for a small wagon. A 130-hp sporty-coupe ZX2 version was added for 1998.

Body styles and prices

	Price range	Trim lines
2-door	$11,580 - $13,080	ZX2 Cool, ZX2 Hot
4-door	$11,330 - $12,630	LX, SE
4-door wagon	$13,830	SE

Safety information

Safety belt pretensioners .... No
Center rear safety belt .... Lap
Dual air bags .... Standard
Side air bags .... Not offered
Antilock brakes .... Optional
Traction control .... Not offered
Gov't front-crash test, driver/front passenger .... ○/○
Gov't side-crash test, driver/rear passenger .... ○/○
IIHS offset crash test .... Acceptable
Injury claim rate compared with all cars/type .... NA/NA

Reliability history

TROUBLE SPOTS	Ford Escort 90	91	92	93	94	95	96	97
Engine								●
Cooling								●
Fuel								●
Ignition								●
Auto. transmission								●
Man. transmission								●
Clutch								●
Electrical								◓
Air conditioning								●
Suspension								●
Brakes								●
Exhaust								●
Body rust								●
Paint/trim								●
Body integrity								◓
Body hardware								◓

Test judgments

Performance
Acceleration .... ○
Transmission .... ◓
Routine handling .... ◓
Emergency handling .... ◓
Braking .... ○

Comfort
Ride, normal load .... ○
Ride, full load .... ○
Noise .... ○
Driving position .... ◓
Front-seat comfort .... ◓
Rear-seat comfort .... ◒
Climate-control system .... ●

Convenience
Access .... ○
Controls and displays .... ●
Trunk .... ○

Other
Fuel economy .... ◓
Predicted reliability .... ○
Predicted depreciation .... NA

Test data

Acceleration
0-30 mph, sec. 3.8
0-60 mph, sec. 11.2
Quarter mile, sec. 18.4
Quarter mile, mph 76
45-65 mph, sec. 7.4

Fuel economy (regular)
EPA city/highway, mpg 25/34
CU's overall mileage, mpg 28
CU's city/highway, mpg 18/42
CU's 150-mile trip, mpg 33
Fuel refill capacity, gal. 12.7
Cruising range, mi. 385
Annual fuel: gal./cost .... 545/$650

Braking from 60 mph
Dry pavement, ft. 147
Wet pavement, ft. 181
Pedal effort, 1st stop, lb. 15
Pedal effort, 10th stop, lb. 20

Specifications

Drive wheels
Front

Seating
Passengers, front/rear 2/3

Dimensions and weight
Length, in. 175
Width, in. 66
Wheelbase, in. 98
Turning circle, ft. 36
Curb weight, lb. 2585
Percent weight, front/rear 64/36
Max. load, lb. 830

Interior room
Front shoulder room, in. 51.5
Front leg room, in. 40.5
Front head room, in. 4.0
Rear shoulder room, in. 52.0
Rear fore-aft room, in. 27.5
Rear head room, in. 1.5
Door top to ground, in. 49.0
Luggage capacity .... 4+1

Engines available
2.0-liter 4 (110 or 130 hp)

Transmissions available
5-speed manual
4-speed automatic

Tested model
1997 LX 4-door, 2.0-liter Four, 4-speed automatic

Tires as tested
Uniroyal Tiger Paw, size P185/65R14

Sport-utility vehicle

Ford Expedition

RECOMMENDED

The Expedition is based on the F-150 pickup truck, and is about the same size as the Chevrolet Tahoe. The Expedition corners capably for its heft. Without a full load of cargo, the ride is firm and a bit jiggly. You can leave the selectable all-wheel-drive system permanently engaged, and doing so doesn't worsen the voracious fuel consumption. Seating is roomy and quite comfortable. The optional third-row seat is supposed to hold three, but it's cramped. First-year reliability has been average, although the four-wheel-drive version fared slightly worse than the two-wheel-drive version.

Body styles and prices

	Price range	Trim lines
4-door wagon 2WD	$28,465 - $32,155	XLT, Eddie Bauer
4-door wagon 4WD	$31,065 - $34,790	XLT, Eddie Bauer

Safety information

Safety belt pretensioners	No
Center rear safety belt	Lap
Dual air bags	Standard
Side air bags	Not offered
Antilock brakes	Standard
Traction control	Not offered
Gov't front-crash test, driver/front passenger	◒/◒
Gov't side-crash test, driver/rear passenger	NA/NA
IIHS offset crash test	NA
Injury claim rate compared with all cars/type	NA/NA

Reliability history

TROUBLE SPOTS	Ford Expedition (4WD) 90	91	92	93	94	95	96	97
Engine								◉
Cooling								◉
Fuel								◉
Ignition								◉
Auto. transmission								◉
Man. transmission								
Clutch								
Electrical								◒
Air conditioning								◒
Suspension								◒
Brakes								◉
Exhaust								◉
Body rust								◉
Paint/trim								◉
Body integrity								◒
Body hardware								◒

Test judgments

Performance

Acceleration	○
Transmission	◉
Routine handling	○
Emergency handling	○
Braking	○

Comfort

Ride, normal load	○
Ride, full load	◒
Noise	◒
Driving position	◒
Front-seat comfort	○
Middle-seat comfort	◒
Rear-seat comfort	◓
Climate-control system	◒

Convenience

Access	○
Controls and displays	◉
Cargo area	◉

Other

Fuel economy	●
Predicted reliability	○
Predicted depreciation	NA

Test data

Acceleration

0-30 mph, sec.	3.6
0-60 mph, sec.	11.2
Quarter mile, sec.	18.2
Quarter mile, mph	76
45-65 mph, sec.	7.7

Fuel economy (regular)

EPA city/highway, mpg	13/18
CU's overall mileage, mpg	13
CU's city/highway, mpg	8/22
CU's 150-mile trip, mpg	16
Fuel refill capacity, gal.	30.0
Cruising range, mi.	465
Annual fuel: gal./cost	1120/$1345

Braking from 60 mph

Dry pavement, ft.	143
Wet pavement, ft.	180
Pedal effort, 1st stop, lb.	15
Pedal effort, 10th stop, lb.	25

Specifications

Drive wheels

Rear or selectable 4WD

Seating

Passengers,front/mid/rear......3/3/3

Dimensions and weight

Length, in.	205
Width, in.	79
Wheelbase, in.	119
Turning circle, ft.	42
Curb weight, lb.	5290
Percent weight, front/rear	52/48
Max. load, lb.	1710

Interior room

Front shoulder room, in.	63.5
Front leg room, in.	42.0
Front head room, in.	5.5
Middle shoulder room, in.	63.5
Middle fore-aft room, in.	33.5
Middle head room, in.	5.5
Rear shoulder room, in.	60.0
Rear fore-aft room, in.	26.5
Rear head room, in.	0.5
Door top to ground, in.	69.5
Cargo volume, cu.ft.	70.0

Engines available

4.6-liter V8 (215 hp)
5.4-liter V8 (230 hp)

Transmissions available

4-speed automatic

Tested model

1997 XLT 4-door wagon 4WD, 4.6-liter V8, 4-speed automatic

Tires as tested

Goodyear Wrangler AP, size P255/70R16

Sport-utility vehicle

Ford Explorer

The best-selling Explorer has much to offer. The 1998 model has a redesigned liftgate. The interior is exceptionally roomy. With its rear seat folded, it offers generous cargo space. The Explorer handles soundly and steers nicely. The five-speed automatic transmission shifts smoothly and the permanent four-wheel-drive system works well. The brakes are competent. But the ride is stiff and choppy on bumpy roads and a little jiggly even on the highway. The 205-hp V6 performs about as well as the 215-hp V8, although it's fairly noisy; its 16-mpg fuel use is nothing to brag about.

Body styles and prices

	Price range	Trim lines
2-door wagon 2WD	$19,880	Sport
2-door wagon 4WD	$22,800	Sport
4-door wagon 2WD	$21,635 - $31,740	XL, XLT, E. Bauer, Ltd.
4-door wagon 4WD	$23,555 - $33,745	XL, XLT, E. Bauer, Ltd.
4-door wagon AWD	$26,770 - $33,295	XLT, E. Bauer, Ltd.

Safety information

Safety belt pretensioners .... No
Center rear safety belt .... Lap
Dual air bags .... Standard
Side air bags .... Not offered
Antilock brakes .... Standard
Traction control .... Not offered
Gov't front-crash test, driver/front passenger .... ◓/◓
Gov't side-crash test, driver/rear passenger .... NA/NA
IIHS offset crash test .... Acceptable
Injury claim rate compared with all cars/type .... ◓/◓

Reliability history

TROUBLE SPOTS	Ford Explorer 90	91	92	93	94	95	96	97
Engine		◒	◒	◓	⊙	⊙	⊙	⊙
Cooling		●	○	◓	◓	◓	⊙	⊙
Fuel		○	◓	◓	◓	◓	◓	⊙
Ignition		○	○	◓	◓	⊙	⊙	⊙
Auto. transmission		○	○	◓	◓	◓	⊙	⊙
Man. transmission		◒	◒	○	◓	◓	⊙	*
Clutch		◒	◒	○	○	◓	◓	*
Electrical		◒	○	○	○	◒	○	◓
Air conditioning		●	●	○	◓	◓	⊙	⊙
Suspension		●	◒	○	○	○	◓	⊙
Brakes		●	●	●	●	◓	⊙	⊙
Exhaust		●	●	○	○	⊙	⊙	⊙
Body rust		◒	◓	⊙	⊙	⊙	⊙	⊙
Paint/trim		◒	○	◓	○	◓	◓	⊙
Body integrity		○	○	○	◓	○	○	◓
Body hardware		◒	◒	○	◒	○	○	◓

Test judgments

Performance
Acceleration .... ◓
Transmission .... ⊙
Routine handling .... ◓
Emergency handling .... ○
Braking .... ◓

Comfort
Ride, normal load .... ○
Ride, full load .... ○
Noise .... ◓
Driving position .... ◓
Front-seat comfort .... ◓
Rear-seat comfort .... ◓
Climate-control system .... ⊙

Convenience
Access .... ◓
Controls and displays .... ⊙
Cargo area .... ⊙

Other
Fuel economy .... ●
Predicted reliability .... ○
Predicted depreciation .... ◓

Test data

Acceleration
0-30 mph, sec. 3.2
0-60 mph, sec. 9.0
Quarter mile, sec. 17.0
Quarter mile, mph 83
45-65 mph, sec. 6.2

Fuel economy (regular)
EPA city/highway, mpg 15/19
CU's overall mileage, mpg 16
CU's city/highway, mpg 10/24
CU's 150-mile trip, mpg 19
Fuel refill capacity, gal. 21.0
Cruising range, mi. 365
Annual fuel: gal./cost .... 965/$1160

Braking from 60 mph
Dry pavement, ft. 138
Wet pavement, ft. 178
Pedal effort, 1st stop, lb. 20
Pedal effort, 10th stop, lb. 20

Specifications

Drive wheels
Rear, permanent 4WD or all

Seating
Passengers,front/rear 3/3

Dimensions and weight
Length, in. 189
Width, in. 70
Wheelbase, in. 112
Turning circle, ft. 40
Curb weight, lb. 4325
Percent weight, front/rear 54/46
Max. load, lb. 1025

Interior room
Front shoulder room, in. 56.5
Front leg room, in. 43.0
Front head room, in. 5.0
Rear shoulder room, in. 56.5
Rear fore-aft room, in. 30.5
Rear head room, in. 4.5
Door top to ground, in. 62.0
Cargo volume, cu.ft. 52.0

Engines available
4.0-liter V6 (160 or 205 hp)
5.0-liter V8 (215 hp)

Transmissions available
5-speed manual, 4-speed automatic, 5-speed automatic

Tested model
1997 XLT 4-door wagon AWD, 4.0-liter V6, 5-speed automatic

Tires as tested
Firestone Wilderness AT, size P235/75R15

Pickup truck

Ford F-150

Redesigned for 1997, this full-sized pickup set new standards for its class. The 4.6-liter V8 accelerates strongly, and the ride is composed and fairly quiet. The F-150 feels remarkably nimble for a big truck. The passenger-side air bag can be switched off—a must if you mount a rear-facing infant seat there. The extended-cab model includes a handy third door on the passenger's side. Four-door versions will be available later this year. The four-wheel-drive version's reliability was slightly worse than the two-wheel-drive version's.

Body styles and prices

	Price range	Trim lines
Regular cab 2WD	$14,835 - $21,960	Std., XL, XLT, Lariat
Regular cab 4WD	$18,055 - $24,765	Std., XL, XLT, Lariat
Extended cab 2WD	$17,190 - $24,395	Std., XL, XLT, Lariat
Extended cab 4WD	$20,810 - $27,395	Std., XL, XLT, Lariat

Safety information

Safety belt pretensioners .... No
Center rear safety belt .... Lap
Dual air bags .... Standard
Side air bags .... Not offered
Antilock brakes .... Optional
Traction control .... Not offered
Gov't front-crash test, driver/front passenger .... ⊙/◒
Gov't side-crash test, driver/rear passenger .... NA/NA
IIHS offset crash test .... NA
Injury claim rate compared with all cars/type .... NA/NA

Reliability history

TROUBLE SPOTS	Ford F150 Pickup (2WD) 90	91	92	93	94	95	96	97
Engine								⊙
Cooling								⊙
Fuel								⊙
Ignition								⊙
Auto. transmission								⊙
Man. transmission								⊙
Clutch								⊙
Electrical								◒
Air conditioning								⊙
Suspension								◒
Brakes								⊙
Exhaust								⊙
Body rust								⊙
Paint/trim								⊙
Body integrity								◒
Body hardware								◒

Test judgments

Performance
Acceleration .... ◒
Transmission .... ◒
Routine handling .... ◒
Emergency handling .... ○
Braking .... ○

Comfort
Ride, normal load .... ○
Ride, full load .... ○
Noise .... ◒
Driving position .... ◒
Front-seat comfort .... ◒
Rear-seat comfort .... ◓
Climate-control system .... ◒

Convenience
Access .... ◒
Controls and displays .... ⊙
Cargo area .... ◒

Other
Fuel economy .... ●
Predicted reliability .... ○
Predicted depreciation .... ◒

Test data

Acceleration
0-30 mph, sec. 3.3
0-60 mph, sec. 9.6
Quarter mile, sec. 17.3
Quarter mile, mph 80
45-65 mph, sec 6.5

Fuel economy (regular)
EPA city/highway, mpg 16/21
CU's overall mileage, mpg 16
CU's city/highway, mpg 10/23
CU's 150-mile trip, mpg 20
Fuel refill capacity, gal. 25.0
Cruising range, mi. 480
Annual fuel: gal./cost .... 955/$1150

Braking from 60 mph
Dry pavement, ft. 153
Wet pavement, ft. 189
Pedal effort, 1st stop, lb. 25
Pedal effort, 10th stop, lb. 30

Specifications

Drive wheels
Rear or part-time 4WD

Seating
Passengers, front/rear 3/3

Dimensions and weight
Length, in. 221
Width, in. 78
Wheelbase, in. 139
Turning circle, ft. 47
Curb weight, lb. 4450
Percent weight, front/rear 58/42
Max. load, lb. 1550

Interior room
Front shoulder room, in. 63.5
Front leg room, in. 42.5
Front head room, in. 6.0
Rear shoulder room, in. 62.5
Rear fore-aft room, in. 27.0
Rear head room, in. 3.5
Door top to ground, in. 67.0

Engines available
4.2-liter V6 (205 hp)
4.6-liter V8 (210 hp)
5.4-liter V8 (235 hp)

Transmissions available
5-speed manual, 4-speed auto.

Tested model
1997 XLT Extended cab 2WD, 4.6-liter V8, 4-speed automatic

Tires as tested
Firestone Wilderness HT II, size P235/70R16

Medium car under $25,000

Ford Taurus

The Taurus and similar Mercury Sable remain little changed for 1998. First-year reliability for the Taurus was worse than average, and it worsened some more in its second year, according to our latest survey of owners. Curiously, the Sable's reliability has been average. In view of those results, we can recommend only the Sable. Otherwise, the Taurus is a good car: roomy, comfortable, quiet, and nimble. We prefer the more powerful and polished 200-hp V6 engine over the older 145-hp V6. The front seats are supportive enough. The rear bench seat can hold three adults comfortably.

Body styles and prices

	Price range	Trim lines
4-door	$18,345 - $28,920	LX, SE, SHO
4-door wagon	$21,205	SE

Safety information

Safety belt pretensioners	No
Center rear safety belt	3-point
Dual air bags	Standard
Side air bags	Not offered
Antilock brakes	Optional
Traction control	Not offered
Gov't front-crash test, driver/front passenger	/
Gov't side-crash test, driver/rear passenger	/
IIHS offset crash test	Good
Injury claim rate compared with all cars/type	/

Reliability history

TROUBLE SPOTS	Ford Taurus 90	91	92	93	94	95	96	97
Engine								
Cooling								
Fuel								
Ignition								
Auto. transmission								
Man. transmission								
Clutch								
Electrical								
Air conditioning								
Suspension								
Brakes								
Exhaust								
Body rust								
Paint/trim								
Body integrity								
Body hardware								

Test judgments

Performance

Acceleration	
Transmission	
Routine handling	
Emergency handling	
Braking	

Comfort

Ride, normal load	
Ride, full load	
Noise	
Driving position	
Front-seat comfort	
Rear-seat comfort	
Climate-control system	

Convenience

Access	
Controls and displays	
Trunk	

Other

Fuel economy	
Predicted reliability	
Predicted depreciation	NA

Test data

Acceleration

0-30 mph, sec.	3.5
0-60 mph, sec.	9.4
Quarter mile, sec.	17.2
Quarter mile, mph	84
45-65 mph, sec.	5.8

Fuel economy (regular)

EPA city/highway, mpg	19/28
CU's overall mileage, mpg	21
CU's city/highway, mpg	13/36
CU's 150-mile trip, mpg	27
Fuel refill capacity, gal.	16.0
Cruising range, mi.	395
Annual fuel: gal./cost	710/$850

Braking from 60 mph

Dry pavement, ft.	142
Wet pavement, ft.	165
Pedal effort, 1st stop, lb.	25
Pedal effort, 10th stop, lb.	30

Specifications

Drive wheels

Front

Seating

Passengers,front/rear	3/3

Dimensions and weight

Length, in.	198
Width, in.	73
Wheelbase, in.	109
Turning circle, ft.	40
Curb weight, lb.	3515
Percent weight, front/rear	64/36
Max. load, lb.	1100

Interior room

Front shoulder room, in.	58.5
Front leg room, in.	43.0
Front head room, in.	5.5
Rear shoulder room, in.	56.0
Rear fore-aft room, in.	31.5
Rear head room, in.	2.0
Door top to ground, in.	50.0
Luggage capacity	4+3

Engines available

3.0-liter V6 (145 or 200hp)
3.4-liter V8 (235 hp)

Transmissions available

4-speed automatic

Tested model

1996 LX 4-door, 3.0-liter V6, 4-speed automatic

Tires as tested

General Ameri G4S, size P205/65R15

Minivan

Ford Windstar

The Windstar rides as smoothly, quietly, and comfortably as many sedans. The 3.8-liter V6 delivers plenty of power, and the automatic transmission shifts smoothly. A low floor eases access and loading. The seats are comfortable. The interior is not as spacious as that of GM's and Chrysler's extended-length vans. The Windstar lacks a second sliding door. Instead, it has a long driver's door and a front seat that slides far forward to enable left-side loading. (That long door is a liability in tight parking spots.) We'd still prefer a second door. Reliability has been below average.

Body styles and prices

	Price range	Trim lines
Minivan	$19,380 - $29,705	Base, GL, LX, Limited

Safety information

Safety belt pretensioners	No
Center rear safety belt	Lap
Dual air bags	Standard
Side air bags	Not offered
Antilock brakes	Standard
Traction control	Optional
Gov't front-crash test, driver/front passenger	⊙/⊙
Gov't side-crash test, driver/rear passenger	NA/NA
IIHS offset crash test	Good
Injury claim rate compared with all cars/type	◓/◓

Reliability history

TROUBLE SPOTS	Ford Windstar 90	91	92	93	94	95	96	97
Engine						◓	⊙	⊙
Cooling						◓	⊙	⊙
Fuel						◓	◓	⊙
Ignition						◓	⊙	◓
Auto. transmission						○	◓	⊙
Man. transmission								
Clutch								
Electrical						●	◒	○
Air conditioning						◓	◓	⊙
Suspension						○	◓	⊙
Brakes						●	○	◓
Exhaust						⊙	⊙	⊙
Body rust						⊙	⊙	⊙
Paint/trim						◓	◓	⊙
Body integrity						◒	○	◓
Body hardware						●	◒	○

Test judgments

Performance

Acceleration	◓
Transmission	⊙
Routine handling	○
Emergency handling	○
Braking	○

Comfort

Ride, normal load	◓
Ride, full load	◓
Noise	◓
Driving position	◓
Front-seat comfort	◓
Middle-seat comfort	◓
Rear-seat comfort	○
Climate-control system	⊙

Convenience

Access	◓
Controls and displays	◓
Cargo area	◓

Other

Fuel economy	◒
Predicted reliability	◒
Predicted depreciation	○

Test data

Acceleration

0-30 mph, sec.	3.5
0-60 mph, sec.	9.5
Quarter mile, sec.	17.3
Quarter mile, mph	81
45-65 mph, sec.	6.2

Fuel economy (regular)

EPA city/highway, mpg	18/25
CU's overall mileage, mpg	19
CU's city/highway, mpg	12/31
CU's 150-mile trip, mpg	23
Fuel refill capacity, gal.	25.0
Cruising range, mi.	555
Annual fuel: gal./cost	785/$940

Braking from 60 mph

Dry pavement, ft.	140
Wet pavement, ft.	167
Pedal effort, 1st stop, lb.	15
Pedal effort, 10th stop, lb.	20

Specifications

Drive wheels

Front

Seating

Passengers, front/mid/rear......2/2/3

Dimensions and weight

Length, in.	201
Width, in.	75
Wheelbase, in.	121
Turning circle, ft.	44
Curb weight, lb.	4055
Percent weight, front/rear	61/39
Max. load, lb.	1325

Interior room

Front shoulder room, in.	61.0
Front leg room, in.	41.0
Front head room, in.	5.5
Middle shoulder room, in.	63.0
Middle fore-aft room, in.	28.0
Middle head room, in.	4.5
Rear shoulder room, in.	57.0
Rear fore-aft room, in.	28.0
Rear head room, in.	4.0
Door top to ground, in.	61.5
Cargo volume, cu.ft.	66.5

Engines available

3.0-liter V6 (150 hp)
3.8-liter V6 (200 hp)

Transmissions available

4-speed automatic

Tested model

1998 LX Minivan, 3.8-liter V6, 4-speed automatic

Tires as tested

Goodyear Invicta GS, size P215/70R15

Sport-utility vehicle

GMC Jimmy

The 1998 Jimmy and similar Chevrolet Blazer and Olds Bravada finally have dual air bags. This year also brought a new dashboard and revised front styling, but the biggest improvement was in the brakes, which used to be distinctly subpar but are now OK. Ride and handling are both so-so. A wide turning circle makes for clumsy maneuvering around town. The engine accelerates powerfully but sounds coarse. The Jimmy's and Blazer's optional four-wheel-drive system is part-time only. The Bravada has a type of full-time four-wheel drive. The rear seat is a bit skimpy, but the split seatback folds down easily to form a generous cargo hold. Reliability has been poor. The Bravada has held up better.

Body styles and prices

	Price range	Trim lines
2-door wagon 2WD	$21,786 - $24,770	SL, SLS
2-door wagon 4WD	$23,774 - $26,758	SL, SLS
4-door wagon 2WD	$23,867 - $29,023	SL, SLS, SLE, SLT
4-door wagon 4WD	$25,855 - $34,135	SL, SLS, SLE, SLT, Envoy

Safety information

Safety belt pretensioners ....No
Center rear safety belt ....Lap
Dual air bags ....Standard
Side air bags....Not offered
Antilock brakes....Standard
Traction control ....Not offered
Gov't front-crash test, driver/front passenger ....⊖/⊖
Gov't side-crash test, driver/rear passenger ....NA/NA
IIHS offset crash test ....Poor
Injury claim rate compared with all cars/type....NA/NA

Reliability history

TROUBLE SPOTS	90	91	92	93	94	95	96	97
Engine						○	○	◉
Cooling						◉	◉	◉
Fuel						◒	○	⊖
Ignition						○	⊖	◉
Auto. transmission						⊖	⊖	◉
Man. transmission						*	*	*
Clutch						*	*	*
Electrical						◒	○	⊖
Air conditioning						⊖	⊖	◉
Suspension						⊖	⊖	◉
Brakes						●	○	⊖
Exhaust						◉	◉	◉
Body rust						◉	◉	◉
Paint/trim						○	⊖	◉
Body integrity						●	○	○
Body hardware						●	○	⊖

(GMC Jimmy)

Test judgments

Performance
Acceleration ....○
Transmission ....⊖
Routine handling ....○
Emergency handling ....●
Braking ....○

Comfort
Ride, normal load ....○
Ride, full load ....○
Noise ....⊖
Driving position ....⊖
Front-seat comfort ....⊖
Rear-seat comfort ....○
Climate-control system ....◉

Convenience
Access ....⊖
Controls and displays ....⊖
Cargo area ....⊖

Other
Fuel economy ....●
Predicted reliability ....●
Predicted depreciation ....○

Test data

Acceleration
0-30 mph, sec. 3.4
0-60 mph, sec. 10.4
Quarter mile, sec. 17.9
Quarter mile, mph 77
45-65 mph, sec. 7.0

Fuel economy (regular)
EPA city/highway, mpg 16/20
CU's overall mileage, mpg 15
CU's city/highway, mpg....10/25
CU's 150-mile trip, mpg 19
Fuel refill capacity, gal. 18.0
Cruising range, mi. 310
Annual fuel: gal./cost ....975/$1170

Braking from 60 mph
Dry pavement, ft. 144
Wet pavement, ft. 163
Pedal effort, 1st stop, lb. 20
Pedal effort, 10th stop, lb. 25

Specifications

Drive wheels
Rear or part-time 4WD

Seating
Passengers,front/rear....2/3

Dimensions and weight
Length, in. 183
Width, in. 68
Wheelbase, in. 107
Turning circle, ft. 46
Curb weight, lb. 4225
Percent weight, front/rear 55/45
Max. load, lb. 1040

Interior room
Front shoulder room, in. 56.5
Front leg room, in. 42.5
Front head room, in. 4.5
Rear shoulder room, in. 57.0
Rear fore-aft room, in. 30.0
Rear head room, in. 4.0
Door top to ground, in. 60.5
Cargo volume, cu.ft. 40.0

Engines available
4.3-liter V6 (190 hp)

Transmissions available
5-speed manual
4-speed automatic

Tested model
1998 Chevrolet Blazer LT 4-door wagon 4WD, 4.3-liter V6, 4-speed automatic

Tires as tested
Michelin XW4, size P235/70R15

Minivan

GMC Safari

The rear-wheel-drive Safari and similar Chevrolet Astro can haul lots of cargo or tow a heavy trailer. They also offer optional all-wheel drive—handy for slippery roads and snowy climes. But these medium-sized vans feel far more like a truck than a car. They handle ponderously, and they ride uncomfortably on bumpy roads—especially when fully loaded. Some controls are inconveniently located. The wheel wells and engine compartment rob foot room in front. Optional Dutch (upper and lower) rear doors aid loading but are cumbersome to manage. Reliability has been notably poor.

Body styles and prices

	Price range	Trim lines
Minivan 2WD	$20,238 - $24,869	SLX, SLE, SLT
Minivan AWD	$22,538 - $27,169	SLX, SLE, SLT

Safety information

Safety belt pretensioners	No
Center rear safety belt	Lap
Dual air bags	Standard
Side air bags	Not offered
Antilock brakes	Standard
Traction control	Not offered
Gov't front-crash test, driver/front passenger	○/○
Gov't side-crash test, driver/rear passenger	NA/NA
IIHS offset crash test	Poor
Injury claim rate compared with all cars/type	◓/◓

Reliability history

TROUBLE SPOTS	GMC Safari 90	91	92	93	94	95	96	97
Engine	○	○	○	○	◓	◓	◉	◉
Cooling	◒	◓	◓	◓	◓	◉	◓	◉
Fuel	◓	◓	◓	○	○	○	◓	○
Ignition	◒	◒	◒	●	○	◓	◓	◓
Auto. transmission	○	○	◓	○	◓	◓	◓	◓
Man. transmission								
Clutch								
Electrical	●	●	◒	●	●	○	○	◓
Air conditioning	◒	◒	○	○	◒	◓	◓	◓
Suspension	◒	◒	◒	◒	○	○	◓	◓
Brakes	●	●	●	●	●	◒	○	◉
Exhaust	◒	◒	○	◒	◓	◉	◓	◉
Body rust	◓	◓	◓	◉	◓	◉	◉	◉
Paint/trim	●	●	◒	◒	○	◓	◓	◓
Body integrity	●	●	●	●	●	●	●	◒
Body hardware	●	●	●	●	●	◒	●	◒

Test judgments

Performance

Acceleration	○
Transmission	◉
Routine handling	◒
Emergency handling	◒
Braking	◒

Comfort

Ride, normal load	○
Ride, full load	○
Noise	○
Driving position	○
Front-seat comfort	◓
Middle-seat comfort	◓
Rear-seat comfort	◓
Climate-control system	◉

Convenience

Access	○
Controls and displays	◓
Cargo area	◉

Other

Fuel economy	●
Predicted reliability	●
Predicted depreciation	○

Test data

Acceleration

0-30 mph, sec.	3.4
0-60 mph, sec.	10.2
Quarter mile, sec.	17.8
Quarter mile, mph	77
45-65 mph, sec.	6.8

Fuel economy (regular)

EPA city/highway, mpg	16/20
CU's overall mileage, mpg	15
CU's city/highway, mpg	10/24
CU's 150-mile trip, mpg	18
Fuel refill capacity, gal.	25.0
Cruising range, mi.	460
Annual fuel: gal./cost	1000/$1200

Braking from 60 mph

Dry pavement, ft.	158
Wet pavement, ft.	184
Pedal effort, 1st stop, lb.	20
Pedal effort, 10th stop, lb.	25

Specifications

Drive wheels

Rear or all

Seating

Passengers, front/mid/rear	2/3/3

Dimensions and weight

Length, in.	190
Width, in.	78
Wheelbase, in.	111
Turning circle, ft.	45
Curb weight, lb.	4520
Percent weight, front/rear	53/47
Max. load, lb.	1425

Interior room

Front shoulder room, in.	64.5
Front leg room, in.	41.0
Front head room, in.	4.0
Middle shoulder room, in.	67.5
Middle fore-aft room, in.	33.5
Middle head room, in.	4.0
Rear shoulder room, in.	66.5
Rear fore-aft room, in.	28.5
Rear head room, in.	3.0
Door top to ground, in.	68.0
Cargo volume, cu.ft.	98.0

Engines available

4.3-liter V6 (190 hp)

Transmissions available

4-speed automatic

Tested model

1996 SLE Minivan 2WD, 4.3-liter V6, 4-speed automatic

Tires as tested

Goodyear Eagle GA, size P215/75R15

Pickup truck

GMC Sierra C/K 1500

The GMC Sierra and similar Chevrolet C/K 1500 pickups received dual air bags last year. These trucks are pleasant enough to drive on straight roads, and the cabin is very quiet. But braking is mediocre, the steering feels sluggish, and rough roads provoke sharp jolts. Front seats are soft but unsupportive. An optional third door on the passenger's side makes loading people or cargo easier. Reliability of the four-wheel-drive version has been worse than average; the two-wheel-drive version has been average. A redesign is due for 1999.

Body styles and prices

	Price range	Trim lines
Regular cab 2WD	$15,100 - $21,168	SL, SLE, SLT
Regular cab 4WD	$18,800 - $24,168	SL, SLE, SLT
Extended cab 2WD	$18,525 - $27,848	SL, SLE, SLT
Extended cab 4WD	$21,525 - $30,848	SL, SLE, SLT

Safety information

Safety belt pretensioners ... No
Center rear safety belt ... Lap
Dual air bags ... Standard
Side air bags ... Not offered
Antilock brakes ... Standard
Traction control ... Not offered
Gov't front-crash test, driver/front passenger ... ◓/○
Gov't side-crash test, driver/rear passenger ... NA/NA
IIHS offset crash test ... NA
Injury claim rate compared with all cars/type ... ◉/◉

Reliability history

TROUBLE SPOTS	GMC Sierra C1500 Pickup 90	91	92	93	94	95	96	97
Engine	○	◓	◓	◓	◓	◓	◓	◉
Cooling	○	○	◓	◓	◓	◉	◓	◉
Fuel	◓	◓	◓	◓	◓	◉	◓	◓
Ignition	◒	◒	◒	○	◓	◓	◓	◉
Auto. transmission	○	○	◒	◓	◓	◉	◓	◉
Man. transmission	◓	○	◓	*	*	◓	*	*
Clutch	◒	●	◒	*	*	◒	*	*
Electrical	◒	◒	◒	○	○	○	◓	◓
Air conditioning	○	◒	○	◓	○	◓	◓	◉
Suspension	○	○	○	◓	◓	◓	○	○
Brakes	◒	◒	○	○	○	◓	○	◉
Exhaust	●	●	◒	○	◓	◉	◓	◉
Body rust	◓	◉	◉	◉	◉	◉	◉	◉
Paint/trim	●	◒	◒	○	◓	◓	◓	◉
Body integrity	○	○	○	○	○	○	○	○
Body hardware	○	◒	◒	○	○	○	◒	○

Test judgments

Performance
Acceleration ... ◓
Transmission ... ◉
Routine handling ... ○
Emergency handling ... ◒
Braking ... ◒

Comfort
Ride, normal load ... ◒
Ride, full load ... ○
Noise ... ◓
Driving position ... ○
Front-seat comfort ... ○
Rear-seat comfort ... ●
Climate-control system ... ◉

Convenience
Access ... ◓
Controls and displays ... ◓
Cargo area ... ◓

Other
Fuel economy ... ●
Predicted reliability ... ○
Predicted depreciation ... ◓

Test data

Acceleration
0-30 mph, sec. ... 3.5
0-60 mph, sec. ... 9.6
Quarter mile, sec. ... 17.3
Quarter mile, mph ... 81
45-65 mph, sec. ... 6.2

Fuel economy (regular)
EPA city/highway, mpg ... 15/20
CU's overall mileage, mpg ... 15
CU's city/highway, mpg ... 10/24
CU's 150-mile trip, mpg ... 18
Fuel refill capacity, gal. ... 25.0
Cruising range, mi. ... 430
Annual fuel: gal./cost .. 1000/$1200

Braking from 60 mph
Dry pavement, ft. ... 149
Wet pavement, ft. ... 175
Pedal effort, 1st stop, lb. ... 15
Pedal effort, 10th stop, lb. ... 30

Specifications

Drive wheels
Rear or part-time 4WD

Seating
Passengers, front/rear ... 3/3

Dimensions and weight
Length, in. ... 218
Width, in. ... 77
Wheelbase, in. ... 142
Turning circle, ft. ... 50
Curb weight, lb. ... 4605
Percent weight, front/rear ... 58/42
Max. load, lb. ... 1595

Interior room
Front shoulder room, in. ... 65.0
Front leg room, in. ... 40.5
Front head room, in. ... 5.0
Rear shoulder room, in. ... 59.5
Rear fore-aft room, in. ... 22.5
Rear head room, in. ... 2.5
Door top to ground, in. ... 64.5

Engines available
4.3-liter V6 (200 hp), 5.0-liter V8 (230 hp), 5.7-liter V8 (255 hp) 6.5-liter V8 turbodiesel (180 hp)

Transmissions available
5-speed manual, 4-speed auto.

Tested model
1996 Chevrolet C/K 1500 Silverado Extended cab 2WD, 5.0-liter V8, 4-speed automatic

Tires as tested
Uniroyal Tiger Paw, size P235/75R15

Pickup truck

GMC Sonoma

The compact Sonoma pickup and its twin, the Chevrolet S-Series, finally get a passenger-side air bag (with a deactivation switch) for 1998. Both still ride stiffly and lean a lot in corners. The steering feels vague and heavy, and the rear wheels hop on washboard roads. The cabin is commendably quiet. The 4.3-liter V6 feels sprightly. And an optional third door aids loading and unloading on extended-cab versions. Reliability has been a problem, particularly with four-wheel-drive models.

Body styles and prices

	Price range	Trim lines
Regular cab 2WD	$11,717 - $13,264	SL, SLS
Regular cab 4WD	$16,417 - $18,014	SL, SLS
Extended cab 2WD	$14,814 - $15,264	SLS
Extended cab 4WD	$19,464 - $19,914	SLS

Safety information

Safety belt pretensioners .... No
Center rear safety belt .... NA
Dual air bags .... Standard
Side air bags .... Not offered
Antilock brakes .... Standard
Traction control .... Not offered
Gov't front-crash test, driver/front passenger .... ◓/◓
Gov't side-crash test, driver/rear passenger .... NA/NA
IIHS offset crash test .... NA
Injury claim rate compared with all cars/type .... NA/NA

Reliability history

TROUBLE SPOTS	GMC S-15 Sonoma Pickup V6 (2WD) 90	91	92	93	94	95	96	97
Engine					◓	◓	○	◉
Cooling					◓	◉	◓	◉
Fuel					○	○	○	◉
Ignition					○	○	◓	◉
Auto. transmission					◓	◉	◓	◉
Man. transmission					*	◓	*	*
Clutch					*	◓	*	*
Electrical					◒	◒	◓	◓
Air conditioning					○	◓	◓	◉
Suspension					○	◓	◓	◉
Brakes					●	◒	○	◉
Exhaust					◓	◉	◉	◉
Body rust					◉	◉	◉	◉
Paint/trim					○	○	◓	◓
Body integrity					○	◒	◒	○
Body hardware					◒	◒	○	○

Test judgments

Performance
Acceleration .... ◓
Transmission .... ◉
Routine handling .... ○
Emergency handling .... ○
Braking .... ◒

Comfort
Ride, normal load .... ◒
Ride, full load .... ◒
Noise .... ◓
Driving position .... ◓
Front-seat comfort .... ○
Rear-seat comfort .... ●
Climate-control system .... ◉

Convenience
Access .... ○
Controls and displays .... ◓
Cargo area .... ○

Other
Fuel economy .... ●
Predicted reliability .... ◒
Predicted depreciation .... ○

Test data

Acceleration
0-30 mph, sec. 3.3
0-60 mph, sec. 9.2
Quarter mile, sec. 17.2
Quarter mile, mph 82
45-65 mph, sec. 6.0

Fuel economy (regular)
EPA city/highway, mpg 17/22
CU's overall mileage, mpg 17
CU's city/highway, mpg 11/30
CU's 150-mile trip, mpg 20
Fuel refill capacity, gal. 19.0
Cruising range, mi. 405
Annual fuel: gal./cost .... 865/$1035

Braking from 60 mph
Dry pavement, ft. 156
Wet pavement, ft. 178
Pedal effort, 1st stop, lb. 20
Pedal effort, 10th stop, lb. 25

Specifications

Drive wheels
Rear or part-time 4WD

Seating
Passengers, front/rear 3/2

Dimensions and weight
Length, in. 204
Width, in. 68
Wheelbase, in. 123
Turning circle, ft. 43
Curb weight, lb. 3560
Percent weight, front/rear 61/39
Max. load, lb. 1042

Interior room
Front shoulder room, in. 57.0
Front leg room, in. 42.0
Front head room, in. 4.5
Rear shoulder room, in. 18.5
Rear fore-aft room, in. 46.0
Rear head room, in. 2.0
Door top to ground, in. 58.5

Engines available
2.2-liter 4 (120 hp)
4.3-liter V6 (175, 180, or 190 hp)

Transmissions available
5-speed manual
4-speed automatic

Tested model
1995 SLE Extended cab 2WD, 4.3-liter V6, 4-speed automatic

Tires as tested
Uniroyal Tiger Paw, size P205/75R15

Sport-utility vehicle

GMC Yukon

The Yukon and its twin, the Chevrolet Tahoe, fill the gap between the compact GMC Jimmy and the enormous GMC Suburban. The cargo bay is almost as roomy as a minivan's. For 1998, selectable full-time four-wheel drive has been added as an option. The Yukon rides relatively well for a truck. The spacious cabin is generally quiet. The steering feels a little vague, but it's responsive, and the 5.7-liter V8 provides plenty of torque for towing. The transmission shifts smoothly. On the downside, fuel economy is dismal and the brakes are mediocre.

Body styles and prices

	Price range	Trim lines
4-door wagon 2WD	$29,919 - $31,896	SLE, SLT
4-door wagon 4WD	$32,919 - $42,855	SLE, SLT, Denali

Safety information

Safety belt pretensioners	No
Center rear safety belt	Lap
Dual air bags	Standard
Side air bags	Not offered
Antilock brakes	Standard
Traction control	Not offered
Gov't front-crash test, driver/front passenger	◓/○
Gov't side-crash test, driver/rear passenger	NA/NA
IIHS offset crash test	NA
Injury claim rate compared with all cars/type	◉/◉

Reliability history

TROUBLE SPOTS	90	91	92	93	94	95	96	97
Engine						◓	◓	◉
Cooling						◉	◉	◉
Fuel						◓	◓	◓
Ignition						○	◉	◉
Auto. transmission						◉	◓	◉
Man. transmission						*		
Clutch						*		
Electrical						○	○	◓
Air conditioning						◓	◓	◉
Suspension						○	◓	◓
Brakes						◒	○	◉
Exhaust						◉	◉	◉
Body rust						◉	◉	◉
Paint/trim						◓	◓	◉
Body integrity						◒	○	◓
Body hardware						◒	○	◓

Test judgments

Performance

Acceleration	◓
Transmission	◉
Routine handling	○
Emergency handling	◒
Braking	◒

Comfort

Ride, normal load	○
Ride, full load	○
Noise	◓
Driving position	◓
Front-seat comfort	◓
Rear-seat comfort	◓
Climate-control system	◉

Convenience

Access	○
Controls and displays	◓
Cargo area	◉

Other

Fuel economy	●
Predicted reliability	○
Predicted depreciation	◉

Test data

Acceleration

0-30 mph, sec.	3.3
0-60 mph, sec.	9.7
Quarter mile, sec.	17.4
Quarter mile, mph	79
45-65 mph, sec.	6.2

Fuel economy (regular)

EPA city/highway, mpg	15/19
CU's overall mileage, mpg	13
CU's city/highway, mpg	8/21
CU's 150-mile trip, mpg	16
Fuel refill capacity, gal.	30.0
Cruising range, mi.	450
Annual fuel: gal./cost	1160/$1390

Braking from 60 mph

Dry pavement, ft.	158
Wet pavement, ft.	187
Pedal effort, 1st stop, lb.	20
Pedal effort, 10th stop, lb.	25

Specifications

Drive wheels

Rear or selectable 4WD

Seating

Passengers,front/rear	3/3

Dimensions and weight

Length, in.	200
Width, in.	77
Wheelbase, in.	118
Turning circle, ft.	45
Curb weight, lb.	5335
Percent weight, front/rear	52/48
Max. load, lb.	1465

Interior room

Front shoulder room, in.	65.0
Front leg room, in.	41.5
Front head room, in.	5.0
Rear shoulder room, in.	65.0
Rear fore-aft room, in.	30.0
Rear head room, in.	4.5
Door top to ground, in.	66.5
Cargo volume, cu.ft.	66.0

Engines available

5.7-liter V8 (255 hp)

Transmissions available

4-speed automatic

Tested model

1996 Chevrolet Tahoe LS 4-door wagon 4WD, 5.7-liter V8, 4-speed automatic

Tires as tested

BF Goodrich Radial Long Trail T/A, size P245/75R16

Medium car under $25,000

Honda Accord

The Accord has long been a very good, reliable car. In its 1998 redesign the Accord became slightly bigger and better. It inherited several components from the Acura CL, including a Four and a V6 VTEC engine. The V6 is sprightlier and quieter, the Four is a little more economical but noisier. The car handles fairly nimbly, but the cabin is not as quiet as it could be. The front seats are comfortable for most people. The rear seat has more room than before. Handling is sound and the ride is comfortable enough. Controls are logical and well executed. The LX with a V6 is a better value than the EX with a Four.

Body styles and prices

	Price range	Trim lines
2-door	$18,290 - $24,150	LX, EX
4-door	$15,100 - $24,150	DX, LX, EX

Safety information

Safety belt pretensioners .... No
Center rear safety belt 3-point
Dual air bags .... Standard
Side air bags .... Not offered
Antilock brakes .... Optional (standard on EX and V6)
Traction control .... Not offered
Gov't front-crash test, driver/front passenger .... ◓/◓
Gov't side-crash test, driver/rear passenger .... NA/NA
IIHS offset crash test .... Acceptable
Injury claim rate compared with all cars/type .... NA/NA

Reliability history

TROUBLE SPOTS	Honda Accord 90	91	92	93	94	95	96	97
Engine	◓	◓	◓	●	●	●	●	●
Cooling	◓	◓	◓	●	●	●	●	●
Fuel	●	●	●	●	●	●	●	●
Ignition	○	○	◓	◓	●	●	●	●
Auto. transmission	◓	◓	◓	●	●	●	●	●
Man. transmission	●	●	●	●	●	●	●	●
Clutch	○	◓	●	●	●	●	●	●
Electrical	○	○	◓	◓	◓	◓	◓	●
Air conditioning	○	○	○	◓	○	◓	●	●
Suspension	○	◓	◓	●	●	●	●	●
Brakes	◒	◒	○	◓	○	◓	◓	●
Exhaust	◒	○	○	◓	●	●	●	●
Body rust	○	◓	●	●	●	●	●	●
Paint/trim	◓	◓	◓	●	◓	◓	◓	●
Body integrity	○	○	○	○	○	◓	◓	●
Body hardware	◒	◒	◒	○	○	○	◓	●

Test judgments

Performance
Acceleration .... ○
Transmission .... ◓
Routine handling .... ◓
Emergency handling .... ○
Braking .... ◓

Comfort
Ride, normal load .... ◓
Ride, full load .... ◓
Noise .... ◓
Driving position .... ◓
Front-seat comfort .... ◓
Rear-seat comfort .... ◓
Climate-control system .... ●

Convenience
Access .... ◓
Controls and displays .... ●
Trunk .... ◓

Other
Fuel economy .... ◓
Predicted reliability .... ●
Predicted depreciation .... NA

Test data

Acceleration
0-30 mph, sec. 3.8
0-60 mph, sec. 10.5
Quarter mile, sec. 18.0
Quarter mile, mph 79
45-65 mph, sec. 6.6

Fuel economy (regular)
EPA city/highway, mpg 23/30
CU's overall mileage, mpg 25
CU's city/highway, mpg 16/39
CU's 150-mile trip, mpg 30
Fuel refill capacity, gal. 17.1
Cruising range, mi. 490
Annual fuel: gal./cost .... 600/$720

Braking from 60 mph
Dry pavement, ft. 132
Wet pavement, ft. 158
Pedal effort, 1st stop, lb. 15
Pedal effort, 10th stop, lb. 20

Specifications

Drive wheels
Front

Seating
Passengers, front/rear 2/3

Dimensions and weight
Length, in. 189
Width, in. 70
Wheelbase, in. 107
Turning circle, ft. 40
Curb weight, lb. 3105
Percent weight, front/rear 61/39
Max. load, lb. 850

Interior room
Front shoulder room, in. 56.5
Front leg room, in. 40.5
Front head room, in. 2.0
Rear shoulder room, in. 54.5
Rear fore-aft room, in. 30.0
Rear head room, in. 2.5
Door top to ground, in. 50.5
Luggage capacity .... 5+1

Engines available
2.3-liter 4 (135, 148, or 150 hp)
3.0-liter V6 (200 hp)

Transmissions available
5-speed manual
4-speed automatic

Tested model
1998 EX 4-door, 2.3-liter Four, 4-speed automatic

Tires as tested
Michelin Energy MXV4, size P195/65R15

Sport-utility vehicle

Honda CR-V

The CR-V was new in 1997. Roughly based on the Civic platform, it competes directly against the ground-breaking Toyota RAV4 and Subaru Forester. It offers a permanent all-wheel-drive system that isn't meant for serious off-roading. The ride is compliant and carlike, but handling is just OK. The engine is fairly noisy, and acceleration is less than sizzling. And while the seats are reasonably comfortable, the driving position is tiring. Some controls are oddly placed, and the tailgate is cumbersome to operate. The rear seat is roomy. Changes for 1998 include the addition of a five-speed manual transmission and a front-wheel-drive model.

Body styles and prices

	Price range	Trim lines
4-door wagon 2WD	$18,350	LX
4-door wagon AWD	$18,750 - $20,250	LX, EX

Safety information

Safety belt pretensioners ....Front
Center rear safety belt ....Lap
Dual air bags ....Standard
Side air bags ....Not offered
Antilock brakes ....Optional
Traction control ....Not offered
Gov't front-crash test, driver/front passenger .... ◓/●
Gov't side-crash test, driver/rear passenger ....NA/NA
IIHS offset crash test ....NA
Injury claim rate compared with all cars/type....................NA/NA

Reliability history

TROUBLE SPOTS	Honda CR-V 90	91	92	93	94	95	96	97
Engine								●
Cooling								●
Fuel								●
Ignition								●
Auto. transmission								○
Man. transmission								
Clutch								
Electrical								●
Air conditioning								●
Suspension								●
Brakes								●
Exhaust								●
Body rust								●
Paint/trim								●
Body integrity								●
Body hardware								●

Test judgments

Performance
Acceleration .... ○
Transmission .... ◓
Routine handling .... ◓
Emergency handling .... ◒
Braking .... ○

Comfort
Ride, normal load .... ○
Ride, full load .... ◓
Noise .... ◓
Driving position .... ○
Front-seat comfort .... ◓
Rear-seat comfort .... ◓
Climate-control system .... ●

Convenience
Access .... ◓
Controls and displays .... ○
Cargo area .... ◒

Other
Fuel economy .... ○
Predicted reliability .... ◓
Predicted depreciation ....NA

Test data

Acceleration
0-30 mph, sec. 4.5
0-60 mph, sec. 12.2
Quarter mile, sec. 19.1
Quarter mile, mph 74
45-65 mph, sec. 7.5

Fuel economy (regular)
EPA city/highway, mpg 22/25
CU's overall mileage, mpg 24
CU's city/highway, mpg....................16/34
CU's 150-mile trip, mpg 28
Fuel refill capacity, gal. 15.3
Cruising range, mi. 395
Annual fuel: gal./cost ......630/$760

Braking from 60 mph
Dry pavement, ft. 143
Wet pavement, ft. 162
Pedal effort, 1st stop, lb. 15
Pedal effort, 10th stop, lb. 20

Specifications

Drive wheels
Front or all

Seating
Passengers,front/rear....................2/3

Dimensions and weight
Length, in. 178
Width, in. 69
Wheelbase, in. 103
Turning circle, ft. 38
Curb weight, lb. 3155
Percent weight, front/rear 55/45
Max. load, lb. 970

Interior room
Front shoulder room, in. 56.0
Front leg room, in. 41.0
Front head room, in. 5.5
Rear shoulder room, in. 55.0
Rear fore-aft room, in. 29.5
Rear head room, in. 5.0
Door top to ground, in. 59.5
Cargo volume, cu.ft. 31.0

Engines available
2.0-liter 4 (126 hp)

Transmissions available
5-speed manual
4-speed automatic

Tested model
1997 4-door wagon AWD, 2.0-liter Four, 4-speed automatic

Tires as tested
BF Goodrich T/A SR4, size 205/70R15

Small car

Honda Civic

Although relatively pricey, this is still one of the best small cars on the market. The four-door LX sedan's 1.6-liter Four and optional four-speed automatic transmission make a good team, providing smooth acceleration. The Civic glides surefootedly through twists and turns. It also delivers an unusually comfortable ride for a small car. The interior is roomy and well laid out. The Civic's trunk is roomy. The EX coupe delivers a supple ride, but its 127-hp VTEC Four doesn't feel responsive enough. However, fuel economy is good.

Body styles and prices

	Price range	Trim lines
2-door	$12,580 - $15,250	DX, HX, EX
2-door hatchback	$10,650 - $12,100	CX, DX
4-door	$12,735 - $16,480	DX, LX, EX

Safety information

Safety belt pretensioners ... No
Center rear safety belt ... Lap
Dual air bags ... Standard
Side air bags ... Not offered
Antilock brakes ... Opt. EX Coupe auto; std. EX sedan
Traction control ... Not offered
Gov't front-crash test, driver/front passenger ... ◒/◒
Gov't side-crash test, driver/rear passenger ... ○/○
IIHS offset crash test ... Acceptable
Injury claim rate compared with all cars/type ... ◓/◒

Reliability history

TROUBLE SPOTS	Honda Civic 90	91	92	93	94	95	96	97
Engine							●	●
Cooling							●	●
Fuel							●	●
Ignition							●	●
Auto. transmission							●	●
Man. transmission							●	●
Clutch							●	●
Electrical							◒	●
Air conditioning							◒	●
Suspension							●	●
Brakes							○	●
Exhaust							●	●
Body rust							●	●
Paint/trim							◒	●
Body integrity							○	◒
Body hardware							○	◒

Test judgments

Performance
Acceleration ... ○
Transmission ... ◒
Routine handling ... ◒
Emergency handling ... ◒
Braking ... ○*

Comfort
Ride, normal load ... ◒
Ride, full load ... ○
Noise ... ○
Driving position ... ◒
Front-seat comfort ... ◒
Rear-seat comfort ... ○
Climate-control system ... ●

Convenience
Access ... ○
Controls and displays ... ◒
Trunk ... ○

Other
Fuel economy ... ◒
Predicted reliability ... ◒
Predicted depreciation ... ◒
*No antilock brakes

Test data

Acceleration
0-30 mph, sec. ... 3.9
0-60 mph, sec. ... 11.1
Quarter mile, sec. ... 18.5
Quarter mile, mph ... 75
45-65 mph, sec. ... 7.4

Fuel economy (regular)
EPA city/highway, mpg ... 28/35
CU's overall mileage, mpg ... 31
CU's city/highway, mpg ... 21/45
CU's 150-mile trip, mpg ... 35
Fuel refill capacity, gal. ... 11.9
Cruising range, mi. ... 385
Annual fuel: gal./cost ... 490/$585

Braking from 60 mph
Dry pavement, ft. ... 144
Wet pavement, ft. ... 153
Pedal effort, 1st stop, lb. ... 20
Pedal effort, 10th stop, lb. ... 25

Specifications

Drive wheels
Front

Seating
Passengers,front/rear ... 2/3

Dimensions and weight
Length, in. ... 175
Width, in. ... 67
Wheelbase, in. ... 103
Turning circle, ft. ... 37
Curb weight, lb. ... 2440
Percent weight, front/rear ... 62/38
Max. load, lb. ... 850

Interior room
Front shoulder room, in. ... 52.0
Front leg room, in. ... 42.0
Front head room, in. ... 5.5
Rear shoulder room, in. ... 51.0
Rear fore-aft room, in. ... 28.5
Rear head room, in. ... 3.0
Door top to ground, in. ... 49.0
Luggage capacity ... 4+1

Engines available
1.6-liter 4 (106, 115, or 127 hp)

Transmissions available
5-speed manual
Continuously variable transmission
4-speed automatic

Tested model
1996 LX 4-door, 1.6-liter Four, 4-speed automatic

Tires as tested
Firestone FR680, size P185/65R14

Minivan

Honda Odyssey

The Odyssey, based on the pre-1998 Honda Accord, has a supple, well-controlled ride. Its four-cylinder engine gained a shade more power this year. People who dislike sliding doors may appreciate the Odyssey's four conventional doors. The seats are comfortable. The rearmost bench seat folds into the floor, leaving a large cargo space. Think of the Odyssey as a six- or seven-passenger car with little luggage space or a four- or five-passenger car with ample luggage space. The Isuzu Oasis is a clone. Honda will replace the Odyssey with a larger, V6-powered van in the fall.

Body styles and prices

	Price range	Trim lines
4-door minivan	$23,810 - $25,800	LX, EX

Safety information

Safety belt pretensioners	No
Center rear safety belt	Lap
Dual air bags	Standard
Side air bags	Not offered
Antilock brakes	Standard
Traction control	Not offered
Gov't front-crash test, driver/front passenger	◓/◓
Gov't side-crash test, driver/rear passenger	NA/NA
IIHS offset crash test	Marginal
Injury claim rate compared with all cars/type	◓/◓

Reliability history

TROUBLE SPOTS	90	91	92	93	94	95	96	97
Engine						●	●	●
Cooling						●	●	●
Fuel						●	●	●
Ignition						●	●	●
Auto. transmission						●	●	●
Man. transmission								
Clutch								
Electrical						◓	●	●
Air conditioning						◓	●	●
Suspension						◓	●	●
Brakes						◓	●	●
Exhaust						●	●	●
Body rust						●	●	●
Paint/trim						●	●	●
Body integrity						●	●	●
Body hardware						○	●	●

Honda Odyssey

Test judgments

Performance

Acceleration	○
Transmission	◓
Routine handling	◓
Emergency handling	○
Braking	◓

Comfort

Ride, normal load	◓
Ride, full load	◓
Noise	◓
Driving position	◓
Front-seat comfort	◓
Middle-seat comfort	◓
Rear-seat comfort	◒
Climate-control system	◓

Convenience

Access	◓
Controls and displays	◓
Cargo area	◒

Other

Fuel economy	◒
Predicted reliability	●
Predicted depreciation	○

Test data

Acceleration

0-30 mph, sec.	4.4
0-60 mph, sec.	12.2
Quarter mile, sec.	19.1
Quarter mile, mph	75
45-65 mph, sec.	7.9

Fuel economy (regular)

EPA city/highway, mpg	21/26
CU's overall mileage, mpg	21
CU's city/highway, mpg	14/31
CU's 150-mile trip, mpg	24
Fuel refill capacity, gal.	17.2
Cruising range, mi.	390
Annual fuel: gal./cost	730/$880

Braking from 60 mph

Dry pavement, ft.	143
Wet pavement, ft.	158
Pedal effort, 1st stop, lb.	20
Pedal effort, 10th stop, lb.	20

Specifications

Drive wheels

Front

Seating

Passengers,front/mid/rear......2/3/2

Dimensions and weight

Length, in.	187
Width, in.	71
Wheelbase, in.	111
Turning circle, ft.	41
Curb weight, lb.	3480
Percent weight, front/rear	59/41
Max. load, lb.	1150

Interior room

Front shoulder room, in.	57.5
Front leg room, in.	42.0
Front head room, in.	4.0
Middle shoulder room, in.	57.5
Middle fore-aft room, in.	30.5
Middle head room, in.	4.0
Rear shoulder room, in.	49.0
Rear fore-aft room, in.	26.5
Rear head room, in.	2.5
Door top to ground, in.	56.0
Cargo volume, cu.ft.	47.5

Engines available

2.3-liter 4 (150 hp)

Transmissions available

4-speed automatic

Tested model

1995 EX 4-door minivan, 2.2-liter Four, 4-speed automatic

Tires as tested

Goodyear Conquest, size P205/65R15

Sport-utility vehicle

Honda Passport

The Passport is a clone of the revamped Isuzu Rodeo. Extensive enhancements for 1998 include an improved instrument panel and a much better, stronger V6 engine that delivers good acceleration and reasonable fuel economy. But this remains an old-school, truck-based SUV: Sharp bumps make the suspension slam hard, and even the highway ride is busy and jittery. The steering feels vague and rubbery, and handling is rather sluggish in quick maneuvers. The front seats are well shaped but too low, and leg room is snug. The rear seat is low, too, but there's ample head and knee room and the backs recline. A low cargo floor and flush sill make loading easy, but folding the rear seats to expand it is cumbersome and the rear gate is a nuisance to open and close. The four-wheel-drive system is part-time only.

Body styles and prices

	Price range	Trim lines
4-door wagon 2WD	$22,700 - $26,500	LX, EX
4-door wagon 4WD	$25,450 - $28,950	LX, EX

Safety information

Safety belt pretensioners	No
Center rear safety belt	Lap
Dual air bags	Standard
Side air bags	Not offered
Antilock brakes	Standard
Traction control	Not offered
Gov't front-crash test, driver/front passenger	○/◓
Gov't side-crash test, driver/rear passenger	NA/NA
IIHS offset crash test	NA
Injury claim rate compared with all cars/type	NA/NA

Reliability history

TROUBLE SPOTS	90	91	92	93	94	95	96	97
Engine								
Cooling								
Fuel								
Ignition								
Auto. transmission								
Man. transmission								
Clutch								
Electrical								
Air conditioning								
Suspension								
Brakes								
Exhaust								
Body rust								
Paint/trim								
Body integrity								
Body hardware								

NO DATA NEW MODEL

Test judgments

Performance

Acceleration	◓
Transmission	◓
Routine handling	○
Emergency handling	◒
Braking	◒

Comfort

Ride, normal load	○
Ride, full load	◒
Noise	◓
Driving position	○
Front-seat comfort	◓
Rear-seat comfort	○
Climate-control system	◓

Convenience

Access	◓
Controls and displays	◓
Cargo area	◓

Other

Fuel economy	◒
Predicted reliability	New
Predicted depreciation	NA

Test data

Acceleration

0-30 mph, sec.	3.2
0-60 mph, sec.	9.1
Quarter mile, sec.	17.0
Quarter mile, mph	82
45-65 mph, sec.	5.9

Fuel economy (regular)

EPA city/highway, mpg	16/20
CU's overall mileage, mpg	18
CU's city/highway, mpg	12/28
CU's 150-mile trip, mpg	21
Fuel refill capacity, gal.	21.1
Cruising range, mi.	410
Annual fuel: gal./cost	830/$995

Braking from 60 mph

Dry pavement, ft.	156
Wet pavement, ft.	191
Pedal effort, 1st stop, lb.	25
Pedal effort, 10th stop, lb.	30

Specifications

Drive wheels

Rear or part-time 4WD

Seating

Passengers,front/rear	2/3

Dimensions and weight

Length, in.	177
Width, in.	70
Wheelbase, in.	106
Turning circle, ft.	41
Curb weight, lb.	3935
Percent weight, front/rear	54/46
Max. load, lb.	915

Interior room

Front shoulder room, in.	56.0
Front leg room, in.	41.0
Front head room, in.	4.0
Rear shoulder room, in.	56.0
Rear fore-aft room, in.	30.0
Rear head room, in.	3.5
Door top to ground, in.	60.0
Cargo volume, cu.ft.	39.5

Engines available

3.2-liter V6 (205 hp)

Transmissions available

5-speed manual
4-speed automatic

Tested model

1998 Isuzu Rodeo S 4-door wagon 4WD, 3.2-liter V6, 4-speed automatic

Tires as tested

Goodyear Wrangler RT/S, size P235/75R15

Small car

Hyundai Accent

The Accent, Hyundai's least expensive model, competes with the Toyota Tercel, Chevrolet Metro, and other small low-budget cars. Its 92-hp, 1.5-liter Four accelerates adequately. An Accent with antilock brakes can be hard to find, but the nonantilock brakes work fairly well. Thankfully, power steering has been made standard on all but the L model. The ride is choppy but relatively quiet. The rear seat is a bit tight for tall people. The Accent scores fairly well among the very smallest models. Minor cosmetic enhancements are all that's new for 1998.

Body styles and prices

	Price range	Trim lines
2-door hatchback	$9,099 - $10,699	L, GS, GSi
4-door	$10,299	GL

Safety information

- Safety belt pretensioners ..... No
- Center rear safety belt ..... Lap
- Dual air bags ..... Standard
- Side air bags ..... Not offered
- Antilock brakes ..... Optional (not offered on L)
- Traction control ..... Not offered
- Gov't front-crash test, driver/front passenger ..... ○/○
- Gov't side-crash test, driver/rear passenger ..... NA/NA
- IIHS offset crash test ..... NA
- Injury claim rate compared with all cars/type ..... ●/●

Reliability history

TROUBLE SPOTS	90 91 92 93 94 95 96 97
Engine	
Cooling	
Fuel	
Ignition	
Auto. transmission	NOT
Man. transmission	
Clutch	ENOUGH
Electrical	
Air conditioning	DATA
Suspension	
Brakes	TO
Exhaust	
Body rust	RATE
Paint/trim	
Body integrity	
Body hardware	

Test judgments

Performance
- Acceleration ..... ◒
- Transmission ..... ○
- Routine handling ..... ◓
- Emergency handling ..... ◓
- Braking ..... ○*

Comfort
- Ride, normal load ..... ◒
- Ride, full load ..... ◒
- Noise ..... ○
- Driving position ..... ◓
- Front-seat comfort ..... ◓
- Rear-seat comfort ..... ◒
- Climate-control system ..... ◓

Convenience
- Access ..... ○
- Controls and displays ..... ◓
- Trunk ..... ◒

Other
- Fuel economy ..... ◓
- Predicted reliability ..... NA
- Predicted depreciation ..... ○

*No antilock brakes

Test data

Acceleration
- 0-30 mph, sec. 4.5
- 0-60 mph, sec. 13.3
- Quarter mile, sec. 19.6
- Quarter mile, mph 72
- 45-65 mph, sec. 8.7

Fuel economy (regular)
- EPA city/highway, mpg 27/35
- CU's overall mileage, mpg 28
- CU's city/highway, mpg 18/45
- CU's 150-mile trip, mpg 34
- Fuel refill capacity, gal. 11.9
- Cruising range, mi. 375
- Annual fuel: gal./cost ..... 540/$645

Braking from 60 mph
- Dry pavement, ft. 137
- Wet pavement, ft. 172
- Pedal effort, 1st stop, lb. 15
- Pedal effort, 10th stop, lb. 25

Specifications

Drive wheels
Front

Seating
- Passengers, front/rear 2/3

Dimensions and weight
- Length, in. 162
- Width, in. 64
- Wheelbase, in. 95
- Turning circle, ft. 35
- Curb weight, lb. 2290
- Percent weight, front/rear 63/37
- Max. load, lb. 850

Interior room
- Front shoulder room, in. 52.5
- Front leg room, in. 40.5
- Front head room, in. 3.5
- Rear shoulder room, in. 51.5
- Rear fore-aft room, in. 27.5
- Rear head room, in. 2.5
- Door top to ground, in. 49.0
- Luggage capacity ..... 4+0

Engines available
1.5-liter 4 (92 hp)

Transmissions available
5-speed manual
4-speed automatic

Tested model
1995 Base 4-door, 1.5-liter Four, 4-speed automatic

Tires as tested
Uniroyal , size P175/70R13

Small car

Hyundai Elantra

This is a well-equipped car, but it still needs more refinement. The Elantra is larger than the Hyundai Accent, but smaller than the midsized Hyundai Sonata. It doesn't enjoy the price advantage Hyundais used to claim. Nimble handling and a well-appointed cabin are the Elantra's long suits. But the ride is jittery even on smooth roads, and the automatic transmission downshifts reluctantly, blunting engine performance. A five-speed manual is available. Plenty of engine, wind, and road noise enters the cabin. The front seats are supportive. The rear seat feels hard, but it's relatively roomy.

Body styles and prices

	Price range	Trim lines
4-door	$11,499 - $12,549	Base, GLS
4-door wagon	$12,399 - $13,999	Base, GLS

Safety information

Safety belt pretensioners .... No
Center rear safety belt .... Lap
Dual air bags .... Standard
Side air bags .... Not offered
Antilock brakes .... Optional on GLS
Traction control .... Not offered
Gov't front-crash test, driver/front passenger .... ○/○
Gov't side-crash test, driver/rear passenger .... NA/NA
IIHS offset crash test .... Acceptable
Injury claim rate compared with all cars/type .... NA/NA

Reliability history

TROUBLE SPOTS	90 91 92 93 94 95 96 97
Engine	NOT ENOUGH DATA TO RATE
Cooling	
Fuel	
Ignition	
Auto. transmission	
Man. transmission	
Clutch	
Electrical	
Air conditioning	
Suspension	
Brakes	
Exhaust	
Body rust	
Paint/trim	
Body integrity	
Body hardware	

Test judgments

Performance
Acceleration .... ○
Transmission .... ○
Routine handling .... ◓
Emergency handling .... ◓
Braking .... ○

Comfort
Ride, normal load .... ◒
Ride, full load .... ◒
Noise .... ○
Driving position .... ◓
Front-seat comfort .... ◓
Rear-seat comfort .... ○
Climate-control system .... ◉

Convenience
Access .... ○
Controls and displays .... ◓
Trunk .... ○

Other
Fuel economy .... ◓
Predicted reliability .... NA
Predicted depreciation .... NA

Test data

Acceleration
0-30 mph, sec. 4.1
0-60 mph, sec. 10.9
Quarter mile, sec. 18.2
Quarter mile, mph 79
45-65 mph, sec. 7.0

Fuel economy (regular)
EPA city/highway, mpg 23/31
CU's overall mileage, mpg 25
CU's city/highway, mpg 15/41
CU's 150-mile trip, mpg 30
Fuel refill capacity, gal. 14.5
Cruising range, mi. 410
Annual fuel: gal./cost .... 610/$735

Braking from 60 mph
Dry pavement, ft. 140
Wet pavement, ft. 166
Pedal effort, 1st stop, lb. 20
Pedal effort, 10th stop, lb. 25

Specifications

Drive wheels
Front

Seating
Passengers, front/rear 2/3

Dimensions and weight
Length, in. 174
Width, in. 67
Wheelbase, in. 100
Turning circle, ft. 36
Curb weight, lb. 2725
Percent weight, front/rear 63/37
Max. load, lb. 850

Interior room
Front shoulder room, in. 55.0
Front leg room, in. 41.5
Front head room, in. 3.5
Rear shoulder room, in. 53.5
Rear fore-aft room, in. 28.5
Rear head room, in. 2.0
Door top to ground, in. 49.5
Luggage capacity .... 4+1

Engines available
1.8-liter 4 (130 hp)

Transmissions available
5-speed manual
4-speed automatic

Tested model
1996 GLS 4-door, 1.8-liter Four, 4-speed automatic

Tires as tested
Michelin XGT H4, size P195/60R14

Hyundai Tiburon

The Tiburon, new for 1997, has a lot going for it, provided that you're not too tall or portly to fit in the cramped cockpit. Though it's based on the rather pedestrian Hyundai Elantra sedan, it's fun to drive. The Tiburon handles crisply and competently. It also steers as responsively as many true sports cars. The standard 140-hp, 2.0-liter Four accelerates eagerly and attains decent fuel economy. The seats are reasonably well shaped but very firm and mounted low. The rear seat is tiny. You may forgive the Tiburon's stiff, noisy ride, since those are qualities one lives with in most sporty coupes.

Body styles and prices

	Price range	Trim lines
2-door	$13,599 - $14,899	Base, FX

Safety information

Safety belt pretensioners	No
Center rear safety belt	NA
Dual air bags	Standard
Side air bags	Not offered
Antilock brakes	Optional on FX
Traction control	Not offered
Gov't front-crash test, driver/front passenger	NA/NA
Gov't side-crash test, driver/rear passenger	NA/NA
IIHS offset crash test	NA
Injury claim rate compared with all cars/type	NA/NA

Reliability history

TROUBLE SPOTS	90 91 92 93 94 95 96 97
Engine	
Cooling	
Fuel	
Ignition	NOT
Auto. transmission	
Man. transmission	ENOUGH
Clutch	
Electrical	
Air conditioning	DATA
Suspension	
Brakes	TO
Exhaust	
Body rust	RATE
Paint/trim	
Body integrity	
Body hardware	

Test judgments

Performance

Acceleration	◓
Transmission	◓
Routine handling	◉
Emergency handling	◓
Braking	○

Comfort

Ride, normal load	○
Ride, full load	○
Noise	○
Driving position	◓
Front-seat comfort	◓
Rear-seat comfort	●
Climate-control system	◉

Convenience

Access	○
Controls and displays	◓
Trunk	◒

Other

Fuel economy	◓
Predicted reliability	NA
Predicted depreciation	NA

Test data

Acceleration

0-30 mph, sec.	3.2
0-60 mph, sec.	8.8
Quarter mile, sec.	16.8
Quarter mile, mph	84
45-65 mph, sec.	5.7

Fuel economy (regular)

EPA city/highway, mpg	22/29
CU's overall mileage, mpg	27
CU's city/highway, mpg	19/39
CU's 150-mile trip, mpg	31
Fuel refill capacity, gal.	14.5
Cruising range, mi.	420
Annual fuel: gal./cost	550/$660

Braking from 60 mph

Dry pavement, ft.	143
Wet pavement, ft.	167
Pedal effort, 1st stop, lb.	15
Pedal effort, 10th stop, lb.	15

Specifications

Drive wheels

Front

Seating

Passengers,front/rear ... 2/2

Dimensions and weight

Length, in.	171
Width, in.	68
Wheelbase, in.	97
Turning circle, ft.	37
Curb weight, lb.	2705
Percent weight, front/rear	63/37
Max. load, lb.	700

Interior room

Front shoulder room, in.	53.0
Front leg room, in.	41.5
Front head room, in.	1.5
Rear shoulder room, in.	46.0
Rear fore-aft room, in.	25.0
Rear head room, in.	0.0
Door top to ground, in.	46.5
Luggage capacity	3+1

Engines available

2.0-liter 4 (140 hp)

Transmissions available

5-speed manual
4-speed automatic

Tested model

1997 FX 2-door, 2.0-liter Four, 5-speed manual

Tires as tested

Michelin XGT H4, size P195/60R14

Medium car over $25,000

Infiniti I30

The I30 is essentially a Nissan Maxima with extra sound-deadening material and a more plush interior. Side-impact air bags in front and minor styling changes are new for 1998. A silky-smooth V6 is this car's best feature. It accelerates nicely and attains pretty good fuel economy. The interior is roomy, but the ride is unexceptional. And handling is just adequate: The body leans considerably during cornering. Some testers found the driving position tiring. The front seats offer firm support except for the thighs. The rear seat is roomy.

RECOMMENDED

Body styles and prices

	Price range	Trim lines
4-door	$28,900 - $31,500	I30, I30t

Safety information

Safety belt pretensioners	No
Center rear safety belt	Lap
Dual air bags	Standard
Side air bags	Standard
Antilock brakes	Standard
Traction control	Not offered
Gov't front-crash test, driver/front passenger	◒/◒
Gov't side-crash test, driver/rear passenger	◒/○
IIHS offset crash test	Poor
Injury claim rate compared with all cars/type	◒/◒

Reliability history

TROUBLE SPOTS (Infiniti I30)	90	91	92	93	94	95	96	97
Engine							●	●
Cooling							●	●
Fuel							●	●
Ignition							●	●
Auto. transmission							●	●
Man. transmission							*	*
Clutch							*	*
Electrical							◒	●
Air conditioning							●	●
Suspension							●	●
Brakes							●	●
Exhaust							●	●
Body rust							●	●
Paint/trim							●	●
Body integrity							◒	●
Body hardware							◒	●

Test judgments

Performance

Acceleration	◒
Transmission	●
Routine handling	◒
Emergency handling	○
Braking	◒

Comfort

Ride, normal load	◒
Ride, full load	○
Noise	◒
Driving position	◒
Front-seat comfort	◒
Rear-seat comfort	◒
Climate-control system	●

Convenience

Access	◒
Controls and displays	●
Trunk	○

Other

Fuel economy	○
Predicted reliability	●
Predicted depreciation	NA

Test data

Acceleration

0-30 mph, sec.	3.5
0-60 mph, sec.	8.8
Quarter mile, sec.	16.8
Quarter mile, mph	85
45-65 mph, sec.	5.6

Fuel economy (premium)

EPA city/highway, mpg	21/28
CU's overall mileage, mpg	23
CU's city/highway, mpg	16/36
CU's 150-mile trip, mpg	27
Fuel refill capacity, gal.	18.5
Cruising range, mi.	470
Annual fuel: gal./cost	640/$900

Braking from 60 mph

Dry pavement, ft.	138
Wet pavement, ft.	156
Pedal effort, 1st stop, lb.	20
Pedal effort, 10th stop, lb.	25

Specifications

Drive wheels

Front

Seating

Passengers,front/rear	2/3

Dimensions and weight

Length, in.	190
Width, in.	70
Wheelbase, in.	106
Turning circle, ft.	38
Curb weight, lb.	3195
Percent weight, front/rear	63/37
Max. load, lb.	900

Interior room

Front shoulder room, in.	57.0
Front leg room, in.	42.0
Front head room, in.	3.0
Rear shoulder room, in.	56.5
Rear fore-aft room, in.	30.0
Rear head room, in.	2.5
Door top to ground, in.	50.0
Luggage capacity	5+0

Engines available

3.0-liter V6 (190 hp)

Transmissions available

5-speed manual
4-speed automatic

Tested model

1996 4-door, 3.0-liter V6, 4-speed automatic

Tires as tested

Bridgestone Pontenza RE92, size 205/65R15

Minivan

Isuzu Oasis

The Oasis is actually a Honda Odyssey with an Isuzu nameplate; it's based on the pre-1998 Honda Accord. The four-cylinder engine gained a little more power this year. The ride is supple and well controlled. People who dislike sliding doors will appreciate this minivan's four conventional doors. The seats are comfortable. The rearmost bench seat folds flush with the floor, leaving a large cargo space behind the middle seats. Consider this a six- or seven-passenger car with little luggage space or a four- or five-passenger car with ample luggage space. Reliability has been excellent.

Body styles and prices

	Price range	Trim lines
4-door minivan	$23,532 - $25,802	S, LS

Safety information

Safety belt pretensioners .... No
Center rear safety belt .... Lap
Dual air bags .... Standard
Side air bags .... Not offered
Antilock brakes .... Standard
Traction control .... Not offered
Gov't front-crash test, driver/front passenger .... ◓/◓
Gov't side-crash test, driver/rear passenger .... NA/NA
IIHS offset crash test .... Marginal
Injury claim rate compared with all cars/type .... ◓/◓

Reliability history

TROUBLE SPOTS	Isuzu Oasis 90	91	92	93	94	95	96	97
Engine							●	●
Cooling							●	●
Fuel							●	●
Ignition							●	●
Auto. transmission							●	●
Man. transmission								
Clutch								
Electrical							●	●
Air conditioning							●	●
Suspension							●	●
Brakes							●	●
Exhaust							●	●
Body rust							●	●
Paint/trim							●	●
Body integrity							●	●
Body hardware							●	●

Test judgments

Performance
Acceleration .... ○
Transmission .... ◓
Routine handling .... ◓
Emergency handling .... ○
Braking .... ◓

Comfort
Ride, normal load .... ◓
Ride, full load .... ◓
Noise .... ◓
Driving position .... ◓
Front-seat comfort .... ◓
Middle-seat comfort .... ◓
Rear-seat comfort .... ◒
Climate-control system .... ◓

Convenience
Access .... ◓
Controls and displays .... ◓
Cargo area .... ◒

Other
Fuel economy .... ◒
Predicted reliability .... ●
Predicted depreciation .... NA

Test data

Acceleration
0-30 mph, sec. 4.4
0-60 mph, sec. 12.2
Quarter mile, sec. 19.1
Quarter mile, mph 75
45-65 mph, sec. 7.9

Fuel economy (regular)
EPA city/highway, mpg 21/26
CU's overall mileage, mpg 21
CU's city/highway, mpg 14/31
CU's 150-mile trip, mpg 24
Fuel refill capacity, gal. 17.2
Cruising range, mi. 390
Annual fuel: gal./cost .... 730/$880

Braking from 60 mph
Dry pavement, ft. 143
Wet pavement, ft. 158
Pedal effort, 1st stop, lb. 20
Pedal effort, 10th stop, lb. 20

Specifications

Drive wheels
Front

Seating
Passengers,front/mid/rear 2/3/2

Dimensions and weight
Length, in. 187
Width, in. 71
Wheelbase, in. 111
Turning circle, ft. 41
Curb weight, lb. 3480
Percent weight, front/rear 59/41
Max. load, lb. 1150

Interior room
Front shoulder room, in. 57.5
Front leg room, in. 42.0
Front head room, in. 4.0
Middle shoulder room, in. 57.5
Middle fore-aft room, in. 30.5
Middle head room, in. 4.0
Rear shoulder room, in. 49.0
Rear fore-aft room, in. 26.5
Rear head room, in. 2.5
Door top to ground, in. 56.0
Cargo volume, cu.ft. 47.5

Engines available
2.3-liter 4 (150 hp)

Transmissions available
4-speed automatic

Tested model
1995 Honda Odyssey EX 4-door minivan, 2.2-liter Four, 4-speed automatic

Tires as tested
Goodyear Conquest, size P205/65R15

Isuzu Rodeo

The Rodeo and its Honda Passport clone were redesigned for 1998. Extensive enhancements include an improved instrument panel and a much better, stronger V6 engine that delivers good acceleration and reasonable fuel economy. But this remains an old-school, truck-based SUV: Sharp bumps make the suspension slam hard, and even the highway ride is busy and jittery. The steering feels vague and rubbery, and handling is rather sluggish in quick maneuvers. The front seats are well shaped but too low, and leg room is snug. The rear seat is low, too, but there's ample head and knee room and the backs recline. A low cargo floor and flush sill make loading easy, but folding the rear seats to expand it is cumbersome and the rear gate is a nuisance to open and close. The four-wheel-drive system is part-time only.

Body styles and prices

	Price range	Trim lines
4-door wagon 2WD	$17,995 - $26,390	S, LS
4-door wagon 4WD	$23,240 - $27,910	S, LS

Safety information

Safety belt pretensioners	No
Center rear safety belt	Lap
Dual air bags	Standard
Side air bags	Not offered
Antilock brakes	Optional
Traction control	Not offered
Gov't front-crash test, driver/front passenger	○/◓
Gov't side-crash test, driver/rear passenger	NA/NA
IIHS offset crash test	NA
Injury claim rate compared with all cars/type	NA/NA

Reliability history

TROUBLE SPOTS	90	91	92	93	94	95	96	97
Engine								
Cooling								
Fuel								
Ignition								
Auto. transmission								
Man. transmission								
Clutch								
Electrical								
Air conditioning								
Suspension								
Brakes								
Exhaust								
Body rust								
Paint/trim								
Body integrity								
Body hardware								

NO DATA NEW MODEL

Test judgments

Performance

Acceleration	◓
Transmission	◓
Routine handling	○
Emergency handling	◒
Braking	◒

Comfort

Ride, normal load	○
Ride, full load	◒
Noise	◓
Driving position	○
Front-seat comfort	◓
Rear-seat comfort	○
Climate-control system	◓

Convenience

Access	◓
Controls and displays	◓
Cargo area	◓

Other

Fuel economy	◒
Predicted reliability	New
Predicted depreciation	NA

Test data

Acceleration

0-30 mph, sec.	3.2
0-60 mph, sec.	9.1
Quarter mile, sec.	17.0
Quarter mile, mph	82
45-65 mph, sec.	5.9

Fuel economy (regular)

EPA city/highway, mpg	16/20
CU's overall mileage, mpg	18
CU's city/highway, mpg	12/28
CU's 150-mile trip, mpg	21
Fuel refill capacity, gal.	21.1
Cruising range, mi.	410
Annual fuel: gal./cost	830/$995

Braking from 60 mph

Dry pavement, ft.	156
Wet pavement, ft.	191
Pedal effort, 1st stop, lb.	25
Pedal effort, 10th stop, lb.	30

Specifications

Drive wheels

Rear or part-time 4WD

Seating

Passengers,front/rear	2/3

Dimensions and weight

Length, in.	177
Width, in.	70
Wheelbase, in.	106
Turning circle, ft.	41
Curb weight, lb.	3935
Percent weight, front/rear	54/46
Max. load, lb.	915

Interior room

Front shoulder room, in.	56.0
Front leg room, in.	41.0
Front head room, in.	4.0
Rear shoulder room, in.	56.0
Rear fore-aft room, in.	30.0
Rear head room, in.	3.5
Door top to ground, in.	60.0
Cargo volume, cu.ft.	39.5

Engines available

2.2-liter 4 (130 hp)
3.2-liter V6 (205 hp)

Transmissions available

5-speed manual
4-speed automatic

Tested model

1998 S 4-door wagon 4WD, 3.2-liter V6, 4-speed automatic

Tires as tested

Goodyear Wrangler RT/S, size P235/75R15

Sport-utility vehicle

Jeep Cherokee

Last year the Cherokee received an exterior face-lift, a passenger-side air bag, and improved controls, but it's still very trucklike. The Cherokee is a good off-roader, but it pitches and rocks even on good roads; cornering isn't crisp. The 4.0-liter Six is much more powerful than the standard 2.5-liter Four. Selectable full-time four-wheel drive is optional. Finding a comfortable driving position is a challenge. The rear seats are cramped and uncomfortable and access is difficult. Cargo space is so-so for a vehicle this large.

Body styles and prices

	Price range	Trim lines
2-door wagon 2WD	$15,540 - $18,175	SE, Sport
2-door wagon 4WD	$17,055 - $19,685	SE, Sport
4-door wagon 2WD	$16,580 - $22,570	SE, Sport, Classic, Limited
4-door wagon 4WD	$18,090 - $24,480	SE, Sport, Classic, Limited

Safety information

Safety belt pretensioners .... No
Center rear safety belt .... Lap
Dual air bags .... Standard
Side air bags .... Not offered
Antilock brakes .... Optional with 6 cyl.
Traction control .... Not offered
Gov't front-crash test, driver/front passenger .... ○/○
Gov't side-crash test, driver/rear passenger .... NA/NA
IIHS offset crash test .... NA
Injury claim rate compared with all cars/type .... ◓/○

Reliability history

TROUBLE SPOTS	90	91	92	93	94	95	96	97
Jeep Cherokee, Wagoneer								
Engine	◒	○	○	◓	◓	◓	◉	Insufficient data
Cooling	●	◒	○	○	◓	◓	◉	
Fuel	◒	○	◓	◓	◉	◉	◓	
Ignition	◒	○	◓	◓	◓	◓	◓	
Auto. transmission	○	○	◓	◓	◓	◓	◓	
Man. transmission	*	*	*	*	*	*	*	
Clutch	*	*	*	*	*	*	*	
Electrical	●	◒	○	◒	◒	○	○	
Air conditioning	◒	○	◓	◓	◓	◓	◓	
Suspension	○	○	○	◓	◓	◓	◉	
Brakes	●	●	●	◒	○	○	○	
Exhaust	●	●	●	◉	◉	◉	◉	
Body rust	○	◓	◓	◉	◉	◉	◉	
Paint/trim	●	◒	○	○	○	○	○	
Body integrity	●	◒	●	◒	◒	◒	◒	
Body hardware	●	◒	○	○	◒	○	◒	

Test judgments

Performance
Acceleration .... ◓
Transmission .... ◓
Routine handling .... ○
Emergency handling .... ○
Braking .... ○

Comfort
Ride, normal load .... ◒
Ride, full load .... ◒
Noise .... ○
Driving position .... ○
Front-seat comfort .... ○
Rear-seat comfort .... ◒
Climate-control system .... ◉

Convenience
Access .... ◒
Controls and displays .... ◓
Cargo area .... ○

Other
Fuel economy .... ●
Predicted reliability .... ○
Predicted depreciation .... ○

Test data

Acceleration
0-30 mph, sec. 3.4
0-60 mph, sec. 9.3
Quarter mile, sec. 17.1
Quarter mile, mph 83
45-65 mph, sec. 5.9

Fuel economy (regular)
EPA city/highway, mpg 15/21
CU's overall mileage, mpg 16
CU's city/highway, mpg 10/25
CU's 150-mile trip, mpg 20
Fuel refill capacity, gal. 20.0
Cruising range, mi. 360
Annual fuel: gal./cost .... 945/$1135

Braking from 60 mph
Dry pavement, ft. 143
Wet pavement, ft. 160
Pedal effort, 1st stop, lb. 25
Pedal effort, 10th stop, lb. 25

Specifications

Drive wheels
Rear, part-time, or selectable 4WD

Seating
Passengers, front/rear 2/3

Dimensions and weight
Length, in. 168
Width, in. 68
Wheelbase, in. 101
Turning circle, ft. 38
Curb weight, lb. 3540
Percent weight, front/rear 56/44
Max. load, lb. 1360

Interior room
Front shoulder room, in. 54.5
Front leg room, in. 40.5
Front head room, in. 3.5
Rear shoulder room, in. 54.5
Rear fore-aft room, in. 26.0
Rear head room, in. 4.0
Door top to ground, in. 58.5
Cargo volume, cu.ft. 36.5

Engines available
2.5-liter 4 (125 hp)
4.0-liter 6 (190 hp)

Transmissions available
5-speed manual
3 or 4-speed automatic

Tested model
1997 Sport 4-door wagon 4WD, 4.0-liter Six, 4-speed automatic

Tires as tested
Goodyear Wrangler RT/S, size P225/75R15

Sport-utility vehicle

Jeep Grand Cherokee

The Grand Cherokee's ride is as good as any SUV's, but the steering is vague. The 4.0-liter Six accelerates adequately. The 5.2-liter V8 is more responsive. Fuel economy, 15 mpg overall with either engine, isn't great. A 245-hp 5.9-liter V8 has been added for 1998. The front seats are soft but unsupportive. The rear seat is cramped, and the cargo capacity is modest. The sophisticated Quadra-Trac full-time all-wheel-drive system is desirable. This model will be replaced for 1999.

Body styles and prices

	Price range	Trim lines
4-door wagon 2WD	$25,945 - $31,460	Laredo, Limited
4-door wagon 4WD	$27,915 - $38,275	Laredo, Limited

Safety information

Safety belt pretensioners	No
Center rear safety belt	Lap
Dual air bags	Standard
Side air bags	Not offered
Antilock brakes	Standard
Traction control	Not offered
Gov't front-crash test, driver/front passenger	○/○
Gov't side-crash test, driver/rear passenger	NA/NA
IIHS offset crash test	Marginal
Injury claim rate compared with all cars/type	◓/◓

Reliability history

TROUBLE SPOTS	90	91	92	93	94	95	96	97
Engine				○	◓	◓	◉	◉
Cooling				○	◓	◓	◉	◉
Fuel				◓	◓	◉	◓	◉
Ignition				○	○	◓	◓	◉
Auto. transmission				○	○	○	○	◉
Man. transmission				*	*	*		
Clutch				*	*	*		
Electrical				◒	◒	○	◒	○
Air conditioning				●	◒	◒	◓	◉
Suspension				○	◓	◓	◓	◉
Brakes				●	◒	○	◓	◉
Exhaust				◓	◉	◉	◉	◉
Body rust				◓	◓	◉	◉	◉
Paint/trim				○	◓	◉	◓	◉
Body integrity				◒	○	○	○	◓
Body hardware				◒	○	○	○	◓

Test judgments

Performance

Acceleration	○
Transmission	◓
Routine handling	○
Emergency handling	○
Braking	○

Comfort

Ride, normal load	◓
Ride, full load	○
Noise	◓
Driving position	◓
Front-seat comfort	◓
Rear-seat comfort	○
Climate-control system	◉

Convenience

Access	◓
Controls and displays	◉
Cargo area	○

Other

Fuel economy	●
Predicted reliability	○
Predicted depreciation	○

Test data

Acceleration

0-30 mph, sec.	3.9
0-60 mph, sec.	10.4
Quarter mile, sec.	17.9
Quarter mile, mph	79
45-65 mph, sec.	6.4

Fuel economy (regular)

EPA city/highway, mpg	15/20
CU's overall mileage, mpg	15
CU's city/highway, mpg	10/25
CU's 150-mile trip, mpg	19
Fuel refill capacity, gal.	23.0
Cruising range, mi.	415
Annual fuel: gal./cost	980/$1175

Braking from 60 mph

Dry pavement, ft.	137
Wet pavement, ft.	181
Pedal effort, 1st stop, lb.	20
Pedal effort, 10th stop, lb.	25

Specifications

Drive wheels

Rear, selectable, or permanent 4WD

Seating

Passengers, front/rear	2/3

Dimensions and weight

Length, in.	177
Width, in.	69
Wheelbase, in.	106
Turning circle, ft.	41
Curb weight, lb.	3885
Percent weight, front/rear	56/44
Max. load, lb.	1150

Interior room

Front shoulder room, in.	58.0
Front leg room, in.	42.0
Front head room, in.	4.5
Rear shoulder room, in.	57.0
Rear fore-aft room, in.	28.0
Rear head room, in.	4.0
Door top to ground, in.	60.0
Cargo volume, cu.ft.	34.0

Engines available

4.0-liter 6 (185 hp)
5.2-liter V8 (220 hp)
5.9-liter V8 (245 hp)

Transmissions available

4-speed automatic

Tested model

1997 Laredo 4-door wagon 4WD, 4.0-liter Six, 4-speed automatic

Tires as tested

Goodyear Wrangler AP, size P225/75R15

Sport-utility vehicle

Jeep Wrangler

The Wrangler is the smallest and crudest Jeep. It was redesigned for 1997, with no important changes made for 1998. Consider the Wrangler for off-road use rather than highway travel. The ride is dreadful: noisy and uncomfortable, with a snappy, rubbery impact from nearly any pavement irregularity. The steering is vague and imprecise. The optional 4.0-liter Six is responsive, but the three-speed optional automatic transmission blunts its performance. The driving position is unpleasant, with the steering wheel too close to the driver's chest.

Body styles and prices

	Price range	Trim lines
2-door 4WD	$14,845 - $20,540	SE, Sport, Sahara
Convertible 4WD	$14,090 - $19,615	SE, Sport, Sahara

Safety information

Safety belt pretensioners	No
Center rear safety belt	NA
Dual air bags	Standard
Side air bags	Not offered
Antilock brakes	Optional with 6 cyl.
Traction control	Not offered
Gov't front-crash test, driver/front passenger	◉/◉
Gov't side-crash test, driver/rear passenger	NA/NA
IIHS offset crash test	NA
Injury claim rate compared with all cars/type	NA/NA

Reliability history

TROUBLE SPOTS	90	91	92	93	94	95	96	97
Engine								◉
Cooling								◉
Fuel								◉
Ignition								◉
Auto. transmission								*
Man. transmission								◓
Clutch								◉
Electrical								◓
Air conditioning								◉
Suspension								◉
Brakes								◉
Exhaust								◉
Body rust								◉
Paint/trim								◉
Body integrity								◓
Body hardware								◓

(Jeep Wrangler)

Test judgments

Performance

Acceleration	○
Transmission	○
Routine handling	◒
Emergency handling	◒
Braking	○

Comfort

Ride, normal load	◒
Ride, full load	◒
Noise	◒
Driving position	○
Front-seat comfort	○
Rear-seat comfort	◒
Climate-control system	◓

Convenience

Access	●
Controls and displays	○
Cargo area	●

Other

Fuel economy	●
Predicted reliability	○
Predicted depreciation	◓

Test data

Acceleration

0-30 mph, sec.	3.6
0-60 mph, sec.	9.9
Quarter mile, sec.	17.6
Quarter mile, mph	79
45-65 mph, sec.	6.2

Fuel economy (regular)

EPA city/highway, mpg	15/18
CU's overall mileage, mpg	15
CU's city/highway, mpg	10/19
CU's 150-mile trip, mpg	18
Fuel refill capacity, gal.	19.0
Cruising range, mi.	320
Annual fuel: gal./cost	1005/$1205

Braking from 60 mph

Dry pavement, ft.	137
Wet pavement, ft.	152
Pedal effort, 1st stop, lb.	20
Pedal effort, 10th stop, lb.	30

Specifications

Drive wheels

Part-time 4WD

Seating

Passengers, front/rear ... 2/2

Dimensions and weight

Length, in.	152
Width, in.	67
Wheelbase, in.	93
Turning circle, ft.	36
Curb weight, lb.	3510
Percent weight, front/rear	50/50
Max. load, lb.	820

Interior room

Front shoulder room, in.	51.5
Front leg room, in.	41.0
Front head room, in.	6.5
Rear shoulder room, in.	57.0
Rear fore-aft room, in.	25.0
Rear head room, in.	4.5
Door top to ground, in.	64.5
Cargo volume, cu.ft.	17.0

Engines available

2.5-liter 4 (120 hp)
4.0-liter 6 (181 hp)

Transmissions available

5-speed manual
3-speed automatic

Tested model

1997 Sahara 2-door 4WD, 4.0-liter Six, 3-speed automatic

Tires as tested

Goodyear Wrangler GS-A, size P225/75R15

Sport-utility vehicle

Land Rover Discovery

The Discovery is a good off-roader, perhaps, but not a great vehicle for everyday driving. The standard 4.0-liter V8 delivers not only slow acceleration but miserable fuel economy. The automatic transmission is slow to downshift, the steering feels vague, and the body leans a lot in turns. The ride is relatively good. Permanent four-wheel drive is standard. The cargo bay is high though short. For those who aren't planning to go off-road, there are several better choices available. A redesign is due for 1999.

Body styles and prices

	Price range	Trim lines
4-door wagon AWD	$34,500 - $38,000	LE, LSE

Safety information

Safety belt pretensioners	No
Center rear safety belt	Lap
Dual air bags	Standard
Side air bags	Not offered
Antilock brakes	Standard
Traction control	Not offered
Gov't front-crash test, driver/front passenger	NA/NA
Gov't side-crash test, driver/rear passenger	NA/NA
IIHS offset crash test	Acceptable
Injury claim rate compared with all cars/type	◒/◒

Reliability history

TROUBLE SPOTS	90 91 92 93 94 95 96 97
Engine	
Cooling	
Fuel	
Ignition	NOT
Auto. transmission	
Man. transmission	ENOUGH
Clutch	
Electrical	
Air conditioning	DATA
Suspension	
Brakes	TO
Exhaust	
Body rust	RATE
Paint/trim	
Body integrity	
Body hardware	

Test judgments

Performance

Acceleration	○
Transmission	○
Routine handling	◓
Emergency handling	◓
Braking	○

Comfort

Ride, normal load	○
Ride, full load	○
Noise	○
Driving position	○
Front-seat comfort	○
Rear-seat comfort	◒
Climate-control system	○

Convenience

Access	○
Controls and displays	○
Cargo area	◉

Other

Fuel economy	●
Predicted reliability	NA
Predicted depreciation	○

Test data

Acceleration

0-30 mph, sec.	4.2
0-60 mph, sec.	12.2
Quarter mile, sec.	18.9
Quarter mile, mph	74
45-65 mph, sec.	7.3

Fuel economy (premium)

EPA city/highway, mpg	14/17
CU's overall mileage, mpg	13
CU's city/highway, mpg	9/19
CU's 150-mile trip, mpg	16
Fuel refill capacity, gal.	23.4
Cruicing range, mi	335
Annual fuel: gal./cost	1120/$1570

Braking from 60 mph

Dry pavement, ft.	143
Wet pavement, ft.	202
Pedal effort, 1st stop, lb.	20
Pedal effort, 10th stop, lb.	30

Specifications

Drive wheels

Permanent 4WD

Seating

Passengers, front/mid/rear	2/3/2

Dimensions and weight

Length, in.	179
Width, in.	71
Wheelbase, in.	100
Turning circle, ft.	42
Curb weight, lb.	4535
Percent weight, front/rear	48/52
Max. load, lb.	1483

Interior room

Front shoulder room, in.	58.0
Front leg room, in.	39.5
Front head room, in.	5.5
Rear shoulder room, in.	58.0
Rear fore-aft room, in.	26.5
Rear head room, in.	7.0
Door top to ground, in.	65.0
Cargo volume, cu.ft.	42.0

Engines available

4.0-liter V8 (182 hp)

Transmissions available

5-speed manual
4-speed automatic

Tested model

1995 4-door wagon AWD, 3.9-liter V8, 4-speed automatic

Tires as tested

Michelin XPC 4x4, size P235/70R16

Medium car over $25,000

Lexus ES300

The ES300 and its cheaper, less lavish cousin, the Toyota Camry, were redesigned for the 1997 model year. Except for side air bags, little else is new for 1998. The Lexus rides smoothly and is exceptionally quiet inside. The 3.0-liter V6 accelerates briskly, and the car handles surely and predictably. As with previous Lexus models, the steering is too light to communicate much road feel, detracting from the driving experience. The four-speed automatic transmission shifts flawlessly. The front seats are amply supportive. The rear is fine for two adults, but three feel crowded. Fit and finish are all first-rate.

Body styles and prices

	Price range	Trim lines
4-door	$30,790	—

Safety information

Safety belt pretensioners	Front
Center rear safety belt	3-point
Dual air bags	Standard
Side air bags	Standard
Antilock brakes	Standard
Traction control	Optional
Gov't front-crash test, driver/front passenger	◓/◓
Gov't side-crash test, driver/rear passenger	NA/NA
IIHS offset crash test	NA
Injury claim rate compared with all cars/type	NA/NA

Reliability history

TROUBLE SPOTS	Lexus ES300 90	91	92	93	94	95	96	97
Engine								●
Cooling								●
Fuel								●
Ignition								●
Auto. transmission								●
Man. transmission								
Clutch								
Electrical								●
Air conditioning								●
Suspension								●
Brakes								●
Exhaust								●
Body rust								●
Paint/trim								●
Body integrity								◓
Body hardware								●

Test judgments

Performance

Acceleration	◓
Transmission	●
Routine handling	◓
Emergency handling	○
Braking	◓

Comfort

Ride, normal load	◓
Ride, full load	◓
Noise	●
Driving position	◓
Front-seat comfort	●
Rear-seat comfort	◓
Climate-control system	●

Convenience

Access	◓
Controls and displays	●
Trunk	◓

Other

Fuel economy	○
Predicted reliability	◓
Predicted depreciation	NA

Test data

Acceleration

0-30 mph, sec.	3.2
0-60 mph, sec.	8.4
Quarter mile, sec.	16.6
Quarter mile, mph	86
45-65 mph, sec.	5.0

Fuel economy (premium)

EPA city/highway, mpg	19/26
CU's overall mileage, mpg	22
CU's city/highway, mpg	14/35
CU's 150-mile trip, mpg	27
Fuel refill capacity, gal.	18.5
Cruising range, mi.	475
Annual fuel: gal./cost	675/$945

Braking from 60 mph

Dry pavement, ft.	130
Wet pavement, ft.	154
Pedal effort, 1st stop, lb.	20
Pedal effort, 10th stop, lb.	25

Specifications

Drive wheels

Front

Seating

Passengers, front/rear	2/3

Dimensions and weight

Length, in.	190
Width, in.	71
Wheelbase, in.	105
Turning circle, ft.	40
Curb weight, lb.	3390
Percent weight, front/rear	62/38
Max. load, lb.	900

Interior room

Front shoulder room, in.	55.0
Front leg room, in.	41.0
Front head room, in.	2.0
Rear shoulder room, in.	53.5
Rear fore-aft room, in.	27.5
Rear head room, in.	1.5
Door top to ground, in.	50.0
Luggage capacity	5+0

Engines available

3.0-liter V6 (200 hp)

Transmissions available

4-speed automatic

Tested model

1997 4-door, 3.0-liter V6, 4-speed automatic

Tires as tested

Michelin MXV4, size P205/65R15

Luxury car

Lincoln Continental

The Continental received a face-lift for 1998. It aspires to compete with the finest luxury models, but it falls short of world standards. The Continental's biggest asset is its muscular V8, which accelerates with gusto. Fuel economy, however, is unimpressive. The ride, noise isolation, and general feel should be much better for what this luxury car costs. Antilock brakes and traction control are standard. The rear seat is roomy and comfortable. The Continental accommodates five with ease, and the trunk is huge. Depreciation is among the worst of any new model.

Body styles and prices

	Price range	Trim lines
4-door	$37,830	—

Safety information

Safety belt pretensioners	No
Center rear safety belt	3-point
Dual air bags	Standard
Side air bags	Not offered
Antilock brakes	Standard
Traction control	Standard
Gov't front-crash test, driver/front passenger	NA/NA
Gov't side-crash test, driver/rear passenger	NA/NA
IIHS offset crash test	Acceptable
Injury claim rate compared with all cars/type	⦿/◓

Reliability history

TROUBLE SPOTS	Lincoln Continental 90	91	92	93	94	95	96	97
Engine	●	●	●	○	○	⦿	⦿	⦿
Cooling	◒	○	○	○	◓	⦿	⦿	◓
Fuel	○	○	◓	◓	◓	○	◓	◓
Ignition	●	◒	○	○	◓	○	◓	⦿
Auto. transmission	◒	●	○	○	◓	◓	○	⦿
Man. transmission								
Clutch								
Electrical	●	●	●	●	◒	●	◒	○
Air conditioning	●	●	●	●	◒	◓	⦿	⦿
Suspension	●	●	●	◒	○	◒	○	○
Brakes	●	●	●	●	○	○	◓	⦿
Exhaust	◓	◓	◓	⦿	⦿	⦿	⦿	⦿
Body rust	◓	⦿	⦿	⦿	⦿	⦿	⦿	⦿
Paint/trim	◒	◒	◓	◓	◓	◓	⦿	⦿
Body integrity	○	◒	○	◒	○	◒	○	◓
Body hardware	●	●	●	◒	●	◒	○	◓

Test judgments

Performance

Acceleration	◓
Transmission	◓
Routine handling	◓
Emergency handling	○
Braking	◓

Comfort

Ride, normal load	◓
Ride, full load	◓
Noise	◓
Driving position	◓
Front-seat comfort	◓
Rear-seat comfort	◓
Climate-control system	⦿

Convenience

Access	◓
Controls and displays	◓
Trunk	◓

Other

Fuel economy	◒
Predicted reliability	○
Predicted depreciation	●

Test data

Acceleration

0-30 mph, sec.	3.1
0-60 mph, sec.	8.1
Quarter mile, sec.	16.2
Quarter mile, mph	89
45-65 mph, sec.	5.2

Fuel economy (premium)

EPA city/highway, mpg	17/25
CU's overall mileage, mpg	18
CU's city/highway, mpg	12/31
CU's 150-mile trip, mpg	21
Fuel refill capacity, gal.	20.0
Cruising range, mi.	340
Annual fuel: gal./cost	835/$1170

Braking from 60 mph

Dry pavement, ft.	137
Wet pavement, ft.	156
Pedal effort, 1st stop, lb.	20
Pedal effort, 10th stop, lb.	30

Specifications

Drive wheels

Front

Seating

Passengers, front/rear	3/3

Dimensions and weight

Length, in.	207
Width, in.	74
Wheelbase, in.	109
Turning circle, ft.	44
Curb weight, lb.	3930
Percent weight, front/rear	63/37
Max. load, lb.	950

Interior room

Front shoulder room, in.	57.0
Front leg room, in.	43.0
Front head room, in.	3.0
Rear shoulder room, in.	56.5
Rear fore-aft room, in.	30.5
Rear head room, in.	3.0
Door top to ground, in.	51.0
Luggage capacity	6+0

Engines available

4.6-liter V8 (260 hp)

Transmissions available

4-speed automatic

Tested model

1996 4-door, 4.6-liter V8, 4-speed automatic

Tires as tested

Michelin MXV4, size P225/60R16

Large car over $30,000

Lincoln Town Car

The Town Car is the last of the domestic, rear-wheel-drive luxury cruisers. This favorite of the car-service and limousine business was dramatically restyled for 1998, but under the skin it has a familiar 4.6-liter V8 engine and an old-tech suspension. Nevertheless, the ride is about as smooth and comfortable as any you'll find. The Town Car also handles quite well for such a large car. Traction control is standard, but side air bags are not. The engine provides adequate acceleration but it's not as refined as that in the Town Car's major competitor, the Cadillac DeVille. The front seats are soft enough but not well shaped for optimal support. The front bench notionally seats three, but the center position is all but uninhabitable. The rear seats three adults with ease. The trunk is very large but oddly shaped.

Body styles and prices

	Price range	Trim lines
4-door	$37,830 - $41,830	Executive, Signature, Cartier

Safety information

Safety belt pretensioners .... No
Center rear safety belt 3-point
Dual air bags .... Standard
Side air bags .... Not offered
Antilock brakes .... Standard
Traction control .... Standard
Gov't front-crash test, driver/front passenger .... NA/NA
Gov't side-crash test, driver/rear passenger .... NA/NA
IIHS offset crash test .... NA
Injury claim rate compared with all cars/type .... NA/NA

Reliability history

TROUBLE SPOTS	90	91	92	93	94	95	96	97
Engine								
Cooling								
Fuel								
Ignition								
Auto. transmission								
Man. transmission								
Clutch								
Electrical								
Air conditioning								
Suspension								
Brakes								
Exhaust								
Body rust								
Paint/trim								
Body integrity								
Body hardware								

NO DATA NEW MODEL

Test judgments

Performance
Acceleration .... ◓
Transmission .... ◓
Routine handling .... ◓
Emergency handling .... ○
Braking .... ◓

Comfort
Ride, normal load .... ◓
Ride, full load .... ◓
Noise .... ●
Driving position .... ◓
Front-seat comfort .... ◓
Rear-seat comfort .... ◓
Climate-control system .... ●

Convenience
Access .... ◓
Controls and displays .... ◓
Trunk .... ◓

Other
Fuel economy .... ◒
Predicted reliability .... ○
Predicted depreciation .... NA

Test data

Acceleration
0-30 mph, sec. 3.3
0-60 mph, sec. 9.3
Quarter mile, sec. 17.2
Quarter mile, mph 81
45-65 mph, sec. 6.2

Fuel economy (premium)
EPA city/highway, mpg 17/24
CU's overall mileage, mpg 19
CU's city/highway, mpg 12/29
CU's 150-mile trip, mpg 23
Fuel refill capacity, gal. 19.0
Cruising range, mi. 405
Annual fuel: gal./cost .... 800/$1120

Braking from 60 mph
Dry pavement, ft. 135
Wet pavement, ft. 148
Pedal effort, 1st stop, lb. 20
Pedal effort, 10th stop, lb. 25

Specifications

Drive wheels
Rear

Seating
Passengers, front/rear 3/3

Dimensions and weight
Length, in. 215
Width, in. 78
Wheelbase, in. 118
Turning circle, ft. 45
Curb weight, lb. 4050
Percent weight, front/rear 56/44
Max. load, lb. 1100

Interior room
Front shoulder room, in. 61.0
Front leg room, in. 42.5
Front head room, in. 5.0
Rear shoulder room, in. 60.0
Rear fore-aft room, in. 32.0
Rear head room, in. 3.5
Door top to ground, in. 51.5
Luggage capacity .... 6+2

Engines available
4.6-liter V8 (200 or 220 hp)

Transmissions available
4-speed automatic

Tested model
1998 Executive 4-door, 4.6-liter V8, 4-speed automatic

Tires as tested
Michelin Symmetry, size P225/60R16

Medium car under $25,000

Mazda 626

The 626 was redesigned for 1998, but it wasn't improved. We liked the old car better. Ride and handling are both mediocre. The driving position is too low. The rear seats are too low and unsupportive. A low roof makes access difficult. The displays are legible, and most controls are easy to reach. The trunk is roomy, and the rear seatback folds down to expand it, but the pass-through port is only a foot high. The versions with a V6 are a far better choice than the four-cylinder models, which are slow and noisy.

Body styles and prices

	Price range	Trim lines
4-door	$15,550 - $23,240	DX, LX, ES

Safety information

Safety belt pretensioners	No
Center rear safety belt	3-point
Dual air bags	Standard
Side air bags	Not offered
Antilock brakes	Optional (standard with V6)
Traction control	Standard with V6
Gov't front-crash test, driver/front passenger	NA/NA
Gov't side-crash test, driver/rear passenger	○/○
IIHS offset crash test	NA
Injury claim rate compared with all cars/type	NA/NA

Reliability history

TROUBLE SPOTS	90 91 92 93 94 95 96 97
Engine	
Cooling	
Fuel	
Ignition	
Auto. transmission	NO
Man. transmission	
Clutch	DATA
Electrical	
Air conditioning	NEW
Suspension	
Brakes	MODEL
Exhaust	
Body rust	
Paint/trim	
Body integrity	
Body hardware	

Test judgments

Performance

Acceleration	○
Transmission	◓
Routine handling	◓
Emergency handling	○
Braking	◓

Comfort

Ride, normal load	◓
Ride, full load	○
Noise	◓
Driving position	○
Front-seat comfort	○
Rear-seat comfort	○
Climate-control system	◓

Convenience

Access	◓
Controls and displays	◓
Trunk	◓

Other

Fuel economy	○
Predicted reliability	New
Predicted depreciation	NA

Test data

Acceleration

0-30 mph, sec.	4.2
0-60 mph, sec.	12.5
Quarter mile, sec.	19.1
Quarter mile, mph	73
45-65 mph, sec.	8.2

Fuel economy (regular)

EPA city/highway, mpg	22/29
CU's overall mileage, mpg	24
CU's city/highway, mpg	16/36
CU's 150-mile trip, mpg	27
Fuel refill capacity, gal.	16.9
Cruising range, mi.	435
Annual fuel: gal./cost	640/$765

Braking from 60 mph

Dry pavement, ft.	137
Wet pavement, ft.	165
Pedal effort, 1st stop, lb.	20
Pedal effort, 10th stop, lb.	30

Specifications

Drive wheels

Front

Seating

Passengers,front/rear	2/3

Dimensions and weight

Length, in.	187
Width, in.	69
Wheelbase, in.	105
Turning circle, ft.	39
Curb weight, lb.	2910
Percent weight, front/rear	62/38
Max. load, lb.	850

Interior room

Front shoulder room, in.	56.0
Front leg room, in.	41.5
Front head room, in.	3.5
Rear shoulder room, in.	56.0
Rear fore-aft room, in.	30.5
Rear head room, in.	2.5
Door top to ground, in.	49.5
Luggage capacity	5+1

Engines available

2.0-liter 4 (125 hp)
2.5-liter V6 (170 hp)

Transmissions available

5-speed manual
4-speed automatic

Tested model

1998 LX 4 4-door, 2.0-liter Four, 4-speed automatic

Tires as tested

Bridgestone Potenza RE92, size P205/60R15

Minivan

Mazda MPV

By offering all-wheel drive, Mazda has tried to blur the line between sport-utility vehicle and minivan with this model. But under the skin it's an out-of-date minivan. The ride is stiff and jiggly even on good roads. The steering is slow, vague, and heavy. The body leans a lot in turns. Interior space is limited. The all-wheel-drive option improves handling somewhat, but the MPV doesn't make the grade as an SUV or a minivan. Newer minivan designs seriously outclass the MPV.

Body styles and prices

	Price range	Trim lines
Minivan 2WD	$23,095 - $26,395	LX, ES
Minivan AWD	$26,895 - $28,895	LX, ES

Safety information

Safety belt pretensioners	No
Center rear safety belt	Lap
Dual air bags	Standard
Side air bags	Not offered
Antilock brakes	Standard
Traction control	Not offered
Gov't front-crash test, driver/front passenger	◓/◓
Gov't side-crash test, driver/rear passenger	NA/NA
IIHS offset crash test	Marginal
Injury claim rate compared with all cars/type	NA/NA

Reliability history

TROUBLE SPOTS	Mazda MPV V6 (2WD) 90	91	92	93	94	95	96	97
Engine	●	●	◒	●	Insufficient data	Insufficient data	Insufficient data	Insufficient data
Cooling	◒	◒	◒	◓				
Fuel	◓	◓	○	◓				
Ignition	○	○	○	◓				
Auto. transmission	◒	○	○	◓				
Man. transmission	*							
Clutch	*							
Electrical	○	◒	○	○				
Air conditioning	●	○	○	◓				
Suspension	○	○	○	◓				
Brakes	●	●	●	◓				
Exhaust	◒	◒	◓	◉				
Body rust	◉	◓	◉	◉				
Paint/trim	○	○	○	◉				
Body integrity	◓	◓	◓	◓				
Body hardware	◒	◒	○	○				

Test judgments

Performance

Acceleration	○
Transmission	◓
Routine handling	◒
Emergency handling	◒
Braking	○

Comfort

Ride, normal load	◒
Ride, full load	◒
Noise	◓
Driving position	○
Front-seat comfort	◓
Middle-seat comfort	○
Rear-seat comfort	◒
Climate-control system	◉

Convenience

Access	○
Controls and displays	◓
Cargo area	●

Other

Fuel economy	●
Predicted reliability	NA
Predicted depreciation	◒

Test data

Acceleration

0-30 mph, sec.	4.1
0-60 mph, sec.	12.2
Quarter mile, sec.	19.0
Quarter mile, mph	73
45-65 mph, sec.	8.0

Fuel economy (regular)

EPA city/highway, mpg	15/19
CU's overall mileage, mpg	16
CU's city/highway, mpg	10/24
CU's 150-mile trip, mpg	20
Fuel refill capacity, gal.	19.8
Cruising range, mi.	360
Annual fuel: gal./cost	940/$1125

Braking from 60 mph

Dry pavement, ft.	144
Wet pavement, ft.	160
Pedal effort, 1st stop, lb.	20
Pedal effort, 10th stop, lb.	20

Specifications

Drive wheels

Rear or all

Seating

Passengers,front/mid/rear......2/3/3

Dimensions and weight

Length, in.	184
Width, in.	72
Wheelbase, in.	110
Turning circle, ft.	42
Curb weight, lb.	4135
Percent weight, front/rear	57/43
Max. load, lb.	1265

Interior room

Front shoulder room, in.	58.0
Front leg room, in.	41.0
Front head room, in.	5.0
Middle shoulder room, in.	57.5
Middle fore-aft room, in.	27.5
Middle head room, in.	5.5
Rear shoulder room, in.	55.0
Rear fore-aft room, in.	25.0
Rear head room, in.	3.0
Door top to ground, in.	64.0
Cargo volume, cu.ft.	37.0

Engines available

3.0-liter V6 (155 hp)

Transmissions available

4-speed automatic

Tested model

1996 LX AWD Minivan AWD, 3.0-liter V6, 4-speed automatic

Tires as tested

BF Goodrich Touring T/A, size P215/70R15

Medium car over $25,000

Mazda Millenia

RECOMMENDED

The Millenia carries over virtually unchanged for 1998. Sensible design and a high level of refinement make this a comfortable car. It compares favorably with such competitors as the Acura TL, Infiniti I30, and Lexus ES300. The S version's supercharged 2.3-liter V6 puts out 210 hp—impressive for so small an engine. The car handles well, though it leans a bit in turns. The suspension soaks up ripples and ruts with quiet aplomb. The front seats are very comfortable. The rear seat can hold two adults comfortably or three adults less comfortably. The trunk is roomy.

Body styles and prices

	Price range	Trim lines
4-door	$28,995 - $36,595	Base, S

Safety information

Safety belt pretensioners .... No
Center rear safety belt .... Lap
Dual air bags .... Standard
Side air bags .... Not offered
Antilock brakes .... Standard
Traction control .... Optional (standard on S)
Gov't front-crash test, driver/front passenger .... /
Gov't side-crash test, driver/rear passenger .... NA/NA
IIHS offset crash test .... Acceptable
Injury claim rate compared with all cars/type .... /

Reliability history

TROUBLE SPOTS	Mazda Millenia 90	91	92	93	94	95	96	97
Engine								Insufficient data
Cooling								
Fuel								
Ignition								
Auto. transmission								
Man. transmission								
Clutch								
Electrical								
Air conditioning								
Suspension								
Brakes								
Exhaust								
Body rust								
Paint/trim								
Body integrity								
Body hardware								

Test judgments

Performance
Acceleration
Transmission
Routine handling
Emergency handling
Braking

Comfort
Ride, normal load
Ride, full load
Noise
Driving position
Front-seat comfort
Rear-seat comfort
Climate-control system

Convenience
Access
Controls and displays
Trunk

Other
Fuel economy
Predicted reliability
Predicted depreciation

Test data

Acceleration
0-30 mph, sec. 3.5
0-60 mph, sec. 8.7
Quarter mile, sec. 16.8
Quarter mile, mph 87
45-65 mph, sec. 5.1

Fuel economy (premium)
EPA city/highway, mpg 20/28
CU's overall mileage, mpg 22
CU's city/highway, mpg 14/35
CU's 150-mile trip, mpg 26
Fuel refill capacity, gal. 18.0
Cruising range, mi. 435
Annual fuel: gal./cost .... 690/$965

Braking from 60 mph
Dry pavement, ft. 136
Wet pavement, ft. 157
Pedal effort, 1st stop, lb. 15
Pedal effort, 10th stop, lb. 20

Specifications

Drive wheels
Front

Seating
Passengers, front/rear 2/3

Dimensions and weight
Length, in. 190
Width, in. 70
Wheelbase, in. 108
Turning circle, ft. 42
Curb weight, lb. 3415
Percent weight, front/rear 63/37
Max. load, lb. 850

Interior room
Front shoulder room, in. 55.0
Front leg room, in. 41.5
Front head room, in. 2.5
Rear shoulder room, in. 54.0
Rear fore-aft room, in. 29.0
Rear head room, in. 2.5
Door top to ground, in. 48.5
Luggage capacity .... 5+0

Engines available
2.3-liter V6 supercharged (210 hp)
2.5-liter V6 (170 hp)

Transmissions available
4-speed automatic

Tested model
1995 S 4-door, 2.3-liter supercharged V6, 4-speed automatic

Tires as tested
Michelin XGT V4, size P215/55R16

Small car

Mazda Protegé

Mazda's small sedan is, in its high-trim ES version, one of the best and roomiest small cars on the market. It handles well and rides satisfactorily. The 1.8-liter Four provides good acceleration. Lower-trim LX and DX models get a noisy but economical 1.5-liter engine and different suspension tuning, which together degrade the car's overall performance markedly. The driving position is very good. The front seats are well padded and nicely shaped and supportive. The rear seat can hold three adults in reasonable comfort—unusual in a car this small. The trunk is relatively roomy.

Body styles and prices

	Price range	Trim lines
4-door	$12,145 - $15,295	DX, LX, ES

Safety information

Safety belt pretensioners ....No
Center rear safety belt ....Lap
Dual air bags ....Standard
Side air bags............Not offered
Antilock brakes ....Optional (not offered on DX)
Traction control ....Not offered
Gov't front-crash test, driver/front passenger ....○/◒
Gov't side-crash test, driver/rear passenger ....NA/NA
IIHS offset crash test ....Acceptable
Injury claim rate compared with all cars/type............●/○

Reliability history

TROUBLE SPOTS	Mazda Protegé 90	91	92	93	94	95	96	97
Engine	○	○	◓	◓	◓	◉	◉	◉
Cooling	◒	○	◓	◓	◉	◉	◉	◉
Fuel	◓	◓	◓	◓	◓	◉	◉	◓
Ignition	○	◓	○	○	◓	◓	◉	◉
Auto. transmission	○	◓	◉	◉	◓	◓	◉	◉
Man. transmission	◉	◓	◉	◉	◉	◉	◉	*
Clutch	◓	◓	◓	◓	◉	◉	◉	*
Electrical	◒	○	◒	○	○	●	○	○
Air conditioning	◒	◓	○	○	◓	◉	◉	◉
Suspension	○	◓	○	◓	◉	◓	◉	◉
Brakes	◒	●	●	◒	○	◓	◓	◉
Exhaust	●	●	◒	○	◓	◉	◉	◉
Body rust	○	◓	◉	◉	◉	◉	◉	◉
Paint/trim	◒	◒	○	◓	◓	◓	◓	◉
Body integrity	○	○	○	○	○	○	◓	○
Body hardware	◒	◒	◒	◒	◒	○	◓	◓

Test judgments

Performance
Acceleration ....◒
Transmission ....◓
Routine handling ....◓
Emergency handling ....◓
Braking ....○

Comfort
Ride, normal load ....○
Ride, full load ....○
Noise ....○
Driving position ....◓
Front-seat comfort ....◓
Rear-seat comfort ....○
Climate-control system ....◓

Convenience
Access ....○
Controls and displays ....◓
Trunk ....○

Other
Fuel economy ....◉
Predicted reliability ....◓
Predicted depreciation ....◒

Test data

Acceleration
0-30 mph, sec. 4.6
0-60 mph, sec. 13.6
Quarter mile, sec. 19.8
Quarter mile, mph 71
45-65 mph, sec. 8.7

Fuel economy (regular)
EPA city/highway, mpg 25/32
CU's overall mileage, mpg 31
CU's city/highway, mpg............20/47
CU's 150-mile trip, mpg 37
Fuel refill capacity, gal. 13.2
Cruising range, mi. 455
Annual fuel: gal./cost ......490/$590

Braking from 60 mph
Dry pavement, ft. 147
Wet pavement, ft. 194
Pedal effort, 1st stop, lb. 20
Pedal effort, 10th stop, lb. 25

Specifications

Drive wheels
Front

Seating
Passengers,front/rear............2/3

Dimensions and weight
Length, in. 175
Width, in. 67
Wheelbase, in. 103
Turning circle, ft. 37
Curb weight, lb. 2500
Percent weight, front/rear 63/37
Max. load, lb. 850

Interior room
Front shoulder room, in. 53.5
Front leg room, in. 41.0
Front head room, in. 4.0
Rear shoulder room, in. 51.5
Rear fore-aft room, in. 30.0
Rear head room, in. 3.0
Door top to ground, in. 50.0
Luggage capacity ....4+2

Engines available
1.5-liter 4 (90 or 92 hp)
1.8-liter 4 (122 hp)

Transmissions available
5-speed manual
4-speed automatic

Tested model
1998 LX 4-door, 1.5-liter Four,
4-speed automatic

Tires as tested
Uniroyal Tiger Paw,
size P185/65R14

Medium car over $25,000

Mercedes-Benz C-Class

The C-Class is Mercedes's smallest sedan line and includes the four-cylinder C230, V6 C280, and the newly introduced V8-powered C43. Updates to the 1998 models also include side air bags and a few minor styling changes. The C-Class is a competent, well-rounded package, but it's not cheap: You can easily drop $40,000 on a C280 by including only a few options. Still, it's one of the nicest cars on the road: well-built, quiet-riding, and very maneuverable. The 2.8-liter V6 is smooth and powerful. The five-speed automatic transmission is responsive. The ride is taut but supple, handling is very capable, and tire grip is tenacious.

Body styles and prices

	Price range	Trim lines
4-door	$30,450 - $52,750	C230, C280, C43

Safety information

Safety belt pretensioners	Front
Center rear safety belt	Lap
Dual air bags	Standard
Side air bags	Standard
Antilock brakes	Standard
Traction control	Standard
Gov't front-crash test, driver/front passenger	◓/◓
Gov't side-crash test, driver/rear passenger	○/◓
IIHS offset crash test	NA
Injury claim rate compared with all cars/type	○/○

Reliability history

TROUBLE SPOTS	Mercedes-Benz C-Class 90	91	92	93	94	95	96	97
Engine					○	◓	●	●
Cooling					◓	●	●	●
Fuel					◓	◓	◓	●
Ignition					◓	◓	◓	●
Auto. transmission					●	○	●	●
Man. transmission								
Clutch								
Electrical					◒	⬤	○	◓
Air conditioning					○	○	◓	○
Suspension					●	●	●	●
Brakes					◒	○	●	●
Exhaust					●	●	●	●
Body rust					●	●	●	●
Paint/trim					●	●	●	●
Body integrity					◓	◓	◓	●
Body hardware					⬤	◒	●	◓

Test judgments

Performance

Acceleration	◓
Transmission	◓
Routine handling	●
Emergency handling	◓
Braking	◓

Comfort

Ride, normal load	◓
Ride, full load	◓
Noise	◓
Driving position	●
Front-seat comfort	●
Rear-seat comfort	◓
Climate-control system	●

Convenience

Access	◓
Controls and displays	●
Trunk	○

Other

Fuel economy	○
Predicted reliability	○
Predicted depreciation	◓

Test data

Acceleration

0-30 mph, sec.	3.3
0-60 mph, sec.	8.5
Quarter mile, sec.	16.7
Quarter mile, mph	88
45-65 mph, sec	5.7

Fuel economy (premium)

EPA city/highway, mpg	21/27
CU's overall mileage, mpg	24
CU's city/highway, mpg	16/37
CU's 150-mile trip, mpg	29
Fuel refill capacity, gal.	16.4
Cruising range, mi.	445
Annual fuel: gal./cost	620/$870

Braking from 60 mph

Dry pavement, ft.	133
Wet pavement, ft.	152
Pedal effort, 1st stop, lb.	10
Pedal effort, 10th stop, lb.	10

Specifications

Drive wheels

Rear

Seating

Passengers,front/rear	2/3

Dimensions and weight

Length, in.	177
Width, in.	68
Wheelbase, in.	106
Turning circle, ft.	35
Curb weight, lb.	3320
Percent weight, front/rear	55/45
Max. load, lb.	865

Interior room

Front shoulder room, in.	55.0
Front leg room, in.	43.0
Front head room, in.	3.0
Rear shoulder room, in.	54.0
Rear fore-aft room, in.	27.5
Rear head room, in.	3.0
Door top to ground, in.	51.0
Luggage capacity	4+1

Engines available

2.3-liter 4 (148 hp)
2.8-liter V6 (194 hp)
4.3-liter V8 (302 hp)

Transmissions available

5-speed automatic

Tested model

1997 C280 4-door, 2.8-liter Six, 5-speed automatic

Tires as tested

Continental Conti Touring Contact, size 195/65R15

Luxury car

Mercedes-Benz E-Class

RECOMMENDED

The civilized E-Class is a pleasure to drive. The E320 combines spirited acceleration with acceptable fuel economy, and precise handling with a luxurious ride. The interior is roomy, and the seats and driving position are first-class. Side air bags and a five-speed automatic are included. The current E-Class lineup includes the E300 turbodiesel, the E320 with a new 3.2-liter V6, and the E430 with a new 4.3-liter V8. A station wagon is new for the 1998 model year. Also, all-wheel drive is offered on the E320 sedan and wagon.

Body styles and prices

	Price range	Trim lines
4-door	$41,800 - $49,900	E300 Turbodiesel, E320, E320 AWD, E430
4-door wagon	$46,500 - $49,250	E320, E320 AWD

Safety information

Safety belt pretensioners .... Front
Center rear safety belt 3-point
Dual air bags .... Standard
Side air bags .... Standard
Antilock brakes .... Standard
Traction control .... Standard
Gov't front-crash test, driver/front passenger .... NA/NA
Gov't side-crash test, driver/rear passenger .... NA/NA
IIHS offset crash test .... Acceptable
Injury claim rate compared with all cars/type .... ◓/○

Reliability history

TROUBLE SPOTS	Mercedes-Benz E-Class 6 90	91	92	93	94	95	96	97
Engine							◓	●
Cooling							●	●
Fuel							◓	●
Ignition							●	◓
Auto. transmission							●	◓
Man. transmission								
Clutch								
Electrical							○	●
Air conditioning							●	◓
Suspension							●	●
Brakes							◓	●
Exhaust							●	●
Body rust							●	●
Paint/trim							◓	●
Body integrity							○	●
Body hardware							◓	●

Test judgments

Performance
Acceleration .... ◓
Transmission .... ◓
Routine handling .... ●
Emergency handling .... ◓
Braking .... ●

Comfort
Ride, normal load .... ◓
Ride, full load .... ◓
Noise .... ●
Driving position .... ●
Front-seat comfort .... ●
Rear-seat comfort .... ◓
Climate-control system .... ●

Convenience
Access .... ◓
Controls and displays .... ◓
Trunk .... ○

Other
Fuel economy .... ○
Predicted reliability .... ◓
Predicted depreciation .... ○

Test data

Acceleration
0-30 mph, sec. 3.1
0-60 mph, sec. 7.8
Quarter mile, sec. 16.1
Quarter mile, mph 90
45-65 mph, sec. 5.0

Fuel economy (premium)
EPA city/highway, mpg 21/29
CU's overall mileage, mpg 22
CU's city/highway, mpg 14/34
CU's 150-mile trip, mpg 36
Fuel refill capacity, gal. 21.1
Cruising range, mi. 510
Annual fuel: gal./cost .... 690/$970

Braking from 60 mph
Dry pavement, ft. 125
Wet pavement, ft. 148
Pedal effort, 1st stop, lb. 20
Pedal effort, 10th stop, lb. 20

Specifications

Drive wheels
Rear or all

Seating
Passengers,front/rear 2/3

Dimensions and weight
Length, in. 189
Width, in. 71
Wheelbase, in. 112
Turning circle, ft. 37
Curb weight, lb. 3570
Percent weight, front/rear 54/46
Max. load, lb. 965

Interior room
Front shoulder room, in. 55.5
Front leg room, in. 43.0
Front head room, in. 4.0
Rear shoulder room, in. 55.5
Rear fore-aft room, in. 31.5
Rear head room, in. 3.0
Door top to ground, in. 52.0
Luggage capacity .... 4+1

Engines available
3.0-liter 6 Turbodiesel (174 hp)
3.2-liter V6 (221 hp)
4.3-liter V8 (275 hp)

Transmissions available
5-speed automatic

Tested model
1996 E320 4-door, 3.2-liter Six, 4-speed automatic

Tires as tested
Michelin Energy MXV4, size 215/55R16

Large car under $30,000

Mercury Grand Marquis

The Grand Marquis and the similar Ford Crown Victoria embody the hallmarks of the classic American freeway cruisers, without suffering from that species' traditional ailments. They are almost the last of the full-frame, rear-drive American V8s. 1998 brought a restyled front and rear and improvements to the suspension. If you want a big, quiet, comfortable-riding large sedan for the least money, look no further. Handling is not bad for a car this large, although the steering is a bit light. Braking and emergency-handling are fairly good. Although the powertrain lacks refinement and good fuel economy, readily available power is there for the asking. Traction control effectively keeps the car on course on slippery roads. The front seat feels soft but could use more support. The rear seat is less accommodating than you would expect in a car this large, but the trunk is cavernous.

Body styles and prices

	Price range	Trim lines
4-door	$21,890 - $23,790	GS, LS

Safety information

- Safety belt pretensioners .... No
- Center rear safety belt .... Lap
- Dual air bags .... Standard
- Side air bags .... Not offered
- Antilock brakes .... Optional
- Traction control .... Optional
- Gov't front-crash test, driver/front passenger .... ◉/◉
- Gov't side-crash test, driver/rear passenger .... ◓/◓
- IIHS offset crash test .... NA
- Injury claim rate compared with all cars/type .... ◉/◓

Reliability history

TROUBLE SPOTS	Mercury Grand Marquis 90	91	92	93	94	95	96	97
Engine	○	○	◓	◉	◉	◉	◉	◉
Cooling	◒	○	◉	◉	◉	◉	◉	◉
Fuel	○	○	○	◓	◓	◓	◓	◉
Ignition	◒	◒	●	◒	◓	◓	◓	◉
Auto. transmission	○	○	◒	●	●	○	◓	◉
Man. transmission								
Clutch								
Electrical	●	●	◒	◒	○	◒	○	◓
Air conditioning	●	◒	◒	◓	◓	◓	◉	◉
Suspension	○	○	◓	◓	◓	◓	○	◉
Brakes	●	●	●	●	◒	◒	○	◓
Exhaust	●	●	◒	◉	◉	◉	◉	◉
Body rust	○	○	◉	◉	◉	◉	◉	◉
Paint/trim	◒	○	○	◓	◓	◓	◓	◓
Body integrity	○	○	○	○	○	○	○	◓
Body hardware	●	●	●	◒	○	○	○	◓

Test judgments

Performance
- Acceleration .... ◓
- Transmission .... ◓
- Routine handling .... ○
- Emergency handling .... ○
- Braking .... ◓

Comfort
- Ride, normal load .... ◓
- Ride, full load .... ◉
- Noise .... ◉
- Driving position .... ◓
- Front-seat comfort .... ○
- Rear-seat comfort .... ○
- Climate-control system .... ◉

Convenience
- Access .... ◓
- Controls and displays .... ◓
- Trunk .... ◓

Other
- Fuel economy .... ◒
- Predicted reliability .... ○
- Predicted depreciation .... ○

Test data

Acceleration
- 0-30 mph, sec. 3.3
- 0-60 mph, sec. 9.2
- Quarter mile, sec. 17.0
- Quarter mile, mph 83
- 45-65 mph, sec. 6.2

Fuel economy (regular)
- EPA city/highway, mpg 17/24
- CU's overall mileage, mpg 19
  - CU's city/highway, mpg 12/32
  - CU's 150-mile trip, mpg 23
- Fuel refill capacity, gal. 19.0
- Cruising range, mi. 400
- Annual fuel: gal./cost .... 805/$965

Braking from 60 mph
- Dry pavement, ft. 143
- Wet pavement, ft. 149
- Pedal effort, 1st stop, lb. 20
- Pedal effort, 10th stop, lb. 25

Specifications

Drive wheels
Rear

Seating
- Passengers, front/rear 3/3

Dimensions and weight
- Length, in. 212
- Width, in. 78
- Wheelbase, in. 115
- Turning circle, ft. 44
- Curb weight, lb. 3985
- Percent weight, front/rear 56/44
- Max. load, lb. 1100

Interior room
- Front shoulder room, in. 61.0
- Front leg room, in. 42.0
- Front head room, in. 5.0
- Rear shoulder room, in. 60.0
- Rear fore-aft room, in. 29.5
- Rear head room, in. 4.0
- Door top to ground, in. 52.0
- Luggage capacity .... 6+2

Engines available
4.6-liter V8 (200 or 215 hp)

Transmissions available
4-speed automatic

Tested model
1998 GS 4-door, 4.6-liter V8, 4-speed automatic

Tires as tested
Michelin Symmetry, size P225/60R16

Medium car under $25,000

Mercury Mystique

The Mystique and similar Ford Contour received a freshening last year. The Mystique LS drives like a good, agile European sports sedan. The ride is firm but well controlled (the lower-trim GS suspension gives a softer ride). The steering is precise, quick, and nicely weighted. Engine choices include a rather noisy 2.0-liter Four or a smooth 2.5-liter V6—the one to choose if it fits your budget. The automatic transmission works well. The front seats are comfortable. The rear feels cramped, despite an extra half-inch of room added last year. The trunk is large.

Body styles and prices

	Price range	Trim lines
4-door	$16,285 - $17,645	GS, LS

Safety information

Safety belt pretensioners	No
Center rear safety belt	3-point
Dual air bags	Standard
Side air bags	Not offered
Antilock brakes	Optional
Traction control	Not offered
Gov't front-crash test, driver/front passenger	●/◓
Gov't side-crash test, driver/rear passenger	○/◓
IIHS offset crash test	Poor
Injury claim rate compared with all cars/type	○/○

Reliability history

TROUBLE SPOTS	Mercury Mystique 90	91	92	93	94	95	96	97
Engine						◓	●	●
Cooling						◓	●	●
Fuel						◒	○	◓
Ignition						◓	◓	◓
Auto. transmission						○	●	●
Man. transmission						●	●	*
Clutch						●	●	*
Electrical						◒	○	○
Air conditioning						◓	●	●
Suspension						○	◓	◓
Brakes						◒	◓	◓
Exhaust						●	●	●
Body rust						●	●	●
Paint/trim						○	◓	●
Body integrity						◒	○	○
Body hardware						◒	◒	○

Test judgments

Performance

Acceleration	◓
Transmission	◓
Routine handling	●
Emergency handling	◓
Braking	◓

Comfort

Ride, normal load	◓
Ride, full load	◓
Noise	◓
Driving position	◓
Front-seat comfort	●
Rear-seat comfort	○
Climate-control system	●

Convenience

Access	◓
Controls and displays	◓
Trunk	◓

Other

Fuel economy	○
Predicted reliability	○
Predicted depreciation	◒

Test data

Acceleration

0-30 mph, sec.	3.8
0-60 mph, sec.	9.8
Quarter mile, sec.	17.5
Quarter mile, mph	82
45-65 mph, sec.	6.2

Fuel economy (regular)

EPA city/highway, mpg	21/30
CU's overall mileage, mpg	22
CU's city/highway, mpg	14/35
CU's 150-mile trip, mpg	28
Fuel refill capacity, gal.	14.5
Cruising range, mi.	370
Annual fuel: gal./cost	685/$820

Braking from 60 mph

Dry pavement, ft.	135
Wet pavement, ft.	173
Pedal effort, 1st stop, lb.	20
Pedal effort, 10th stop, lb.	25

Specifications

Drive wheels

Front

Seating

Passengers,front/rear	2/3

Dimensions and weight

Length, in.	185
Width, in.	69
Wheelbase, in.	107
Turning circle, ft.	40
Curb weight, lb.	3115
Percent weight, front/rear	65/35
Max. load, lb.	880

Interior room

Front shoulder room, in.	53.5
Front leg room, in.	41.5
Front head room, in.	4.5
Rear shoulder room, in.	53.0
Rear fore-aft room, in.	28.0
Rear head room, in.	1.0
Door top to ground, in.	50.5
Luggage capacity	5+1

Engines available

2.0-liter 4 (125 hp)
2.5-liter V6 (170 hp)

Transmissions available

5-speed manual
4-speed automatic

Tested model

1998 LS V6 4-door, 2.5-liter V6, 4-speed automatic

Tires as tested

Goodyear Eagle GT+4, size P205/60R15

Medium car under $25,000

Mercury Sable

The Sable is similar to the Ford Taurus. This car is comfortable, quiet, and nimble. We prefer the LS version, which comes with a more powerful and polished drivetrain than the base GS version's. The front seats are supportive. The rear bench seat can hold three adults comfortably, but the swoopy roof line can bang the head of unwary passengers trying to get into the rear seat. Reliability of the Sable has remained average, while the Taurus was far below average in our last survey of owners. We recommend only the Sable.

Body styles and prices

	Price range	Trim lines
4-door	$19,445 - $20,495	GS, LS
4-door wagon	$22,385	LS

Safety information

Safety belt pretensioners	No
Center rear safety belt	3-point
Dual air bags	Standard
Side air bags	Not offered
Antilock brakes	Optional
Traction control	Not offered
Gov't front-crash test, driver/front passenger	◓/◓
Gov't side-crash test, driver/rear passenger	○/○
IIHS offset crash test	Good
Injury claim rate compared with all cars/type	◓/⊙

Reliability history

TROUBLE SPOTS	Mercury Sable 90	91	92	93	94	95	96	97
Engine							⊙	⊙
Cooling							⊙	⊙
Fuel							◓	⊙
Ignition							◓	⊙
Auto. transmission							○	◓
Man. transmission								
Clutch								
Electrical							○	◓
Air conditioning							◓	⊙
Suspension							○	◓
Brakes							◓	⊙
Exhaust							⊙	⊙
Body rust							⊙	⊙
Paint/trim							◓	⊙
Body integrity							●	◓
Body hardware							◒	◓

Test judgments

Performance

Acceleration	○
Transmission	◓
Routine handling	◓
Emergency handling	○
Braking	○

Comfort

Ride, normal load	◓
Ride, full load	◓
Noise	◓
Driving position	◓
Front-seat comfort	◓
Rear-seat comfort	◓
Climate-control system	⊙

Convenience

Access	◓
Controls and displays	⊙
Trunk	⊙

Other

Fuel economy	○
Predicted reliability	○
Predicted depreciation	NA

Test data

Acceleration

0-30 mph, sec.	3.9
0-60 mph, sec.	11.4
Quarter mile, sec.	18.5
Quarter mile, mph	76
45-65 mph, sec.	7.5

Fuel economy (regular)

EPA city/highway, mpg	20/29
CU's overall mileage, mpg	22
CU's city/highway, mpg	14/35
CU's 150-mile trip, mpg	27
Fuel refill capacity, gal.	16.1
Cruising range, mi.	405
Annual fuel: gal./cost	695/$835

Braking from 60 mph

Dry pavement, ft.	140
Wet pavement, ft.	172
Pedal effort, 1st stop, lb.	15
Pedal effort, 10th stop, lb.	20

Specifications

Drive wheels

Front

Seating

Passengers,front/rear	3/3

Dimensions and weight

Length, in.	200
Width, in.	73
Wheelbase, in.	109
Turning circle, ft.	40
Curb weight, lb.	3345
Percent weight, front/rear	65/35
Max. load, lb.	1100

Interior room

Front shoulder room, in.	58.5
Front leg room, in.	42.0
Front head room, in.	5.0
Rear shoulder room, in.	56.0
Rear fore-aft room, in.	32.0
Rear head room, in.	2.0
Door top to ground, in.	50.5
Luggage capacity	6+1

Engines available

3.0-liter V6 (145 or 200hp)

Transmissions available

4-speed automatic

Tested model

1997 GS 4-door, 3.0-liter V6, 4-speed automatic

Tires as tested

General Ameri*G4S, size P205/65R15

Small car

Mercury Tracer

RECOMMENDED

The Tracer and similar Ford Escort were partly redesigned—and greatly improved—for 1997, and they carry over virtually unchanged into 1998. The Tracer corners fairly nimbly. The ride feels choppy but remains composed in bumpy turns. Noise from the engine, road, and wind creeps into the cabin. The transmission shifts smoothly enough but makes the engine labor annoyingly at times. Leg room is a little tight for tall drivers. The front seats are small but supportive. The rear seat is cramped. The wagon version offers respectable cargo space, and it's about the least costly wagon on the market.

Body styles and prices

	Price range	Trim lines
4-door	$11,405 - $12,760	GS, LS
4-door wagon	$14,255	LS

Safety information

Safety belt pretensioners	No
Center rear safety belt	Lap
Dual air bags	Standard
Side air bags	Not offered
Antilock brakes	Optional
Traction control	Not offered
Gov't front-crash test, driver/front passenger	○/○
Gov't side-crash test, driver/rear passenger	○/○
IIHS offset crash test	Acceptable
Injury claim rate compared with all cars/type	NA/NA

Reliability history

TROUBLE SPOTS	Mercury Tracer 90	91	92	93	94	95	96	97
Engine								●
Cooling								●
Fuel								●
Ignition								●
Auto. transmission								●
Man. transmission								●
Clutch								●
Electrical								◓
Air conditioning								●
Suspension								●
Brakes								●
Exhaust								●
Body rust								●
Paint/trim								●
Body integrity								◓
Body hardware								◓

Test judgments

Performance

Acceleration	○
Transmission	◓
Routine handling	◓
Emergency handling	◓
Braking	○

Comfort

Ride, normal load	○
Ride, full load	○
Noise	○
Driving position	◓
Front-seat comfort	◓
Rear-seat comfort	◒
Climate-control system	●

Convenience

Access	○
Controls and displays	●
Trunk	○

Other

Fuel economy	◓
Predicted reliability	○
Predicted depreciation	NA

Test data

Acceleration

0-30 mph, sec.	3.8
0-60 mph, sec.	11.2
Quarter mile, sec.	18.4
Quarter mile, mph	76
45-65 mph, sec.	7.4

Fuel economy (regular)

EPA city/highway, mpg	26/34
CU's overall mileage, mpg	28
CU's city/highway, mpg	18/42
CU's 150-mile trip, mpg	33
Fuel refill capacity, gal.	12.7
Cruising range, mi.	385
Annual fuel: gal./cost	545/$650

Braking from 60 mph

Dry pavement, ft.	147
Wet pavement, ft.	181
Pedal effort, 1st stop, lb.	15
Pedal effort, 10th stop, lb.	20

Specifications

Drive wheels

Front

Seating

Passengers,front/rear	2/3

Dimensions and weight

Length, in.	175
Width, in.	66
Wheelbase, in.	98
Turning circle, ft.	36
Curb weight, lb.	2585
Percent weight, front/rear	64/36
Max. load, lb.	830

Interior room

Front shoulder room, in.	51.5
Front leg room, in.	40.5
Front head room, in.	4.0
Rear shoulder room, in.	52.0
Rear fore-aft room, in.	27.5
Rear head room, in.	1.5
Door top to ground, in.	49.0
Luggage capacity	4+1

Engines available

2.0-liter 4 (110 hp)

Transmissions available

5-speed manual
4-speed automatic

Tested model

1997 Ford Escort LX 4-door, 2.0-liter Four, 4-speed automatic

Tires as tested

Uniroyal Tiger Paw, size P185/65R14

Minivan

Mercury Villager

The Villager and similar Nissan Quest are made in the U.S. jointly by Ford and Nissan. These minivans ride comfortably and quietly. They feel carlike to drive, and the V6 delivers adequate power. But these vans haven't changed much in recent years, and more modern competitors like the Dodge Caravan and Toyota Sienna have eclipsed them. The Villager and Quest lack the cargo space of the Chrysler minivans, and they won't offer a left-side sliding door until the 1999 model year. But a variety of seating arrangements provides some versatility. Reliability has been average.

Body styles and prices

	Price range	Trim lines
Minivan	$20,805 - $26,905	GS, LS, Nautica

Safety information

Safety belt pretensioners	No
Center rear safety belt	Lap
Dual air bags	Standard
Side air bags	Not offered
Antilock brakes	Standard
Traction control	Not offered
Gov't front-crash test, driver/front passenger	◉/○
Gov't side-crash test, driver/rear passenger	NA/NA
IIHS offset crash test	Marginal
Injury claim rate compared with all cars/type	◓/◓

Reliability history

TROUBLE SPOTS	Mercury Villager 90	91	92	93	94	95	96	97
Engine				◓	◓	○	○	◉
Cooling				◓	◓	◉	◉	◉
Fuel				◓	◓	◓	◉	◉
Ignition				◓	◓	◓	◉	◉
Auto. transmission				◓	◉	◉	◉	◉
Man. transmission								
Clutch								
Electrical				●	◒	●	◒	○
Air conditioning				○	○	◓	◓	◉
Suspension				○	◓	◓	◓	◓
Brakes				◒	◒	◒	◓	◉
Exhaust				●	◓	◉	◉	◉
Body rust				◉	◉	◉	◉	◉
Paint/trim				◓	◓	◓	◉	◉
Body integrity				◒	○	◒	◒	○
Body hardware				●	◒	●	◒	○

Test judgments

Performance	
Acceleration	○
Transmission	◓
Routine handling	○
Emergency handling	○
Braking	◓
Comfort	
Ride, normal load	◓
Ride, full load	◓
Noise	◓
Driving position	◓
Front-seat comfort	◓
Middle-seat comfort	◓
Rear-seat comfort	○
Climate-control system	◉
Convenience	
Access	◓
Controls and displays	○
Cargo area	○
Other	
Fuel economy	◒
Predicted reliability	○
Predicted depreciation	○

Test data

Acceleration

0-30 mph, sec.	4.0
0-60 mph, sec.	11.8
Quarter mile, sec.	18.7
Quarter mile, mph	74
45-65 mph, sec.	7.3

Fuel economy (regular)

EPA city/highway, mpg	17/23
CU's overall mileage, mpg	19
CU's city/highway, mpg	12/32
CU's 150-mile trip, mpg	23
Fuel refill capacity, gal.	20.0
Cruising range, mi.	430
Annual fuel: gal./cost	775/$930

Braking from 60 mph

Dry pavement, ft.	140
Wet pavement, ft.	161
Pedal effort, 1st stop, lb.	25
Pedal effort, 10th stop, lb.	30

Specifications

Drive wheels

Front

Seating

Passengers,front/mid/rear......2/2/3

Dimensions and weight

Length, in.	190
Width, in.	74
Wheelbase, in.	112
Turning circle, ft.	41
Curb weight, lb.	3900
Percent weight, front/rear	59/41
Max. load, lb.	1290

Interior room

Front shoulder room, in.	61.5
Front leg room, in.	40.0
Front head room, in.	5.0
Middle shoulder room, in.	63.5
Middle fore-aft room, in.	26.5
Middle head room, in.	5.5
Rear shoulder room, in.	61.5
Rear fore-aft room, in.	27.0
Rear head room, in.	4.0
Door top to ground, in.	60.0
Cargo volume, cu.ft.	55.0

Engines available

3.0-liter V6 (151 hp)

Transmissions available

4-speed automatic

Tested model

1996 GS Minivan, 3.0-liter V6, 4-speed automatic

Tires as tested

General Ameri G4S, size P205/75R15

Medium car under $25,000

Mitsubishi Galant

RECOMMENDED

The Galant is a good midsized sedan, but it scores a notch lower than competing models like the Toyota Camry, Honda Accord, and Subaru Legacy. The highway ride is pleasant enough, but the body rocks and pitches on poor secondary roads. The car handles safely. The 2.4-liter Four delivers lively acceleration and respectable fuel economy. The automatic transmission usually shifts smoothly. The front seats are supportive and firm. The trunk is roomy, and the rear seatback can fold down to expand it further. A new Galant debuts in the fall.

Body styles and prices

	Price range	Trim lines
4-door	$15,680 - $25,310	DE, ES, LS

Safety information

Safety belt pretensioners .... No
Center rear safety belt .... Lap
Dual air bags .... Standard
Side air bags .... Not offered
Antilock brakes .... Std. LS; opt. ES
Traction control .... Not offered
Gov't front-crash test, driver/front passenger .... ◓/◓
Gov't side-crash test, driver/rear passenger .... ○/◒
IIHS offset crash test .... Poor
Injury claim rate compared with all cars/type .... ◒/◒

Reliability history

TROUBLE SPOTS	Mitsubishi Galant 90	91	92	93	94	95	96	97
Engine	◒	○	○	Insufficient data	◓	⦿	◓	◓
Cooling	○	◓	◓		⦿	⦿	⦿	⦿
Fuel	◓	○	⦿		⦿	⦿	◓	⦿
Ignition	○	○	◓		○	◓	◓	⦿
Auto. transmission	○	○	◓		◓	◓	◓	○
Man. transmission	*	*	*		*	*	*	*
Clutch	*	*	*		*	*	*	*
Electrical	○	◓	⦿		◒	◓	◓	◓
Air conditioning	○	◓	◓		◓	◓	◓	⦿
Suspension	○	○	◓		○	○	◓	⦿
Brakes	●	●	○		◒	●	○	⦿
Exhaust	◓	⦿	◓		⦿	⦿	⦿	⦿
Body rust	⦿	◓	⦿		⦿	⦿	⦿	⦿
Paint/trim	○	○	○		◓	◓	◓	⦿
Body integrity	○	◓	○		○	◒	◒	⦿
Body hardware	○	◓	○		●	◒	◒	◓

Test judgments

Performance
Acceleration .... ◓
Transmission .... ◓
Routine handling .... ◓
Emergency handling .... ○
Braking .... ○

Comfort
Ride, normal load .... ◓
Ride, full load .... ◓
Noise .... ◓
Driving position .... ◓
Front-seat comfort .... ◓
Rear-seat comfort .... ○
Climate-control system .... ⦿

Convenience
Access .... ◓
Controls and displays .... ⦿
Trunk .... ◓

Other
Fuel economy .... ◓
Predicted reliability .... ○
Predicted depreciation .... ◒

Test data

Acceleration
0-30 mph, sec. 3.5
0-60 mph, sec. 9.8
Quarter mile, sec. 17.6
Quarter mile, mph 81
45-65 mph, sec. 6.4

Fuel economy (regular)
EPA city/highway, mpg 22/28
CU's overall mileage, mpg 25
CU's city/highway, mpg 17/37
CU's 150-mile trip, mpg 30
Fuel refill capacity, gal. 16.9
Cruising range, mi. 470
Annual fuel: gal./cost .... 590/$710

Braking from 60 mph
Dry pavement, ft. 142
Wet pavement, ft. 171
Pedal effort, 1st stop, lb. 15
Pedal effort, 10th stop, lb. 20

Specifications

Drive wheels
Front

Seating
Passengers, front/rear 2/3

Dimensions and weight
Length, in. 188
Width, in. 68
Wheelbase, in. 104
Turning circle, ft. 39
Curb weight, lb. 2970
Percent weight, front/rear 62/38
Max. load, lb. 827

Interior room
Front shoulder room, in. 54.5
Front leg room, in. 41.5
Front head room, in. 3.5
Rear shoulder room, in. 54.0
Rear fore-aft room, in. 26.5
Rear head room, in. 2.5
Door top to ground, in. 49.0
Luggage capacity .... 5+0

Engines available
2.4-liter 4 (141 hp)

Transmissions available
5-speed manual
4-speed automatic

Tested model
1997 ES 4-door, 2.4-liter Four, 4-speed automatic

Tires as tested
Bridgestone SF-408, size P185/70R14

Small car

Mitsubishi Mirage

Redesigned for 1997, the Mirage is a capable small car. The 1.8-liter Four in the LS model delivers adequate acceleration. (A 1.5-liter Four is standard in the base version.) The Mirage handles securely and predictably, and its ride is supple. The interior feels airy and spacious. The front seats are supportive and roomy enough. The rear seat can hold two adults in moderate comfort, but three won't be happy there. Optional fold-down rear seatbacks let you expand the rather small trunk. Reliability is still unknown due to insufficient responses in our latest survey.

Body styles and prices

	Price range	Trim lines
2-door	$10,830 - $14,330	DE, LS
4-door	$12,360 - $13,300	DE, LS

Safety information

Safety belt pretensioners .... No
Center rear safety belt .... Lap
Dual air bags .... Standard
Side air bags .... Not offered
Antilock brakes .... Optional on LS
Traction control .... Not offered
Gov't front-crash test, driver/front passenger .... NA/NA
Gov't side-crash test, driver/rear passenger .... NA/NA
IIHS offset crash test .... Poor
Injury claim rate compared with all cars/type .... NA/NA

Reliability history

TROUBLE SPOTS	90 91 92 93 94 95 96 97
Engine	
Cooling	
Fuel	
Ignition	
Auto. transmission	NOT
Man. transmission	
Clutch	ENOUGH
Electrical	
Air conditioning	DATA
Suspension	
Brakes	TO
Exhaust	
Body rust	RATE
Paint/trim	
Body integrity	
Body hardware	

Test judgments

Performance
Acceleration .... ○
Transmission .... ◓
Routine handling .... ◓
Emergency handling .... ◓
Braking .... ○

Comfort
Ride, normal load .... ○
Ride, full load .... ○
Noise .... ◓
Driving position .... ◓
Front-seat comfort .... ◓
Rear-seat comfort .... ○
Climate-control system .... ◓

Convenience
Access .... ○
Controls and displays .... ●
Trunk .... ◒

Other
Fuel economy .... ◓
Predicted reliability .... NA
Predicted depreciation .... NA

Test data

Acceleration
0-30 mph, sec. 3.9
0-60 mph, sec. 10.8
Quarter mile, sec. 18.2
Quarter mile, mph 78
45-65 mph, sec. 7.1

Fuel economy (regular)
EPA city/highway, mpg 26/33
CU's overall mileage, mpg 27
CU's city/highway, mpg 18/41
CU's 150-mile trip, mpg 33
Fuel refill capacity, gal. 13.2
Cruising range, mi. 400
Annual fuel: gal./cost .... 560/$670

Braking from 60 mph
Dry pavement, ft. 142
Wet pavement, ft. 167
Pedal effort, 1st stop, lb. 25
Pedal effort, 10th stop, lb. 30

Specifications

Drive wheels
Front

Seating
Passengers, front/rear 2/3

Dimensions and weight
Length, in. 174
Width, in. 67
Wheelbase, in. 98
Turning circle, ft. 36
Curb weight, lb. 2525
Percent weight, front/rear 63/37
Max. load, lb. 825

Interior room
Front shoulder room, in. 53.0
Front leg room, in. 41.0
Front head room, in. 5.0
Rear shoulder room, in. 52.0
Rear fore-aft room, in. 26.0
Rear head room, in. 2.0
Door top to ground, in. 49.0
Luggage capacity .... 3+2

Engines available
1.5-liter 4 (92 hp)
1.8-liter 4 (113 hp)

Transmissions available
5-speed manual
4-speed automatic

Tested model
1997 LS 4-door, 1.8-liter Four, 4-speed automatic

Tires as tested
Michelin Energy MXV4, size P185/65R14

Sport-utility vehicle

Mitsubishi Montero Sport

The Montero Sport was new for 1997 but seemed much older and more trucklike than other existing SUVs. Common road bumps deliver stiff, rubbery kicks, and even the highway ride is jittery. Handling is rather cumbersome. Fuel economy is pretty good for an SUV, but the V6 in the LS model we tested didn't feel particularly lively. The four-wheel drive is only a part-time system. The front seats are reasonably comfortable and supportive. Access is difficult. Cargo space is adequate.

Body styles and prices

	Price range	Trim lines
4-door wagon 2WD	$18,030 - $28,360	ES, LS, XLS
4-door wagon 4WD	$23,920 - $32,250	LS, XLS

Safety information

Safety belt pretensioners	No
Center rear safety belt	Lap
Dual air bags	Standard
Side air bags	Not Offered
Antilock brakes	Standard on XLS and 4WD
Traction control	Not offered
Gov't front-crash test, driver/front passenger	NA/NA
Gov't side-crash test, driver/rear passenger	NA/NA
IIHS offset crash test	NA
Injury claim rate compared with all cars/type	NA/NA

Reliability history

TROUBLE SPOTS	90 91 92 93 94 95 96 97
Engine	
Cooling	
Fuel	
Ignition	NOT
Auto. transmission	
Man. transmission	ENOUGH
Clutch	
Electrical	DATA
Air conditioning	
Suspension	TO
Brakes	
Exhaust	RATE
Body rust	
Paint/trim	
Body integrity	
Body hardware	

Test judgments

Performance	
Acceleration	○
Transmission	◓
Routine handling	○
Emergency handling	○
Braking	○
Comfort	
Ride, normal load	◒
Ride, full load	◒
Noise	◓
Driving position	○
Front-seat comfort	◓
Rear-seat comfort	○
Climate-control system	⦿
Convenience	
Access	○
Controls and displays	⦿
Cargo area	○
Other	
Fuel economy	◒
Predicted reliability	NA
Predicted depreciation	NA

Test data

Acceleration	
0-30 mph, sec.	4.2
0-60 mph, sec.	11.9
Quarter mile, sec.	18.9
Quarter mile, mph	75
45-65 mph, sec.	7.6

Fuel economy (regular)	
EPA city/highway, mpg	18/21
CU's overall mileage, mpg	18
CU's city/highway, mpg	13/25
CU's 150-mile trip, mpg	22
Fuel refill capacity, gal.	19.5
Cruising range, mi.	400
Annual fuel: gal./cost	815/$980

Braking from 60 mph	
Dry pavement, ft.	139
Wet pavement, ft.	173
Pedal effort, 1st stop, lb.	20
Pedal effort, 10th stop, lb.	25

Specifications

Drive wheels
Rear or part-time 4WD

Seating

Passengers, front/rear	2/3

Dimensions and weight	
Length, in.	188
Width, in.	67
Wheelbase, in.	107
Turning circle, ft.	43
Curb weight, lb.	4135
Percent weight, front/rear	55/45
Max. load, lb.	1215

Interior room	
Front shoulder room, in.	55.5
Front leg room, in.	41.5
Front head room, in.	3.5
Rear shoulder room, in.	55.0
Rear fore-aft room, in.	30.5
Rear head room, in.	3.0
Door top to ground, in.	61.0
Cargo volume, cu.ft.	33.0

Engines available
2.4-liter 4 (134 hp)
3.0-liter V6 (173 hp)

Transmissions available
5-speed manual
4-speed automatic

Tested model
1997 LS 4-door wagon 4WD, 3.0-liter V6, 4-speed automatic

Tires as tested
Yokohama Super Digger 815B, size 265/70R15

Sports/sporty car under $25,000

Nissan 200SX

The 200SX is a coupe version of the Nissan Sentra. Except for a few styling tweaks, 1998 brings no changes. With the base 1.6-liter Four, it's just a dowdy Sentra with two doors—well laid out, but not very exciting. The SE-R version's stronger, 140-hp, 2.0-liter Four and stiffer suspension transform the car and allow it to outperform some higher-priced sports coupes. The SE-R offers refined performance along with capable handling and braking (with standard antilock brakes). But the ride is stiff, and the cabin is cramped. With the equipment typically found in the SE-R, expect the real price to climb above $18,000.

Body styles and prices

	Price range	Trim lines
2-door	$13,149 - $16,749	Base, SE, SE-R

Safety information

Safety belt pretensioners .... No
Center rear safety belt .... Lap
Dual air bags .... Standard
Side air bags .... Not offered
Antilock brakes .... Optional
Traction control .... Not offered
Gov't front-crash test, driver/front passenger .... NA/NA
Gov't side-crash test, driver/rear passenger .... NA/NA
IIHS offset crash test .... NA
Injury claim rate compared with all cars/type .... ⬤/⬤

Reliability history

TROUBLE SPOTS	Nissan 200SX 90	91	92	93	94	95	96	97
Engine						◓	●	Insufficient data
Cooling						●	●	
Fuel						○	◓	
Ignition						●	●	
Auto. transmission						*	*	
Man. transmission						*	*	
Clutch						*	*	
Electrical						◓	◓	
Air conditioning						●	◓	
Suspension						○	◓	
Brakes						◓	◓	
Exhaust						◓	●	
Body rust						●	●	
Paint/trim						◓	◓	
Body integrity						◓	◓	
Body hardware						○	○	

Test judgments

Performance
Acceleration .... ◓
Transmission .... ●
Routine handling .... ●
Emergency handling .... ◓
Braking .... ●

Comfort
Ride, normal load .... ○
Ride, full load .... ○
Noise .... ○
Driving position .... ○
Front-seat comfort .... ◓
Rear-seat comfort .... ◒
Climate-control system .... ◓

Convenience
Access .... ○
Controls and displays .... ●
Trunk .... ◒

Other
Fuel economy .... ◓
Predicted reliability .... ◓
Predicted depreciation .... ○

Test data

Acceleration
0-30 mph, sec. 3.2
0-60 mph, sec. 8.6
Quarter mile, sec. 16.8
Quarter mile, mph 84
45-65 mph, sec. 5.5

Fuel economy (regular)
EPA city/highway, mpg 23/31
CU's overall mileage, mpg 28
CU's city/highway, mpg 20/38
CU's 150-mile trip, mpg 31
Fuel refill capacity, gal. 13.2
Cruising range, mi. 385
Annual fuel: gal./cost .... 545/$650

Braking from 60 mph
Dry pavement, ft. 125
Wet pavement, ft. 136
Pedal effort, 1st stop, lb. 25
Pedal effort, 10th stop, lb. 25

Specifications

Drive wheels
Front

Seating
Passengers, front/rear 2/3

Dimensions and weight
Length, in. 170
Width, in. 67
Wheelbase, in. 100
Turning circle, ft. 39
Curb weight, lb. 2580
Percent weight, front/rear 63/37
Max. load, lb. 814

Interior room
Front shoulder room, in. 51.0
Front leg room, in. 41.0
Front head room, in. 2.5
Rear shoulder room, in. 52.5
Rear fore-aft room, in. 25.5
Rear head room, in. 2.0
Door top to ground, in. 49.5
Luggage capacity .... 4+0

Engines available
1.6-liter 4 (115 hp)
2.0-liter 4 (140 hp)

Transmissions available
5-speed manual
4-speed automatic

Tested model
1996 SE-R 2-door, 2.0-liter Four, 5-speed manual

Tires as tested
Goodyear Eagle RS-A, size P195/55R15

Medium car under $25,000

Nissan Altima

Redesigned for 1998, the Altima is a cheaper alternative to the Honda Accord, Mazda 626, and Toyota Camry, but falls a notch below those cars. Though it's larger than last year's version, it still is less polished and less roomy than these competing models. Neither the ride nor the handling are very good. The seats are uncomfortable, and the cabin is a little noisy. Some of the interior fittings are insubstantial. On the positive side, it accelerates fairly well, gets good fuel economy, and should prove to be reliable.

Body styles and prices

	Price range	Trim lines
4-door	$14,990 - $19,890	XE, GXE, SE, GLE

Safety information

Safety belt pretensioners .... No
Center rear safety belt .... Lap
Dual air bags .... Standard
Side air bags .... Not offered
Antilock brakes .... Optional
Traction control .... Not offered
Gov't front-crash test, driver/front passenger .... NA/NA
Gov't side-crash test, driver/rear passenger .... ○/○
IIHS offset crash test .... NA
Injury claim rate compared with all cars/type .... ◒/◒

Reliability history

TROUBLE SPOTS	90	91	92	93	94	95	96	97
Engine				◓	◓	●	●	●
Cooling				●	●	●	●	●
Fuel				◓	●	◓	◓	●
Ignition				◓	◓	◓	●	●
Auto. transmission				●	◓	◓	●	●
Man. transmission				●	●	●	*	*
Clutch				○	●	●	*	*
Electrical				◒	○	○	○	◓
Air conditioning				○	◓	◓	●	●
Suspension				◓	◓	◓	●	●
Brakes				◒	○	○	◓	●
Exhaust				◓	●	●	●	●
Body rust				●	●	●	●	●
Paint/trim				○	◓	◓	◓	●
Body integrity				◓	◓	○	○	◓
Body hardware				○	◓	○	○	○

Test judgments

Performance
Acceleration .... ○
Transmission .... ◓
Routine handling .... ◓
Emergency handling .... ○
Braking .... ○

Comfort
Ride, normal load .... ○
Ride, full load .... ○
Noise .... ◓
Driving position .... ○
Front-seat comfort .... ◓
Rear-seat comfort .... ○
Climate-control system .... ●

Convenience
Access .... ◓
Controls and displays .... ●
Trunk .... ○

Other
Fuel economy .... ◓
Predicted reliability .... ◓
Predicted depreciation .... ○

Test data

Acceleration
0-30 mph, sec. 3.9
0-60 mph, sec. 10.6
Quarter mile, sec. 18.0
Quarter mile, mph 79
45-65 mph, sec. 6.6

Fuel economy (regular)
EPA city/highway, mpg 22/30
CU's overall mileage, mpg 25
CU's city/highway, mpg 15/42
CU's 150-mile trip, mpg 31
Fuel refill capacity, gal. 15.9
Cruising range, mi. 455
Annual fuel: gal./cost .... 605/$725

Braking from 60 mph
Dry pavement, ft. 146
Wet pavement, ft. 173
Pedal effort, 1st stop, lb. 20
Pedal effort, 10th stop, lb. 30

Specifications

Drive wheels
Front

Seating
Passengers,front/rear 2/3

Dimensions and weight
Length, in. 184
Width, in. 69
Wheelbase, in. 103
Turning circle, ft. 41
Curb weight, lb. 3020
Percent weight, front/rear 63/37
Max. load, lb. 860

Interior room
Front shoulder room, in. 55.0
Front leg room, in. 41.0
Front head room, in. 5.0
Rear shoulder room, in. 53.5
Rear fore-aft room, in. 28.5
Rear head room, in. 3.5
Door top to ground, in. 50.5
Luggage capacity .... 5+1

Engines available
2.4-liter 4 (150 hp)

Transmissions available
5-speed manual
4-speed automatic

Tested model
1998 GXE 4-door, 2.4-liter Four, 4-speed automatic

Tires as tested
General XP2000 GT, size P195/65R15

Medium car under $25,000

Nissan Maxima

RECOMMENDED

The only substantial change to Nissan's flagship sedan for 1998 is the availability of side air bags for the front occupants. This model's best features are a strong, refined aluminum V6 and a roomy interior with lots of head room. While the car remains competent, the ride is just so-so, and handling is only adequate. The seats aren't especially comfortable, particularly on long trips. The Infiniti I30 is a plusher, costlier version of the Maxima. Both cars are expensive for what you get. Reliability continues to be excellent.

Body styles and prices

	Price range	Trim lines
4-door	$21,499 - $26,899	GXE, SE, GLE

Safety information

Safety belt pretensioners	No
Center rear safety belt	Lap
Dual air bags	Standard
Side air bags	Optional
Antilock brakes	Optional
Traction control	Not offered
Gov't front-crash test, driver/front passenger	◓/◓
Gov't side-crash test, driver/rear passenger	◓/○
IIHS offset crash test	Acceptable
Injury claim rate compared with all cars/type	○/○

Reliability history

TROUBLE SPOTS	Nissan Maxima 90	91	92	93	94	95	96	97
Engine	◓	◓	○	◓	⊙	⊙	⊙	⊙
Cooling	◓	◓	⊙	⊙	⊙	⊙	⊙	⊙
Fuel	○	○	○	◓	◓	◓	◓	⊙
Ignition	○	○	◓	◓	⊙	◓	⊙	⊙
Auto. transmission	○	◓	⊙	◓	◓	⊙	⊙	⊙
Man. transmission	◒	◓	◓	*	*	⊙	⊙	*
Clutch	◒	◒	◒	*	*	○	⊙	*
Electrical	●	◒	○	○	○	◓	◓	◓
Air conditioning	◓	◓	◓	◓	⊙	⊙	⊙	⊙
Suspension	◓	◓	◓	◓	⊙	⊙	⊙	⊙
Brakes	●	●	●	◒	○	◓	⊙	⊙
Exhaust	◒	○	◓	⊙	⊙	⊙	⊙	⊙
Body rust	◓	◓	◓	⊙	⊙	⊙	⊙	⊙
Paint/trim	○	○	◓	◓	◓	◓	◓	◓
Body integrity	◓	◓	◓	◓	◓	◓	◓	⊙
Body hardware	●	◒	◒	◒	○	◓	◓	⊙

Test judgments

Performance

Acceleration	◓
Transmission	◓
Routine handling	◓
Emergency handling	○
Braking	◓

Comfort

Ride, normal load	○
Ride, full load	○
Noise	◓
Driving position	◓
Front-seat comfort	◓
Rear-seat comfort	◓
Climate-control system	⊙

Convenience

Access	◓
Controls and displays	⊙
Trunk	◓

Other

Fuel economy	○
Predicted reliability	⊙
Predicted depreciation	○

Test data

Acceleration

0-30 mph, sec.	3.4
0-60 mph, sec.	8.9
Quarter mile, sec.	16.9
Quarter mile, mph	84
45-65 mph, sec.	5.6

Fuel economy (regular)

EPA city/highway, mpg	21/28
CU's overall mileage, mpg	23
CU's city/highway, mpg	15/36
CU's 150-mile trip, mpg	28
Fuel refill capacity, gal.	18.5
Cruising range, mi.	480
Annual fuel: gal./cost	655/$790

Braking from 60 mph

Dry pavement, ft.	138
Wet pavement, ft.	165
Pedal effort, 1st stop, lb.	20
Pedal effort, 10th stop, lb.	25

Specifications

Drive wheels

Front

Seating

Passengers, front/rear	2/3

Dimensions and weight

Length, in.	189
Width, in.	70
Wheelbase, in.	106
Turning circle, ft.	39
Curb weight, lb.	3130
Percent weight, front/rear	63/37
Max. load, lb.	900

Interior room

Front shoulder room, in.	57.0
Front leg room, in.	42.5
Front head room, in.	3.0
Rear shoulder room, in.	56.0
Rear fore-aft room, in.	30.5
Rear head room, in.	3.0
Door top to ground, in.	50.0
Luggage capacity	5+1

Engines available

3.0-liter V6 (190 hp)

Transmissions available

5-speed manual
4-speed automatic

Tested model

1998 GXE 4-door, 3.0-liter V6, 4-speed automatic

Tires as tested

Goodyear Eagle GA, size P205/65R15

Sport-utility vehicle

Nissan Pathfinder

The Pathfinder sells in the competitive midsized SUV market. The Pathfinder has a good ride for an SUV, and it handles responsively. Cargo space isn't as commodious as in some other SUVs in this class. The 3.3-liter V6 accelerates adequately, but it's noisy. The four-wheel drive is only a part-time system. The SE trim line is the best value. If you're considering the up-level LE, you'd probably be better off getting its cousin the Infiniti QX4, which has full-time four-wheel drive.

Body styles and prices

	Price range	Trim lines
4-door wagon 2WD	$23,999 - $30,449	XE, LE
4-door wagon 4WD	$25,999 - $32,849	XE, SE, LE

Safety information

Safety belt pretensioners	No
Center rear safety belt	Lap
Dual air bags	Standard
Side air bags	Not offered
Antilock brakes	Standard
Traction control	Not offered
Gov't front-crash test, driver/front passenger	○/○
Gov't side-crash test, driver/rear passenger	NA/NA
IIHS offset crash test	Marginal
Injury claim rate compared with all cars/type	○/◒

Reliability history

TROUBLE SPOTS	Nissan Pathfinder (4WD) 90	91	92	93	94	95	96	97
Engine							◉	◉
Cooling							◉	◉
Fuel							◓	◉
Ignition							◉	◉
Auto. transmission							◉	◉
Man. transmission							*	*
Clutch							*	*
Electrical							○	◓
Air conditioning							◉	◉
Suspension							◒	◉
Brakes							◉	◉
Exhaust							◉	◉
Body rust							◉	◉
Paint/trim							◓	◉
Body integrity							◒	◓
Body hardware							○	◓

Test judgments

Performance

Acceleration	○
Transmission	◓
Routine handling	◓
Emergency handling	○
Braking	○

Comfort

Ride, normal load	◓
Ride, full load	○
Noise	○
Driving position	◓
Front-seat comfort	◓
Rear-seat comfort	○
Climate-control system	◓

Convenience

Access	◓
Controls and displays	◓
Cargo area	○

Other

Fuel economy	●
Predicted reliability	○
Predicted depreciation	○

Test data

Acceleration

0-30 mph, sec.	3.5
0-60 mph, sec.	10.9
Quarter mile, sec.	18.2
Quarter mile, mph	75
45-65 mph, sec.	7.8

Fuel economy (regular)

EPA city/highway, mpg	15/19
CU's overall mileage, mpg	15
CU's city/highway, mpg	10/24
CU's 150-mile trip, mpg	19
Fuel refill capacity, gal.	21.1
Cruising range, mi.	365
Annual fuel: gal./cost	980/$1175

Braking from 60 mph

Dry pavement, ft.	153
Wet pavement, ft.	158
Pedal effort, 1st stop, lb.	25
Pedal effort, 10th stop, lb.	30

Specifications

Drive wheels

Rear or part-time 4WD

Seating

Passengers,front/rear	2/3

Dimensions and weight

Length, in.	178
Width, in.	69
Wheelbase, in.	106
Turning circle, ft.	40
Curb weight, lb.	4090
Percent weight, front/rear	56/44
Max. load, lb.	1060

Interior room

Front shoulder room, in.	56.5
Front leg room, in.	41.5
Front head room, in.	4.0
Rear shoulder room, in.	56.5
Rear fore-aft room, in.	29.0
Rear head room, in.	4.0
Door top to ground, in.	60.0
Cargo volume, cu.ft.	33.0

Engines available

3.3-liter V6 (168 hp)

Transmissions available

5-speed manual
4-speed automatic

Tested model

1996 LE 4-door wagon 4WD, 3.3-liter V6, 4-speed automatic

Tires as tested

General Grabber ST, size P235/70R15

Minivan

Nissan Quest

The Quest and similar Mercury Villager are made in the U.S. jointly by Ford and Nissan. These minivans ride comfortably and quietly, they feel carlike to drive, and the V6 delivers adequate power. But these vans haven't changed much in recent years, and more modern competitors like the Dodge Caravan and Toyota Sienna have eclipsed them. The Villager and Quest lack the cargo space of the Chrysler minivans, and they won't offer a left-side sliding door until the 1999 model year. But a variety of seating arrangements provides some versatility. Reliability has been average.

Body styles and prices

	Price range	Trim lines
Minivan	$23,099 - $26,069	XE, GXE, GLE

Safety information

Safety belt pretensioners	No
Center rear safety belt	Lap
Dual air bags	Standard
Side air bags	Not offered
Antilock brakes	Standard (optional on XE)
Traction control	Not offered
Gov't front-crash test, driver/front passenger	⊙/○
Gov't side-crash test, driver/rear passenger	NA/NA
IIHS offset crash test	Marginal
Injury claim rate compared with all cars/type	◓/◓

Reliability history

TROUBLE SPOTS	Nissan Quest 90	91	92	93	94	95	96	97
Engine				◓	◓	○	○	⊙
Cooling				◓	◓	⊙	⊙	⊙
Fuel				◓	◓	◓	⊙	⊙
Ignition				◓	◓	◓	⊙	⊙
Auto. transmission				◓	⊙	⊙	⊙	⊙
Man. transmission								
Clutch								
Electrical				●	◒	●	◒	○
Air conditioning				○	○	◓	◓	⊙
Suspension				○	◓	◓	◓	◓
Brakes				◒	◒	◒	◓	⊙
Exhaust				●	◓	⊙	⊙	⊙
Body rust				⊙	⊙	⊙	⊙	⊙
Paint/trim				◓	◓	◓	⊙	⊙
Body integrity				◒	○	◒	◒	○
Body hardware				●	◒	●	◒	○

Test judgments

Performance

Acceleration	○
Transmission	◓
Routine handling	○
Emergency handling	○
Braking	◓

Comfort

Ride, normal load	◓
Ride, full load	◓
Noise	◓
Driving position	◓
Front-seat comfort	◓
Middle-seat comfort	◓
Rear-seat comfort	○
Climate-control system	⊙

Convenience

Access	◓
Controls and displays	○
Cargo area	○

Other

Fuel economy	◒
Predicted reliability	○
Predicted depreciation	○

Test data

Acceleration

0-30 mph, sec.	4.0
0-60 mph, sec.	11.8
Quarter mile, sec.	18.7
Quarter mile, mph	74
45-65 mph, sec.	7.3

Fuel economy (regular)

EPA city/highway, mpg	17/23
CU's overall mileage, mpg	19
CU's city/highway, mpg	12/32
CU's 150-mile trip, mpg	23
Fuel refill capacity, gal.	20.0
Cruising range, mi.	430
Annual fuel: gal./cost	775/$930

Braking from 60 mph

Dry pavement, ft.	140
Wet pavement, ft.	161
Pedal effort, 1st stop, lb.	25
Pedal effort, 10th stop, lb.	30

Specifications

Drive wheels

Front

Seating

Passengers,front/mid/rear......2/2/3

Dimensions and weight

Length, in.	190
Width, in.	74
Wheelbase, in.	112
Turning circle, ft.	41
Curb weight, lb.	3900
Percent weight, front/rear	59/41
Max. load, lb.	1290

Interior room

Front shoulder room, in.	61.5
Front leg room, in.	40.0
Front head room, in.	5.0
Middle shoulder room, in.	63.5
Middle fore-aft room, in.	26.5
Middle head room, in.	5.5
Rear shoulder room, in.	61.5
Rear fore-aft room, in.	27.0
Rear head room, in.	4.0
Door top to ground, in.	60.0
Cargo volume, cu.ft.	55.0

Engines available

3.0-liter V6 (151 hp)

Transmissions available

4-speed automatic

Tested model

1996 Mercury Villager GS Minivan, 3.0-liter V6, 4-speed automatic

Tires as tested

General Ameri G4S, size P205/75R15

Small car

Nissan Sentra

Minor styling tweaks and a sportier 2.0-liter, 140-hp SE version are the only 1998 changes to Nissan's smallest sedan. Overall, the Sentra falls a notch or two below the best small cars on the market—the Honda Civic and Mazda Protegé ES, for example. The Sentra's 1.6-liter Four feels a bit slow in everyday driving; the automatic transmission sometimes hunts annoyingly. Steering response borders on sluggish, and the car leans a lot in turns. The ride is satisfactory on most roads. The front seats provide adequate support, but the rear seat is cramped.

Body styles and prices

	Price range	Trim lines
4-door	$11,519 - $16,749	Base, XE, GXE, GLE,SE

Safety information

Safety belt pretensioners	No
Center rear safety belt	Lap
Dual air bags	Standard
Side air bags	Not offered
Antilock brakes	Optional
Traction control	Not offered
Gov't front-crash test, driver/front passenger	○/◓
Gov't side-crash test, driver/rear passenger	○/○
IIHS offset crash test	Acceptable
Injury claim rate compared with all cars/type	●/◒

Reliability history

TROUBLE SPOTS	Nissan Sentra							
	90	91	92	93	94	95	96	97
Engine	◒	◓	◓	⊙	⊙	⊙	⊙	⊙
Cooling	◓	◓	◓	⊙	⊙	⊙	⊙	⊙
Fuel	◓	○	○	◓	◓	◓	◓	⊙
Ignition	◒	○	○	◓	◓	◓	⊙	⊙
Auto. transmission	○	○	◓	◓	◓	◓	○	*
Man. transmission	⊙	⊙	◓	⊙	⊙	⊙	⊙	*
Clutch	○	○	○	⊙	⊙	◓	⊙	*
Electrical	○	○	○	○	○	◒	○	◓
Air conditioning	○	○	◓	◓	◓	⊙	⊙	◓
Suspension	○	◓	◓	◓	⊙	⊙	⊙	⊙
Brakes	●	●	●	●	◒	○	◓	⊙
Exhaust	◒	◒	◓	◓	⊙	⊙	⊙	⊙
Body rust	◒	◓	⊙	◓	⊙	⊙	⊙	⊙
Paint/trim	●	◒	○	○	◓	○	⊙	⊙
Body integrity	◒	◒	○	○	○	○	○	◓
Body hardware	●	◒	○	○	○	○	○	◓

Test judgments

Performance	
Acceleration	○
Transmission	◓
Routine handling	◓
Emergency handling	○
Braking	○
Comfort	
Ride, normal load	○
Ride, full load	○
Noise	○
Driving position	◓
Front-seat comfort	◓
Rear-seat comfort	◒
Climate-control system	◓
Convenience	
Access	◓
Controls and displays	⊙
Trunk	◒
Other	
Fuel economy	◓
Predicted reliability	◓
Predicted depreciation	○

Test data

Acceleration

0-30 mph, sec.	4.0
0-60 mph, sec.	11.7
Quarter mile, sec.	18.7
Quarter mile, mph	74
45-65 mph, sec.	7.5

Fuel economy (regular)

EPA city/highway, mpg	28/37
CU's overall mileage, mpg	28
CU's city/highway, mpg	18/44
CU's 150-mile trip, mpg	34
Fuel refill capacity, gal.	13.2
Cruising range, mi.	415
Annual fuel: gal./cost	545/$655

Braking from 60 mph

Dry pavement, ft.	142
Wet pavement, ft.	158
Pedal effort, 1st stop, lb.	15
Pedal effort, 10th stop, lb.	20

Specifications

Drive wheels

Front

Seating

Passengers,front/rear	2/3

Dimensions and weight

Length, in.	170
Width, in.	67
Wheelbase, in.	100
Turning circle, ft.	38
Curb weight, lb.	2500
Percent weight, front/rear	63/37
Max. load, lb.	814

Interior room

Front shoulder room, in.	53.0
Front leg room, in.	41.0
Front head room, in.	3.5
Rear shoulder room, in.	52.5
Rear fore-aft room, in.	26.5
Rear head room, in.	2.0
Door top to ground, in.	49.5
Luggage capacity	4+0

Engines available

1.6-liter 4 (115 hp)
2.0-liter 4 (140 hp)

Transmissions available

5-speed manual
4-speed automatic

Tested model

1995 GXE 4-door, 1.6-liter Four, 4-speed automatic

Tires as tested

Michelin MX4, size P175/70R13

Medium car over $25,000

Oldsmobile Aurora

The Aurora, Oldsmobile's flagship large sedan, was originally conceived as an alternative to "near-luxury" imports, but it didn't quite work out that way. Its customers are people who mostly prefer large domestic sedans instead. A sophisticated 250-hp aluminum Northstar V8, similar to Cadillac's, is the Aurora's best feature. The ride was improved for 1998, but not improved enough. The Aurora still falls short in handling, braking, and control layout. Overstyling hurts this car: The low roof and steeply raked roof pillars inhibit access and compromise the view out. The cockpit feels claustrophobic, and the driving position is uncomfortable. The nonadjustable shoulder belt anchors can make the belts uncomfortable for tall people. A wide turning circle makes parking harder than it has to be. Reliability has been average lately.

Body styles and prices

	Price range	Trim lines
4-door	$36,020	—

Safety information

Safety belt pretensioners	No
Center rear safety belt	Lap
Dual air bags	Standard
Side air bags	Not offered
Antilock brakes	Standard
Traction control	Standard
Gov't front-crash test, driver/front passenger	○/○
Gov't side-crash test, driver/rear passenger	NA/NA
IIHS offset crash test	NA
Injury claim rate compared with all cars/type	◉/◉

Reliability history

TROUBLE SPOTS	90	91	92	93	94	95	96	97
Engine						◒	◒	◉
Cooling						◒	◉	◉
Fuel						◒	◉	◉
Ignition						◒	◉	◉
Auto. transmission						◒	◉	◒
Man. transmission								
Clutch								
Electrical						◓	◓	●
Air conditioning						○	◒	◒
Suspension						◒	◉	◒
Brakes						◒	◒	◒
Exhaust						◉	◉	◉
Body rust						◉	◉	◉
Paint/trim						◒	◒	◒
Body integrity						◓	◓	◒
Body hardware						●	◒	◒

Test judgments

Performance

Acceleration	◒
Transmission	◉
Routine handling	○
Emergency handling	○
Braking	○

Comfort

Ride, normal load	○
Ride, full load	○
Noise	◒
Driving position	○
Front-seat comfort	◒
Rear-seat comfort	○
Climate-control system	◉

Convenience

Access	○
Controls and displays	○
Trunk	○

Other

Fuel economy	◓
Predicted reliability	○
Predicted depreciation	◓

Test data

Acceleration

0-30 mph, sec.	3.2
0-60 mph, sec.	7.7
Quarter mile, sec.	16.0
Quarter mile, mph	89
45-65 mph, sec.	4.9

Fuel economy (premium)

EPA city/highway, mpg	17/26
CU's overall mileage, mpg	19
CU's city/highway, mpg	12/32
CU's 150-mile trip, mpg	24
Fuel refill capacity, gal.	20.0
Cruising range, mi.	450
Annual fuel: gal./cost	775/$1085

Braking from 60 mph

Dry pavement, ft.	151
Wet pavement, ft.	180
Pedal effort, 1st stop, lb.	15
Pedal effort, 10th stop, lb.	20

Specifications

Drive wheels

Front

Seating

Passengers,front/rear	2/3

Dimensions and weight

Length, in.	205
Width, in.	74
Wheelbase, in.	114
Turning circle, ft.	43
Curb weight, lb.	3990
Percent weight, front/rear	63/37
Max. load, lb.	915

Interior room

Front shoulder room, in.	57.5
Front leg room, in.	41.5
Front head room, in.	2.0
Rear shoulder room, in.	57.5
Rear fore-aft room, in.	30.5
Rear head room, in.	1.5
Door top to ground, in.	50.5
Luggage capacity	4+2

Engines available

4.0-liter V8 (250 hp)

Transmissions available

4-speed automatic

Tested model

1998 4-door, 4.0-liter V8, 4-speed automatic

Tires as tested

Goodyear Eagle GA, size P235/60R16

Medium car under $25,000

Oldsmobile Cutlass

The Cutlass was all-new for 1997. This corporate twin of the Chevrolet Malibu is a well-rounded performer overall, but it needs a little more polish to join the top ranks of midsized, midpriced sedans. The chassis irons out most road bumps well but feels a little jittery and unsettled on good roads. Handling is sound but unexceptional. The 3.1-liter V6 accelerates quite nicely but isn't very refined. The standard automatic transmission shifts very smoothly. The interior is spacious, and the seats are fairly comfortable. Rear seating is fine for three. The trunk is roomy.

Body styles and prices

	Price range	Trim lines
4-door	$17,800 - $19,425	GL, GLS

Safety information

Safety belt pretensioners	No
Center rear safety belt	Lap
Dual air bags	Standard
Side air bags	Not offered
Antilock brakes	Standard
Traction control	Not offered
Gov't front-crash test, driver/front passenger	◒/◒
Gov't side-crash test, driver/rear passenger	●/○
IIHS offset crash test	NA
Injury claim rate compared with all cars/type	NA/NA

Reliability history

TROUBLE SPOTS	Oldsmobile Cutlass 90	91	92	93	94	95	96	97
Engine								⦿
Cooling								⦿
Fuel								⦿
Ignition								⦿
Auto. transmission								⦿
Man. transmission								
Clutch								
Electrical								○
Air conditioning								◒
Suspension								◒
Brakes								○
Exhaust								⦿
Body rust								⦿
Paint/trim								◒
Body integrity								○
Body hardware								⦿

Test judgments

Performance

Acceleration	◒
Transmission	⦿
Routine handling	◒
Emergency handling	○
Braking	◒

Comfort

Ride, normal load	○
Ride, full load	○
Noise	◒
Driving position	◒
Front-seat comfort	◒
Rear-seat comfort	◒
Climate-control system	⦿

Convenience

Access	◒
Controls and displays	⦿
Trunk	◒

Other

Fuel economy	○
Predicted reliability	○
Predicted depreciation	NA

Test data

Acceleration

0-30 mph, sec.	3.2
0-60 mph, sec.	9.2
Quarter mile, sec.	17.0
Quarter mile, mph	83
45-65 mph, sec.	5.8

Fuel economy (regular)

EPA city/highway, mpg	20/29
CU's overall mileage, mpg	24
CU's city/highway, mpg	15/38
CU's 150-mile trip, mpg	30
Fuel refill capacity, gal.	15.2
Cruising range, mi.	425
Annual fuel: gal./cost	635/$760

Braking from 60 mph

Dry pavement, ft.	130
Wet pavement, ft.	170
Pedal effort, 1st stop, lb.	15
Pedal effort, 10th stop, lb.	25

Specifications

Drive wheels

Front

Seating

Passengers,front/rear	2/3

Dimensions and weight

Length, in.	192
Width, in.	69
Wheelbase, in.	107
Turning circle, ft.	40
Curb weight, lb.	3075
Percent weight, front/rear	64/36
Max. load, lb.	915

Interior room

Front shoulder room, in.	55.0
Front leg room, in.	43.0
Front head room, in.	4.5
Rear shoulder room, in.	54.0
Rear fore-aft room, in.	30.5
Rear head room, in.	2.0
Door top to ground, in.	50.5
Luggage capacity	5+1

Engines available

3.1-liter V6 (150 hp)

Transmissions available

4-speed automatic

Tested model

1997 GLS 4-door, 3.1-liter V6, 4-speed automatic

Tires as tested

Firestone Affinity, size P215/60R15

Medium car under $25,000

Oldsmobile Intrigue

PROMISING

The Intrigue was new for 1998, and it represents a giant leap for Oldsmobile: a solid performer that handles well and boasts a well-designed interior. It rides well on most roads. The V6 accelerates briskly, though it's not as refined as those from Toyota, Nissan, or even Ford. The cockpit is roomy, but rear headroom is limited. This fall it's slated to receive a modern 3.5-liter V6 to address this shortcoming. The front seats are adequately comfortable, and the rear seat is fairly accommodating. The trunk is roomy as well, and the split rear seatback folds down to expand it further.

Body styles and prices

	Price range	Trim lines
4-door	$20,890 - $24,110	Base, GL, GLS

Safety information

Safety belt pretensioners	No
Center rear safety belt	Lap
Dual air bags	Standard
Side air bags	Not offered
Antilock brakes	Standard
Traction control	Standard
Gov't front-crash test, driver/front passenger	◒/○
Gov't side-crash test, driver/rear passenger	○/NA
IIHS offset crash test	NA
Injury claim rate compared with all cars/type	NA/NA

Reliability history

TROUBLE SPOTS	90 91 92 93 94 95 96 97
Engine	
Cooling	
Fuel	
Ignition	
Auto. transmission	NO
Man. transmission	
Clutch	DATA
Electrical	
Air conditioning	NEW
Suspension	
Brakes	MODEL
Exhaust	
Body rust	
Paint/trim	
Body integrity	
Body hardware	

Test judgments

Performance

Acceleration	◒
Transmission	●
Routine handling	◒
Emergency handling	○
Braking	◒

Comfort

Ride, normal load	◒
Ride, full load	◒
Noise	◒
Driving position	◒
Front-seat comfort	◒
Rear-seat comfort	◒
Climate-control system	●

Convenience

Access	◒
Controls and displays	●
Trunk	◒

Other

Fuel economy	◓
Predicted reliability	New
Predicted depreciation	NA

Test data

Acceleration

0-30 mph, sec.	3.2
0-60 mph, sec.	9.1
Quarter mile, sec.	16.9
Quarter mile, mph	84
45-65 mph, sec.	5.9

Fuel economy (regular)

EPA city/highway, mpg	19/30
CU's overall mileage, mpg	20
CU's city/highway, mpg	12/34
CU's 150-mile trip, mpg	25
Fuel refill capacity, gal.	18.0
Cruising range, mi.	425
Annual fuel: gal./cost	745/$895

Braking from 60 mph

Dry pavement, ft.	138
Wet pavement, ft.	160
Pedal effort, 1st stop, lb.	20
Pedal effort, 10th stop, lb.	25

Specifications

Drive wheels

Front

Seating

Passengers, front/rear	2/3

Dimensions and weight

Length, in.	196
Width, in.	74
Wheelbase, in.	109
Turning circle, ft.	40
Curb weight, lb.	3470
Percent weight, front/rear	64/36
Max. load, lb.	917

Interior room

Front shoulder room, in.	58.0
Front leg room, in.	43.0
Front head room, in.	4.5
Rear shoulder room, in.	56.0
Rear fore-aft room, in.	29.0
Rear head room, in.	2.5
Door top to ground, in.	51.0
Luggage capacity	5+1

Engines available

3.8-liter V6 (195 hp)

Transmissions available

4-speed automatic

Tested model

1998 GL 4-door, 3.8-liter V6, 4-speed automatic

Tires as tested

Goodyear Eagle RS-A, size P225/60R16

Oldsmobile Silhouette

The Silhouette and similar Chevrolet Venture and Pontiac Trans Sport received side-impact air bags this year. A useful left-side sliding door and powered right-side door are available. Ride and handling are both good. The front seats are quite comfortable. These are among the few front-wheel-drive minivans that offer a three-seat middle row. The Trans Sport did especially poorly in an offset frontal crash test conducted by the Insurance Institute for Highway Safety. We assume the Venture and Silhouette would have fared similarly. First-year reliability was extremely poor.

Body styles and prices

	Price range	Trim lines
Minivan regular	$24,430	GS
Minivan extended	$23,965 - $27,965	GL, GLS

Safety information

Safety belt pretensioners ....Front
Center rear safety belt ....Lap
Dual air bags ....Standard
Side air bags ....Standard
Antilock brakes..Standard
Traction control ....Optional
Gov't front-crash test, driver/front passenger ....◓/○
Gov't side-crash test, driver/rear passenger ....NA/NA
IIHS offset crash test ....Poor
Injury claim rate compared with all cars/type............NA/NA

Reliability history

TROUBLE SPOTS	Oldsmobile Silhouette (ext.) 90	91	92	93	94	95	96	97
Engine								◉
Cooling								◉
Fuel								◓
Ignition								◓
Auto. transmission								◉
Man. transmission								
Clutch								
Electrical								○
Air conditioning								◓
Suspension								◓
Brakes								◓
Exhaust								◓
Body rust								◉
Paint/trim								○
Body integrity								◒
Body hardware								●

Test judgments

Performance
Acceleration ....◓
Transmission ....◉
Routine handling ....○
Emergency handling ....○
Braking ....○

Comfort
Ride, normal load ....◓
Ride, full load ....◓
Noise ....◓
Driving position ....◓
Front-seat comfort ....◓
Middle-seat comfort ....○
Rear-seat comfort ....○
Climate-control system ....◉

Convenience
Access ....◓
Controls and displays ....◓
Cargo area ....◓

Other
Fuel economy ....◒
Predicted reliability ....●
Predicted depreciation ....NA

Test data

Acceleration
0-30 mph, sec. 3.5
0-60 mph, sec. 10.0
Quarter mile, sec. 17.5
Quarter mile, mph 81
45-65 mph, sec. 6.6

Fuel economy (regular)
EPA city/highway, mpg 18/25
CU's overall mileage, mpg 19
CU's city/highway, mpg.......12/33
CU's 150-mile trip, mpg 24
Fuel refill capacity, gal. 25.0
Cruising range, mi. 565
Annual fuel: gal./cost ......785/$940

Braking from 60 mph
Dry pavement, ft. 147
Wet pavement, ft. 176
Pedal effort, 1st stop, lb. 15
Pedal effort, 10th stop, lb. 25

Specifications

Drive wheels
Front

Seating
Passengers,front/mid/rear......2/3/3

Dimensions and weight
Length, in. 201
Width, in. 72
Wheelbase, in. 120
Turning circle, ft. 42
Curb weight, lb. 3890
Percent weight, front/rear 59/41
Max. load, lb. 1475

Interior room
Front shoulder room, in. 60.0
Front leg room, in. 41.0
Front head room, in. 6.0
Middle shoulder room, in. 61.5
Middle fore-aft room, in. 30.0
Middle head room, in. 5.5
Rear shoulder room, in. 60.0
Rear fore-aft room, in. 29.5
Rear head room, in. 5.0
Door top to ground, in. 62.0
Cargo volume, cu.ft. 76.0

Engines available
3.4-liter V6 (180 hp)

Transmissions available
4-speed automatic

Tested model
1997 Chevrolet Venture LS
Minivan extended, 3.4-liter V6,
4-speed automatic

Tires as tested
Firestone FR680, size P215/70R15

Medium car under $25,000

Plymouth Breeze

The Breeze is the least expensive of Chrysler's midsized sedans, which include the upscale Chrysler Cirrus and mid-market Dodge Stratus. It's an adequate performer overall, with a spacious interior. Braking is about average. The ride feels jittery even on smooth roads. The handling is sound but not crisp. The 132-hp, 2.0-liter Four works hard and noisily to pull the car up hills. For 1998, the 150-hp, 2.4-liter Four, also found in the Stratus, joins the options list. The transmission could shift more smoothly. Reliability for the Breeze (but not the Cirrus or Stratus) has been average of late.

Body styles and prices

	Price range	Trim lines
4-door	$14,675	—

Safety information

Safety belt pretensioners .... No
Center rear safety belt .... Lap
Dual air bags .... Standard
Side air bags .... Not offered
Antilock brakes .... Optional
Traction control .... Not offered
Gov't front-crash test, driver/front passenger .... ○/◓
Gov't side-crash test, driver/rear passenger .... ○/◒
IIHS offset crash test .... Poor
Injury claim rate compared with all cars/type .... ○/◓

Reliability history

TROUBLE SPOTS	Plymouth Breeze 90	91	92	93	94	95	96	97
Engine							●	Insufficient data
Cooling							●	
Fuel							●	
Ignition							◓	
Auto. transmission							★	
Man. transmission							★	
Clutch							★	
Electrical							○	
Air conditioning							●	
Suspension							◓	
Brakes							○	
Exhaust							●	
Body rust							●	
Paint/trim							◓	
Body integrity							◒	
Body hardware							○	

Test judgments

Performance
Acceleration .... ○
Transmission .... ◓
Routine handling .... ◓
Emergency handling .... ◓
Braking .... ○

Comfort
Ride, normal load .... ○
Ride, full load .... ○
Noise .... ◓
Driving position .... ◓
Front-seat comfort .... ◓
Rear-seat comfort .... ◓
Climate-control system .... ◓

Convenience
Access .... ◓
Controls and displays .... ●
Trunk .... ◓

Other
Fuel economy .... ○
Predicted reliability .... ○
Predicted depreciation .... NA

Test data

Acceleration
0-30 mph, sec. 3.9
0-60 mph, sec. 11.7
Quarter mile, sec. 18.7
Quarter mile, mph 74
45-65 mph, sec. 7.5

Fuel economy (regular)
EPA city/highway, mpg 22/32
CU's overall mileage, mpg 23
CU's city/highway, mpg 14/40
CU's 150-mile trip, mpg 29
Fuel refill capacity, gal. 16.0
Cruising range, mi. 435
Annual fuel: gal./cost .... 655/$785

Braking from 60 mph
Dry pavement, ft. 146
Wet pavement, ft. 160
Pedal effort, 1st stop, lb. 20
Pedal effort, 10th stop, lb. 25

Specifications

Drive wheels
Front

Seating
Passengers, front/rear 2/3

Dimensions and weight
Length, in. 186
Width, in. 72
Wheelbase, in. 108
Turning circle, ft. 39
Curb weight, lb. 3050
Percent weight, front/rear 63/37
Max. load, lb. 865

Interior room
Front shoulder room, in. 55.5
Front leg room, in. 41.5
Front head room, in. 3.5
Rear shoulder room, in. 54.5
Rear fore-aft room, in. 30.0
Rear head room, in. 2.5
Door top to ground, in. 49.5
Luggage capacity .... 5+0

Engines available
2.0-liter 4 (132 hp)
2.4-liter 4 (150 hp)

Transmissions available
5-speed manual
4-speed automatic

Tested model
1996 4-door, 2.0-liter Four, 4-speed automatic

Tires as tested
Michelin XW4, size P195/70R14

Minivan

Plymouth Grand Voyager

This long-wheelbase version of the Plymouth Voyager is similar to the Dodge Grand Caravan and Chrysler Town & Country. It rides quietly, handles fairly nimbly, and converts easily from people-carrier to roomy cargo-hauler. The 3.3-liter V6 accelerates adequately. The front seats are fairly comfortable, but some of our testers found the padding a little lumpy. The middle and rear seats are very heavy, but they have little wheels underneath to help you move them. A second, left-side sliding door is a handy option. Headlights are weak. Reliability has been spotty.

Body styles and prices

	Price range	Trim lines
Minivan	$20,125 - $22,285	Base, SE

Safety information

Safety belt pretensioners ....No
Center rear safety belt ....Lap
Dual air bags ....Standard
Side air bags ....Not offered
Antilock brakes.......................Standard (optional on Base)
Traction control ....Not offered
Gov't front-crash test, driver/front passenger ....○/◒
Gov't side-crash test, driver/rear passenger ....NA/NA
IIHS offset crash test ....Marginal
Injury claim rate compared with all cars/type ....●/●

Reliability history

TROUBLE SPOTS	Plymouth Grand Voyager V6 90	91	92	93	94	95	96	97
Engine							●	●
Cooling							◓	●
Fuel							○	●
Ignition							●	●
Auto. transmission							◓	●
Man. transmission								
Clutch								
Electrical							◒	○
Air conditioning							◓	●
Suspension							◓	●
Brakes							◒	◓
Exhaust							●	●
Body rust							●	●
Paint/trim							◓	◓
Body integrity							◒	○
Body hardware							◒	○

Test judgments

Performance
Acceleration ....○
Transmission ....●
Routine handling ....○
Emergency handling ....○
Braking ....◓

Comfort
Ride, normal load ....◓
Ride, full load ....◓
Noise ....◓
Driving position ....◓
Front-seat comfort ....◓
Middle-seat comfort ....◓
Rear-seat comfort ....◓
Climate-control system ....●

Convenience
Access ....◓
Controls and displays ....●
Cargo area ....◓

Other
Fuel economy ....◒
Predicted reliability ....◒
Predicted depreciation ....◒

Test data

Acceleration
0-30 mph, sec. 3.7
0-60 mph, sec. 11.2
Quarter mile, sec. 18.4
Quarter mile, mph 75
45-65 mph, sec. 7.2

Fuel economy (regular)
EPA city/highway, mpg 18/24
CU's overall mileage, mpg 18
CU's city/highway, mpg.......11/31
CU's 150-mile trip, mpg 23
Fuel refill capacity, gal. 20.0
Cruising range, mi. 420
Annual fuel: gal./cost ......825/$990

Braking from 60 mph
Dry pavement, ft. 139
Wet pavement, ft. 168
Pedal effort, 1st stop, lb. 20
Pedal effort, 10th stop, lb. 25

Specifications

Drive wheels
Front

Seating
Passengers,front/mid/rear......2/2/3

Dimensions and weight
Length, in. 200
Width, in. 77
Wheelbase, in. 119
Turning circle, ft. 41
Curb weight, lb. 4050
Percent weight, front/rear 58/42
Max. load, lb. 1150

Interior room
Front shoulder room, in. 62.5
Front leg room, in. 41.0
Front head room, in. 5.5
Middle shoulder room, in. 64.0
Middle fore-aft room, in. 29.5
Middle head room, in. 5.0
Rear shoulder room, in. 61.0
Rear fore-aft room, in. 30.0
Rear head room, in. 3.0
Door top to ground, in. 60.5
Cargo volume, cu.ft. 76.0

Engines available
2.4-liter 4 (150 hp), 3.0-liter V6 (150 hp), 3.3-liter V6 (158 hp)

Transmissions available
3-speed automatic
4-speed automatic

Tested model
1997 SE Minivan, 3.3-liter V6, 4-speed automatic

Tires as tested
Goodyear Conquest, size P215/65R15

Small car

Plymouth Neon

The Dodge and Plymouth Neon twins remain basically unchanged for 1998. (A sporty Dodge Neon R/T is due out soon.) The Neon has a relatively roomy interior. The stronger of the two four-cylinder engines is fairly sprightly when it's mated to the five-speed manual transmission, though it sounds harsh. The three-speed automatic transmission robs lots of power from the engine. And with the automatic, fuel economy is unimpressive for a small car. The Neon handles predictably. The front seats are generally comfortable, and three adults can fit in the rear. Reliability has been subpar.

Body styles and prices

	Price range	Trim lines
2-door	$11,200 - $11,455	Base, Highline
4-door	$11,300 - $11,555	Base, Highline

Safety information

Safety belt pretensioners .... No
Center rear safety belt .... Lap
Dual air bags .... Standard
Side air bags .... Not offered
Antilock brakes .... Optional
Traction control .... Not offered
Gov't front-crash test, driver/front passenger .... ○/◓
Gov't side-crash test, driver/rear passenger .... ◒/○
IIHS offset crash test .... Poor
Injury claim rate compared with all cars/type .... ◒/○

Reliability history

TROUBLE SPOTS	Plymouth Neon 90	91	92	93	94	95	96	97
Engine						○	◓	◉
Cooling						◉	◓	◉
Fuel						○	◓	◉
Ignition						○	◓	◉
Auto. transmission						◓	◓	◉
Man. transmission						◓	◉	*
Clutch						◉	◉	*
Electrical						◒	◒	◉
Air conditioning						○	◓	◓
Suspension						◓	◓	◉
Brakes						●	○	◉
Exhaust						◓	◉	◉
Body rust						◉	◉	◉
Paint/trim						○	◓	◉
Body integrity						●	◒	○
Body hardware						◒	◒	◉

Test judgments

Performance
Acceleration .... ◓
Transmission .... ◓
Routine handling .... ◓
Emergency handling .... ◓
Braking .... ○

Comfort
Ride, normal load .... ◒
Ride, full load .... ◒
Noise .... ◒
Driving position .... ◓
Front-seat comfort .... ◓
Rear-seat comfort .... ◒
Climate-control system .... ◉

Convenience
Access .... ○
Controls and displays .... ◓
Trunk .... ◒

Other
Fuel economy .... ◓
Predicted reliability .... ◒
Predicted depreciation .... ○

Test data

Acceleration
0-30 mph, sec. 3.2
0-60 mph, sec. 8.4
Quarter mile, sec. 16.6
Quarter mile, mph 87
45-65 mph, sec. 5.9

Fuel economy (regular)
EPA city/highway, mpg 29/39
CU's overall mileage, mpg 30
CU's city/highway, mpg 21/44
CU's 150-mile trip, mpg 35
Fuel refill capacity, gal. 12.5
Cruising range, mi. 410
Annual fuel: gal./cost .... 495/$595

Braking from 60 mph
Dry pavement, ft. 140
Wet pavement, ft. 153
Pedal effort, 1st stop, lb. 10
Pedal effort, 10th stop, lb. 15

Specifications

Drive wheels
Front

Seating
Passengers, front/rear 2/3

Dimensions and weight
Length, in. 172
Width, in. 68
Wheelbase, in. 104
Turning circle, ft. 38
Curb weight, lb. 2545
Percent weight, front/rear 64/36
Max. load, lb. 865

Interior room
Front shoulder room, in. 51.5
Front leg room, in. 42.0
Front head room, in. 5.0
Rear shoulder room, in. 52.0
Rear fore-aft room, in. 28.0
Rear head room, in. 1.5
Door top to ground, in. 49.0
Luggage capacity .... 3+2

Engines available
2.0-liter 4 (132 hp)
2.0-liter 4 (150 hp)

Transmissions available
5-speed manual, 3-speed auto.

Tested model
1996 Dodge Neon Coupe Sport, 2.0-liter Four, 5-speed manual

Tires as tested
Goodyear Eagle RS-A, size P185/65R14

Minivan

Plymouth Voyager

The short-wheelbase Dodge Caravan/Plymouth Voyager twins perform exceptionally well overall. They ride quietly, handle nimbly, and convert easily from people-carrier to cargo-hauler. A second, left-side sliding door, a handy feature, is either standard or optional, depending on the trim line. The 3.3-liter V6 is the engine of choice. While the middle and rear seats are easy to unhitch, they're very heavy. Small wheels beneath make them easier to wrestle out and store. Headlights are weak. Reliability has been spotty.

Body styles and prices

	Price range	Trim lines
Minivan	$17,415 - $21,290	Base, SE

Safety information

Safety belt pretensioners ..... No
Center rear safety belt ..... Lap
Dual air bags ..... Standard
Side air bags ..... Not offered
Antilock brakes ..... Standard (optional on Base)
Traction control ..... Not offered
Gov't front-crash test, driver/front passenger ..... ○/○
Gov't side-crash test, driver/rear passenger ..... NA/NA
IIHS offset crash test ..... NA
Injury claim rate compared with all cars/type ..... ◒/○

Reliability history

TROUBLE SPOTS	90	91	92	93	94	95	96	97
Engine							◒	◉
Cooling							◉	◉
Fuel							○	◉
Ignition							◉	◉
Auto. transmission							◒	◉
Man. transmission								
Clutch								
Electrical							○	◒
Air conditioning							◒	◉
Suspension							◒	◉
Brakes							◐	◒
Exhaust							◉	◉
Body rust							◉	◉
Paint/trim							◒	◉
Body integrity							○	○
Body hardware							◐	○

Plymouth Voyager V6

Test judgments

Performance
Acceleration ..... ○
Transmission ..... ◉
Routine handling ..... ◒
Emergency handling ..... ○
Braking ..... ○

Comfort
Ride, normal load ..... ◒
Ride, full load ..... ◒
Noise ..... ◒
Driving position ..... ◒
Front-seat comfort ..... ◒
Middle-seat comfort ..... ◒
Rear-seat comfort ..... ◒
Climate-control system ..... ◉

Convenience
Access ..... ◒
Controls and displays ..... ◉
Cargo area ..... ◒

Other
Fuel economy ..... ●
Predicted reliability ..... ○
Predicted depreciation ..... ◐

Test data

Acceleration
0-30 mph, sec. 3.6
0-60 mph, sec. 11.0
Quarter mile, sec. 18.3
Quarter mile, mph 76
45-65 mph, sec. 7.4

Fuel economy (regular)
EPA city/highway, mpg 18/24
CU's overall mileage, mpg 19
CU's city/highway, mpg 12/30
CU's 150-mile trip, mpg 22
Fuel refill capacity, gal. 20.0
Cruising range, mi. 420
Annual fuel: gal./cost ..... 810/$970

Braking from 60 mph
Dry pavement, ft. 144
Wet pavement, ft. 155
Pedal effort, 1st stop, lb. 20
Pedal effort, 10th stop, lb. 30

Specifications

Drive wheels
Front

Seating
Passengers, front/mid/rear 2/2/3

Dimensions and weight
Length, in. 186
Width, in. 76
Wheelbase, in. 113
Turning circle, ft. 40
Curb weight, lb. 3985
Percent weight, front/rear 59/41
Max. load, lb. 1150

Interior room
Front shoulder room, in. 62.5
Front leg room, in. 41.0
Front head room, in. 5.5
Middle shoulder room, in. 64.0
Middle fore-aft room, in. 28.0
Middle head room, in. 5.0
Rear shoulder room, in. 61.5
Rear fore-aft room, in. 26.5
Rear head room, in. 3.0
Door top to ground, in. 60.0
Cargo volume, cu.ft. 64.0

Engines available
2.4-liter 4 (150 hp)
3.0-liter V6 (150 hp)
3.3-liter V6 (158 hp)

Transmissions available
3-speed automatic
4-speed automatic

Tested model
1996 Dodge Caravan LE Minivan, 3.3-liter V6, 4-speed automatic

Tires as tested
Michelin XW4, size P215/65R15

Medium car under $25,000

Pontiac Grand Prix

The Grand Prix is the sportiest of a clan that includes the Buick Century, Buick Regal, and Oldsmobile Intrigue. The Grand Prix corners crisply with little body lean. The steering is nicely weighted and responsive. The 3.8-liter V6 performs nicely. The automatic transmission shifts very smoothly. The front seats are roomy and reasonably comfortable, though their padding is a little skimpy. The rear seat is spacious enough, though the cushion is rather low. The ride is not as comfortable as it should be. First-year reliability has been average.

Body styles and prices

	Price range	Trim lines
2-door	$20,415	GT
4-door	$18,795 - $20,665	SE, GT

Safety information

Safety belt pretensioners	No
Center rear safety belt	Lap
Dual air bags	Standard
Side air bags	Not offered
Antilock brakes	Standard
Traction control	Standard
Gov't front-crash test, driver/front passenger	◒/●
Gov't side-crash test, driver/rear passenger	NA/NA
IIHS offset crash test	Acceptable
Injury claim rate compared with all cars/type	NA/NA

Reliability history

TROUBLE SPOTS	Pontiac Grand Prix 90	91	92	93	94	95	96	97
Engine								●
Cooling								●
Fuel								●
Ignition								●
Auto. transmission								●
Man. transmission								
Clutch								
Electrical								◒
Air conditioning								●
Suspension								●
Brakes								●
Exhaust								●
Body rust								●
Paint/trim								●
Body integrity								○
Body hardware								◒

Test judgments

Performance

Acceleration	◒
Transmission	●
Routine handling	◒
Emergency handling	◒
Braking	○

Comfort

Ride, normal load	○
Ride, full load	○
Noise	◒
Driving position	◒
Front-seat comfort	◒
Rear-seat comfort	○
Climate-control system	●

Convenience

Access	◒
Controls and displays	◒
Trunk	◒

Other

Fuel economy	○
Predicted reliability	○
Predicted depreciation	NA

Test data

Acceleration

0-30 mph, sec.	3.2
0-60 mph, sec.	8.9
Quarter mile, sec.	16.8
Quarter mile, mph	84
45-65 mph, sec.	5.6

Fuel economy (regular)

EPA city/highway, mpg	19/30
CU's overall mileage, mpg	21
CU's city/highway, mpg	13/36
CU's 150-mile trip, mpg	26
Fuel refill capacity, gal.	18.0
Cruising range, mi.	440
Annual fuel: gal./cost	715/$860

Braking from 60 mph

Dry pavement, ft.	143
Wet pavement, ft.	168
Pedal effort, 1st stop, lb.	15
Pedal effort, 10th stop, lb.	20

Specifications

Drive wheels

Front

Seating

Passengers,front/rear	2/3

Dimensions and weight

Length, in.	197
Width, in.	73
Wheelbase, in.	111
Turning circle, ft.	40
Curb weight, lb.	3400
Percent weight, front/rear	65/35
Max. load, lb.	915

Interior room

Front shoulder room, in.	58.0
Front leg room, in.	42.5
Front head room, in.	4.0
Rear shoulder room, in.	56.0
Rear fore-aft room, in.	29.5
Rear head room, in.	2.5
Door top to ground, in.	49.5
Luggage capacity	5+1

Engines available

3.1-liter V6 (160 hp)
3.8-liter V6 (195 hp)
3.8-liter V6 supercharged (240 hp)

Transmissions available

4-speed automatic

Tested model

1997 SE 4-door, 3.8-liter V6, 4-speed automatic

Tires as tested

Goodyear Eagle LS, size P225/60R16

Small car

Pontiac Sunfire

The Sunfire and the Chevrolet Cavalier are cousins. The standard 115-hp, 2.2-liter Four in the sedan we tested sounded raucous when revved, but it accelerated adequately. (Pontiac says the engine is quieter for 1998.) The optional 150-hp, 2.4-liter Four in the coupe we also tested is gutsier. The standard manual transmission feels imprecise. We preferred the smooth-shifting four-speed automatic. The front seats feel comfortable on short trips, but thin padding makes them fatiguing on long journeys. The rear seat is inhospitable, especially in the coupe.

Body styles and prices

	Price range	Trim lines
2-door	$12,495 - $15,495	SE, GT
4-door	$12,495	SE
Convertible	$19,495	SE

Safety information

Safety belt pretensioners	No
Center rear safety belt	Lap
Dual air bags	Standard
Side air bags	Not offered
Antilock brakes	Standard
Traction control	Standard with 4-speed automatic
Gov't front-crash test, driver/front passenger	◓/◓
Gov't side-crash test, driver/rear passenger	●/○
IIHS offset crash test	Poor
Injury claim rate compared with all cars/type	◒/◓

Reliability history

TROUBLE SPOTS	Pontiac Sunfire 90	91	92	93	94	95	96	97
Engine						○	◓	◉
Cooling						◓	◓	◉
Fuel						◓	◓	◉
Ignition						◓	◓	◓
Auto. transmission						◓	◓	◉
Man. transmission						*	◓	◓
Clutch						*	○	◉
Electrical						◒	◒	◓
Air conditioning						◉	◉	◉
Suspension						◓	◓	◓
Brakes						◒	○	◓
Exhaust						◓	◓	◉
Body rust						◉	◉	◉
Paint/trim						◓	◓	◉
Body integrity						◒	●	○
Body hardware						◒	○	◓

Test judgments

Performance	
Acceleration	◓
Transmission	◓
Routine handling	◓
Emergency handling	○
Braking	◓
Comfort	
Ride, normal load	○
Ride, full load	◒
Noise	○
Driving position	○
Front-seat comfort	◓
Rear-seat comfort	◒
Climate-control system	◉
Convenience	
Access	○
Controls and displays	◉
Trunk	◒
Other	
Fuel economy	○
Predicted reliability	○
Predicted depreciation	○

Test data

Acceleration	
0-30 mph, sec.	2.9
0-60 mph, sec.	8.1
Quarter mile, sec.	16.3
Quarter mile, mph	86
45-65 mph, sec.	5.2
Fuel economy (regular)	
EPA city/highway, mpg	23/33
CU's overall mileage, mpg	25
CU's city/highway, mpg	17/36
CU's 150-mile trip, mpg	30
Fuel refill capacity, gal.	15.2
Cruising range, mi.	420
Annual fuel: gal./cost	605/$725
Braking from 60 mph	
Dry pavement, ft.	135
Wet pavement, ft.	153
Pedal effort, 1st stop, lb.	20
Pedal effort, 10th stop, lb.	25

Specifications

Drive wheels
Front

Seating

Passengers, front/rear	2/3

Dimensions and weight

Length, in.	182
Width, in.	67
Wheelbase, in.	104
Turning circle, ft.	38
Curb weight, lb.	2890
Percent weight, front/rear	65/35
Max. load, lb.	882

Interior room

Front shoulder room, in.	54.0
Front leg room, in.	41.0
Front head room, in.	2.5
Rear shoulder room, in.	50.0
Rear fore-aft room, in.	27.0
Rear head room, in.	1.0
Door top to ground, in.	49.0
Luggage capacity	3+1

Engines available
2.2-liter 4 (115 hp)
2.4-liter 4 (150 hp)

Transmissions available
5-speed manual, 3-speed automatic, 4-speed automatic

Tested model
1996 GT 2-door, 2.4-liter Four, 5-speed manual

Tires as tested
Goodyear Eagle RS-A, size P205/55R16

Minivan

Pontiac Trans Sport

The Trans Sport received side air bags for 1998. Equipped with the Montana trim package, it poses as a sport-utility vehicle, but lacks four-wheel drive—and delivers a stiff ride. The Trans Sport, like its Chevrolet Venture and Oldsmobile Silhouette cousins, comes in both regular and longer versions. Options include a useful left-side sliding door and powered right-side door. The front seats are quite comfortable. The Trans Sport did especially poorly in an offset frontal crash test conducted by the Insurance Institute for Highway Safety. First-year reliability has been extremely poor.

Body styles and prices

	Price range	Trim lines
Minivan regular	$20,840 - $22,380	SE
Minivan extended	$23,090	SE

Safety information

Safety belt pretensioners	Front
Center rear safety belt	Lap
Dual air bags	Standard
Side air bags	Standard
Antilock brakes	Standard
Traction control	Optional
Gov't front-crash test, driver/front passenger	◓/○
Gov't side-crash test, driver/rear passenger	NA/NA
IIHS offset crash test	Poor
Injury claim rate compared with all cars/type	NA/NA

Reliability history

TROUBLE SPOTS	Pontiac Trans Sport (ext.) 90	91	92	93	94	95	96	97
Engine								⦿
Cooling								⦿
Fuel								◓
Ignition								◓
Auto. transmission								⦿
Man. transmission								
Clutch								
Electrical								○
Air conditioning								◓
Suspension								◓
Brakes								◓
Exhaust								◓
Body rust								⦿
Paint/trim								○
Body integrity								◒
Body hardware								●

Test judgments

Performance

Acceleration	○
Transmission	⦿
Routine handling	○
Emergency handling	○
Braking	◓

Comfort

Ride, normal load	○
Ride, full load	○
Noise	◓
Driving position	◓
Front-seat comfort	◓
Middle-seat comfort	○
Rear-seat comfort	○
Climate-control system	⦿

Convenience

Access	◓
Controls and displays	◓
Cargo area	◓

Other

Fuel economy	◒
Predicted reliability	●
Predicted depreciation	NA

Test data

Acceleration

0-30 mph, sec.	3.6
0-60 mph, sec.	10.3
Quarter mile, sec.	17.7
Quarter mile, mph	80
45-65 mph, sec.	7.0

Fuel economy (regular)

EPA city/highway, mpg	18/25
CU's overall mileage, mpg	18
CU's city/highway, mpg	11/30
CU's 150-mile trip, mpg	22
Fuel refill capacity, gal.	25.0
Cruising range, mi.	530
Annual fuel: gal./cost	840/$1005

Braking from 60 mph

Dry pavement, ft.	138
Wet pavement, ft.	165
Pedal effort, 1st stop, lb.	20
Pedal effort, 10th stop, lb.	30

Specifications

Drive wheels

Front

Seating

Passengers,front/mid/rear......2/3/3

Dimensions and weight

Length, in.	201
Width, in.	73
Wheelbase, in.	120
Turning circle, ft.	43
Curb weight, lb.	4005
Percent weight, front/rear	58/42
Max. load, lb.	1350

Interior room

Front shoulder room, in.	60.0
Front leg room, in.	41.0
Front head room, in.	6.0
Middle shoulder room, in.	61.5
Middle fore-aft room, in.	30.5
Middle head room, in.	6.0
Rear shoulder room, in.	60.0
Rear fore-aft room, in.	29.5
Rear head room, in.	5.0
Door top to ground, in.	62.5
Cargo volume, cu.ft.	76.0

Engines available

3.4-liter V6 (180 hp)

Transmissions available

4-speed automatic

Tested model

1997 SE Montana Minivan extended, 3.4-liter V6, 4-speed automatic

Tires as tested

General XP2000 GT, size P215/70R15

Saturn

Saturn is one of the few domestic lines that manages to appeal to import-buyers and to be reliable. But the cars themselves have been pretty unremarkable. Acceleration, braking, and fuel economy are good. The SL2 handles fairly nimbly—much better than the SL1. The quick steering conveys pretty good road feel. Accommodations and controls are inferior, and the four-cylinder engine still makes a racket after years of improvements meant to silence it. Saturn says late-1998 models are quieter. The car retains its unusual plastic body panels that rebound after denting from minor impacts. The Saturn holds its value very well for a domestic sedan.

Body styles and prices

	Price range	Trim lines
4-door	\$10,595 - \$12,755	SL, SL1, SL2
4-door wagon	\$12,295 - \$14,255	SW1, SW2

Safety information

Safety belt pretensioners .... No
Center rear safety belt .... Lap
Dual air bags .... Standard
Side air bags .... Not offered
Antilock brakes .... Optional
Traction control .... Optional with ABS
Gov't front-crash test, driver/front passenger .... ●/◓
Gov't side-crash test, driver/rear passenger .... ○/○
IIHS offset crash test .... Acceptable
Injury claim rate compared with all cars/type .... ○/●

Reliability history

TROUBLE SPOTS	Saturn SL Sedan, SW Wagon 90	91	92	93	94	95	96	97
Engine							●	●
Cooling							●	●
Fuel							◓	●
Ignition							◓	●
Auto. transmission							●	●
Man. transmission							●	●
Clutch							●	●
Electrical							○	◓
Air conditioning							●	●
Suspension							●	●
Brakes							○	●
Exhaust							●	●
Body rust							●	●
Paint/trim							●	●
Body integrity							○	◓
Body hardware							○	◓

Test judgments

Performance
Acceleration .... ◓
Transmission .... ◓
Routine handling .... ◓
Emergency handling .... ◓
Braking .... ○

Comfort
Ride, normal load .... ○
Ride, full load .... ○
Noise .... ○
Driving position .... ○
Front-seat comfort .... ○
Rear-seat comfort .... ◒
Climate-control system .... ●

Convenience
Access .... ○
Controls and displays .... ○
Trunk .... ◒

Other
Fuel economy .... ◓
Predicted reliability .... ○
Predicted depreciation .... ◓

Test data

Acceleration
0-30 mph, sec. 3.7
0-60 mph, sec. 9.5
Quarter mile, sec. 17.4
Quarter mile, mph 82
45-65 mph, sec. 5.8

Fuel economy (regular)
EPA city/highway, mpg 24/34
CU's overall mileage, mpg 29
CU's city/highway, mpg 18/43
CU's 150-mile trip, mpg 36
Fuel refill capacity, gal. 12.1
Cruising range, mi. 410
Annual fuel: gal./cost .... 525/\$630

Braking from 60 mph
Dry pavement, ft. 148
Wet pavement, ft. 160
Pedal effort, 1st stop, lb. 20
Pedal effort, 10th stop, lb. 25

Specifications

Drive wheels
Front

Seating
Passengers,front/rear 2/3

Dimensions and weight
Length, in. 177
Width, in. 67
Wheelbase, in. 102
Turning circle, ft. 41
Curb weight, lb. 2465
Percent weight, front/rear 61/39
Max. load, lb. 864

Interior room
Front shoulder room, in. 52.0
Front leg room, in. 41.0
Front head room, in. 5.5
Rear shoulder room, in. 52.5
Rear fore-aft room, in. 26.5
Rear head room, in. 2.5
Door top to ground, in. 48.5
Luggage capacity .... 4+0

Engines available
1.9-liter 4 (100 or 124 hp)

Transmissions available
5-speed manual
4-speed automatic

Tested model
1998 SL2 4-door, 1.9-liter Four, 4-speed automatic

Tires as tested
Firestone Affinity Touring, size P185/65R15

Sports/sporty car under $25,000

Saturn SC

The SC2 holds its own with other sporty coupes. Only minor refinements have been made for 1998. The SC2 accelerates well and handles responsively. The body doesn't lean much in turns, and the tires grip well. The ride is a little unsettled but on a par with many other small cars. The manual transmission's shift lever needs a long throw. Head room is tight, leg room snug. The front seats are uncomfortable. The rear seat is better than in most coupes, but that's not saying much.

Body styles and prices

	Price range	Trim lines
2-door	$12,595 - $14,855	SC1, SC2

Safety information

Safety belt pretensioners	No
Center rear safety belt	NA
Dual air bags	Standard
Side air bags	Not offered
Antilock brakes	Optional
Traction control	Optional with ABS
Gov't front-crash test, driver/front passenger	NA/NA
Gov't side-crash test, driver/rear passenger	NA/NA
IIHS offset crash test	Acceptable
Injury claim rate compared with all cars/type	○/○

Reliability history

TROUBLE SPOTS	Saturn SC Coupe 90	91	92	93	94	95	96	97
Engine								⊙
Cooling								⊙
Fuel								◒
Ignition								⊙
Auto. transmission								⊙
Man. transmission								⊙
Clutch								⊙
Electrical								⊙
Air conditioning								⊙
Suspension								⊙
Brakes								⊙
Exhaust								⊙
Body rust								⊙
Paint/trim								⊙
Body integrity								◒
Body hardware								◒

Test judgments

Performance

Acceleration	◒
Transmission	◒
Routine handling	◒
Emergency handling	◒
Braking	◒

Comfort

Ride, normal load	○
Ride, full load	○
Noise	○
Driving position	○
Front-seat comfort	○
Rear-seat comfort	●
Climate-control system	⊙

Convenience

Access	○
Controls and displays	○
Trunk	◐

Other

Fuel economy	◒
Predicted reliability	○
Predicted depreciation	◒

Test data

Acceleration

0-30 mph, sec.	3.2
0-60 mph, sec.	8.9
Quarter mile, sec.	16.9
Quarter mile, mph	84
45-65 mph, sec.	5.6

Fuel economy (regular)

EPA city/highway, mpg	27/37
CU's overall mileage, mpg	28
CU's city/highway, mpg	19/42
CU's 150-mile trip, mpg	33
Fuel refill capacity, gal.	12.2
Cruising range, mi.	375
Annual fuel: gal./cost	540/$645

Braking from 60 mph

Dry pavement, ft.	134
Wet pavement, ft.	151
Pedal effort, 1st stop, lb.	20
Pedal effort, 10th stop, lb.	25

Specifications

Drive wheels

Front

Seating

Passengers, front/rear	2/2

Dimensions and weight

Length, in.	180
Width, in.	67
Wheelbase, in.	102
Turning circle, ft.	40
Curb weight, lb.	2420
Percent weight, front/rear	61/39
Max. load, lb.	715

Interior room

Front shoulder room, in.	52.5
Front leg room, in.	41.5
Front head room, in.	4.0
Rear shoulder room, in.	50.0
Rear fore-aft room, in.	25.5
Rear head room, in.	0.5
Door top to ground, in.	47.5
Luggage capacity	3+2

Engines available

1.9-liter 4 (100 or 124 hp)

Transmissions available

5-speed manual
4-speed automatic

Tested model

1997 SC2 2-door, 1.9-liter Four, 5-speed manual

Tires as tested

Firestone Firehawk GTA, size P195/60R15

Sport-utility vehicle

Subaru Forester

RECOMMENDED

The Forester is new for 1998, a car/SUV hybrid that joins the growing ranks of car-based small SUVs such as the Toyota RAV4 and Honda CR-V. The Forester is based on the reliable and good-performing Impreza station wagon but with a taller and roomier cargo compartment and more ground clearance. The Forester has a good, compliant ride, and handles quite nimbly. Its four-cylinder engine provides zesty acceleration. It's quite small compared with a conventional SUV like the Ford Explorer, but roomy inside for this class. It has an effective all-wheel-drive system and a responsive automatic transmission. The controls are logically laid out, and the tailgate is easy to manage. The rear seat is cramped, but the cabin has lots of storage compartments.

Body styles and prices

	Price range	Trim lines
4-door wagon AWD	$18,695 - $22,195	Base, L, S

Safety information

Safety belt pretensioners	No
Center rear safety belt	Lap
Dual air bags	Standard
Side air bags	Not offered
Antilock brakes	Optional
Traction control	Not offered
Gov't front-crash test, driver/front passenger	NA/NA
Gov't side-crash test, driver/rear passenger	NA/NA
IIHS offset crash test	NA
Injury claim rate compared with all cars/type	NA/NA

Reliability history

TROUBLE SPOTS	90 91 92 93 94 95 96 97
Engine	
Cooling	
Fuel	
Ignition	
Auto. transmission	NO
Man. transmission	
Clutch	DATA
Electrical	
Air conditioning	NEW
Suspension	
Brakes	MODEL
Exhaust	
Body rust	
Paint/trim	
Body integrity	
Body hardware	

Test judgments

Performance

Acceleration	○
Transmission	◒
Routine handling	◒
Emergency handling	◒
Braking	◒

Comfort

Ride, normal load	◒
Ride, full load	◒
Noise	◒
Driving position	◒
Front-seat comfort	◒
Rear-seat comfort	○
Climate-control system	⊙

Convenience

Access	◒
Controls and displays	⊙
Cargo area	◒

Other

Fuel economy	○
Predicted reliability	⊙
Predicted depreciation	NA

Test data

Acceleration

0-30 mph, sec.	3.6
0-60 mph, sec.	10.5
Quarter mile, sec.	18.1
Quarter mile, mph	76
45-65 mph, sec.	6.9

Fuel economy (regular)

EPA city/highway, mpg	21/26
CU's overall mileage, mpg	22
CU's city/highway, mpg	15/31
CU's 150-mile trip, mpg	26
Fuel refill capacity, gal.	15.9
Cruising range, mi.	380
Annual fuel: gal./cost	690/$830

Braking from 60 mph

Dry pavement, ft.	131
Wet pavement, ft.	170
Pedal effort, 1st stop, lb.	20
Pedal effort, 10th stop, lb.	25

Specifications

Drive wheels

All

Seating

Passengers,front/rear	2/3

Dimensions and weight

Length, in.	175
Width, in.	68
Wheelbase, in.	99
Turning circle, ft.	39
Curb weight, lb.	3195
Percent weight, front/rear	55/45
Max. load, lb.	900

Interior room

Front shoulder room, in.	54.0
Front leg room, in.	41.5
Front head room, in.	6.0
Rear shoulder room, in.	54.0
Rear fore-aft room, in.	28.0
Rear head room, in.	5.5
Door top to ground, in.	54.5
Cargo volume, cu.ft.	35.5

Engines available

2.5-liter 4 (165 hp)

Transmissions available

5-speed manual
4-speed automatic

Tested model

1998 S 4-door wagon AWD, 2.5-liter Four, 4-speed automatic

Tires as tested

Yokohama Geolander H/T, size P215/60R16

Small car

Subaru Impreza

RECOMMENDED

The Impreza is the least expensive all-wheel-drive model on the market. 1998 brings a new dashboard and a new model—the 2.5RS, a sporty two-door with a 165-hp, 2.5-liter engine from the Legacy line. The steering is responsive, and the ride is relatively good for a small car. The front seats provide good support, but the rear seat is cramped. The wagon isn't the roomiest in its class. The Outback Sport version is not a real off-road vehicle, but it's nimble, responsive, and fun to drive.

Body styles and prices

	Price range	Trim lines
2-door AWD	$15,895 - $19,195	L, 2.5 RS
4-door AWD	$15,895	L
4-door wagon AWD	$16,295 - $17,995	L, Outback Sport

Safety information

Safety belt pretensioners	No
Center rear safety belt	Lap
Dual air bags	Standard
Side air bags	Not offered
Antilock brakes	Optional
Traction control	Not offered
Gov't front-crash test, driver/front passenger	◒/◒
Gov't side-crash test, driver/rear passenger	NA/NA
IIHS offset crash test	NA
Injury claim rate compared with all cars/type	○/◒

Reliability history

TROUBLE SPOTS	90	91	92	93	94	95	96	97
Engine				◉		◉	◉	◉
Cooling				◉		◉	◉	◉
Fuel				◉		◒	◉	◉
Ignition				◒		◒	◉	◉
Auto. transmission				◒		◉	◉	◉
Man. transmission				◉		*	◉	*
Clutch				◒	Insufficient data	*	◉	*
Electrical				◒		◒	◒	◒
Air conditioning				◒		◉	◉	◉
Suspension				◒		◉	◉	◉
Brakes				○		◉	◒	◒
Exhaust				◉		◉	◉	◉
Body rust				◉		◉	◉	◉
Paint/trim				◉		◉	◒	◉
Body integrity				◒		○	○	◒
Body hardware				◒		◒	◒	◒

(Column header: Subaru Impreza)

Test judgments

Performance

Acceleration	○
Transmission	◒
Routine handling	◉
Emergency handling	◒
Braking	◒

Comfort

Ride, normal load	◒
Ride, full load	○
Noise	○
Driving position	◒
Front-seat comfort	◒
Rear-seat comfort	○
Climate-control system	◉

Convenience

Access	○
Controls and displays	◒
Cargo area	●

Other

Fuel economy	○
Predicted reliability	◉
Predicted depreciation	○

Test data

Acceleration

0-30 mph, sec.	3.6
0-60 mph, sec.	10.8
Quarter mile, sec.	18.2
Quarter mile, mph	76
45-65 mph, sec.	7.1

Fuel economy (regular)

EPA city/highway, mpg	23/30
CU's overall mileage, mpg	23
CU's city/highway, mpg	16/34
CU's 150-mile trip, mpg	28
Fuel refill capacity, gal.	13.2
Cruising range, mi.	340
Annual fuel: gal./cost	645/$770

Braking from 60 mph

Dry pavement, ft.	130
Wet pavement, ft.	153
Pedal effort, 1st stop, lb.	25
Pedal effort, 10th stop, lb.	30

Specifications

Drive wheels

All

Seating

Passengers, front/rear ... 2/3

Dimensions and weight

Length, in.	172
Width, in.	67
Wheelbase, in.	99
Turning circle, ft.	36
Curb weight, lb.	2895
Percent weight, front/rear	57/43
Max. load, lb.	900

Interior room

Front shoulder room, in.	52.5
Front leg room, in.	42.0
Front head room, in.	4.5
Rear shoulder room, in.	51.0
Rear fore-aft room, in.	27.0
Rear head room, in.	2.5
Door top to ground, in.	50.5
Cargo volume, cu.ft.	19.5

Engines available

2.2-liter 4 (137 hp)
2.5-liter 4 (165 hp)

Transmissions available

5-speed manual, 4-speed auto.

Tested model

1997 Outback Sport 4 door wagon AWD, 2.2-liter Four, 4-speed automatic

Tires as tested

Bridgestone Potenza, size P205/60R15

Medium car under $25,000

Subaru Legacy

This midsized car feels almost as agile as a European sports sedan. Permanent all-wheel drive adds a measure of driver confidence. The ride is firm but supple. The cabin is not as quiet as, say, that of the Toyota Camry. The standard 2.2-liter Four accelerates well enough. A more powerful 2.5-liter Four comes with the GT and Outback models. The seats are comfortable. The rear is roomy enough for two adults. The Legacy wagon, with or without Outback trim, is a good alternative to a sport-utility vehicle.

Body styles and prices

	Price range	Trim lines
4-door AWD	$19,195 - $24,895	L, GT, GT Limited
4-door wagon AWD	$16,895 - $24,595	Brighton, L, Outback, GT, Outback Ltd.

Safety information

Safety belt pretensioners	No
Center rear safety belt	Lap
Dual air bags	Standard
Side air bags	Not offered
Antilock brakes	Standard (not offered on Brighton)
Traction control	Not offered
Gov't front-crash test, driver/front passenger	◓/◓
Gov't side-crash test, driver/rear passenger	○/NA
IIHS offset crash test	Acceptable
Injury claim rate compared with all cars/type	◓/◓

Reliability history

TROUBLE SPOTS	Subaru Legacy 90	91	92	93	94	95	96	97
Engine	◓	◓	◓	◓	◉	◉	◉	◉
Cooling	○	◓	◉	◉	◉	◉	◉	◉
Fuel	◓	◓	◉	◉	◓	◓	◉	◉
Ignition	◓	◓	◓	◓	◓	○	◉	◉
Auto. transmission	○	○	◉	◉	◉	◉	◉	◉
Man. transmission	◓	◓	◉	◉	◉	◉	◉	◉
Clutch	◒	○	○	○	○	◓	◓	◉
Electrical	○	○	◓	◓	○	○	◓	◓
Air conditioning	◒	○	○	◉	◉	◉	◉	◉
Suspension	○	◒	◓	◓	◓	◉	◉	◉
Brakes	●	●	●	◒	○	◓	◓	◉
Exhaust	◓	◓	◉	◉	◉	◉	◉	◉
Body rust	◒	◓	◓	◉	◉	◉	◉	◉
Paint/trim	○	○	○	◓	◓	◉	◓	◉
Body integrity	◒	○	○	○	◓	◓	◓	◉
Body hardware	●	●	◒	○	○	◓	○	◓

Test judgments

Performance

Acceleration	○
Transmission	◓
Routine handling	◓
Emergency handling	◓
Braking	◓

Comfort

Ride, normal load	◓
Ride, full load	◓
Noise	◓
Driving position	◓
Front-seat comfort	◓
Rear-seat comfort	◓
Climate-control system	◓

Convenience

Access	◓
Controls and displays	◉
Trunk	◓

Other

Fuel economy	○
Predicted reliability	◉
Predicted depreciation	◓

Test data

Acceleration

0-30 mph, sec.	3.5
0-60 mph, sec.	10.3
Quarter mile, sec.	17.9
Quarter mile, mph	78
45-65 mph, sec.	6.7

Fuel economy (regular)

EPA city/highway, mpg	23/30
CU's overall mileage, mpg	24
CU's city/highway, mpg	16/36
CU's 150-mile trip, mpg	28
Fuel refill capacity, gal.	15.9
Cruising range, mi.	415
Annual fuel: gal./cost	630/$755

Braking from 60 mph

Dry pavement, ft.	136
Wet pavement, ft.	157
Pedal effort, 1st stop, lb.	20
Pedal effort, 10th stop, lb.	25

Specifications

Drive wheels

All

Seating

Passengers,front/rear	2/3

Dimensions and weight

Length, in.	181
Width, in.	68
Wheelbase, in.	104
Turning circle, ft.	38
Curb weight, lb.	2980
Percent weight, front/rear	56/44
Max. load, lb.	850

Interior room

Front shoulder room, in.	54.0
Front leg room, in.	42.0
Front head room, in.	5.0
Rear shoulder room, in.	53.5
Rear fore-aft room, in.	30.0
Rear head room, in.	3.5
Door top to ground, in.	50.0
Luggage capacity	5+0

Engines available

2.2-liter 4 (137 hp)
2.5-liter 4 (165 hp)

Transmissions available

5-speed manual
4-speed automatic

Tested model

1997 L 4-door AWD, 2.2-liter Four, 4-speed automatic

Tires as tested

Bridgestone SF-411, size P185/70R14

Small car

Suzuki Esteem

The Esteem, introduced in 1995, was Suzuki's first foray into the mainstream sedan market. A wagon joined the lineup for 1998. The Esteem is behind most Japanese competitors in many respects. The car falls short in ride, quietness, and powertrain smoothness. The Esteem accelerates well enough, but its engine sounds harsh when revved. Fuel economy is respectable. The seats are fairly comfortable front and rear, but elbow room suffers because of the car's narrowness.

Body styles and prices

	Price range	Trim lines
4-door	$11,999 - $14,899	GL, GLX, GLX+
4-door wagon	$12,499 - $15,599	GL, GLX, GLX+

Safety information

Safety belt pretensioners	No
Center rear safety belt	Lap
Dual air bags	Standard
Side air bags	Not offered
Antilock brakes	Optional
Traction control	Not offered
Gov't front-crash test, driver/front passenger	NA/NA
Gov't side-crash test, driver/rear passenger	NA/NA
IIHS offset crash test	NA
Injury claim rate compared with all cars/type	NA/NA

Reliability history

TROUBLE SPOTS	90 91 92 93 94 95 96 97
Engine	
Cooling	
Fuel	
Ignition	NOT
Auto. transmission	
Man. transmission	ENOUGH
Clutch	
Electrical	
Air conditioning	DATA
Suspension	
Brakes	TO
Exhaust	
Body rust	RATE
Paint/trim	
Body integrity	
Body hardware	

Test judgments

Performance	
Acceleration	○
Transmission	◓
Routine handling	◓
Emergency handling	○
Braking	○
Comfort	
Ride, normal load	○
Ride, full load	◒
Noise	○
Driving position	○
Front-seat comfort	◓
Rear-seat comfort	○
Climate-control system	●
Convenience	
Access	○
Controls and displays	◓
Trunk	◒
Other	
Fuel economy	◓
Predicted reliability	NA
Predicted depreciation	○

Test data

Acceleration

0-30 mph, sec.	4.0
0-60 mph, sec.	11.8
Quarter mile, sec.	18.7
Quarter mile, mph	75
45-65 mph, sec.	7.7

Fuel economy (regular)

EPA city/highway, mpg	27/34
CU's overall mileage, mpg	29
CU's city/highway, mpg	20/44
CU's 150-mile trip, mpg	33
Fuel refill capacity, gal.	13.5
Cruising range, mi.	415
Annual fuel: gal./cost	520/$625

Braking from 60 mph

Dry pavement, ft.	143
Wet pavement, ft.	162
Pedal effort, 1st stop, lb.	20
Pedal effort, 10th stop, lb.	30

Specifications

Drive wheels
Front

Seating

Passengers, front/rear	2/3

Dimensions and weight

Length, in.	165
Width, in.	66
Wheelbase, in.	98
Turning circle, ft.	35
Curb weight, lb.	2290
Percent weight, front/rear	62/38
Max. load, lb.	870

Interior room

Front shoulder room, in.	52.0
Front leg room, in.	41.0
Front head room, in.	4.5
Rear shoulder room, in.	51.5
Rear fore-aft room, in.	27.5
Rear head room, in.	2.5
Door top to ground, in.	49.0
Luggage capacity	3+1

Engines available
1.6-liter 4 (95 hp)

Transmissions available
5-speed manual
4-speed automatic

Tested model
1995 GLX 4-door, 1.6-liter Four, 4-speed automatic

Tires as tested
Bridgestone All Season SF408, size P175/70R13

Sport-utility vehicle

Suzuki Sidekick

The small Sidekick and similar Chevrolet Tracker come with two or four doors. The two-door version has a soft top. The Sidekick Sport has a larger and more powerful engine—a 120-hp Four unavailable in the Tracker. In all versions, the steering is slow, and the handling is ungainly and imprecise. The ride is punishing on all roads. Overall, the Sidekick/Tracker twins are crude and uncomfortable. They are quite competent off-road, although their four-wheel-drive system is part-time. A redesigned model, called the Vitara, is due for 1999.

Body styles and prices

	Price range	Trim lines
4-door wagon 2WD	$14,399 - $16,899	JS, Sport JS
4-door wagon 4WD	$15,999 - $19,399	JX , Sport JX, Sport JXL
Convertible 2WD	$13,099	JS
Convertible 4WD	$14,869	JX

Safety information

Safety belt pretensioners	No
Center rear safety belt	NA
Dual air bags	Standard
Side air bags	Not offered
Antilock brakes	Optional
Traction control	Not offered
Gov't front-crash test, driver/front passenger	◒/○
Gov't side-crash test, driver/rear passenger	NA/NA
IIHS offset crash test	NA
Injury claim rate compared with all cars/type	●/●

Reliability history

TROUBLE SPOTS	Suzuki Sidekick 90	91	92	93	94	95	96	97
Engine	○	◓	◉	◓	◓	◉	◓	Insufficient data
Cooling	◓	◓	◓	◓	◓	◉	◉	
Fuel	◒	◓	◓	◉	◓	◓	◉	
Ignition	○	○	○	○	○	○	◉	
Auto. transmission	*	*	*	*	*	◉	◓	
Man. transmission	*	*	*	*	◉	◓	◉	
Clutch	*	*	*	*	◓	◓	◉	
Electrical	◒	◒	◒	○	○	○	○	
Air conditioning	*	*	*	○	◓	◓	◓	
Suspension	◓	◉	○	◓	◉	◉	◉	
Brakes	●	●	●	○	○	◓	○	
Exhaust	●	●	◒	○	◉	◉	◉	
Body rust	◒	◓	◉	◓	◉	◓	◉	
Paint/trim	○	◓	○	◉	◉	◓	◓	
Body integrity	◒	◒	◒	◒	●	◒	○	
Body hardware	●	◒	●	○	◒	◒	○	

Test judgments

Performance

Acceleration	○
Transmission	○
Routine handling	○
Emergency handling	○
Braking	○

Comfort

Ride, normal load	◒
Ride, full load	◒
Noise	◒
Driving position	○
Front-seat comfort	◓
Rear-seat comfort	○
Climate-control system	◒

Convenience

Access	◓
Controls and displays	○
Cargo area	◒

Other

Fuel economy	○
Predicted reliability	○
Predicted depreciation	○

Test data

Acceleration

0-30 mph, sec.	4.2
0-60 mph, sec.	11.8
Quarter mile, sec.	18.7
Quarter mile, mph	74
45-65 mph, sec.	7.0

Fuel economy (regular)

EPA city/highway, mpg	22/25
CU's overall mileage, mpg	23
CU's city/highway, mpg	17/30
CU's 150-mile trip, mpg	27
Fuel refill capacity, gal.	18.5
Cruising range, mi.	460
Annual fuel: gal./cost	650/$780

Braking from 60 mph

Dry pavement, ft.	142
Wet pavement, ft.	161
Pedal effort, 1st stop, lb.	20
Pedal effort, 10th stop, lb.	25

Specifications

Drive wheels

Rear or part-time 4WD

Seating

Passengers,front/rear	2/2

Dimensions and weight

Length, in.	162
Width, in.	67
Wheelbase, in.	98
Turning circle, ft.	37
Curb weight, lb.	2910
Percent weight, front/rear	53/47
Max. load, lb.	771

Interior room

Front shoulder room, in.	51.0
Front leg room, in.	42.0
Front head room, in.	5.5
Rear shoulder room, in.	50.5
Rear fore-aft room, in.	26.5
Rear head room, in.	4.5
Door top to ground, in.	59.5
Cargo volume, cu.ft.	24.0

Engines available

1.6-liter 4 (95 hp)
1.8-liter 4 (120 hp)

Transmissions available

5-speed manual, 3 or 4-speed auto.

Tested model

1996 JLX Sport 4-door wagon 4WD, 1.8-liter Four, 5-speed manual

Tires as tested

Uniroyal Tiger Paw, size P215/65R16

Small car

Suzuki Swift

This hatchback, like the similar Chevrolet Metro sedan, is one of the smallest and lightest cars on the road. Except for an additional nine hp in the 1.3-liter engine, there are no changes for 1998. The Swift is too sluggish and clumsy to nip neatly through city traffic, and it's fatiguing to drive on long trips. The ride is choppy and noisy. The rear seat holds just two, and not comfortably.

Body styles and prices

	Price range	Trim lines
2-door hatchback	$9,099	—

Safety information

Safety belt pretensioners	No
Center rear safety belt	NA
Dual air bags	Standard
Side air bags	Not offered
Antilock brakes	Optional
Traction control	Not offered
Gov't front-crash test, driver/front passenger	◓/◓
Gov't side-crash test, driver/rear passenger	NA/NA
IIHS offset crash test	NA
Injury claim rate compared with all cars/type	●/◒

Reliability history

TROUBLE SPOTS	90	91	92	93	94	95	96	97
Engine	○	○	○	◓	◓	◉	◉	Insufficient data
Cooling	◓	◓	◓	◉	◉	◉	◉	
Fuel	○	◓	◓	◉	◉	◓	◉	
Ignition	○	○	◒	◓	◓	◉	◓	
Auto. transmission	*	*	◓	*	*	*	*	
Man. transmission	◓	○	◓	◉	◉	◉	*	
Clutch	◓	◓	◓	◓	◉	◉	*	
Electrical	○	○	◒	◒	○	◒	○	
Air conditioning	●	●	◓	○	○	●	○	
Suspension	○	◓	◓	◓	◓	◓	◉	
Brakes	●	◒	◒	○	○	◓	◉	
Exhaust	●	●	●	◒	◓	◉	◉	
Body rust	○	○	◓	◉	◉	◉	◉	
Paint/trim	◒	○	◓	◓	◉	◓	◓	
Body integrity	●	●	●	○	○	○	◓	
Body hardware	●	●	●	●	◒	◒	○	

Test judgments

Performance	
Acceleration	◒
Transmission	○
Routine handling	○
Emergency handling	○
Braking	○
Comfort	
Ride, normal load	◒
Ride, full load	◒
Noise	◒
Driving position	○
Front-seat comfort	○
Rear-seat comfort	◒
Climate-control system	◓
Convenience	
Access	○
Controls and displays	◓
Trunk	◒
Other	
Fuel economy	◓
Predicted reliability	◓
Predicted depreciation	○

Test data

Acceleration	
0-30 mph, sec.	5.0
0-60 mph, sec.	15.3
Quarter mile, sec.	20.4
Quarter mile, mph	68
45-65 mph, sec.	10.0

Fuel economy (regular)	
EPA city/highway, mpg	30/34
CU's overall mileage, mpg	29
CU's city/highway, mpg	19/42
CU's 150-mile trip, mpg	35
Fuel refill capacity, gal.	10.6
Cruising range, mi.	335
Annual fuel: gal./cost	520/$625

Braking from 60 mph	
Dry pavement, ft.	151
Wet pavement, ft.	172
Pedal effort, 1st stop, lb.	25
Pedal effort, 10th stop, lb.	35

Specifications

Drive wheels
Front

Seating

Passengers,front/rear	2/2

Dimensions and weight

Length, in.	149
Width, in.	63
Wheelbase, in.	93
Turning circle, ft.	35
Curb weight, lb.	1845
Percent weight, front/rear	61/39
Max. load, lb.	688

Interior room

Front shoulder room, in.	49.0
Front leg room, in.	40.5
Front head room, in.	4.5
Rear shoulder room, in.	47.5
Rear fore-aft room, in.	27.5
Rear head room, in.	1.5
Door top to ground, in.	49.5
Luggage capacity	2+0

Engines available
1.3-liter 4 (79 hp)

Transmissions available
5-speed manual
3-speed automatic

Tested model
1995 Geo Metro LSi 4-door, 1.3-liter Four, 3-speed automatic

Tires as tested
Goodyear Invicta GL, size P155/80R13

Sport-utility vehicle

Suzuki X90

The X90 is a small sport-utility vehicle based on the two-door Suzuki Sidekick. This T-top two-seater combines some features of a convertible, a coupe, and an SUV—but it's not a practical alternative to any of the above. The meager 95-hp Four works hard to maintain highway speeds even on mild uphill inclines. The handling can grow twitchy even during normal driving on bumpy or slippery curves. The cabin is noisy and cramped, the trunk is small, and the ride is awful.

Body styles and prices

	Price range	Trim lines
2-door 2WD	$13,399	—
2-door 4WD	$14,799	—

Safety information

Safety belt pretensioners	No
Center rear safety belt	NA
Dual air bags	Standard
Side air bags	Not offered
Antilock brakes	Standard
Traction control	Not offered
Gov't front-crash test, driver/front passenger	NA/NA
Gov't side-crash test, driver/rear passenger	NA/NA
IIHS offset crash test	NA
Injury claim rate compared with all cars/type	NA/NA

Reliability history

TROUBLE SPOTS	90 91 92 93 94 95 96 97
Engine	
Cooling	
Fuel	
Ignition	
Auto. transmission	NOT
Man. transmission	
Clutch	ENOUGH
Electrical	
Air conditioning	DATA
Suspension	
Brakes	TO
Exhaust	
Body rust	RATE
Paint/trim	
Body integrity	
Body hardware	

Test judgments

Performance

Acceleration	○
Transmission	◒
Routine handling	○
Emergency handling	○
Braking	○

Comfort

Ride, normal load	●
Noise	◓
Driving position	○
Front-seat comfort	○
Climate-control system	◒

Convenience

Access	○
Controls and displays	○
Cargo area	○

Other

Fuel economy	◒
Predicted reliability	NA
Predicted depreciation	NA

Test data

Acceleration

0-30 mph, sec.	4.0
0-60 mph, sec.	11.6
Quarter mile, sec.	18.6
Quarter mile, mph	73
45-65 mph, sec.	7.5

Fuel economy (regular)

EPA city/highway, mpg	25/28
CU's overall mileage, mpg	27
CU's city/highway, mpg	20/36
CU's 150-mile trip, mpg	31
Fuel refill capacity, gal.	11.1
Cruising range, mi.	320
Annual fuel: gal./cost	555/$665

Braking from 60 mph

Dry pavement, ft.	149
Wet pavement, ft.	164
Pedal effort, 1st stop, lb.	20
Pedal effort, 10th stop, lb.	30

Specifications

Drive wheels

Rear or part-time 4WD

Seating

Passengers,front	2

Dimensions and weight

Length, in.	146
Width, in.	67
Wheelbase, in.	87
Turning circle, ft.	35
Curb weight, lb.	2490
Percent weight, front/rear	57/43
Max. load, lb.	459

Interior room

Front shoulder room, in.	49.5
Front leg room, in.	41.0
Front head room, in.	4.0
Door top to ground, in.	55.0
Luggage capacity	4+0

Engines available

1.6-liter 4 (95 hp)

Transmissions available

5-speed manual
4-speed automatic

Tested model

1996 2-door 4WD, 1.6-liter Four, 5-speed manual

Tires as tested

Bridgestone Dueler H/T 688, size P195/65R15

Sport-utility vehicle

Toyota 4Runner

RECOMMENDED

The 4Runner is among the better SUVs. It corners well, and the chassis suppresses most road bumps well. The 3.4-liter V6—the engine of choice—is lively, and fuel use is quite frugal for a two-ton SUV. The four-wheel-drive setup remains a part-time-only system—disappointing in such a costly vehicle. The driving position could be better. Front and rear seats are all fairly comfortable, but a high step-up makes getting in and out a chore. Reliability has been average for the four-wheel drive and better than average for the two-wheel drive.

Body styles and prices

	Price range	Trim lines
4-door wagon 2WD	$20,558 - $32,248	Base, SR5, Limited
4-door wagon 4WD	$22,708 - $34,618	Base, SR5, Limited

Safety information

Safety belt pretensioners ....No
Center rear safety belt ....Lap
Dual air bags ....Standard
Side air bags....Not offered
Antilock brakes....Standard on V6; optional on 4
Traction control ....Not offered
Gov't front-crash test, driver/front passenger ....○/○
Gov't side-crash test, driver/rear passenger ....NA/NA
IIHS offset crash test ....Acceptable
Injury claim rate compared with all cars/type....○/◒

Reliability history

TROUBLE SPOTS	Toyota 4Runner (4WD) 90	91	92	93	94	95	96	97
Engine							◒	●
Cooling							◓	●
Fuel							●	●
Ignition							●	●
Auto. transmission							●	●
Man. transmission							●	*
Clutch							●	*
Electrical							◓	●
Air conditioning							●	●
Suspension							◓	●
Brakes							●	●
Exhaust							●	●
Body rust							●	●
Paint/trim							●	●
Body integrity							◓	◓
Body hardware							◓	●

Test judgments

Performance
Acceleration ....○
Transmission ....●
Routine handling ....○
Emergency handling ....○
Braking ....◓

Comfort
Ride, normal load ....○
Ride, full load ....◒
Noise ....◓
Driving position ....○
Front-seat comfort ....◓
Rear-seat comfort ....○
Climate-control system ....◓

Convenience
Access ....○
Controls and displays ....●
Cargo area ....●

Other
Fuel economy ....◒
Predicted reliability ....○
Predicted depreciation ....●

Test data

Acceleration
0-30 mph, sec. 3.5
0-60 mph, sec. 10.0
Quarter mile, sec. 17.6
Quarter mile, mph 79
45-65 mph, sec. 6.3

Fuel economy (regular)
EPA city/highway, mpg 16/19
CU's overall mileage, mpg 18
CU's city/highway, mpg....12/28
CU's 150-mile trip, mpg 22
Fuel refill capacity, gal. 18.5
Cruising range, mi. 370
Annual fuel: gal./cost ....825/$990

Braking from 60 mph
Dry pavement, ft. 132
Wet pavement, ft. 161
Pedal effort, 1st stop, lb. 20
Pedal effort, 10th stop, lb. 30

Specifications

Drive wheels
Rear or part-time 4WD

Seating
Passengers,front/rear....2/3

Dimensions and weight
Length, in. 179
Width, in. 67
Wheelbase, in. 105
Turning circle, ft. 39
Curb weight, lb. 3930
Percent weight, front/rear 55/45
Max. load, lb. 1320

Interior room
Front shoulder room, in. 53.5
Front leg room, in. 42.0
Front head room, in. 2.5
Rear shoulder room, in. 53.5
Rear fore-aft room, in. 31.0
Rear head room, in. 5.0
Door top to ground, in. 63.5
Cargo volume, cu.ft. 44.0

Engines available
2.7-liter 4 (150 hp)
3.4-liter V6 (183 hp)

Transmissions available
5-speed manual
4-speed automatic

Tested model
1996 SR5 4-door wagon 4WD, 3.4-liter V6, 4-speed automatic

Tires as tested
Bridgestone Dueler H/T 689, size P265/70R16

Large car under $30,000

Toyota Avalon

The Avalon is essentially a well-equipped pre-1997 Camry with a stretched, extra-roomy rear seat. The Avalon scores very well in our tests despite being a rather uninspiring, anonymous automobile. It offers either five- or six-passenger seating. Minor tweaks and side-impact air bags are new for 1998. The 3.0-liter V6 is powerful and economical, and the transmission shifts smoothly. Light steering gives little road feel, though. The cabin is commendably quiet. The front seats are large and comfortable. The optional front bench seat is comfortable for two. The rear seat is very roomy and comfortable. Think of the Avalon as a reliable alternative to the largest domestic sedans.

Body styles and prices

	Price range	Trim lines
4-door	$24,278 - $28,128	XL, XLS

Safety information

Safety belt pretensioners .... Front
Center rear safety belt 3-point
Dual air bags .... Standard
Side air bags .... Standard
Antilock brakes .... Standard
Traction control .... Optional
Gov't front-crash test, driver/front passenger .... ◐/●
Gov't side-crash test, driver/rear passenger .... ●/◐
IIHS offset crash test .... Marginal
Injury claim rate compared with all cars/type .... ◐/◒

Reliability history

TROUBLE SPOTS	Toyota Avalon 90	91	92	93	94	95	96	97
Engine						●	●	●
Cooling						●	●	●
Fuel						●	●	●
Ignition						●	●	●
Auto. transmission						●	●	●
Man. transmission								
Clutch								
Electrical						○	○	●
Air conditioning						●	●	●
Suspension						●	◐	●
Brakes						◐	◐	●
Exhaust						●	●	●
Body rust						●	●	●
Paint/trim						●	◐	●
Body integrity						⬤	◒	◐
Body hardware						○	○	◐

Test judgments

Performance
Acceleration .... ◐
Transmission .... ◐
Routine handling .... ◐
Emergency handling .... ○
Braking .... ◐

Comfort
Ride, normal load .... ◐
Ride, full load .... ◐
Noise .... ◐
Driving position .... ◐
Front-seat comfort .... ◐
Rear-seat comfort .... ◐
Climate-control system .... ●

Convenience
Access .... ◐
Controls and displays .... ●
Trunk .... ◐

Other
Fuel economy .... ○
Predicted reliability .... ◐
Predicted depreciation .... ○

Test data

Acceleration
0-30 mph, sec. 3.3
0-60 mph, sec. 8.5
Quarter mile, sec. 16.6
Quarter mile, mph 86
45-65 mph, sec. 5.3

Fuel economy (regular)
EPA city/highway, mpg 21/30
CU's overall mileage, mpg 23
CU's city/highway, mpg 15/37
CU's 150-mile trip, mpg 28
Fuel refill capacity, gal. 18.5
Cruising range, mi. 490
Annual fuel: gal./cost .... 640/$765

Braking from 60 mph
Dry pavement, ft. 128
Wet pavement, ft. 172
Pedal effort, 1st stop, lb. 20
Pedal effort, 10th stop, lb. 25

Specifications

Drive wheels
Front

Seating
Passengers,front/rear 3/3

Dimensions and weight
Length, in. 192
Width, in. 71
Wheelbase, in. 107
Turning circle, ft. 40
Curb weight, lb. 3355
Percent weight, front/rear 62/38
Max. load, lb. 1045

Interior room
Front shoulder room, in. 57.0
Front leg room, in. 42.0
Front head room, in. 5.0
Rear shoulder room, in. 57.0
Rear fore-aft room, in. 33.5
Rear head room, in. 2.5
Door top to ground, in. 51.5
Luggage capacity .... 5+1

Engines available
3.0-liter V6 (200 hp)

Transmissions available
4-speed automatic

Tested model
1998 XL 4-door, 3.0-liter V6, 4-speed automatic

Tires as tested
Bridgestone Potenza RE92, size P205/65R15

Medium car under $25,000

Toyota Camry

The Camry is a fine car overall. It offers side air bags for 1998. The ride is quiet and compliant. Handling is secure and predictable. The steering feels a bit too light at times but responds quickly and precisely. The optional 3.0-liter V6 delivers plenty of thrust and comes nicely mated to a slick, smooth-shifting, four-speed automatic transmission. The standard 2.2-liter Four accelerates adequately and costs about $2,000 less than the V6. Fuel economy for the Four is also slightly better. The seats are fairly comfortable, and the rear is roomy.

Body styles and prices

	Price range	Trim lines
4-door	$16,938 - $24,868	CE, LE, XLE

Safety information

Safety belt pretensioners	Front
Center rear safety belt	3-point
Dual air bags	Standard
Side air bags	Optional
Antilock brakes	Standard (optional on CE)
Traction control	Optional with V6
Gov't front-crash test, driver/front passenger	◒/◒
Gov't side-crash test, driver/rear passenger	○/○
IIHS offset crash test	Good
Injury claim rate compared with all cars/type	NA/NA

Reliability history

TROUBLE SPOTS	Toyota Camry 90	91	92	93	94	95	96	97
Engine								●
Cooling								●
Fuel								●
Ignition								●
Auto. transmission								●
Man. transmission								*
Clutch								*
Electrical								●
Air conditioning								●
Suspension								●
Brakes								●
Exhaust								●
Body rust								●
Paint/trim								●
Body integrity								◒
Body hardware								◒

Test judgments

Performance

Acceleration	○
Transmission	●
Routine handling	◒
Emergency handling	○
Braking	◒

Comfort

Ride, normal load	◒
Ride, full load	◒
Noise	◒
Driving position	◒
Front-seat comfort	◒
Rear-seat comfort	◒
Climate-control system	●

Convenience

Access	◒
Controls and displays	●
Trunk	◒

Other

Fuel economy	◒
Predicted reliability	◒
Predicted depreciation	NA

Test data

Acceleration

0-30 mph, sec.	3.9
0-60 mph, sec.	11.4
Quarter mile, sec.	18.5
Quarter mile, mph	76
45-65 mph, sec.	6.9

Fuel economy (regular)

EPA city/highway, mpg	23/30
CU's overall mileage, mpg	25
CU's city/highway, mpg	16/42
CU's 150-mile trip, mpg	30
Fuel refill capacity, gal.	18.0
Cruising range, mi.	520
Annual fuel: gal./cost	590/$710

Braking from 60 mph

Dry pavement, ft.	139
Wet pavement, ft.	173
Pedal effort, 1st stop, lb.	20
Pedal effort, 10th stop, lb.	25

Specifications

Drive wheels
Front

Seating

Passengers,front/rear	2/3

Dimensions and weight

Length, in.	189
Width, in.	70
Wheelbase, in.	105
Turning circle, ft.	37
Curb weight, lb.	3135
Percent weight, front/rear	62/38
Max. load, lb.	900

Interior room

Front shoulder room, in.	57.0
Front leg room, in.	42.0
Front head room, in.	4.5
Rear shoulder room, in.	56.5
Rear fore-aft room, in.	29.5
Rear head room, in.	2.0
Door top to ground, in.	50.0
Luggage capacity	5+1

Engines available
2.2-liter 4 (133 hp)
3.0-liter V6 (194 hp)

Transmissions available
5-speed manual
4-speed automatic

Tested model
1997 LE 4 4-door, 2.2-liter Four, 4-speed automatic

Tires as tested
Dunlop SP40 A/S, size P195/70R14

Small car

Toyota Corolla

RECOMMENDED

The Corolla was redesigned for 1998, with a more powerful engine. It's built in North America. The Corolla and the Chevrolet Prizm differ only in cosmetic details. These are among the first economy cars to offer side air bags. The Corolla rides comfortably and the engine is quite responsive. Leg room may be a little tight for tall drivers but head room is generous. The front seats are nicely shaped and supportive. Historically the Corolla has been a slightly better value than the Prizm. Some lower-trim Corolla models made before April 1998 (all the VE and some CE models) lacked a front stabilizer bar and didn't handle well in tight, fast turns. Models with that bar handle more safely and nimbly. (The presence of the bar is noted on the car's window sticker.)

Body styles and prices

	Price range	Trim lines
4-door	$11,908 - $14,798	VE, CE, LE

Safety information

Safety belt pretensioners	Front
Center rear safety belt	3-point
Dual air bags	Standard
Side air bags	Optional
Antilock brakes	Optional
Traction control	Not offered
Gov't front-crash test, driver/front passenger	◓/◓
Gov't side-crash test, driver/rear passenger	○/○
IIHS offset crash test	Acceptable
Injury claim rate compared with all cars/type	NA/NA

Reliability history

TROUBLE SPOTS	90 91 92 93 94 95 96 97
Engine	
Cooling	
Fuel	
Ignition	
Auto. transmission	NO
Man. transmission	
Clutch	DATA
Electrical	
Air conditioning	NEW
Suspension	
Brakes	MODEL
Exhaust	
Body rust	
Paint/trim	
Body integrity	
Body hardware	

Test judgments

Performance

Acceleration	○
Transmission	◓
Routine handling	○
Emergency handling	◒
Braking	○

Comfort

Ride, normal load	◓
Ride, full load	○
Noise	◓
Driving position	◓
Front-seat comfort	◓
Rear-seat comfort	◒
Climate-control system	◉

Convenience

Access	○
Controls and displays	◓
Trunk	○

Other

Fuel economy	◓
Predicted reliability	◉
Predicted depreciation	NA

Test data

Acceleration

0-30 mph, sec.	3.8
0-60 mph, sec.	10.7
Quarter mile, sec.	18.0
Quarter mile, mph	79
45-65 mph, sec.	6.2

Fuel economy (regular)

EPA city/highway, mpg	28/36
CU's overall mileage, mpg	30
CU's city/highway, mpg	21/44
CU's 150-mile trip, mpg	36
Fuel refill capacity, gal.	13.2
Cruising range, mi.	440
Annual fuel: gal./cost	495/$595

Braking from 60 mph

Dry pavement, ft.	146
Wet pavement, ft.	171
Pedal effort, 1st stop, lb.	20
Pedal effort, 10th stop, lb.	25

Specifications

Drive wheels

Front

Seating

Passengers, front/rear	2/3

Dimensions and weight

Length, in.	174
Width, in.	67
Wheelbase, in.	97
Turning circle, ft.	35
Curb weight, lb.	2525
Percent weight, front/rear	61/39
Max. load, lb.	850

Interior room

Front shoulder room, in.	53.0
Front leg room, in.	40.5
Front head room, in.	4.0
Rear shoulder room, in.	52.0
Rear fore-aft room, in.	25.5
Rear head room, in.	1.5
Door top to ground, in.	48.0
Luggage capacity	4+1

Engines available

1.8-liter 4 (120 hp)

Transmissions available

5-speed manual
3-speed automatic
4-speed automatic

Tested model

1998 CE 4-door, 1.8-liter Four, 4-speed automatic

Tires as tested

Michelin MX4, size P175/65R14

Sport-utility vehicle

Toyota RAV4

The RAV4 competes with other car-based small SUVs, such as the Subaru Forester and Honda CR-V. Unit-body construction and independent suspension help the RAV4 feel more carlike than trucklike. Nimble handling makes the RAV4 fun to drive. It comes with either front-wheel drive or all-wheel drive. It has no low-range facility for serious off-roading. The manual-shift version feels sprightlier than the automatic. The front seats are small but firm and supportive. Minor styling tweaks and a few more horsepower are new for 1998.

Body styles and prices

	Price range	Trim lines
2-door wagon 2WD	$15,388	—
2-door wagon AWD	$16,798	—
4-door wagon 2WD	$16,248	—
4-door wagon AWD	$17,658	—
Convertible 2WD or AWD	$15,388 - $16,798	—

Safety information

Safety belt pretensioners	Front
Center rear safety belt	Lap
Dual air bags	Standard
Side air bags	Not offered
Antilock brakes	Optional
Traction control	Not offered
Gov't front-crash test, driver/front passenger	○/○
Gov't side-crash test, driver/rear passenger	NA/NA
IIHS offset crash test	NA
Injury claim rate compared with all cars/type	●/●

Reliability history

TROUBLE SPOTS (Toyota RAV4)	90	91	92	93	94	95	96	97
Engine							◉	◉
Cooling							◉	◉
Fuel							◉	◉
Ignition							◉	◉
Auto. transmission							◓	◉
Man. transmission							◉	◉
Clutch							◉	◉
Electrical							◉	◉
Air conditioning							◉	◉
Suspension							◉	◉
Brakes							◉	◉
Exhaust							◉	◉
Body rust							◉	◉
Paint/trim							◉	◉
Body integrity							◓	◓
Body hardware							◓	◉

Test judgments

Performance

Acceleration	◒
Transmission	◓
Routine handling	◓
Emergency handling	○
Braking	◓

Comfort

Ride, normal load	○
Ride, full load	○
Noise	○
Driving position	◓
Front-seat comfort	◓
Rear-seat comfort	○
Climate-control system	◉

Convenience

Access	◓
Controls and displays	◉
Cargo area	◒

Other

Fuel economy	○
Predicted reliability	◉
Predicted depreciation	NA

Test data

Acceleration

0-30 mph, sec.	4.5
0-60 mph, sec.	12.7
Quarter mile, sec.	19.3
Quarter mile, mph	73
45-65 mph, sec	7.9

Fuel economy (regular)

EPA city/highway, mpg	22/26
CU's overall mileage, mpg	22
CU's city/highway, mpg	15/33
CU's 150-mile trip, mpg	27
Fuel refill capacity, gal.	15.3
Cruising range, mi.	385
Annual fuel: gal./cost	670/$805

Braking from 60 mph

Dry pavement, ft.	136
Wet pavement, ft.	159
Pedal effort, 1st stop, lb.	20
Pedal effort, 10th stop, lb.	25

Specifications

Drive wheels

Front or all

Seating

Passengers,front/rear	2/3

Dimensions and weight

Length, in.	163
Width, in.	67
Wheelbase, in.	95
Turning circle, ft.	38
Curb weight, lb.	3000
Percent weight, front/rear	59/41
Max. load, lb.	895

Interior room

Front shoulder room, in.	53.0
Front leg room, in.	39.5
Front head room, in.	3.5
Rear shoulder room, in.	52.5
Rear fore-aft room, in.	24.5
Rear head room, in.	4.5
Door top to ground, in.	59.0
Cargo volume, cu.ft.	28.0

Engines available

2.0-liter 4 (127 hp)

Transmissions available

5-speed manual
4-speed automatic

Tested model

1997 4-door wagon AWD, 2.0-liter Four, 4-speed automatic

Tires as tested

Bridgestone Dueler H/T 687, size 215/70R16

Minivan

Toyota Sienna

The Sienna is our highest-rated minivan. Introduced as a 1998 model, the Sienna is based on the Camry sedan, and it rides quietly and handles competently—much like a Camry. The standard V6 accelerates eagerly, and the transmission shifts smoothly. Both tall and short drivers can see out well. Front- and middle-row seats are quite comfortable, and accessing them is easy. The rearmost seat is well padded and its back reclines, but it's tight for tall people and hard to reach. The Sienna has both left-side and right-side sliding doors, a significant convenience. Cargo space is comparable to the Dodge Caravan's. We expect reliability to be top-notch.

Body styles and prices

	Price range	Trim lines
Minivan	$21,140 - $27,100	CE, LE, XLE

Safety information

Safety belt pretensioners	Front
Center rear safety belt	Lap
Dual air bags	Standard
Side air bags	Not offered
Antilock brakes	Standard
Traction control	Not offered
Gov't front-crash test, driver/front passenger	●/●
Gov't side-crash test, driver/rear passenger	NA/NA
IIHS offset crash test	Good
Injury claim rate compared with all cars/type	NA/NA

Reliability history

TROUBLE SPOTS	90 91 92 93 94 95 96 97
Engine	
Cooling	
Fuel	
Ignition	
Auto. transmission	NO
Man. transmission	
Clutch	DATA
Electrical	
Air conditioning	NEW
Suspension	
Brakes	MODEL
Exhaust	
Body rust	
Paint/trim	
Body integrity	
Body hardware	

Test judgments

Performance

Acceleration	○
Transmission	●
Routine handling	◓
Emergency handling	○
Braking	○

Comfort

Ride, normal load	◓
Ride, full load	◓
Noise	◓
Driving position	◓
Front-seat comfort	◓
Middle-seat comfort	●
Rear-seat comfort	○
Climate-control system	◓

Convenience

Access	◓
Controls and displays	◓
Cargo area	○

Other

Fuel economy	◒
Predicted reliability	◓
Predicted depreciation	NA

Test data

Acceleration

0-30 mph, sec.	3.8
0-60 mph, sec.	10.3
Quarter mile, sec.	17.8
Quarter mile, mph	81
45-65 mph, sec.	6.1

Fuel economy (regular)

EPA city/highway, mpg	18/24
CU's overall mileage, mpg	19
CU's city/highway, mpg	12/30
CU's 150-mile trip, mpg	23
Fuel refill capacity, gal.	21.0
Cruising range, mi.	450
Annual fuel: gal./cost	790/$945

Braking from 60 mph

Dry pavement, ft.	144
Wet pavement, ft.	198
Pedal effort, 1st stop, lb.	25
Pedal effort, 10th stop, lb.	30

Specifications

Drive wheels

Front

Seating

Passengers,front/mid/rear	2/2/3

Dimensions and weight

Length, in.	194
Width, in.	73
Wheelbase, in.	114
Turning circle, ft.	44
Curb weight, lb.	3990
Percent weight, front/rear	58/42
Max. load, lb.	1259

Interior room

Front shoulder room, in.	60.0
Front leg room, in.	41.5
Front head room, in.	6.5
Middle shoulder room, in.	62.0
Middle fore-aft room, in.	33.0
Middle head room, in.	4.5
Rear shoulder room, in.	59.0
Rear fore-aft room, in.	25.0
Rear head room, in.	2.0
Door top to ground, in.	60.5
Cargo volume, cu.ft.	63.5

Engines available

3.0-liter V6 (194 hp)

Transmissions available

4-speed automatic

Tested model

1998 LE Minivan, 3.0-liter V6, 4-speed automatic

Tires as tested

Dunlop SP40 A/S, size P215/65R15

Small car

Toyota Tercel

The Tercel comes now only as a two-door. This is one of the more reliable cars—but it's dull. Assets are a zesty powertrain and excellent fuel economy. Drawbacks include a rough, noisy ride, handling that's rather clumsy for a small car, and a cramped rear seat. The nonantilock brakes are mediocre—and a Tercel with the optional antilock brakes is nearly impossible to find. Leg room is skimpy for tall drivers. With the arrival of a more competitively priced Corolla, the Tercel's days may be numbered.

Body styles and prices

	Price range	Trim lines
2-door	$12,690	CE

Safety information

Safety belt pretensioners ... No
Center rear safety belt ... Lap
Dual air bags ... Standard
Side air bags ... Not offered
Antilock brakes ... Optional
Traction control ... Not offered
Gov't front-crash test, driver/front passenger ... NA/NA
Gov't side-crash test, driver/rear passenger ... ○/◓
IIHS offset crash test ... NA
Injury claim rate compared with all cars/type ... ●/●

Reliability history

TROUBLE SPOTS	90	91	92	93	94	95	96	97
Engine	◒	○	◓	◓	◉	◉	◉	Insufficient data
Cooling	○	○	◓	○	◓	◉	◉	
Fuel	◒	◉	◉	◉	◉	◉	◉	
Ignition	◒	◓	◓	◓	◉	◉	◉	
Auto. transmission	◓	◓	◉	◉	◉	◓	*	
Man. transmission	◉	◉	◉	◉	◉	*	*	
Clutch	○	◓	◓	◉	◉	*	*	
Electrical	○	○	○	◉	◓	◉	◉	
Air conditioning	○	◒	○	○	◓	◉	◉	
Suspension	○	◉	◉	◉	◉	◓	◉	
Brakes	●	○	◒	◓	◓	◉	◉	
Exhaust	●	○	◓	◓	◉	◉	◉	
Body rust	◒	◉	◉	◉	◉	◉	◉	
Paint/trim	○	○	○	○	◓	◓	○	
Body integrity	○	○	○	◓	◓	◒	◓	
Body hardware	○	○	○	◓	◓	○	◓	

Test judgments

Performance
Acceleration ... ◓
Transmission ... ◓
Routine handling ... ○
Emergency handling ... ○
Braking ... ◒*

Comfort
Ride, normal load ... ○
Ride, full load ... ◒
Noise ... ◒
Driving position ... ○
Front-seat comfort ... ○
Rear-seat comfort ... ●
Climate-control system ... ◓

Convenience
Access ... ○
Controls and displays ... ◓
Trunk ... ◒

Other
Fuel economy ... ◉
Predicted reliability ... ◉
Predicted depreciation ... ○
* no antilock brakes

Test data

Acceleration
0-30 mph, sec. ... 3.4
0-60 mph, sec. ... 10.2
Quarter mile, sec. ... 17.7
Quarter mile, mph ... 80
45-65 mph, sec ... 6.4

Fuel economy (regular)
EPA city/highway, mpg ... 34/40
CU's overall mileage, mpg ... 39
CU's city/highway, mpg ... 28/51
CU's 150-mile trip, mpg ... 47
Fuel refill capacity, gal. ... 11.9
Cruising range, mi. ... 525
Annual fuel: gal./cost ... 380/$460

Braking from 60 mph
Dry pavement, ft. ... 153
Wet pavement, ft. ... 193
Pedal effort, 1st stop, lb. ... 15
Pedal effort, 10th stop, lb. ... 20

Specifications

Drive wheels
Front

Seating
Passengers,front/rear ... 2/3

Dimensions and weight
Length, in. ... 162
Width, in. ... 65
Wheelbase, in. ... 94
Turning circle, ft. ... 36
Curb weight, lb. ... 2015
Percent weight, front/rear ... 61/39
Max. load, lb. ... 775

Interior room
Front shoulder room, in. ... 51.5
Front leg room, in. ... 41.0
Front head room, in. ... 3.5
Rear shoulder room, in. ... 49.0
Rear fore-aft room, in. ... 25.0
Rear head room, in. ... 2.0
Door top to ground, in. ... 48.0
Luggage capacity ... 4+0

Engines available
1.5-liter 4 (93 hp)

Transmissions available
5-speed manual
3-speed automatic
4-speed automatic

Tested model
1995 Base 2-door, 1.5-liter Four, 5-speed manual

Tires as tested
Michelin MX4, size P155/80R13

Small car

Volkswagen Golf

This well-designed small hatchback handles capably and uses its space efficiently. The responsive 2.0-liter Four and easy-shifting manual transmission perform well together. The ride is supple. The front seats offer good, firm support. The four-cylinder GTI handles with finesse, but its acceleration is unexceptional. The GTI VR6 version comes with a smooth, powerful V6. Side-impact air bags became optional this year. Reliability has improved to average of late. A redesigned Golf is expected this summer as a 1999 model.

Body styles and prices

	Price range	Trim lines
2-door hatchback	$16,670 - $20,235	GTI, GTI VR6
4-door hatchback	$13,495	GL
Convertible	$17,975 - $22,290	GL, GLS

Safety information

Safety belt pretensioners	Front
Center rear safety belt	Lap
Dual air bags	Standard
Side air bags	Optional
Antilock brakes	Optional (standard on Cabrio, GTI VR6)
Traction control	Standard on GTI VR6
Gov't front-crash test, driver/front passenger	○/○
Gov't side-crash test, driver/rear passenger	NA/NA
IIHS offset crash test	Marginal
Injury claim rate compared with all cars/type	○/◉

Reliability history

TROUBLE SPOTS	Volkswagen Golf, GTI, Golf III 90	91	92	93	94	95	96	97
Engine					◓	◓	◉	◉
Cooling					◓	◉	◉	◉
Fuel					○	○	◓	◉
Ignition					○	○	◓	◉
Auto. transmission					○	○	○	*
Man. transmission					◓	◉	◉	◓
Clutch					◓	◉	◉	◉
Electrical					◒	●	◒	◓
Air conditioning					○	◓	◉	◉
Suspension					◉	◓	◓	◉
Brakes					○	◓	◉	◉
Exhaust					◓	◉	◉	◉
Body rust					◓	◉	◉	◉
Paint/trim					○	○	◓	◓
Body integrity					○	○	○	◓
Body hardware					●	●	◒	◓

Test judgments

Performance

Acceleration	○
Transmission	◓
Routine handling	◉
Emergency handling	◓
Braking	◓

Comfort

Ride, normal load	○
Ride, full load	○
Noise	◓
Driving position	◓
Front-seat comfort	◓
Rear-seat comfort	○
Climate-control system	○

Convenience

Access	◓
Controls and displays	○
Trunk	○

Other

Fuel economy	◓
Predicted reliability	○
Predicted depreciation	○

Test data

Acceleration

0-30 mph, sec.	3.6
0-60 mph, sec.	10.8
Quarter mile, sec.	18.0
Quarter mile, mph	79
45-65 mph, sec.	7.2

Fuel economy (regular)

EPA city/highway, mpg	24/31
CU's overall mileage, mpg	27
CU's city/highway, mpg	18/38
CU's 150-mile trip, mpg	31
Fuel refill capacity, gal.	14.5
Cruising range, mi.	415
Annual fuel: gal./cost	565/$680

Braking from 60 mph

Dry pavement, ft.	134
Wet pavement, ft.	149
Pedal effort, 1st stop, lb.	15
Pedal effort, 10th stop, lb.	20

Specifications

Drive wheels

Front

Seating

Passengers, front/rear	2/3

Dimensions and weight

Length, in.	160
Width, in.	67
Wheelbase, in.	97
Turning circle, ft.	36
Curb weight, lb.	2570
Percent weight, front/rear	63/37
Max. load, lb.	1067

Interior room

Front shoulder room, in.	53.5
Front leg room, in.	42.0
Front head room, in.	2.5
Rear shoulder room, in.	53.0
Rear fore-aft room, in.	27.0
Rear head room, in.	3.0
Door top to ground, in.	51.5
Luggage capacity	3+1

Engines available

2.0-liter 4 (115 hp)
2.8-liter V6 (172 hp)

Transmissions available

5-speed manual
4-speed automatic

Tested model

1996 GTI 2-door hatchback, 2.0-liter Four, 5-speed manual

Tires as tested

Goodyear Eagle GA, size P195/60R14

Medium car under $25,000

Volkswagen Passat

The Passat was redesigned and greatly improved for 1998. Based on the Audi A4, the new Passat is an excellent car overall. It's roomy and comfortable, with front seats and a driving position that are close to ideal. It handles smoothly and precisely, and delivers a firm yet supple ride.The turbocharged 1.8-liter Four accelerates well but sounds a bit harsh. The optional five-speed automatic transmission shifts smoothly, and the brakes are excellent. The interior appointments have a quality feel. V6 and wagon versions have joined the lineup recently. All-wheel-drive versions are due later this year.

Body styles and prices

	Price range	Trim lines
4-door	$20,750 - $26,250	GLS, TDI, GLX
4-door wagon	$21,300	GLS

Safety information

Safety belt pretensioners	Front & rear
Center rear safety belt	Lap
Dual air bags	Standard
Side air bags	Standard
Antilock brakes	Standard
Traction control	Standard
Gov't front-crash test, driver/front passenger	NA/NA
Gov't side-crash test, driver/rear passenger	NA/NA
IIHS offset crash test	Good
Injury claim rate compared with all cars/type	NA/NA

Reliability history

TROUBLE SPOTS	90 91 92 93 94 95 96 97
Engine	
Cooling	
Fuel	
Ignition	
Auto. transmission	NO
Man. transmission	
Clutch	DATA
Electrical	
Air conditioning	NEW
Suspension	
Brakes	MODEL
Exhaust	
Body rust	
Paint/trim	
Body integrity	
Body hardware	

Test judgments

Performance

Acceleration	○
Transmission	◒
Routine handling	◒
Emergency handling	◒
Braking	●

Comfort

Ride, normal load	◒
Ride, full load	◒
Noise	◒
Driving position	◒
Front-seat comfort	●
Rear-seat comfort	◒
Climate-control system	◒

Convenience

Access	◒
Controls and displays	◒
Trunk	◒

Other

Fuel economy	○
Predicted reliability	New
Predicted depreciation	NA

Test data

Acceleration

0-30 mph, sec.	3.8
0-60 mph, sec.	10.3
Quarter mile, sec.	17.9
Quarter mile, mph	82
45-65 mph, sec.	6.3

Fuel economy (premium)

EPA city/highway, mpg	21/31
CU's overall mileage, mpg	24
CU's city/highway, mpg	16/38
CU's 150-mile trip, mpg	30
Fuel refill capacity, gal.	18.5
Cruising range, mi.	520
Annual fuel: gal./cost	615/$860

Braking from 60 mph

Dry pavement, ft.	129
Wet pavement, ft.	154
Pedal effort, 1st stop, lb.	20
Pedal effort, 10th stop, lb.	20

Specifications

Drive wheels
Front

Seating

Passengers,front/rear	2/3

Dimensions and weight

Length, in.	184
Width, in.	69
Wheelbase, in.	106
Turning circle, ft.	38
Curb weight, lb.	3175
Percent weight, front/rear	61/39
Max. load, lb.	990

Interior room

Front shoulder room, in.	55.5
Front leg room, in.	42.5
Front head room, in.	6.5
Rear shoulder room, in.	53.5
Rear fore-aft room, in.	29.0
Rear head room, in.	3.0
Door top to ground, in.	51.0
Luggage capacity	5+0

Engines available
1.8-liter 4 Turbo (150 hp), 1.9-liter 4 turbodiesel (90 hp), 2.8-liter V6 (190 hp)

Transmissions available
5-speed manual, 4 or 5-speed auto.

Tested model
1998 GLS 4-door, 1.8-liter Turbo Four, 5-speed automatic

Tires as tested
Continental Conti Touring, size 195/65R15

Medium car over $25,000

Volvo S70/V70

Sedan or wagon, this is one of our highest rated cars. It has a full complement of safety equipment. The engine of choice is the 190-hp "light pressure" turbo found in the GLT. With that engine, the car is quick, fairly quiet, and gets reasonable fuel economy. Tire grip is tenacious, and braking is first-class. Large, comfortable seats only partially make up for a stiff ride, however. The rear easily holds three, and the trunk is spacious. The automatic climate system works very well. The wagon version is roomy and well thought out. The all-wheel-drive wagon is a sensible alternative to an SUV.

Body styles and prices

	Price range	Trim lines
4-door	$26,985 - $34,010	Base, GT, GLT, T5
4-door wagon AWD	$34,420 - $40,995	GLT, XC, R
4-door wagon FWD	$28,285 - $35,310	Base, GT, GLT, T5

Safety information

Safety belt pretensioners	Front
Center rear safety belt	3-point
Dual air bags	Standard
Side air bags	Standard
Antilock brakes	Standard
Traction control	Optional
Gov't front-crash test, driver/front passenger	●/●
Gov't side-crash test, driver/rear passenger	◓/NA
IIHS offset crash test	Good
Injury claim rate compared with all cars/type	◓/◓

Reliability history

TROUBLE SPOTS	Volvo 850 Series 90	91	92	93	94	95	96	97
Engine				◓	◓	●	●	●
Cooling				●	◓	●	●	●
Fuel				◓	◓	◓	●	●
Ignition				○	○	◓	●	●
Auto. transmission				○	◓	◓	●	●
Man. transmission				◓	◓	●	●	*
Clutch				○	●	●	●	*
Electrical				◒	◒	◒	○	◓
Air conditioning				○	○	◓	●	●
Suspension				○	◓	●	●	●
Brakes				◓	○	◓	○	●
Exhaust				●	●	●	●	●
Body rust				●	●	●	●	●
Paint/trim				◓	○	◓	●	●
Body integrity				○	◒	○	◓	●
Body hardware				◒	◒	○	◓	◓

Test judgments

Performance

Acceleration	●
Transmission	◓
Routine handling	◓
Emergency handling	◓
Braking	◓

Comfort

Ride, normal load	○
Ride, full load	○
Noise	◓
Driving position	◓
Front-seat comfort	●
Rear-seat comfort	◓
Climate-control system	●

Convenience

Access	◓
Controls and displays	◓
Cargo area	○

Other

Fuel economy	○
Predicted reliability	◓
Predicted depreciation	○

Test data

Acceleration

0-30 mph, sec.	3.0
0-60 mph, sec.	7.6
Quarter mile, sec.	15.9
Quarter mile, mph	91
45-65 mph, sec.	4.4

Fuel economy (premium)

EPA city/highway, mpg	19/27
CU's overall mileage, mpg	21
CU's city/highway, mpg	13/34
CU's 150-mile trip, mpg	26
Fuel refill capacity, gal.	18.4
Cruising range, mi.	445
Annual fuel: gal./cost	715/$1005

Braking from 60 mph

Dry pavement, ft.	128
Wet pavement, ft.	159
Pedal effort, 1st stop, lb.	15
Pedal effort, 10th stop, lb.	15

Specifications

Drive wheels

Front or all

Seating

Passengers,front/rear	2/3

Dimensions and weight

Length, in.	186
Width, in.	69
Wheelbase, in.	105
Turning circle, ft.	37
Curb weight, lb.	3380
Percent weight, front/rear	60/40
Max. load, lb.	960

Interior room

Front shoulder room, in.	56.0
Front leg room, in.	42.0
Front head room, in.	3.0
Rear shoulder room, in.	56.5
Rear fore-aft room, in.	29.5
Rear head room, in.	3.5
Door top to ground, in.	49.5
Cargo volume, cu.ft.	34.5

Engines available

2.3-liter 5 turbo (236 hp)
2.4-liter 5 (168 hp)
2.4-liter 5 turbo (190 hp)

Transmissions available

5-speed manual
4-speed automatic

Tested model

1998 GLT 4-door wagon FWD, 2.4-liter turbo Five, 4-speed auto.

Tires as tested

Michelin MXV4, size 195/60R15

Coupe

Acura CL

■ **Trim line:** 2.3CL, 3.0CL ■ **Body style:** 2-door ■ **Price:** $22,310-$26,660 ■ **Predicted depreciation:** NA ■ **Predicted reliability:** ○ ■ This model is based on the pre-1998 Honda Accord coupe. For 1998, the base model is the 2.3CL, which receives a slightly larger, 150 hp, 2.3-liter VTEC Four. A five-speed manual or four-speed automatic transmission is available with the Four. The 3.0CL comes standard with a smooth, refined 200-hp, 3.0-liter V6 and a slick automatic transmission. Expect a comfortable ride but a small interior.

Specifications

Dimensions *Length,* 190 in.; *Width,* 70 in.; *Curb weight,* 3050 lb.; *Passengers, front/rear,* 2/3 **Drive wheels** Front **Engines** 2.3-liter 4 (150 hp), 3.0-liter V6 (200 hp) **Transmissions** 5-speed manual, 4-speed automatic

Safety information

Side air bags .... Not offered
Antilock brakes .... Standard
Gov't front-crash test, driver/front passenger ... NA/NA
IIHS offset crash test .... NA

Reliability history

TROUBLE SPOTS	90	91	92	93	94	95	96	97
Engine								●
Cooling								●
Fuel								●
Ignition								●
Auto. trans.								●
Man. trans.								●
Clutch								●
Electrical								●
A/C								●
Suspension								●
Brakes								●
Exhaust								●
Body rust								●
Paint/trim								●
Integrity								○
Hardware								○

(Acura CL)

Sport-utility vehicle

Acura SLX

■ **Trim line:** — ■ **Body style:** 4-door wagon 4WD ■ **Price:** $36,300 ■ **Predicted depreciation:** NA ■ **Predicted reliability:** NA ■ The SLX is an Isuzu Trooper with Honda's Acura nameplate. We rated the 1996-1997 Acura SLX and similar 1995-1997 Isuzu Trooper Not Acceptable because of their pronounced tendency to roll over in our emergency-handling tests, based on our tests of the 1996 SLX and the 1995 and 1996 Trooper. The 1998 model has a revised engine, transmission, and body. Because we have not tested this model, we don't know if the changes have affected its handling. We cannot judge its performance.

Specifications

Dimensions *Length,* 184 in.; *Width,* 72 in.; *Curb weight,* 4430 lb.; *Passengers, front/rear,* 2/3 **Drive wheels** Selectable 4WD **Engines** 3.5-liter V6 (215 hp) **Transmissions** 4-speed automatic

Safety information

Side air bags .... Not offered
Antilock brakes .... Standard
Gov't front-crash test, driver/front passenger ..... ○/○
IIHS offset crash test .... NA

Reliability history

TROUBLE SPOTS	90 91 92 93 94 95 96 97
Engine	
Cooling	
Fuel	
Ignition	NOT
Auto. trans.	
Man. trans.	ENOUGH
Clutch	
Electrical	
A/C	DATA
Suspension	
Brakes	TO
Exhaust	
Body rust	
Paint/trim	RATE
Integrity	
Hardware	

Medium car over $25,000

Audi A6

■ **Trim line:** Avant ■ **Body style:** 4-door, 4-door wagon AWD ■ **Price:** $33,750-$36,600 ■ **Predicted depreciation:** NA ■ **Predicted reliability:** New ■ This German-made sedan, larger than the A4, has been redesigned for 1998. Highlights include a new body and chassis with a longer wheelbase, and a more potent 200-hp V6. A new A6 wagon has just been introduced. This is a well-engineered, quiet, comfortable car with secure and responsive handling. The popular Quattro all-wheel-drive option is available on all versions, and standard on the wagon. Audi provides all scheduled maintenance free for three years or 50,000 miles.

Specifications

Dimensions *Length,* 193 in.; *Width,* 70 in.; *Curb weight,* 3785 lb.; *Passengers, front/rear,* 2/3 **Drive wheels** Front or all **Engines** 2.8-liter V6 (200 hp) **Transmissions** 5-speed automatic

Safety information

Side air bags .... Standard
Antilock brakes .... Standard
Gov't front-crash test, driver/front passenger ... NA/NA
IIHS offset crash test .... NA

Reliability history

TROUBLE SPOTS	90 91 92 93 94 95 96 97
Engine	
Cooling	
Fuel	
Ignition	NO
Auto. trans.	
Man. trans.	DATA
Clutch	
Electrical	
A/C	NEW
Suspension	
Brakes	MODEL
Exhaust	
Body rust	
Paint/trim	
Integrity	
Hardware	

Luxury car

Audi A8

■ **Trim line:** 3.7, 4.2Quattro ■ **Body style:** 4-door ■ **Price:** $57,400-$65,000 ■ **Predicted depreciation:** NA ■ **Predicted reliability:** NA ■ Audi's top-of-the-line A8 is a full-sized luxury car that competes with the BMW 7-Series, Mercedes S-Class, and Lexus LS400. The A8 has an all-aluminum body and offers a choice of two V8s and front-wheel or all-wheel drive. A five-speed automatic transmission is standard. The transmission has a Tiptronic feature that allows easy manual shifts with a flick of the lever. The A8 comes with every conceivable feature, including six air bags—two up front and one in each of the four doors. Both front and rear seats are heated. A comprehensive warranty covers everything for the first three years.

Specifications

Dimensions *Length,* 198 in.; *Width,* 74 in.; *Curb weight,* 3950 lb.; *Passengers, front/rear,* 2/3 **Drive wheels** Front or all **Engines** 3.7-liter V8 (230 hp), 4.2-liter V8 (300 hp) **Transmissions** 5-speed automatic

Safety information

Side air bags .... Standard
Antilock brakes .... Standard
Gov't front-crash test, driver/front passenger ... NA/NA
IIHS offset crash test .... NA

Reliability history

TROUBLE SPOTS	90 91 92 93 94 95 96 97
Engine	
Cooling	
Fuel	
Ignition	NOT
Auto. trans.	
Man. trans.	ENOUGH
Clutch	
Electrical	
A/C	DATA
Suspension	
Brakes	TO
Exhaust	
Body rust	
Paint/trim	RATE
Integrity	
Hardware	

Sports/sporty car under $25,000

BMW 318ti

■ **Trim line:** — ■ **Body style:** 2-door hatchback ■ **Price:** $21,390 ■ **Predicted depreciation:** ○ ■ **Predicted reliability:** NA ■ The 318ti is the "entry level" BMW, but it quickly gets expensive if you add a few desirable options. This hatchback coupe is similar in many ways to the 3-Series, but it's shorter and lighter. The rear-wheel-drive 318ti is fun to drive, with precise handling, tenacious tire grip, plus a firm but comfortable ride. A 138-hp, 1.9-liter Four is the only engine available. Traction control is standard—and a must on slick roads. Side-impact air bags are now standard.

Specifications

Dimensions *Length,* 166 in.; *Width,* 67 in.; *Curb weight,* 2790 lb.; *Passengers, front/rear,* 2/3 **Drive wheels** Rear **Engines** 1.9-liter 4 (138 hp) **Transmissions** 5-speed manual, 4-speed automatic

Safety information

Side air bags .... Standard
Antilock brakes .... Standard
Gov't front-crash test, driver/front passenger ... NA/NA
IIHS offset crash test .... NA

Reliability history

TROUBLE SPOTS	90 91 92 93 94 95 96 97
Engine	
Cooling	
Fuel	
Ignition	NOT
Auto. trans.	
Man. trans.	ENOUGH
Clutch	
Electrical	
A/C	DATA
Suspension	
Brakes	TO
Exhaust	
Body rust	
Paint/trim	RATE
Integrity	
Hardware	

Luxury car

BMW 740iL

■ **Trim line:** 740i, 740iL ■ **Body style:** 4-door ■ **Price:** $61,500-$65,500 ■ **Predicted depreciation:** ○ ■ **Predicted reliability:** ○ ■ The top-of-the-line 7-Series BMW competes with the world's premier luxury sedans. Both long- and short-wheelbase versions are available. New safety items for 1998 include an anti-skid system as well as front side- and head-level air bags. Rear side air bags are optional. The 4.4-liter V8 produces 282 hp. The 740i handles superbly for a car its size. Nearly all controls are easy to use, once you figure out what they all do.

Specifications

Dimensions *Length,* 196 in.; *Width,* 73 in.; *Curb weight,* 4145 lb.; *Passengers, front/rear,* 2/3 **Drive wheels** Rear **Engines** 4.4-liter V8 (282 hp) **Transmissions** 5-speed automatic

Safety information

Side air bags .... Standard
Antilock brakes .... Standard
Gov't front-crash test, driver/front passenger ... NA/NA
IIHS offset crash test .... NA

Reliability history

TROUBLE SPOTS	BMW 7-Series							
	90	91	92	93	94	95	96	97
Engine						○		
Cooling						◉		
Fuel						○		
Ignition						◓		
Auto. trans.						◉		
Man. trans.	Insufficient data	Insufficient data	Insufficient data	Insufficient data	Insufficient data		Insufficient data	Insufficient data
Clutch								
Electrical						●		
A/C						◒		
Suspension						◉		
Brakes						◓		
Exhaust						◉		
Body rust						◉		
Paint/trim						◓		
Integrity						◓		
Hardware						○		

Sports/sporty car over $25,000

BMW Z3

■ **Trim line:** M, 1.9, 2.8, M Roadster ■ **Body style:** 2-door, Convertible ■ **Price:** $29,425-$42,200 ■ **Predicted depreciation:** NA ■ **Predicted reliability:** ○ ■ BMW uses components from the less expensive 318ti to build this sleek roadster in Spartanburg, S.C. The Z3 interior is cramped—not surprising in a two-seater—and you can't recline the seat very far. The 138-hp, 1.9-liter Four feels a little flat, but the ride is tolerable by any standard, and handling is good. The 189-hp, 2.8-liter inline Six makes this a far more exciting car. Sadly, the Six adds a whopping $6,000, putting the Z3 closer in price to the Porsche Boxster and Mercedes SLK than to, say, the Mazda Miata. Two high-performance, 240-hp M models, a roadster and a coupe, join the lineup for 1998.

Specifications

Dimensions *Length,* 159 in.; *Width,* 67 in.; *Curb weight,* 2960 lb.; *Passengers, front,* 2 **Drive wheels** Rear **Engines** 1.9-liter 4 (138 hp), 2.8-liter 6 (189 hp), 3.2-liter 6 (240 hp) **Transmissions** 5-speed manual, 4-speed automatic

Safety information

Side air bags .... Not offered
Antilock brakes .... Standard
Gov't front-crash test, driver/front passenger ... NA/NA
IIHS offset crash test .... NA

Reliability history

TROUBLE SPOTS	90	91	92	93	94	95	96	97
Engine							Insufficient data	◉
Cooling								◉
Fuel								◉
Ignition								◉
Auto. trans.								*
Man. trans.								*
Clutch								*
Electrical								◓
A/C								◉
Suspension								◉
Brakes								◉
Exhaust								◉
Body rust								◓
Paint/trim								◉
Integrity								○
Hardware								◓

Coupe

Cadillac Eldorado

■ **Trim line:** Base, Touring Coupe ■ **Body style:** 2-door ■ **Price:** $38,495-$42,695 ■ **Predicted depreciation:** ◒ ■ **Predicted reliability:** ● ■ This luxury coupe comes with lots of high-tech equipment, including a 4.6-liter, 32-valve, aluminum Northstar V8. Stability control—a sophisticated device that helps prevent sideways skids—is part of the antilock brake system. The higher-priced Touring Coupe provides strong acceleration, though handling is less than precise. The front seat is roomy. The rear seat is fairly comfortable for two, but access is awkward.

Specifications

Dimensions *Length,* 202 in.; *Width,* 76 in.; *Curb weight,* 3840 lb.; *Passengers, front/rear,* 2/3 **Drive wheels** Front **Engines** 4.6-liter V8 (275 hp), 4.6-liter V8 (300 hp) **Transmissions** 4-speed automatic

Safety information

Side air bags .... Not offered
Antilock brakes .... Standard
Gov't front-crash test, driver/front passenger ... NA/NA
IIHS offset crash test .... NA

Reliability history

TROUBLE SPOTS	90	91	92	93	94	95	96	97
Engine	○	Insufficient data	○	Insufficient data	◓	◓	◓	Insufficient data
Cooling	◒		○		◉	◉	◓	
Fuel	○		○		◓	◓	◓	
Ignition	◒		○		◒	◓	◓	
Auto. trans.	○		◓		◉	◓	◓	
Man. trans.								
Clutch								
Electrical	●		●		◒	◒	◒	
A/C	●		◒		○	○	○	
Suspension	○		●		◓	◉	◓	
Brakes	●		●		○	◓	○	
Exhaust	◓		◓		◉	◉	◉	
Body rust	◓		◓		◉	◉	◉	
Paint/trim	◓		◓		◓	◓	○	
Integrity	◓		●		◒	●	●	
Hardware	◒		●		●	●	○	

Luxury car

Cadillac Seville

■ **Trim line:** SLS, STS ■ **Body style:** 4-door ■ **Price:** $42,495-$46,995 ■ **Predicted depreciation:** NA ■ **Predicted reliability:** New ■ The Seville has been redesigned for 1998, and now shares its basic platform with the Oldsmobile Aurora and Buick Riviera. Cadillac seems to want to position the Seville as an alternative to European luxury sedans and the Lexus LS400. It retains the sophisticated Northstar V8. Still, it has a world-class powertrain and good ride and handling. The rear seat is a little bit cramped.

Specifications

Dimensions *Length,* 201 in.; *Width,* 75 in.; *Curb weight,* 4050 lb.; *Passengers, front/rear,* 2/3 **Drive wheels** Front **Engines** 4.6-liter V8 (275 hp), 4.6-liter V8 (300 hp) **Transmissions** 4-speed automatic

Safety information

Side air bags .... Standard
Antilock brakes .... Standard
Gov't front-crash test, driver/front passenger ... NA/NA
IIHS offset crash test .... NA

Reliability history

TROUBLE SPOTS	90	91	92	93	94	95	96	97
Engine								
Cooling								
Fuel								
Ignition	NO							
Auto. trans.								
Man. trans.	DATA							
Clutch								
Electrical								
A/C	NEW							
Suspension								
Brakes	MODEL							
Exhaust								
Body rust								
Paint/trim								
Integrity								
Hardware								

Sports/sporty car under $25,000

Chevrolet Camaro

■ **Trim line:** Base, Z28 ■ **Body style:** 2-door, Convertible ■ **Price:** $16,625-$27,450 ■ **Predicted depreciation:** ○ ■ **Predicted reliability:** ● ■ Changes for 1998 include a minor face-lift and a 305-hp version of the Chevy Corvette's V8. The standard engine is a 200-hp, 3.8-liter V6. The Camaro is too bulky to be nimble. Traction control is a worthy option on V8-powered models. A six-speed manual transmission is standard in the Z28; a four-speed automatic is optional. The ride is uncomfortable. Braking is very good. The V8 has been substantially less reliable than the V6.

Specifications

Dimensions *Length,* 193 in.; *Width,* 74 in.; *Curb weight,* 3545 lb.; *Passengers, front/rear,* 2/2 **Drive wheels** Rear **Engines** 3.8-liter V6 (200 hp), 5.7-liter V8 (305 hp), 5.7-liter V8 (320 hp) **Transmissions** 5-speed manual, 6-speed manual, 4-speed automatic

Safety information

Side air bags ....Not offered
Antilock brakes ....Standard
Gov't front-crash test, driver/front passenger .....◓/◉
IIHS offset crash test ....NA

Reliability history

TROUBLE SPOTS	Chevrolet Camaro V8							
	90	91	92	93	94	95	96	97
Engine	Insufficient data	○	Insufficient data	Insufficient data	○	◒	◒	Insufficient data
Cooling		◒			○	◓	◉	
Fuel		●			◓	◓	◓	
Ignition		●			◒	○	◉	
Auto. trans.		*			◉	◉	*	
Man. trans.		*			*	*	*	
Clutch		*			*	*	*	
Electrical		◒			◒	●	◒	
A/C		○			◓	○	◉	
Suspension		○			◓	◓	◓	
Brakes		◒			◒	○	◓	
Exhaust		◒			◉	◓	◉	
Body rust		◉			◉	◉	◉	
Paint/trim		●			◓	◓	○	
Integrity		●			●	●	◒	
Hardware		●			●	◒	◒	

Sports/sporty car over $25,000

Chevrolet Corvette

■ **Trim line:** — ■ **Body style:** 2-door, Convertible ■ **Price:** $37,495-$44,425 ■ **Predicted depreciation:** NA ■ **Predicted reliability:** New ■ This legendary two-seat sports car was extensively redesigned recently. The Corvette has a potent 345-hp, 5.7-liter V8. The cockpit is less confining than the previous model, and has lower door sills for easier access. Handling has improved but this car still puts thrust before finesse. Controls and displays have improved. The transmission is now in the rear for better weight distribution and more interior room. The huge tires make a lot of noise. A convertible model and stability-control option are new for this model year. Raising and lowering the soft top is an aggravating chore.

Specifications

Dimensions *Length,* 180 in.; *Width,* 74 in.; *Curb weight,* 3220 lb.; *Passengers, front,* 2 **Drive wheels** Rear **Engines** 5.7-liter V8 (345 hp) **Transmissions** 6-speed manual, 4-speed automatic

Safety information

Side air bags ....Not offered
Antilock brakes ....Standard
Gov't front-crash test, driver/front passenger ...NA/NA
IIHS offset crash test ....NA

Reliability history

TROUBLE SPOTS	90 91 92 93 94 95 96 97
Engine	
Cooling	
Fuel	
Ignition	NO
Auto. trans.	
Man. trans.	DATA
Clutch	
Electrical	
A/C	NEW
Suspension	
Brakes	MODEL
Exhaust	
Body rust	
Paint/trim	
Integrity	
Hardware	

Sport-utility vehicle

Chevrolet Suburban

■ **Trim line:** Base, LS, LT ■ **Body style:** 4-door wagon 2WD, 4-door wagon 4WD ■ **Price:** $25,555-$38,425 ■ **Predicted depreciation:** ◉ ■ **Predicted reliability:** ◒ ■ This largest of sport-utilities and its GMC twin can seat as many as nine or tow a trailer weighing up to 10,000 pounds. These outsized station wagons come with rear-wheel or four-wheel drive. Selectable full-time four-wheel drive is a new option for 1998. Both the big V8s offered are powerful, but they burn a lot of fuel. The 6.5-liter turbodiesel V8 is more economical. For most people, the 5.7-liter V8 is the best choice, especially since it comes with a more compliant suspension.

Specifications

Dimensions *Length,* 220 in.; *Width,* 76 in.; *Curb weight,* 5640 lb.; *Passengers, front/mid/rear,* 3/3/3 **Drive wheels** Rear or selectable 4WD **Engines** 5.7-liter V8 (255 hp), 6.5-liter V8 turbodiesel (195 hp), 7.4-liter V8 (290 hp) **Transmissions** 4-speed automatic

Safety information

Side air bags ....Not offered
Antilock brakes ....Standard
Gov't front-crash test, driver/front passenger .....◓/◓
IIHS offset crash test ....NA

Reliability history

TROUBLE SPOTS	Chevrolet Suburban							
	90	91	92	93	94	95	96	97
Engine	○	○	○	◓	◓	◉	◉	◉
Cooling	●	◒	●	●	◉	◉	◉	◉
Fuel	◓	◓	◓	◉	◓	◉	◓	◉
Ignition	●	●	◒	○	○	◓	◓	◉
Auto. trans.	◒	●	◒	○	◓	◓	◓	◉
Man. trans.	*							
Clutch	*							
Electrical	●	◒	◒	◒	◒	◒	○	◓
A/C	●	◒	○	○	◒	○	◓	◉
Suspension	◒	○	○	○	◓	◓	◓	◓
Brakes	●	●	●	●	●	◒	○	○
Exhaust	◒	●	○	○	◓	◉	◉	◉
Body rust	◒	○	◓	◓	◉	◉	◉	◉
Paint/trim	●	●	◒	○	◓	◓	◉	◉
Integrity	●	●	●	◒	◒	○	○	◓
Hardware	●	●	◒	●	◒	●	◒	◓

Large car over $30,000

Chrysler 300M

■ **Trim line:** — ■ **Body style:** 4-door ■ **Price:** $28,300 ■ **Predicted depreciation:** NA ■ **Predicted reliability:** New ■ Released this spring as a 1999 model, the 300M resurrects a Chrysler naming scheme from the '50s and '60s. The 300M is an upscale sibling of the Dodge Intrepid and Chrysler Concorde, and is powered by the same new aluminum, 3.5-liter, 253-hp V6 as the Chrysler LHS. The roomy 300M is positioned to appeal to the buyer of a "near luxury" car who would ordinarily consider an import first. Reliability of new Chrysler products has been spotty, so it may be prudent to wait one model year.

Specifications

Dimensions *Length,* 198 in.; *Width,* 75 in.; *Curb weight,* 3560 lb.; *Passengers, front/rear,* 3/3 **Drive wheels** Front **Engines** 3.5-liter V6 (253 hp) **Transmissions** 4-speed automatic

Safety information

Side air bags ....Not offered
Antilock brakes ....Standard
Gov't front-crash test, driver/front passenger ...NA/NA
IIHS offset crash test ....NA

Reliability history

TROUBLE SPOTS	90 91 92 93 94 95 96 97
Engine	
Cooling	
Fuel	
Ignition	NO
Auto. trans.	
Man. trans.	DATA
Clutch	
Electrical	
A/C	NEW
Suspension	
Brakes	MODEL
Exhaust	
Body rust	
Paint/trim	
Integrity	
Hardware	

Large car over $30,000

Chrysler LHS

■ **Trim line:** — ■ **Body style:** 4-door ■ **Price:** $28,400 ■ **Predicted depreciation:** NA ■ **Predicted reliability:** New ■ The LHS is an upscale version of the new Chrysler Concorde. It's a large four-door sedan styled to look like a sporty coupe. It comes loaded with standard equipment like heated, powered, leather-trimmed seats, an upgraded sound system, and touches of fake wood throughout the cabin. The standard engine is a brand-new 253-hp aluminum V6. The LHS may turn out to be a sound performer, but the reliability of Chrysler products in their first year of production has not been encouraging.

Specifications

Dimensions *Length,* 208 in.; *Width,* 74 in.; *Curb weight,* 3580 lb.; *Passengers, front/rear,* 3/3 **Drive wheels** Front **Engines** 3.5-liter V6 (253 hp) **Transmissions** 4-speed automatic

Safety information

Side air bags ....Not offered
Antilock brakes ....Standard
Gov't front-crash test, driver/front passenger ...NA/NA
IIHS offset crash test ....NA

Reliability history

TROUBLE SPOTS	90 91 92 93 94 95 96 97
Engine	
Cooling	
Fuel	
Ignition	NO
Auto. trans.	
Man. trans.	DATA
Clutch	
Electrical	
A/C	NEW
Suspension	
Brakes	MODEL
Exhaust	
Body rust	
Paint/trim	
Integrity	
Hardware	

Sports/sporty car under $25,000

Ford Mustang

■ **Trim line:** Base, GT, Cobra ■ **Body style:** 2-door, Convertible ■ **Price:** $16,150-$28,430 ■ **Predicted depreciation:** ○ ■ **Predicted reliability:** ○ ■ This old-fashioned muscle car hasn't changed significantly since its 1994 redesign. The Mustang doesn't feel as sporty as its Chevrolet Camaro and Pontiac Firebird competitors. The 150-hp, 3.8-liter V6 version feels sluggish. The 225-hp, 4.6-liter V8 in the GT version has more punch. The Mustang steps to the side on bumps and delivers a jerky ride. The front seats provide generally adequate support but little comfort. Adults won't be happy in the rear seat, but practicality isn't what this car is about.

Specifications

Dimensions *Length,* 182 in.; *Width,* 72 in.; *Curb weight,* 3450 lb.; *Passengers, front/rear,* 2/2 **Drive wheels** Rear **Engines** 3.8-liter V6 (150 hp), 4.6-liter V8 (225 hp), 4.6-liter V8 (305 hp) **Transmissions** 5-speed manual, 4-speed automatic

Safety information

Side air bags ....Not offered
Antilock brakes ....Optional
Gov't front-crash test, driver/front passenger .....⊙/◓
IIHS offset crash test ....NA

Reliability history

TROUBLE SPOTS	Ford Mustang 90	91	92	93	94	95	96	97
Engine					⊙	◓	⊙	Insufficient data
Cooling					⊙	⊙	⊙	
Fuel					⊙	◓	⊙	
Ignition					○	◓	◓	
Auto. trans.					●	○	◓	
Man. trans.					◓	○	◓	
Clutch					◓	⊙	◓	
Electrical					○	○	○	
A/C					○	◓	⊙	
Suspension					○	◓	○	
Brakes					◒	○	◓	
Exhaust					◓	⊙	⊙	
Body rust					⊙	⊙	⊙	
Paint/trim					○	○	◓	
Integrity					◒	◒	◒	
Hardware					◒	○	○	

Pickup truck

Ford Ranger

■ **Trim line:** XL, XLT, Splash ■ **Body style:** Regular cab 2WD, Regular cab 4WD, Extended cab 2WD, Extended cab 4WD ■ **Price:** $11,485-$19,695 ■ **Predicted depreciation:** NA ■ **Predicted reliability:** New ■ The Ranger has been redesigned for 1998, with a new front suspension, longer wheelbase, and better engines. We haven't tested it yet, but expect it to remain a good truck. A cutoff switch allows you to deactivate the passenger-side air bag—a must if you mount an infant seat there. The regular-cab version is roomier inside, while the extended-cab stays the same size. A longer, four-door-cab model appears in early summer.

Specifications

Dimensions *Length,* 203 in.; *Width,* 69 in.; *Curb weight,* 3315 lb.; *Passengers, front/rear,* 3/2 **Drive wheels** Rear or part-time 4WD **Engines** 2.5-liter 4 (117 hp), 3.0-liter V6 (145 hp), 4.0-liter V6 (158 hp) **Transmissions** 5-speed manual, 4-speed auto., 5-speed auto.

Safety information

Side air bags ....Not offered
Antilock brakes ....Optional
Gov't front-crash test, driver/front passenger .....◓/◓
IIHS offset crash test ....NA

Reliability history

TROUBLE SPOTS	90 91 92 93 94 95 96 97
Engine	
Cooling	
Fuel	
Ignition	NO
Auto. trans.	
Man. trans.	DATA
Clutch	
Electrical	
A/C	NEW
Suspension	
Brakes	MODEL
Exhaust	
Body rust	
Paint/trim	
Integrity	
Hardware	

Sport-utility vehicle

GMC Suburban

■ **Trim line:** SL, SLE, SLT ■ **Body style:** 4-door wagon 2WD, 4-door wagon 4WD ■ **Price:** $25,619-$36,058 ■ **Predicted depreciation:** ◉ ■ **Predicted reliability:** ◒ ■ This largest of sport-utilities and its Chevrolet twin emphasize utility. They can seat as many as nine or tow a trailer weighing up to 10,000 pounds. These outsized station wagons come with rear-wheel or four-wheel drive. Selectable full-time four-wheel drive is a new option for 1998. Both the 5.7-liter V8 and mammoth 7.4-liter V8 are powerful, but they burn a lot of fuel. The 6.5-liter turbodiesel V8 is more economical. For most people, the 5.7-liter V8 is the best choice, especially since it comes with a more compliant suspension.

Specifications

Dimensions *Length,* 220 in.; *Width,* 77 in.; *Curb weight,* 5640 lb.; *Passengers, front/mid/rear,* 3/3/3 **Drive wheels** Rear or selectable 4WD **Engines** 5.7-liter V8 (255 hp), 6.5-liter V8 turbodiesel (190 hp), 7.4-liter V8 (290 hp) **Transmissions** 4-speed auto.

Safety information

Side air bags ....Not offered
Antilock brakes ....Standard
Gov't front-crash test, driver/front passenger .....◓/◓
IIHS offset crash test ....NA

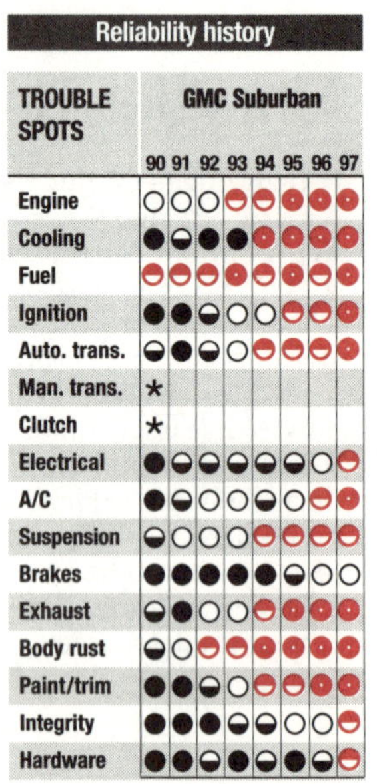

Reliability history

TROUBLE SPOTS	GMC Suburban							
	90	91	92	93	94	95	96	97
Engine	○	○	○	◓	◓	◉	◉	◉
Cooling	●	◒	●	●	◉	◉	◉	◉
Fuel	◓	◓	◓	◉	◓	◉	◓	◉
Ignition	●	●	◒	○	○	◓	◓	◉
Auto. trans.	◒	●	◒	○	◓	◓	◓	◉
Man. trans.	*							
Clutch	*							
Electrical	●	◒	◒	◒	◒	◒	○	◓
A/C	●	◒	○	○	◒	○	◓	◉
Suspension	◒	○	○	○	◓	◓	◓	◓
Brakes	●	●	●	●	●	◒	○	○
Exhaust	◒	●	○	○	◓	◉	◉	◉
Body rust	◒	○	◓	◓	◉	◉	◉	◉
Paint/trim	●	●	◒	○	◓	◓	◉	◉
Integrity	●	●	●	◒	◒	○	○	◓
Hardware	●	●	◒	●	◒	●	◒	◓

Sports/sporty car under $25,000

RECOMMENDED

Honda Prelude

■ **Trim line:** Base, Type SH ■ **Body style:** 2-door ■ **Price:** $23,300-$25,800 ■ **Predicted depreciation:** NA ■ **Predicted reliability:** ◉ ■ The Prelude was redesigned for the 1997 model year. It's a little roomier, and the dash looks cleaner than the previous version's. It also offers an automatic transmission that can be shifted manually, as well as a sophisticated limited-slip differential that improves tire grip during hard turns. The most potent version of Honda's VTEC Fours is standard in both base and SH versions. It puts out 195 hp when teamed with the manual transmission.

Specifications

Dimensions *Length,* 178 in.; *Width,* 69 in.; *Curb weight,* 3040 lb.; *Passengers, front/rear,* 2/2 **Drive wheels** Front **Engines** 2.2-liter 4 (190 hp), 2.2-liter 4 (195 hp) **Transmissions** 5-speed manual, 4-speed automatic

Safety information

Side air bags ....Not offered
Antilock brakes ....Standard
Gov't front-crash test, driver/front passenger ...NA/NA
IIHS offset crash test ....NA

Reliability history

TROUBLE SPOTS	Honda Prelude							
	90	91	92	93	94	95	96	97
Engine	○	○	◉	◉	Insufficient data	◉	Insufficient data	Insufficient data
Cooling	◓	○	◉	◉		◉		
Fuel	◓	◓	◉	◉		◉		
Ignition	◓	◓	◓	◓		◉		
Auto. trans.	*	*	◉	*		*		
Man. trans.	◉	◉	◉	*		*		
Clutch	○	◒	◓	*		*		
Electrical	○	○	◓	○		◓		
A/C	◒	○	◓	◉		○		
Suspension	○	◓	◓	◉		◉		
Brakes	◒	◒	◓	◓		◓		
Exhaust	○	○	○	◉		◉		
Body rust	◉	◉	◓	◉		◉		
Paint/trim	◓	○	○	○		◉		
Integrity	◓	○	◒	◓		○		
Hardware	○	◒	○	○		◒		

Medium car under $25,000

Hyundai Sonata

■ **Trim line:** Base, GL, GLS ■ **Body style:** 4-door ■ **Price:** $14,749-$18,549 ■ **Predicted depreciation:** ◒ ■ **Predicted reliability:** NA ■ The Sonata carries over virtually unchanged into 1998. It's well equipped but needs more polish to measure up. The ride, handling, and powertrain are not competitive. Every tiny road bump finds its way to the occupants; snaps and jiggles mar the ride on poor roads. The front seats are fairly comfortable; the rear seat is adequate for two, snug for three. The trunk is roomy, and the rear seatbacks can fold for additional cargo room. Hyundais used to compete well in price, if nothing else. But with reasonable equipment, the Sonata's price advantage all but disappears. A redesigned model is due for 1999.

Specifications

Dimensions *Length,* 185 in.; *Width,* 70 in.; *Curb weight,* 3095 lb.; *Passengers, front/rear,* 2/3 **Drive wheels** Front **Engines** 2.0-liter 4 (137 hp), 3.0-liter V6 (142 hp) **Transmissions** 5-speed manual, 4-speed automatic

Safety information

Side air bags .... Not offered
Antilock brakes .... Optional with V6
Gov't front-crash test, driver/front passenger ..... ○/◓
IIHS offset crash test .... Poor

Reliability history

TROUBLE SPOTS	90 91 92 93 94 95 96 97
Engine	
Cooling	
Fuel	
Ignition	NOT
Auto. trans.	
Man. trans.	ENOUGH
Clutch	
Electrical	DATA
A/C	
Suspension	
Brakes	TO
Exhaust	
Body rust	RATE
Paint/trim	
Integrity	
Hardware	

Luxury car

Infiniti Q45

RECOMMENDED

■ **Trim line:** Q45, Q45t ■ **Body style:** 4-door ■ **Price:** $47,900-$49,900 ■ **Predicted depreciation:** ● ■ **Predicted reliability:** ⊙ ■ This flagship of Nissan's luxury Infiniti line was completely redesigned for 1997. Front safety-belt pretensioners—which instantly take up slack in a crash—are new for 1998. The "Big Q" is positioned to compete against other luxury models such as the Lexus LS400 and Mercedes-Benz E-430. The Q45's 4.1-liter V8 is strong and smooth. Dual front and side-impact air bags are standard, as is traction control—especially useful with the Q45's rear-wheel drive. But in this luxury class, the lack of features such as dual-zone air conditioning is disappointing.

Specifications

Dimensions *Length,* 200 in.; *Width,* 72 in.; *Curb weight,* 3840 lb.; *Passengers, front/rear,* 2/3 **Drive wheels** Rear **Engines** 4.1-liter V8 (266 hp) **Transmissions** 4-speed automatic

Safety information

Side air bags .... Standard
Antilock brakes .... Standard
Gov't front-crash test, driver/front passenger ... NA/NA
IIHS offset crash test .... Marginal

Reliability history

TROUBLE SPOTS (Infiniti Q45)	90	91	92	93	94	95	96	97
	Insufficient data			Insufficient data		Insufficient data	Insufficient data	Insufficient data
Engine		○	◓		⊙			
Cooling		○	◓		⊙			
Fuel		○	○		◓			
Ignition		⊙	◓		◓			
Auto. trans.		○	◒		⊙			
Man. trans.								
Clutch								
Electrical		●	○		○			
A/C		○	○		◓			
Suspension		◓	○		◒			
Brakes		●	●		○			
Exhaust		⊙	⊙		⊙			
Body rust		◓	◓		◓			
Paint/trim		◓	◓		◓			
Integrity		○	◓		⊙			
Hardware		●	◒		◓			

Sport-utility vehicle

Infiniti QX4

■ **Trim line:** — ■ **Body style:** 4-door wagon 4WD ■ **Price:** $35,550 ■ **Predicted depreciation:** NA ■ **Predicted reliability:** NA ■ This is one of several gussied-up, higher-priced versions of lower-line SUVs. The QX4 is basically an upscale version of the Nissan Pathfinder. It has a relatively comfortable ride and good front seats. The rear seats are not comfortable, though. The interior, and hence the cargo space, is quite modest. That leaves the QX4 more maneuverable and easier to park than some elephantine competitors, but also a little less useful. Unlike the Pathfinder, the QX4 has a selectable full-time four-wheel-drive system.

Specifications

Dimensions *Length,* 184 in.; *Width,* 72 in.; *Curb weight,* 4355 lb.; *Passengers, front/rear,* 2/3 **Drive wheels** Selectable 4WD **Engines** 3.3-liter V6 (168 hp) **Transmissions** 4-speed automatic

Safety information

Side air bags .... Not offered
Antilock brakes .... Standard
Gov't front-crash test, driver/front passenger ... NA/NA
IIHS offset crash test .... Marginal

Reliability history

TROUBLE SPOTS	90 91 92 93 94 95 96 97
Engine	
Cooling	
Fuel	
Ignition	NOT
Auto. trans.	
Man. trans.	ENOUGH
Clutch	
Electrical	DATA
A/C	
Suspension	
Brakes	TO
Exhaust	
Body rust	RATE
Paint/trim	
Integrity	
Hardware	

Sport-utility vehicle

Isuzu Amigo

■ **Trim line:** — ■ **Body style:** 2-door wagon 2WD, 2-door wagon 4WD, Convertible 2WD, Convertible 4WD ■ **Price:** $14,995-$19,500E ■ **Predicted depreciation:** NA ■ **Predicted reliability:** New ■ The Amigo was redesigned and reintroduced for 1998 after a three-year absence from the market. It's aimed at young buyers: a small-sized two-door SUV with a partial canvas top covering the rear seats and cargo area. It shares the same optional 205-hp V6 as in the Rodeo. But as an old-style, truck-based vehicle, don't expect it to boast a good ride or nimble handling. The four-wheel-drive system is part-time only.

Specifications

Dimensions *Length,* 168 in.; *Width,* 70 in.; *Curb weight,* 3675 lb.; *Passengers, front/rear,* 2/3 **Drive wheels** Rear or part-time 4WD **Engines** 2.2-liter 4 (130 hp), 3.2-liter V6 (205 hp) **Transmissions** 5-speed manual, 4-speed automatic

Safety information

Side air bags ....Not offered
Antilock brakes ....Standard
Gov't front-crash test, driver/front passenger ...NA/NA
IIHS offset crash test ....NA

Reliability history

TROUBLE SPOTS	90 91 92 93 94 95 96 97
Engine	
Cooling	
Fuel	
Ignition	NO
Auto. trans.	
Man. trans.	DATA
Clutch	
Electrical	
A/C	NEW
Suspension	
Brakes	MODEL
Exhaust	
Body rust	
Paint/trim	
Integrity	
Hardware	

Pickup truck

Isuzu Hombre

■ **Trim line:** S, XS ■ **Body style:** Regular cab 2WD, Regular cab 4WD, Extended cab 2WD, Extended cab 4WD ■ **Price:** $11,449-$20,178 ■ **Predicted depreciation:** NA ■ **Predicted reliability:** NA ■ The Hombre is essentially Chevrolet's compact S pickup with slightly different sheet metal. It offers an extended cab with small rear jump seats for 1998, as well as optional four-wheel drive. The standard setup remains a regular-cab pickup with a four-cylinder engine and a five-speed manual transmission. Other changes for 1998 include a passenger-side air bag (with a deactivation switch) and a redesigned instrument panel.

Specifications

Dimensions *Length,* 189 in.; *Width,* 68 in.; *Curb weight,* 2850 lb.; *Passengers, front/rear,* 3/2 **Drive wheels** Rear or part-time 4WD **Engines** 2.2-liter 4 (120 hp), 4.3-liter V6 (175 hp) **Transmissions** 5-speed manual, 4-speed automatic

Safety information

Side air bags ....Not offered
Antilock brakes ....Standard
Gov't front-crash test, driver/front passenger .....◓/◓
IIHS offset crash test ....NA

Reliability history

TROUBLE SPOTS	90 91 92 93 94 95 96 97
Engine	
Cooling	
Fuel	
Ignition	NOT
Auto. trans.	
Man. trans.	ENOUGH
Clutch	
Electrical	DATA
A/C	
Suspension	
Brakes	TO
Exhaust	
Body rust	RATE
Paint/trim	
Integrity	
Hardware	

Sport-utility vehicle

Isuzu Trooper

■ **Trim line:** S ■ **Body style:** 4-door wagon 4WD ■ **Price:** $26,550 ■ **Predicted depreciation:** NA ■ **Predicted reliability:** ◉ ■ The Isuzu Trooper is the same as the Acura SLX. We rated the 1995-1997 Isuzu Trooper and similar 1996-1997 Acura SLX Not Acceptable because of their pronounced tendency to roll over in our emergency-handling tests, based on our tests of the 1995 and 1996 Trooper and the 1996 SLX. The 1998 model has a revised engine, transmission, and body. Because we have not tested this model, we don't know if the changes have affected its handling. We cannot judge its performance.

Specifications

Dimensions *Length,* 184 in.; *Width,* 72 in.; *Curb weight,* 4430 lb.; *Passengers, front/rear,* 2/3 **Drive wheels** Selectable 4WD **Engines** 3.5-liter V6 (215 hp) **Transmissions** 5-speed manual, 4-speed automatic

Safety information

Side air bags ....Not offered
Antilock brakes ....Standard
Gov't front-crash test, driver/front passenger .....○/○
IIHS offset crash test ....NA

Reliability history

TROUBLE SPOTS	Isuzu Trooper							
	90	91	92	93	94	95	96	97
Engine	●	○	○	◓	○	◉	◉	Insufficient data
Cooling	◒	○	◉	◉	◉	◉	◉	
Fuel	◓	◓	◓	◓	◉	◓	◉	
Ignition	○	◓	◓	◓	◓	◉	◉	
Auto. trans.	*	*	*	*	○	◉	*	
Man. trans.	○	◓	*	*	*	*	*	
Clutch	◒	●	*	*	*	*	*	
Electrical	◓	○	●	○	○	◓	◓	
A/C	◒	◒	◓	◓	◓	◓	◉	
Suspension	◓	○	◓	◉	◓	◉	◉	
Brakes	●	●	○	◉	◓	◉	◉	
Exhaust	●	●	◒	◉	◓	◓	◉	
Body rust	●	◒	◉	◉	◓	◉	◉	
Paint/trim	○	◒	◉	○	○	◓	◉	
Integrity	◒	○	◓	◓	○	○	◓	
Hardware	◒	◒	◒	○	○	○	◓	

Luxury car

Jaguar XJ8

■ **Trim line:** Base, Vanden Plas, XJR, XJ8L ■ **Body style:** 4-door, 4-door LWB ■ **Price:** $54,750-$67,400 ■ **Predicted depreciation:** ◒ ■ **Predicted reliability:** NA ■ This British-made luxury sedan changed its name from XJ6 to XJ8 this year, heralding a switch to a new V8 engine. A new five-speed automatic transmission contributes to a fine, slick, spirited drivetrain that should make the Jag more competitive with other premium models from Mercedes, BMW, and Lexus. The ride was already one of the best in the world. Accommodations are apt to be tight for this class. For a roomier back seat, consider the extended-wheelbase L model.

Specifications

Dimensions *Length,* 198 in.; *Width,* 71 in.; *Curb weight,* 4040 lb.; *Passengers, front/rear,* 2/3 **Drive wheels** Rear **Engines** 4.0-liter V8 (290 hp), 4.0-liter V8 supercharged (370 hp) **Transmissions** 5-speed automatic

Safety information

Side air bags ....Standard
Antilock brakes ....Standard
Gov't front-crash test, driver/front passenger ...NA/NA
IIHS offset crash test ....NA

Reliability history

TROUBLE SPOTS	90 91 92 93 94 95 96 97
Engine	
Cooling	
Fuel	
Ignition	NOT
Auto. trans.	
Man. trans.	ENOUGH
Clutch	
Electrical	DATA
A/C	
Suspension	
Brakes	TO
Exhaust	
Body rust	RATE
Paint/trim	
Integrity	
Hardware	

Small car

Kia Sephia

■ **Trim line:** Base, LS ■ **Body style:** 4-door ■ **Price:** $9,995-$10,995 ■ **Predicted depreciation:** NA ■ **Predicted reliability:** New ■ The Korean carmaker Kia has been trying to establish an American beachhead for several years. Still, it may not be easy to find a dealer in your area. Up until the 1998 model year, the Sephia was a small sedan based on an old-generation Mazda 323, and except for price, it trailed the competition badly. The Sephia has been redesigned for 1998, and it now incorporates components made by Kia itself, including a more powerful 1.8-liter Four. It remains to be seen whether it catches on in the competitive and declining small-car market.

Specifications

Dimensions *Length,* 174 in.; *Width,* 67 in.; *Curb weight,* 2620 lb.; *Passengers, front/rear,* 2/3 **Drive wheels** Front **Engines** 1.8-liter 4 (125 hp) **Transmissions** 5-speed manual, 4-speed automatic

Safety information

Side air bags ....Not offered
Antilock brakes ....Optional
Gov't front-crash test, driver/front passenger .....◓/◓
IIHS offset crash test ....Poor

Reliability history

TROUBLE SPOTS	90 91 92 93 94 95 96 97
Engine	
Cooling	
Fuel	
Ignition	NO
Auto. trans.	
Man. trans.	DATA
Clutch	
Electrical	
A/C	NEW
Suspension	
Brakes	MODEL
Exhaust	
Body rust	
Paint/trim	
Integrity	
Hardware	

Sport-utility vehicle

Kia Sportage

■ **Trim line:** Base, EX ■ **Body style:** 4-door wagon 2WD, 4-door wagon 4WD, Convertible 2WD, Convertible 4WD ■ **Price:** $14,000-$18,495E ■ **Predicted depreciation:** NA ■ **Predicted reliability:** NA ■ Kia has been selling the Sportage, a small trucklike sport-utility vehicle, for a few years. It's made in the mold of the Chevrolet Tracker and Suzuki Sidekick. A shorter-wheelbase two-door soft top model is new for 1998. The Sportage offers only a part-time four-wheel-drive system and is nowhere near as sophisticated or up-to-date as a Toyota RAV4, Honda CR-V, or Subaru Forester. It has an uncomfortable ride, clumsy handling, and a crude powertrain. Four-wheel antilock brakes are finally optional.

Specifications

Dimensions *Length,* 162 in.; *Width,* 68 in.; *Curb weight,* 3355 lb.; *Passengers, front/rear,* 2/3 **Drive wheels** Rear or part-time 4WD **Engines** 2.0-liter 4 (130 hp) **Transmissions** 5-speed manual, 4-speed automatic

Safety information

Side air bags ....Not offered
Antilock brakes ....Optional
Gov't front-crash test, driver/front passenger .....○/◒
IIHS offset crash test ....NA

Reliability history

TROUBLE SPOTS	90 91 92 93 94 95 96 97
Engine	
Cooling	
Fuel	
Ignition	NOT
Auto. trans.	
Man. trans.	ENOUGH
Clutch	
Electrical	DATA
A/C	
Suspension	
Brakes	TO
Exhaust	
Body rust	RATE
Paint/trim	
Integrity	
Hardware	

Sport-utility vehicle

Land Rover Range Rover

■ **Trim line:** 4.0 SE, 4.6 HSE ■ **Body style:** 4-door wagon AWD ■ **Price:** $56,000-$63,500 ■ **Predicted depreciation:** ○ ■ **Predicted reliability:** NA ■ Land Rover's upscale Range Rover is essentially unchanged for 1998, and comes with all sorts of luxury-car amenities and leather galore. It also includes a number of advanced engineering features such as a sophisticated all-wheel-drive system and air suspension. When you park, the body can lower itself to ease getting in and out. Once underway, it rises again. It rises still more when you select "low range," the better to clear off-road obstructions. This year, the Range Rover has more competition from the new Mercedes-Benz M-Class and Lexus LX470.

Specifications

Dimensions *Length,* 186 in.; *Width,* 74 in.; *Curb weight,* 4875 lb.; *Passengers, front/rear,* 3/3 **Drive wheels** Permanent 4WD **Engines** 4.0-liter V8 (190 hp), 4.6-liter V8 (225 hp) **Transmissions** 4-speed automatic

Safety information

Side air bags ....Not offered
Antilock brakes ....Standard
Gov't front-crash test, driver/front passenger...NA/NA
IIHS offset crash test ....NA

Reliability history

TROUBLE SPOTS	90 91 92 93 94 95 96 97
Engine	
Cooling	
Fuel	
Ignition	NOT
Auto. trans.	
Man. trans.	ENOUGH
Clutch	
Electrical	
A/C	DATA
Suspension	
Brakes	TO
Exhaust	
Body rust	
Paint/trim	RATE
Integrity	
Hardware	

Luxury car

Lexus GS300/GS400

RECOMMENDED

■ **Trim line:** GS300, GS400 ■ **Body style:** 4-door ■ **Price:** $36,800-$44,800 ■ **Predicted depreciation:** ○ ■ **Predicted reliability:** ● ■ This rear-wheel-drive car was redesigned for 1998 with a new body and—in GS400 versions—a new V8. Traction control, side air bags, and antilock brakes are standard. Toyota has conjured up significantly more rear-seat and trunk room for the new car; the old one was sadly deficient in those areas. The new GS competes with the Mercedes-Benz E-Class and BMW 5-Series. While the new GS performs and handles better than its predecessor, it's still not as crisp-handling or as comfortable-riding as a BMW or Mercedes. It should prove to be very reliable.

Specifications

Dimensions *Length,* 189 in.; *Width,* 71 in.; *Curb weight,* 3750 lb.; *Passengers, front/rear,* 2/3 **Drive wheels** Rear **Engines** 3.0-liter 6 (225 hp), 4.0-liter V8 (300 hp) **Transmissions** 5-speed automatic

Safety information

Side air bags ....Standard
Antilock brakes ....Standard
Gov't front-crash test, driver/front passenger...NA/NA
IIHS offset crash test ....NA

Reliability history

TROUBLE SPOTS	Lexus GS300							
	90	91	92	93	94	95	96	97
Engine				◓	●	Insufficient data	Insufficient data	Insufficient data
Cooling				●	●			
Fuel				●	●			
Ignition				◓	●			
Auto. trans.				●	●			
Man. trans.								
Clutch								
Electrical				○	◓			
A/C				●	●			
Suspension				◓	◓			
Brakes				○	◓			
Exhaust				●	●			
Body rust				●	●			
Paint/trim				◓	●			
Integrity				○	◓			
Hardware				○	◓			

Luxury car

Lexus LS400

RECOMMENDED

■ **Trim line:** — ■ **Body style:** 4-door ■ **Price:** $52,900 ■ **Predicted depreciation:** ○ ■ **Predicted reliability:** ◓ ■ This flagship of Toyota's upscale Lexus division is one of the world's finest luxury sedans. The ride is very comfortable, but handling is not so crisp. The 4.0-liter V8 is smooth and powerful. It combines a sophisticated rear-wheel-drive powertrain with a plush, quiet, leather-wrapped interior. Side air bags are standard, as is a more powerful V8 and a new five-speed automatic transmission.

Specifications

Dimensions *Length,* 197 in.; *Width,* 72 in.; *Curb weight,* 3800 lb.; *Passengers, front/rear,* 2/3 **Drive wheels** Rear **Engines** 4.0-liter V8 (290 hp) **Transmissions** 5-speed automatic

Safety information

Side air bags ....Standard
Antilock brakes ....Standard
Gov't front-crash test, driver/front passenger...NA/NA
IIHS offset crash test..Good

Reliability history

TROUBLE SPOTS	Lexus LS400							
	90	91	92	93	94	95	96	97
Engine	●	●	●	●	●	●	●	●
Cooling	●	●	●	●	●	●	●	●
Fuel	●	●	●	●	●	◓	●	●
Ignition	◓	◓	●	◓	●	◓	●	●
Auto. trans.	●	●	●	●	●	◓	●	●
Man. trans.								
Clutch								
Electrical	○	○	◓	◓	◓	○	◓	◓
A/C	◒	◒	○	●	●	◓	●	●
Suspension	◒	◒	○	●	◓	◓	●	●
Brakes	○	○	○	◓	◒	○	◓	●
Exhaust	●	●	●	●	●	●	●	●
Body rust	●	●	●	●	●	●	●	●
Paint/trim	●	●	●	●	●	●	●	●
Integrity	◓	◓	●	◓	◓	◓	◓	◓
Hardware	○	◓	◓	◓	◓	◓	○	◓

Sport-utility vehicle

Lexus LX470

■ **Trim line:** — ■ **Body style:** 4-door wagon AWD ■ **Price:** $54,950 ■ **Predicted depreciation:** NA ■ **Predicted reliability:** New ■ This luxury-priced SUV is based on the big, imposing Toyota Land Cruiser and competes at the high end of the SUV market. The 1998 model has a 4.7-liter V8, a longer wheelbase, an independent front suspension, and a mild exterior restyling. It has a height-adjustable suspension that the Land Cruiser lacks and a fancier interior. Full-time four-wheel drive ensures good traction. Five adults can fit comfortably. With the small third-row passenger seats folded, cargo space almost rivals a minivan's.

Specifications

Dimensions *Length,* 193 in.; *Width,* 76 in.; *Curb weight,* 5400 lb.; *Passengers, front/mid/rear,* 2/3/2 **Drive wheels** Permanent 4WD **Engines** 4.7-liter V8 (230 hp) **Transmissions** 4-speed automatic

Safety information

Side air bags .... Not offered
Antilock brakes .... Standard
Gov't front-crash test, driver/front passenger ... NA/NA
IIHS offset crash test .... NA

Reliability history

TROUBLE SPOTS	90 91 92 93 94 95 96 97
Engine	NO
Cooling	
Fuel	DATA
Ignition	
Auto. trans.	NEW
Man. trans.	
Clutch	MODEL
Electrical	
A/C	
Suspension	
Brakes	
Exhaust	
Body rust	
Paint/trim	
Integrity	
Hardware	

Sport-utility vehicle

Lexus RX300

■ **Trim line:** — ■ **Body style:** 4-door wagon 2WD, 4-door wagon AWD ■ **Price:** $31,550-$32,950 ■ **Predicted depreciation:** NA ■ **Predicted reliability:** New ■ The RX300, new in 1998, is a medium-sized sport-utility vehicle based on the ES300 (and Toyota Camry) sedan. As such, it takes the RAV4 and CR-V concept further upmarket. The RX300 is available as a front-wheel-drive or all-wheel-drive model. It competes with other luxury-priced SUVs like the Mercedes M-Class and Infiniti QX4. This Lexus has a refined powertrain and nice controls, but the rear seat and cargo area are a bit small. It also has no serious off-road capability.

Specifications

Dimensions *Length,* 180 in.; *Width,* 72 in.; *Curb weight,* 4040 lb.; *Passengers, front/rear,* 2/3 **Drive wheels** Front or all **Engines** 3.0-liter V6 (220 hp) **Transmissions** 4-speed automatic

Safety information

Side air bags .... Standard
Antilock brakes .... Standard
Gov't front-crash test, driver/front passenger ... NA/NA
IIHS offset crash test .... NA

Reliability history

TROUBLE SPOTS	90 91 92 93 94 95 96 97
Engine	NO
Cooling	
Fuel	DATA
Ignition	
Auto. trans.	NEW
Man. trans.	
Clutch	MODEL
Electrical	
A/C	
Suspension	
Brakes	
Exhaust	
Body rust	
Paint/trim	
Integrity	
Hardware	

Coupe

Lexus SC300/SC400

RECOMMENDED

■ **Trim line:** SC300, SC400 ■ **Body style:** 2-door ■ **Price:** $40,900-$52,700 ■ **Predicted depreciation:** ○ ■ **Predicted reliability:** ● ■ This rear-wheel-drive luxury coupe emphasizes both slick refinement and crisp performance. The SC300 comes with a spirited Six. The SC400 has a new, more powerful aluminum V8, but you'll pay thousands of dollars more to get it. A new five-speed automatic transmission for the SC400 debuted for 1998; the manual transmission in the SC300 was dropped. The ride is firm. The front seats offer generally fine accommodations. The rear is better left uninhabited, and the trunk is very small. Reliability, however, has been top-notch.

Specifications

Dimensions *Length,* 193 in.; *Width,* 71 in.; *Curb weight,* 3710 lb.; *Passengers, front/rear,* 2/3 **Drive wheels** Rear **Engines** 3.0-liter 6 (225 hp), 4.0-liter V8 (290 hp) **Transmissions** 4-speed automatic, 5-speed automatic

Safety information

Side air bags .... Not offered
Antilock brakes .... Standard
Gov't front-crash test, driver/front passenger ... NA/NA
IIHS offset crash test .... NA

Reliability history

TROUBLE SPOTS	Lexus SC300/400							
	90	91	92	93	94	95	96	97
Engine			●	●	Insufficient data	●	Insufficient data	Insufficient data
Cooling			●	●		●		
Fuel			●	●		●		
Ignition			●	●		●		
Auto. trans.			●	●		◒		
Man. trans.			*	*		*		
Clutch			*	*		*		
Electrical			○	○		◒		
A/C			◒	◒		◒		
Suspension			◒	●		◒		
Brakes			◒	●		●		
Exhaust			●	●		●		
Body rust			●	●		●		
Paint/trim			◒	◒		○		
Integrity			◒	◒		◒		
Hardware			○	○		◒		

Sport-utility vehicle

Lincoln Navigator

■ **Trim line:** — ■ **Body style:** 4-door wagon 2WD, 4-door wagon 4WD ■ **Price:** $39,310-$42,960 ■ **Predicted depreciation:** NA ■ **Predicted reliability:** New ■ Think of the Navigator as a Ford Expedition traveling business class. It has more leather and wood interior trim, and a second row that features two individual seats with a large console between them.The Navigator's selectable all-wheel-drive system can be left permanently engaged. We haven't tested a Navigator. If it's like the Expedition, expect sound handling but terrible fuel economy. And it's so high that getting in or out takes real agility. Parking and maneuvering around town can try one's patience, too.

Specifications

Dimensions *Length,* 205 in.; *Width,* 80 in.; *Curb weight,* 5400 lb.; *Passengers, front/mid/rear,* 2/3/3 **Drive wheels** Rear or selectable 4WD **Engines** 5.4-liter V8 (230 hp) **Transmissions** 4-speed automatic

Safety information

Side air bags ....Not offered
Antilock brakes ....Standard
Gov't front-crash test, driver/front passenger .....◓/◓
IIHS offset crash test ....NA

Reliability history

TROUBLE SPOTS	90 91 92 93 94 95 96 97
Engine	
Cooling	
Fuel	
Ignition	NO
Auto. trans.	
Man. trans.	DATA
Clutch	
Electrical	
A/C	NEW
Suspension	
Brakes	MODEL
Exhaust	
Body rust	
Paint/trim	
Integrity	
Hardware	

Pickup truck

Mazda B-Series

■ **Trim line:** SX, SE ■ **Body style:** Regular cab 2WD, Regular cab 4WD, Extended cab 2WD, Extended cab 4WD ■ **Price:** $10,370-$19,485 ■ **Predicted depreciation:** NA ■ **Predicted reliability:** New ■ This is essentially a Ranger that Ford makes for Mazda. A 1998 redesign gives it a new front suspension and longer wheelbase. A cutoff switch allows you to deactivate the passenger-side air bag. Both rear-wheel-drive and four-wheel-drive models are available. The regular-cab version is roomier inside, while the extended-cab stays the same size. Extended-cab models with four doors will be available this summer. We haven't tested the B-Series but expect it to remain a good truck.

Specifications

Dimensions *Length,* 203 in.; *Width,* 69 in.; *Curb weight,* 3315 lb.; *Passengers, front/rear,* 3/2 **Drive wheels** Rear or part-time 4WD **Engines** 2.5-liter 4 (119 hp), 3.0-liter V6 (150 hp), 4.0-liter V6 (160 hp) **Transmissions** 5-speed manual, 4-speed auto., 5-speed automatic

Safety information

Side air bags ....Not offered
Antilock brakes ....Optional
Gov't front-crash test, driver/front passenger .....◓/◓
IIHS offset crash test ....NA

Reliability history

TROUBLE SPOTS	90 91 92 93 94 95 96 97
Engine	
Cooling	
Fuel	
Ignition	NO
Auto. trans.	
Man. trans.	DATA
Clutch	
Electrical	
A/C	NEW
Suspension	
Brakes	MODEL
Exhaust	
Body rust	
Paint/trim	
Integrity	
Hardware	

RECOMMENDED

Sports/sporty car under $25,000

Mazda MX-5 Miata

■ **Trim line:** — ■ **Body style:** Convertible ■ **Price:** $19,770 ■ **Predicted depreciation:** NA ■ **Predicted reliability:** ● ■ For the 1998 model year, this entertaining, open-top two-seater gets its first revision since its introduction. Large fixed headlights replace the pop-up lights, the car grows a shade larger, and the engine increases its horsepower to 140. Also, a glass rear window is finally made standard. Zesty performance, nimble handling, and precise and direct steering have always made this car fun to drive. It's also been a cramped, noisy, hard-riding car, too small inside for a tall person. The new one maintains the same list of virtues with fewer vices.

Specifications

Dimensions *Length,* 155 in.; *Width,* 66 in.; *Curb weight,* 2335 lb.; *Passengers, front,* 2 **Drive wheels** Rear **Engines** 1.8-liter 4 (140 hp) **Transmissions** 5-speed manual, 4-speed automatic

Safety information

Side air bags ....Not offered
Antilock brakes ....Optional
Gov't front-crash test, driver/front passenger ...NA/NA
IIHS offset crash test ....NA

Reliability history

TROUBLE SPOTS (Mazda MX-5 Miata)	90	91	92	93	94	95	96	97
Engine	◓	◓	◓	◓	◓	●	●	Insufficient data
Cooling	◓	●	●	●	●	●	●	
Fuel	●	●	●	●	◓	●	●	
Ignition	◓	◓	○	◓	◒	◓	●	
Auto. trans.		*	*	*	*	*	*	
Man. trans.	●	●	●	●	●	◓	●	
Clutch	○	◒	◓	●	●	●	●	
Electrical	○	○	◒	○	○	◓	◓	
A/C	◓	◓	●	◓	◓	●	●	
Suspension	●	●	●	●	◓	◓	●	
Brakes	◓	○	○	●	●	◓	●	
Exhaust	●	◓	●	●	●	●	●	
Body rust	●	●	●	●	●	●	●	
Paint/trim	◒	○	○	◓	◓	◓	◓	
Integrity	○	○	○	○	○	◒	◓	
Hardware	○	◒	◒	◓	○	●	◓	

Coupe

Mercedes-Benz CLK

■ **Trim line:** CLK320 ■ **Body style:** 2-door ■ **Price:** $39,850 ■ **Predicted depreciation:** NA ■ **Predicted reliability:** New ■ The CLK, new for 1998, is a coupe version of the C-Class sedan that's styled to look like the larger E-Class. The two rear seats are reasonably hospitable for a coupe. The engine is a good-performing 215-hp, 3.2-liter V6. Side air bags and a five-speed automatic transmission are standard. Based on our brief experience, this car handles well and is fast, frugal, and comfortable, though not as exuberant and rewarding to drive as a BMW 328iS or M3.

Specifications

Dimensions *Length,* 180 in.; *Width,* 68 in.; *Curb weight,* 3295 lb.; *Passengers, front/rear,* 2/2 **Drive wheels** Rear **Engines** 3.2-liter V6 (215 hp) **Transmissions** 5-speed automatic

Safety information

Side air bags .... Standard
Antilock brakes .... Standard
Gov't front-crash test, driver/front passenger ... NA/NA
IIHS offset crash test .... NA

Reliability history

TROUBLE SPOTS	90 91 92 93 94 95 96 97
Engine	
Cooling	
Fuel	
Ignition	NO
Auto. trans.	
Man. trans.	DATA
Clutch	
Electrical	
A/C	NEW
Suspension	
Brakes	MODEL
Exhaust	
Body rust	
Paint/trim	
Integrity	
Hardware	

Sport-utility vehicle

Mercedes-Benz M-class

■ **Trim line:** ML320 ■ **Body style:** 4-door wagon AWD ■ **Price:** $33,950 ■ **Predicted depreciation:** NA ■ **Predicted reliability:** New ■ The M-Class breaks new ground for SUVs. It's medium-sized, like the Ford Explorer or Jeep Grand Cherokee. A third row of seats will be optional for 1999. The M-Class has a fully independent suspension and a sophisticated full-time four-wheel-drive system. It is powered by a spirited 3.2-liter V6, and has a five-speed automatic transmission. The M-Class handles well and rides quietly and comfortably. It's also roomy inside and relatively easy to climb into and out of. The frame height is constructed so the M-Class won't override the bumper of a normal passenger car in a collision.

Specifications

Dimensions *Length,* 181 in.; *Width,* 72 in.; *Curb weight,* 4200 lb.; *Passengers, front/mid/rear,* 2/3/2 **Drive wheels** Permanent 4WD **Engines** 3.2-liter V6 (215 hp) **Transmissions** 5-speed automatic

Safety information

Side air bags .... Standard
Antilock brakes .... Standard
Gov't front-crash test, driver/front passenger ... NA/NA
IIHS offset crash test .... NA

Reliability history

TROUBLE SPOTS	90 91 92 93 94 95 96 97
Engine	
Cooling	
Fuel	
Ignition	NO
Auto. trans.	
Man. trans.	DATA
Clutch	
Electrical	
A/C	NEW
Suspension	
Brakes	MODEL
Exhaust	
Body rust	
Paint/trim	
Integrity	
Hardware	

Luxury car

Mercedes-Benz S320

■ **Trim line:** — ■ **Body style:** 4-door LWB, 4-door SWB ■ **Price:** $64,000-$67,300 ■ **Predicted depreciation:** NA ■ **Predicted reliability:** ○ ■ The S-Class sedans, powered by a range of 6-, 8-, and 12-cylinder engines, keep company with the world's most expensive luxury cars. The S320 is a large car, quiet, roomy, and very comfortable for long-distance cruising. Despite its bulk and weight, it handles with surprising agility. The ride is as good as any you'll find. You can expect the leading edge in safety engineering and equipment as well. But for the price of the S320, most competitors offer a V8. A redesigned S320 sedan is due for 1999.

Specifications

Dimensions *Length,* 201 in.; *Width,* 74 in.; *Curb weight,* 4420 lb.; *Passengers, front/rear,* 2/3 **Drive wheels** Rear **Engines** 3.2-liter 6 (228 hp) **Transmissions** 5-speed automatic

Safety information

Side air bags .... Standard
Antilock brakes .... Standard
Gov't front-crash test, driver/front passenger ... NA/NA
IIHS offset crash test .... NA

Reliability history

Mercedes-Benz S-Class

TROUBLE SPOTS	90 91	92	93	94	95	96	97
Engine		Insufficient data	Insufficient data	Insufficient data	◓	Insufficient data	Insufficient data
Cooling					◉		
Fuel					○		
Ignition					◓		
Auto. trans.					◓		
Man. trans.							
Clutch							
Electrical					●		
A/C					○		
Suspension					◉		
Brakes					○		
Exhaust					◓		
Body rust					◉		
Paint/trim					◉		
Integrity					○		
Hardware					●		

Sports/sporty car over $25,000

Mercedes-Benz SLK

■ **Trim line:** SLK230 ■ **Body style:** Convertible ■ **Price:** $39,700 ■ **Predicted depreciation:** NA ■ **Predicted reliability:** New ■ This two-seat convertible is a thoroughly modern design with many innovative technical and safety features. It's powered by a supercharged, intercooled, 2.3-liter Four. An electrically retractable hardtop (that folds and stows itself in the trunk when lowered) makes this convertible feel almost as solid as a fixed-roof coupe. A sensor deactivates the passenger-side air bag if a specially designed child seat is mounted there. The SLK also has side air bags and a sophisticated all-speed traction-control system. The only transmission so far is a five-speed automatic; a manual will be available soon.

Specifications

Dimensions *Length,* 157 in.; *Width,* 68 in.; *Curb weight,* 3020 lb.; *Passengers, front,* 2 **Drive wheels** Rear **Engines** 2.3-liter 4 supercharged (191 hp) **Transmissions** 5-speed automatic

Safety information

Side air bags	Standard
Antilock brakes	Standard
Gov't front-crash test, driver/front passenger	NA/NA
IIHS offset crash test	NA

Reliability history

TROUBLE SPOTS	90 91 92 93 94 95 96 97
Engine	
Cooling	
Fuel	
Ignition	NO
Auto. trans.	
Man. trans.	DATA
Clutch	
Electrical	
A/C	NEW
Suspension	
Brakes	MODEL
Exhaust	
Body rust	
Paint/trim	
Integrity	
Hardware	

Sports/sporty car under $25,000

Mercury Cougar

■ **Trim line:** Base, LS ■ **Body style:** 2-door ■ **Price:** $16,195-$18,095 ■ **Predicted depreciation:** NA ■ **Predicted reliability:** New ■ The previous Cougar was a clone of the Ford Thunderbird, an old-time rear-drive coupe that's been discontinued. This year's Cougar is a brand-new car, introduced as a 1999 model. It's a front-drive hatchback coupe based on the same underpinnings as the Ford Contour/ Mercury Mystique. It's also the first model to showcase a design scheme Ford calls New Edge, a movement toward angular planes rather than curves and ovals. We expect the Cougar to be a quick, agile-handling, up-to-date car.

Specifications

Dimensions *Length,* 185 in.; *Width,* 70 in.; *Curb weight,* 3385 lb.; *Passengers, front/rear,* 2/2 **Drive wheels** Front **Engines** 2.0-liter 4 (125 hp), 2.5-liter V6 (170 hp) **Transmissions** 5-speed manual, 4-speed automatic

Safety information

Side air bags	Optional
Antilock brakes	Optional
Gov't front-crash test, driver/front passenger	NA/NA
IIHS offset crash test	NA

Reliability history

TROUBLE SPOTS	90 91 92 93 94 95 96 97
Engine	
Cooling	
Fuel	
Ignition	NO
Auto. trans.	
Man. trans.	DATA
Clutch	
Electrical	
A/C	NEW
Suspension	
Brakes	MODEL
Exhaust	
Body rust	
Paint/trim	
Integrity	
Hardware	

Sport-utility vehicle

Mercury Mountaineer

■ **Trim line:** — ■ **Body style:** 4-door wagon 2WD, 4-door wagon AWD ■ **Price:** $26,730-$28,730 ■ **Predicted depreciation:** NA ■ **Predicted reliability:** ○ ■ This SUV is actually a relabeled Ford Explorer. The standard engine for 1998 is a 4.0-liter V6 with a very smooth five-speed automatic transmission. The 5.0-liter V8 from last year remains an option. The Mountaineer handles and brakes well, but the ride is stiff and choppy. The permanent all-wheel-drive system, standard with the V8, lacks a low-range setting for serious off-road conditions.

Specifications

Dimensions *Length,* 189 in.; *Width,* 70 in.; *Curb weight,* 4440 lb.; *Passengers, front/rear,* 2/3 **Drive wheels** Rear, permanent 4WD or all **Engines** 4.0-liter V6 (205 hp), 5.0-liter V8 (215 hp) **Transmissions** 4-speed automatic, 5-speed automatic

Safety information

Side air bags	Not offered
Antilock brakes	Standard
Gov't front-crash test, driver/front passenger	◒/◒
IIHS offset crash test	Acceptable

Reliability history

TROUBLE SPOTS	Mercury Mountaineer 90	91	92	93	94	95	96	97
Engine								●
Cooling								●
Fuel								●
Ignition								●
Auto. trans.								●
Man. trans.								
Clutch								
Electrical								◒
A/C								●
Suspension								●
Brakes								●
Exhaust								●
Body rust								●
Paint/trim								●
Integrity								◒
Hardware								◒

Sports/sporty car over $25,000

Mitsubishi 3000GT

■ **Trim line:** Base, SL, VR-4 ■ **Body style:** 2-door hatchback ■ **Price:** $27,770-$46,230 ■ **Predicted depreciation:** ◒ ■ **Predicted reliability:** NA ■ The top-of-the-line 320-hp VR-4 is loaded with techno-gadgets: twin turbochargers and intercoolers, four-wheel steering, electronically adjustable suspension, and all-wheel drive. The front-wheel drive, 161-hp base version is far less costly but much less interesting. The VR-4 model delivers fierce acceleration, exceptionally short stops, and good cornering grip. But the 3000GT is too heavy and wide to feel nimble. And its rear seat is just for show. Even with all the available high-tech equipment, this design is pretty old—it's been around since 1991.

Specifications

Dimensions *Length,* 180 in.; *Width,* 72 in.; *Curb weight,* 3805 lb.; *Passengers, front/rear,* 2/3 **Drive wheels** Front or all **Engines** 3.0-liter V6 (161 hp), 3.0-liter V6 (218 hp), 3.0-liter V6 turbo (320 hp) **Transmissions** 5-speed manual, 6-speed manual, 4-speed automatic

Safety information

Side air bags ....Not offered
Antilock brakes ....Standard (not offered on Base)
Gov't front-crash test, driver/front passenger ...NA/NA
IIHS offset crash test ....NA

Reliability history

TROUBLE SPOTS	Mitsubishi 3000GT (2WD)							
	90	91	92	93	94	95	96	97
Engine		◓	○	◓	◉	Insufficient data	Insufficient data	Insufficient data
Cooling		○	◓	◓	◉			
Fuel		◉	◉	◉	◉			
Ignition		○	○	◓	○			
Auto. trans.		*	*	*	*			
Man. trans.		*	*	*	*			
Clutch		*	*	*	*			
Electrical		◒	●	◒	○			
A/C		○	◉	◓	◓			
Suspension		◓	○	○	◉			
Brakes		○	○	◒	◓			
Exhaust		◉	◉	◉	◉			
Body rust		◉	◉	◉	◉			
Paint/trim		◒	○	◒	○			
Integrity		◒	◒	○	○			
Hardware		●	◒	◒	◒			

Medium car over $25,000

Mitsubishi Diamante

■ **Trim line:** ES, LS ■ **Body style:** 4-door ■ **Price:** $27,650-$33,050 ■ **Predicted depreciation:** ● ■ **Predicted reliability:** NA ■ Mitsubishi's front-wheel-drive, luxury-car flagship was redesigned for 1997 and continues virtually unchanged for 1998. It competes with other mid-luxury sedans, such as the Infiniti I30, Lexus ES300, and Mazda Millenia. Power comes from a 210-hp, 3.5-liter V6. Antilock brakes and a remote keyless entry system became standard in 1998, while traction control remains optional.

Specifications

Dimensions *Length,* 194 in.; *Width,* 70 in.; *Curb weight,* 3385 lb.; *Passengers, front/rear,* 2/3 **Drive wheels** Front **Engines** 3.5-liter V6 (210 hp) **Transmissions** 4-speed automatic

Safety information

Side air bags ....Not offered
Antilock brakes ....Standard
Gov't front-crash test, driver/front passenger ...NA/NA
IIHS offset crash test ....NA

Reliability history

TROUBLE SPOTS	90	91	92	93	94	95	96	97
Engine								
Cooling								
Fuel								
Ignition	NOT							
Auto. trans.								
Man. trans.	ENOUGH							
Clutch								
Electrical								
A/C	DATA							
Suspension								
Brakes	TO							
Exhaust								
Body rust	RATE							
Paint/trim								
Integrity								
Hardware								

Sports/sporty car under $25,000

Mitsubishi Eclipse

■ **Trim line:** RS, GS, GS-T, GSX ■ **Body style:** 2-door hatchback, Convertible ■ **Price:** $15,740-$26,660 ■ **Predicted depreciation:** ◓ ■ **Predicted reliability:** ● ■ The Eclipse is similar to the now-discontinued Eagle Talon, but it comes as a convertible as well as a coupe. The basic versions aren't very sporty. The standard 2.0-liter Four needs a lot of revving to produce much power. Turbocharged versions are quicker and smoother, but also more expensive. The Eclipse comes with either front-wheel or all-wheel drive. As with most sports coupes, the rear seat is almost unusable. Reliability has been poor.

Specifications

Dimensions *Length,* 172 in.; *Width,* 68 in.; *Curb weight,* 3235 lb.; *Passengers, front/rear,* 2/2 **Drive wheels** Front or all **Engines** 2.0-liter 4 (140 hp), 2.0-liter 4 turbo (205 hp), 2.0-liter 4 turbo (210 hp), 2.4-liter 4 (141 hp) **Transmissions** 5-speed manual, 4-speed auto.

Safety information

Side air bags ....Not offered
Antilock brakes ....Optional (not offered on RS)
Gov't front-crash test, driver/front passenger .....◓/◉
IIHS offset crash test ....NA

Reliability history

TROUBLE SPOTS	Mitsubishi Eclipse							
	90	91	92	93	94	95	96	97
Engine						○	◓	Insufficient data
Cooling						◓	◉	
Fuel						◒	○	
Ignition						○	○	
Auto. trans.						◓	*	
Man. trans.						◓	*	
Clutch						◓	*	
Electrical						●	◒	
A/C						◓	◉	
Suspension						◓	○	
Brakes						◒	○	
Exhaust						◉	◉	
Body rust						◉	◉	
Paint/trim						○	◓	
Integrity						●	◒	
Hardware						●	●	

Sport-utility vehicle

Mitsubishi Montero

■ **Trim line:** — ■ **Body style:** 4-door wagon 4WD ■ **Price:** $33,530 ■ **Predicted depreciation:** ○ ■ **Predicted reliability:** ○ ■ The large, boxy, and aging Montero has been slightly freshened for 1998. It competes among the more luxurious SUVs, and it has a long list of standard equipment. The Montero is powered by a 200-hp, 3.5-liter V6. A four-speed automatic is the only available transmission. The Montero feels ponderous in normal driving. The selectable four-wheel-drive system can remain permanently engaged. The middle seat provides decent space for two six-footers, but not three. Two extra child-sized seats are available for the rear, so you can seat seven in a pinch.

Specifications

Dimensions *Length,* 187 in.; *Width,* 70 in.; *Curb weight,* 4445 lb.; *Passengers, front/mid/rear,* 2/3/2 **Drive wheels** Selectable 4WD **Engines** 3.5-liter V6 (200 hp) **Transmissions** 4-speed automatic

Safety information

Side air bags ....Not offered
Antilock brakes ....Standard
Gov't front-crash test, driver/front passenger ...NA/NA
IIHS offset crash test ....Acceptable

Reliability history

TROUBLE SPOTS	Mitsubishi Montero							
	90	91	92	93	94	95	96	97
Engine	◒					◓		
Cooling	○					◉		
Fuel	○					◉		
Ignition	○					◉		
Auto. trans.	*					*		
Man. trans.	*					*		
Clutch	*					*		
Electrical	○	Insufficient data	Insufficient data	Insufficient data	Insufficient data	◓	Insufficient data	Insufficient data
A/C	◉					◓		
Suspension	○					○		
Brakes	◒					◒		
Exhaust	◓					◉		
Body rust	◓					◓		
Paint/trim	◓					◓		
Integrity	○					○		
Hardware	●					◒		

Sports/sporty car under $25,000

Nissan 240SX

■ **Trim line:** Base, SE, LE ■ **Body style:** 2-door ■ **Price:** $18,359-$24,449 ■ **Predicted depreciation:** ◒ ■ **Predicted reliability:** NA ■ This front-engined, rear-wheel-drive coupe competes against such front-wheel-drive models as the Honda Prelude and Toyota Celica. The 240SX received minor body refinements last year. Our limited experience suggests that it provides very good handling and a reasonably comfortable ride. The 2.4-liter Four offers adequate if noisy acceleration. Both automatic and manual transmissions are offered. Full, clear instrumentation complements generally well-designed controls. The firm front seats provide adequate support. As in most sports coupes, the rear seat is best left vacant.

Specifications

Dimensions *Length,* 177 in.; *Width,* 68 in.; *Curb weight,* 2880 lb.; *Passengers, front/rear,* 2/3 **Drive wheels** Rear **Engines** 2.4-liter 4 (155 hp) **Transmissions** 5-speed manual, 4-speed automatic

Safety information

Side air bags ....Not offered
Antilock brakes ....Optional
Gov't front-crash test, driver/front passenger .....○/◓
IIHS offset crash test ....NA

Reliability history

TROUBLE SPOTS	Nissan 240SX							
	90	91	92	93	94	95	96	97
Engine	○	◓	◓	◓				
Cooling	◓	◉	◉	◉				
Fuel	○	○	◓	◉				
Ignition	○	◓	○	◓				
Auto. trans.	*	*	*	*				
Man. trans.	◓	◉	*	*				
Clutch	◒	○	*	*				
Electrical	◒	○	○	◓	Insufficient data	Insufficient data	Insufficient data	Insufficient data
A/C	○	◓	◓	◓				
Suspension	◓	◓	◓	◓				
Brakes	●	●	○	○				
Exhaust	●	◒	◓	◉				
Body rust	○	◓	◉	◉				
Paint/trim	○	◓	◓	◓				
Integrity	○	◓	◓	○				
Hardware	●	◒	◓	○				

Pickup truck

Nissan Frontier

■ **Trim line:** Standard, XE, SE ■ **Body style:** Regular cab 2WD, Regular cab 4WD, Extended cab 2WD, Extended cab 4WD ■ **Price:** $12,010-$21,010 ■ **Predicted depreciation:** NA ■ **Predicted reliability:** New ■ The Frontier is a new compact pickup truck built by Nissan in Tennessee. The previous Nissan pickup, unofficially called Hardbody, was a fairly crude vehicle. So is the Frontier. Only a 2.4-liter Four is currently available. A V6 will follow, perhaps for 1999. Antilock brakes are standard with four-wheel-drive models, but only rear ABS comes with two-wheel-drive versions.

Specifications

Dimensions *Length,* 196 in.; *Width,* 66 in.; *Curb weight,* 3235 lb.; *Passengers, front/rear,* 2/2 **Drive wheels** Rear or part-time 4WD **Engines** 2.4-liter 4 (143 hp) **Transmissions** 5-speed manual, 4-speed automatic

Safety information

Side air bags ....Not offered
Antilock brakes ....Standard with 4WD
Gov't front-crash test, driver/front passenger .....○/◓
IIHS offset crash test ....NA

Reliability history

TROUBLE SPOTS	90	91	92	93	94	95	96	97
Engine								
Cooling								
Fuel								
Ignition	NO							
Auto. trans.								
Man. trans.	DATA							
Clutch								
Electrical								
A/C	NEW							
Suspension								
Brakes	MODEL							
Exhaust								
Body rust								
Paint/trim								
Integrity								
Hardware								

Large car under $30,000

Oldsmobile 88

■ **Trim line:** Base, LS, LSS, Regency ■ **Body style:** 4-door ■ **Price:** $22,795-$28,395 ■ **Predicted depreciation:** ◒ ■ **Predicted reliability:** ○ ■ This is a quiet, softly sprung car in the old American tradition. The standard model has a split bench seat in front, while the LS and LSS versions have individual seats. The cushiest version is the six-passenger Regency. The standard 205-hp, 3.8-liter V6 accelerates responsively. A 240-hp, supercharged version of this engine is also available. The four-speed automatic transmission shifts very smoothly. The seating is comfortable for five, less so for six.

Specifications

Dimensions *Length,* 200 in.; *Width,* 74 in.; *Curb weight,* 3470 lb.; *Passengers, front/rear,* 3/3 **Drive wheels** Front **Engines** 3.8-liter V6 (205 hp), 3.8-liter V6 supercharged (240 hp) **Transmissions** 4-speed automatic

Safety information

Side air bags ....Not offered
Antilock brakes ....Standard
Gov't front-crash test, driver/front passenger .....◉/○
IIHS offset crash test ....NA

Reliability history

TROUBLE SPOTS	Oldsmobile 88							
	90	91	92	93	94	95	96	97
Engine	◓	◓	◓	◓	○	◓	◉	◉
Cooling	◒	○	◒	◒	◓	◉	◉	◉
Fuel	○	○	◓	◓	◓	◓	◉	◉
Ignition	●	●	●	◒	◒	◓	◓	◉
Auto. trans.	○	◓	◓	○	◓	◓	◉	◉
Man. trans.								
Clutch								
Electrical	●	◒	●	◒	◒	◒	○	○
A/C	●	◒	◒	○	◓	◓	◉	◉
Suspension	○	○	○	◓	◓	◓	◓	◓
Brakes	●	●	●	●	○	○	◉	◓
Exhaust	◓	◉	◉	◓	◉	◓	◉	◉
Body rust	○	◓	◉	◉	◉	◉	◉	◉
Paint/trim	◒	◒	○	◓	○	◓	◉	◓
Integrity	○	◓	○	○	◒	◒	◒	○
Hardware	○	●	◒	◒	●	●	○	◓

Medium car under $25,000

Oldsmobile Alero

■ **Trim line:** GX, GL, GLS ■ **Body style:** 2-door, 4-door ■ **Price:** $15,000-$18,000E ■ **Predicted depreciation:** NA ■ **Predicted reliability:** New ■ The Alero is new this year, due out this summer as a 1999 model. It is Oldsmobile's entry-level midsized sedan. The Alero is a sister car to the Pontiac Grand Am, with which it shares many parts. It looks like a somewhat smaller version of the Olds Intrigue, with contemporary styling inside and out. It comes as either a sedan or as a coupe. The standard engine, a 2.4-liter Four, is the same as that found in the Chevy Malibu, where it sounds rather noisy and unrefined. The Alero joins a crowded market that includes a host of domestic and Japanese-nameplate competitors.

Specifications

Dimensions *Length,* 187 in.; *Width,* 70 in.; *Curb weight,* 3020 lb.; *Passengers, front/rear,* 2/3 **Drive wheels** Front **Engines** 2.4-liter 4 (150 hp), 3.4-liter V6 (170 hp) **Transmissions** 4-speed automatic

Safety information

Side air bags ....Not offered
Antilock brakes ....Standard
Gov't front-crash test, driver/front passenger ...NA/NA
IIHS offset crash test ....NA

Reliability history

TROUBLE SPOTS	90	91	92	93	94	95	96	97
Engine	NO DATA NEW MODEL							
Cooling								
Fuel								
Ignition								
Auto. trans.								
Man. trans.								
Clutch								
Electrical								
A/C								
Suspension								
Brakes								
Exhaust								
Body rust								
Paint/trim								
Integrity								
Hardware								

Sport-utility vehicle

Oldsmobile Bravada

■ **Trim line:** — ■ **Body style:** 4-door wagon AWD ■ **Price:** $30,645 ■ **Predicted depreciation:** NA ■ **Predicted reliability:** ◓ ■ This is an upscale version of the Chevrolet Blazer and GMC Jimmy. Some exterior cosmetic changes and a new dashboard are the major changes for 1998, and GM has also improved the brakes markedly. Standard equipment includes permanent all-wheel drive—though without a low range. Ride and handling are both so-so. The engine accelerates powerfully but sounds coarse. Overall, the Bravada has the same strengths and weaknesses as the cheaper GM models, but the Bravada has had above-average reliability.

Specifications

Dimensions *Length,* 184 in.; *Width,* 68 in.; *Curb weight,* 4200 lb.; *Passengers, front/rear,* 2/3 **Drive wheels** All **Engines** 4.3-liter V6 (190 hp) **Transmissions** 4-speed automatic

Safety information

Side air bags ....Not offered
Antilock brakes ....Standard
Gov't front-crash test, driver/front passenger .....◓/◓
IIHS offset crash test ....Poor

Reliability history

TROUBLE SPOTS	Oldsmobile Bravada							
	90	91	92	93	94	95	96	97
Engine							◉	Insufficient data
Cooling							◉	
Fuel							◓	
Ignition							◉	
Auto. trans.							◉	
Man. trans.								
Clutch								
Electrical							◉	
A/C							◉	
Suspension							◉	
Brakes							○	
Exhaust							◉	
Body rust							◉	
Paint/trim							◉	
Integrity							◓	
Hardware							◉	

Large car under $30,000

Pontiac Bonneville

■ **Trim line:** SE, SSE ■ **Body style:** 4-door ■ **Price:** $22,390-$29,390 ■ **Predicted depreciation:** ○ ■ **Predicted reliability:** ○ ■ The Bonneville has changed little since we last tested one, in 1994. The ride is tightly controlled, and steering response is quick. The optional firm suspension and touring tires improve handling markedly. The optional supercharged 240-hp, 3.8-liter V6 is powerful, and even the nonsupercharged 205-hp V6 accelerates well. The four-speed automatic transmission shifts smoothly. The front seats are comfortable. The rear seat is roomy enough for three adults. Reliability has remained average.

Specifications

Dimensions *Length,* 201 in.; *Width,* 75 in.; *Curb weight,* 3665 lb.; *Passengers, front/rear,* 3/3 **Drive wheels** Front **Engines** 3.8-liter V6 (205 hp), 3.8-liter V6 supercharged (240 hp) **Transmissions** 4-speed automatic

Safety information

Side air bags ....Not offered
Antilock brakes ....Standard
Gov't front-crash test, driver/front passenger .....◉/○
IIHS offset crash test ....NA

Reliability history

TROUBLE SPOTS	Pontiac Bonneville							
	90	91	92	93	94	95	96	97
Engine	◓	◓	◓	◓	◓	◓	◉	◉
Cooling	◒	○	○	◒	◓	◉	◉	◉
Fuel	◒	○	◓	◓	◓	◓	◉	◉
Ignition	●	●	●	◒	◒	◓	◉	◉
Auto. trans.	◓	◓	◓	◓	◓	◓	◉	◉
Man. trans.								
Clutch								
Electrical	●	●	●	●	◒	◒	◒	○
A/C	◒	◒	◒	○	○	◓	◉	◉
Suspension	○	○	○	◓	◓	◓	◓	◓
Brakes	●	●	●	●	○	◓	◓	◉
Exhaust	◉	◉	◓	◓	◉	◓	◓	◉
Body rust	○	○	◉	◉	◓	◓	◉	◉
Paint/trim	◒	○	◒	◓	◓	◓	◓	◉
Integrity	○	○	◒	○	◒	◒	◒	○
Hardware	◒	●	●	●	●	◒	○	◓

Symbol key: ◉ = much better, ◓ = better, ○ = average, ◒ = worse, ● = much worse

---

Sports/sporty car under $25,000

Pontiac Firebird

■ **Trim line:** Base, Formula, Trans Am ■ **Body style:** 2-door hatchback, Convertible ■ **Price:** $18,015-$29,715 ■ **Predicted depreciation:** ○ ■ **Predicted reliability:** ● ■ The Pontiac Firebird and its cousin, the Chevrolet Camaro, are among the last of the rear-wheel-drive muscle cars. Changes for 1998 include a minor face-lift and a 305-hp version of the Chevy Corvette's V8. The standard engine is a 200-hp, 3.8-liter V6. Traction control is optional on V8 models. Braking is very good. Still, this car is too bulky to be nimble, and the ride is uncomfortable. Reliability of the V8 has been substantially worse than the V6.

Specifications

Dimensions *Length,* 194 in.; *Width,* 75 in.; *Curb weight,* 3545 lb.; *Passengers, front/rear,* 2/2 **Drive wheels** Rear **Engines** 3.8-liter V6 (200 hp), 5.7-liter V8 (305 hp), 5.7-liter V8 (320 hp) **Transmissions** 5-speed manual, 6-speed manual, 4-speed automatic

Safety information

Side air bags ....Not offered
Antilock brakes ....Standard
Gov't front-crash test, driver/front passenger .....◓/◉
IIHS offset crash test ....NA

Reliability history

TROUBLE SPOTS	Pontiac Firebird V8							
	90	91	92	93	94	95	96	97
Engine	Insufficient data	○	Insufficient data	Insufficient data	○	◒	◒	Insufficient data
Cooling		◒			○	◓	◉	
Fuel		●			◓	◓	◓	
Ignition		●			◒	○	◉	
Auto. trans.		*			◉	◉	*	
Man. trans.		*			*	*	*	
Clutch		*			*	*	*	
Electrical		◒			◒	●	◒	
A/C		○			◓	○	◉	
Suspension		○			◓	◓	◓	
Brakes		◒			◒	○	◓	
Exhaust		◒			◉	◓	◉	
Body rust		◉			◉	◉	◉	
Paint/trim		●			◓	◓	○	
Integrity		●			●	●	◒	
Hardware		●			●	◒	◒	

Symbol key: ◉ = much better, ◓ = better, ○ = average, ◒ = worse, ● = much worse; * as printed

---

Medium car under $25,000

Pontiac Grand Am

■ **Trim line:** SE, SE1, SE2 ■ **Body style:** 2-door, 4-door ■ **Price:** $15,870-$18,970 ■ **Predicted depreciation:** NA ■ **Predicted reliability:** New ■ The Grand Am has been Pontiac's best-seller for years, providing flashy-looking but run-of-the-mill transportation. It has been redesigned this year and released as a 1999 model. The new Grand Am looks similar to the car it replaces, but the wheelbase is longer, the overall length is a little shorter, and it has more interior room. The base engine, a 2.4-liter Four, is the same as that in the Chevrolet Malibu—an adequate but somewhat unrefined power plant. An optional 170-hp 3.4-liter V6 will let this car compete more credibly against such alternatives as the Ford Contour and Nissan Altima.

Specifications

Dimensions *Length,* 186 in.; *Width,* 70 in.; *Curb weight,* 3115 lb.; *Passengers, front/rear,* 2/3 **Drive wheels** Front **Engines** 2.4-liter 4 (150 hp), 3.4-liter V6 (170 hp) **Transmissions** 5-speed manual, 4-speed automatic

Safety information

Side air bags ....Not offered
Antilock brakes ....Standard
Gov't front-crash test, driver/front passenger ...NA/NA
IIHS offset crash test ....NA

Reliability history

TROUBLE SPOTS	90	91	92	93	94	95	96	97
Engine								
Cooling								
Fuel								
Ignition	NO							
Auto. trans.								
Man. trans.	DATA							
Clutch								
Electrical								
A/C	NEW							
Suspension								
Brakes	MODEL							
Exhaust								
Body rust								
Paint/trim								
Integrity								
Hardware								

Sports/sporty car over $25,000

Porsche Boxster

■ **Trim line:** — ■ **Body style:** Convertible ■ **Price:** $41,000 ■ **Predicted depreciation:** NA ■ **Predicted reliability:** NA ■ The rear-drive Boxster has a flat-Six "boxer" engine, and either a crisp five-speed manual or five-speed Tiptronic automatic transmission. Side air bags are new for 1998. A powered convertible soft top is standard. Handling is superb, and the ride's acceptable. The engine and manual transmission are well matched and provide quick acceleration. Routine options quickly push the price close to $50,000. Demand has been strong, so don't expect to find a bargain-priced Boxster on a dealer's lot anytime soon.

Specifications

Dimensions *Length,* 171 in.; *Width,* 70 in.; *Curb weight,* 2890 lb.; *Passengers, front,* 2 **Drive wheels** Rear **Engines** 2.5-liter 6 (201 hp) **Transmissions** 5-speed manual, 5-speed automatic

Safety information

Side air bags ....Standard
Antilock brakes ....Standard
Gov't front-crash test, driver/front passenger ...NA/NA
IIHS offset crash test ....NA

Reliability history

TROUBLE SPOTS	90 91 92 93 94 95 96 97
Engine	
Cooling	
Fuel	
Ignition	NOT
Auto. trans.	
Man. trans.	ENOUGH
Clutch	
Electrical	
A/C	DATA
Suspension	
Brakes	TO
Exhaust	
Body rust	
Paint/trim	RATE
Integrity	
Hardware	

Medium car over $25,000

Saab 9-3

■ **Trim line:** S, SE ■ **Body style:** 2-door hatchback, 4-door hatchback, Convertible ■ **Price:** $25,500-$41,500 ■ **Predicted depreciation:** ○ ■ **Predicted reliability:** ◒ ■ The 9-3 is the new name for the Saab 900. It blends strong acceleration with Saab quirkiness. The only available engine is a 2.0-liter turbocharged Four. A V6 was previously available, but was dropped due to a lack of interest. The 9-3 has a taut ride and corners soundly. This is really a four-passenger car; three in the rear is one too many. The hatchback design provides ample storage space, and it gets larger still when you fold down the rear seatbacks. Reliability of the 900 has not been good, but appears to have improved lately.

Specifications

Dimensions *Length,* 182 in.; *Width,* 67 in.; *Curb weight,* 3145 lb.; *Passengers, front/rear,* 2/3 **Drive wheels** Front **Engines** 2.0-liter 4 Turbo (185 hp) **Transmissions** 5-speed manual, 4-speed automatic

Safety information

Side air bags ....Standard
Antilock brakes ....Standard
Gov't front-crash test, driver/front passenger .....◓/◓
IIHS offset crash test ....Marginal

Reliability history

TROUBLE SPOTS	Saab 900							
	90	91	92	93	94	95	96	97
Engine					◒	◓	◓	Insufficient data
Cooling					◒	○	⊙	
Fuel					◓	◓	⊙	
Ignition					○	○	◓	
Auto. trans.					○	◓	⊙	
Man. trans.					○	◓	⊙	
Clutch					○	◓	⊙	
Electrical					◒	●	◒	
A/C					○	○	◓	
Suspension					○	○	◓	
Brakes					○	○	◓	
Exhaust					○	◓	⊙	
Body rust					⊙	⊙	⊙	
Paint/trim					◓	◓	⊙	
Integrity					○	◒	○	
Hardware					◒	◒	◒	

Medium car over $25,000

Saab 9-5

■ **Trim line:** Base, SE ■ **Body style:** 4-door ■ **Price:** $29,995-$36,800 ■ **Predicted depreciation:** NA ■ **Predicted reliability:** New ■ The new 9-5 is a long-overdue replacement for the Saab 9000. This is the larger and fancier of Saab's two sports sedans. It faces stiff competition from German and Japanese nameplates in the near-luxury market. The 9-5 will sport a turbocharged four-cylinder engine and, for the first time, a turbocharged V6. Side air bags and a unique active head restraint are standard. Old Saab fans will be gratified to find that Saab quirks remain, such as the ignition switch located between the front seats. A wagon version is due in 1999.

Specifications

Dimensions *Length,* 189 in.; *Width,* 71 in.; *Curb weight,* 3590 lb.; *Passengers, front/rear,* 2/3 **Drive wheels** Front **Engines** 2.3-liter 4 Turbo (170 hp), 3.0-liter V6 Turbo (200 hp) **Transmissions** 5-speed manual, 4-speed automatic

Safety information

Side air bags ....Standard
Antilock brakes ....Standard
Gov't front-crash test, driver/front passenger ...NA/NA
IIHS offset crash test ....NA

Reliability history

TROUBLE SPOTS	90 91 92 93 94 95 96 97
Engine	
Cooling	
Fuel	
Ignition	NO
Auto. trans.	
Man. trans.	DATA
Clutch	
Electrical	
A/C	NEW
Suspension	
Brakes	MODEL
Exhaust	
Body rust	
Paint/trim	
Integrity	
Hardware	

Sports/sporty car under $25,000

Toyota Celica

■ **Trim line:** GT ■ **Body style:** 2-door hatchback, Convertible ■ **Price:** $20,536-$24,550 ■ **Predicted depreciation:** ○ ■ **Predicted reliability:** ⊙ ■ The Celica has changed little since its 1994 redesign and continues to offer a balanced combination of good handling, fuel economy, and reliability. The 135-hp, 2.2-liter Four in the GT accelerates adequately but is still not as quick as some competitors. The five-speed manual transmission shifts precisely. The car responds quickly to its steering, and the tires grip well. The front seats offer good support.

Specifications

Dimensions *Length,* 174 in.; *Width,* 69 in.; *Curb weight,* 2720 lb.; *Passengers, front/rear,* 2/2 **Drive wheels** Front **Engines** 2.2-liter 4 (135 hp) **Transmissions** 5-speed manual, 4-speed automatic

Safety information

Side air bags	Not offered
Antilock brakes	Optional
Gov't front-crash test, driver/front passenger	NA/NA
IIHS offset crash test	NA

Reliability history

TROUBLE SPOTS (Toyota Celica)	90	91	92	93	94	95	96	97
Engine	◓	◓	◓	◓	⊙	⊙	⊙	Insufficient data
Cooling	○	◓	◓	⊙	⊙	⊙	⊙	
Fuel	◓	⊙	⊙	⊙	⊙	⊙	⊙	
Ignition	○	◓	◓	◓	⊙	◓	⊙	
Auto. trans.	⊙	◓	⊙	*	⊙	*	*	
Man. trans.	⊙	⊙	⊙	*	⊙	*	*	
Clutch	○	◓	○	*	⊙	*	*	
Electrical	◒	◒	○	○	⊙	○	⊙	
A/C	●	●	◒	◓	⊙	◓	⊙	
Suspension	◓	◓	⊙	⊙	◓	⊙	◓	
Brakes	○	○	○	○	⊙	◓	◓	
Exhaust	◓	◓	⊙	⊙	⊙	⊙	⊙	
Body rust	◓	⊙	⊙	⊙	⊙	⊙	⊙	
Paint/trim	○	○	○	◓	⊙	◓	⊙	
Integrity	○	○	○	○	◓	○	◓	
Hardware	○	○	◒	◒	○	○	◓	

Sport-utility vehicle

Toyota Land Cruiser

■ **Trim line:** — ■ **Body style:** 4-door wagon AWD ■ **Price:** $45,950 ■ **Predicted depreciation:** ⊙ ■ **Predicted reliability:** New ■ The big, expensive Land Cruiser has been redesigned. It now sports a 4.7-liter V8 and independent front suspension. The interior is nicely laid out and offers lots of cargo room. A third-row rear seat is optional. Full-time four-wheel-drive is standard. The new Land Cruiser aims to be a premium SUV in every respect. It's a heavy, high-dollar elephant, more in the mold of the Lincoln Navigator than the smart, sophisticated Mercedes M-Class.

Specifications

Dimensions *Length,* 193 in.; *Width,* 76 in.; *Curb weight,* 6470 lb.; *Passengers, front/mid/rear,* 2/3/2 **Drive wheels** Permanent 4WD **Engines** 4.7-liter V8 (230 hp) **Transmissions** 4-speed automatic

Safety information

Side air bags	Not offered
Antilock brakes	Standard
Gov't front-crash test, driver/front passenger	NA/NA
IIHS offset crash test	NA

Reliability history

TROUBLE SPOTS	90 91 92 93 94 95 96 97
Engine	
Cooling	
Fuel	NO
Ignition	
Auto. trans.	
Man. trans.	DATA
Clutch	
Electrical	
A/C	NEW
Suspension	
Brakes	MODEL
Exhaust	
Body rust	
Paint/trim	
Integrity	
Hardware	

Sports/sporty car over $25,000

Toyota Supra

■ **Trim line:** Base, Turbo ■ **Body style:** 2-door hatchback ■ **Price:** $30,918-$40,308 ■ **Predicted depreciation:** ○ ■ **Predicted reliability:** NA ■ The Supra Turbo, with a 320-hp turbo Six, seems designed to travel at triple the speed limit. The base, nonturbo model has 225 hp. Sophisticated traction control works at all speeds, and is almost mandatory for piloting this rear-wheel-drive sports car in wet or slippery conditions. There's very little body lean during hard cornering. The ride is very stiff. Low front seats make seeing out difficult. The rear seat is almost unusable. The Supra is one of the last remaining Japanese sports cars in what was once a very crowded market.

Specifications

Dimensions *Length,* 178 in.; *Width,* 71 in.; *Curb weight,* 3555 lb.; *Passengers, front/rear,* 2/2 **Drive wheels** Rear **Engines** 3.0-liter 6 (225 hp), 3.0-liter 6 turbo (320 hp) **Transmissions** 6-speed manual, 4-speed automatic

Safety information

Side air bags	Not offered
Antilock brakes	Standard
Gov't front-crash test, driver/front passenger	NA/NA
IIHS offset crash test	NA

Reliability history

TROUBLE SPOTS	90 91 92 93 94 95 96 97
Engine	
Cooling	
Fuel	
Ignition	NOT
Auto. trans.	
Man. trans.	ENOUGH
Clutch	
Electrical	
A/C	DATA
Suspension	
Brakes	TO
Exhaust	
Body rust	
Paint/trim	RATE
Integrity	
Hardware	

Pickup truck

Toyota T100

■ **Trim line:** Base, DX, SR5 ■ **Body style:** Regular cab 2WD, Extended cab 2WD, Extended cab 4WD ■ **Price:** $14,828-$24,398 ■ **Predicted depreciation:** ○ ■ **Predicted reliability:** ◓ ■ The T100 is the only pickup truck imported into the U.S.—not all that surprising, when you consider that imported trucks carry a steep 25 percent tariff. The T100 is almost a full-sized pickup, designed for hauling and towing—but if you expect to do much of either, choose the V6 instead of the standard Four. Controls and displays are easy to reach and see. A passenger-side air bag is not offered. The T100 costs quite a bit for what you get, but it has proved reliable. A new V8 version, manufactured in the U.S., will replace it in 1999.

Specifications

Dimensions *Length,* 209 in.; *Width,* 75 in.; *Curb weight,* 3460 lb.; *Passengers, front/rear,* 3/3 **Drive wheels** Rear or part-time 4WD **Engines** 2.7-liter 4 (150 hp), 3.4-liter V6 (190 hp) **Transmissions** 5-speed manual, 4-speed automatic

Safety information

Side air bags ....Not offered
Antilock brakes ....Optional with V6
Gov't front-crash test, driver/front passenger .....◓/◉
IIHS offset crash test ....NA

Reliability history

TROUBLE SPOTS	Toyota T100 Pickup (2WD) 90	91	92	93	94	95	96	97
Engine				○	Insufficient data	◓	◓	Insufficient data
Cooling				◓		◉	◉	
Fuel				◉		◉	◉	
Ignition				◉		◉	◉	
Auto. trans.				*		◉	○	
Man. trans.				*		*	*	
Clutch				*		*	*	
Electrical				◓		◓	◓	
A/C				*		◉	◉	
Suspension				◓		◓	◓	
Brakes				◓		◉	◉	
Exhaust				◉		◉	◉	
Body rust				◓		◉	◉	
Paint/trim				◉		◉	◓	
Integrity				◉		○	◓	
Hardware				○		○	◓	

Pickup truck

Toyota Tacoma

■ **Trim line:** Base, Sport, SR5, Limited ■ **Body style:** Regular cab 2WD, Regular cab 4WD, Extended cab 2WD, Extended cab 4WD ■ **Price:** $12,538-$24,028 ■ **Predicted depreciation:** ◓ ■ **Predicted reliability:** ◓ ■ Some minor styling changes and a passenger-side air bag with a cutoff switch are new this year for the U.S.-made Tacoma. In several respects this small pickup has been a disappointment. Its powertrain is responsive, especially with the optional V6, and the controls are good. But the seats are not comfortable, the handling was unimpressive, and the ride was awful in the last model we tested. Bumpy curves make the truck leap and bound. Antilock brakes are hard to find, and without them stops are very long.

Specifications

Dimensions *Length,* 199 in.; *Width,* 67 in.; *Curb weight,* 3040 lb.; *Passengers, front/rear,* 3/2 **Drive wheels** Rear or part-time 4WD **Engines** 2.4-liter 4 (142 hp), 2.7-liter 4 (150 hp), 3.4-liter V6 (190 hp) **Transmissions** 5-speed manual, 4-speed automatic

Safety information

Side air bags ....Not offered
Antilock brakes ....Optional
Gov't front-crash test, driver/front passenger .....◓/○
IIHS offset crash test ....NA

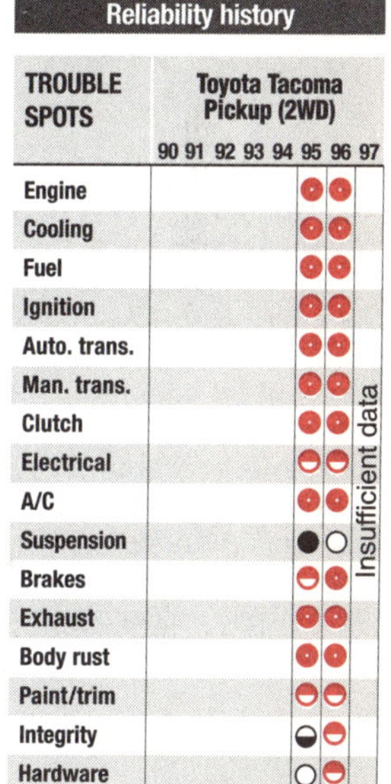

Reliability history

TROUBLE SPOTS	Toyota Tacoma Pickup (2WD) 90	91	92	93	94	95	96	97
Engine						◉	◉	Insufficient data
Cooling						◉	◉	
Fuel						◉	◉	
Ignition						◉	◉	
Auto. trans.						◉	◉	
Man. trans.						◉	◉	
Clutch						◉	◉	
Electrical						◓	◓	
A/C						◉	◉	
Suspension						●	○	
Brakes						◓	◉	
Exhaust						◉	◉	
Body rust						◉	◉	
Paint/trim						◓	◓	
Integrity						◒	◓	
Hardware						○	◓	

Small car

Volkswagen Jetta

RECOMMENDED

■ **Trim line:** GL, GT, GLS, TDI, GLX ■ **Body style:** 4-door ■ **Price:** $14,595-$20,955 ■ **Predicted depreciation:** ○ ■ **Predicted reliability:** ○ ■ Think of the Jetta as a Golf with a very large trunk. Side-impact air bags became optional this year. The basic engine is a responsive 2.0-liter Four. We'd choose the manual transmission over the automatic. The GLX version comes with a smooth and powerful V6 and sporty suspension, seats, and tires. All versions offer excellent handling, crisp steering, and good tire grip. The front seats provide good, firm support. The rear seat is adequate for two adults, but not three. The Jetta's reliability record has improved to average of late. A replacement is due for 1999.

Specifications

Dimensions *Length,* 173 in.; *Width,* 67 in.; *Curb weight,* 2955 lb.; *Passengers, front/rear,* 2/3 **Drive wheels** Front **Engines** 1.9-liter 4 Turbodiesel (90 hp), 2.0-liter 4 (115 hp), 2.8-liter V6 (172 hp) **Transmissions** 5-speed manual, 4-speed automatic

Safety information

Side air bags ....Optional
Antilock brakes.................Optional (standard on GLX)
Gov't front-crash test, driver/front passenger .....○/○
IIHS offset crash test ....Marginal

Reliability history

TROUBLE SPOTS	Volkswagen Jetta, Jetta III 90	91	92	93	94	95	96	97
Engine					◓	◓	◉	◉
Cooling					◓	◉	◉	◉
Fuel					○	○	◓	◉
Ignition					○	○	◓	◉
Auto. trans.					○	○	○	*
Man. trans.					◓	◉	◉	◓
Clutch					◓	◉	◉	◉
Electrical					◒	●	◒	◓
A/C					○	◓	◉	◉
Suspension					◉	◓	◓	◉
Brakes					○	◓	◉	◉
Exhaust					◓	◉	◉	◉
Body rust					◓	◉	◉	◉
Paint/trim					○	○	◓	◓
Integrity					○	○	○	◓
Hardware					●	●	◒	◓

Small car

Volkswagen New Beetle

■ **Trim line:** Base, TDI ■ **Body style:** 2-door hatchback ■ **Price:** $15,200-$16,475 ■ **Predicted depreciation:** NA ■ **Predicted reliability:** New ■ The New Beetle bears a vague family resemblance to the famous rear-engined Beetle that VW scrapped 20 years ago, but the new car is entirely different and far better. The New Beetle is really a two-door version of the next-generation Golf, and the current Golf is a capable small car. The New Beetle comes well equipped. It has front-wheel drive and a front-mounted engine. The airy interior has a neat, retro look. The low swooping roofline robs head room from the rear seats, but the rear hatch adds versatility.

Specifications

Dimensions *Length,* 161 in.; *Width,* 68 in.; *Curb weight,* 2715 lb.; *Passengers, front/rear,* 2/2 **Drive wheels** Front **Engines** 1.8-liter 4 Turbo (150 hp), 1.9-liter 4 Turbodiesel (90 hp), 2.0-liter 4 (115 hp) **Transmissions** 5-speed manual, 4-speed automatic, 5-speed auto.

Safety information

Side air bags ....Standard
Antilock brakes ....Optional
Gov't front-crash test, driver/front passenger ...NA/NA
IIHS offset crash test ....NA

Reliability history

TROUBLE SPOTS	90 91 92 93 94 95 96 97
Engine	
Cooling	
Fuel	
Ignition	NO
Auto. trans.	
Man. trans.	DATA
Clutch	
Electrical	
A/C	NEW
Suspension	
Brakes	MODEL
Exhaust	
Body rust	
Paint/trim	
Integrity	
Hardware	

Coupe

Volvo C70

■ **Trim line:** — ■ **Body style:** 2-door ■ **Price:** $38,995 ■ **Predicted depreciation:** NA ■ **Predicted reliability:** New ■ The C70, introduced for the 1998 model year, is a coupe based on the Volvo S70. A convertible is due later this year. This car is an attempt by Volvo to shed its stodgy, workhorse image and add something a little more fun and frivolous—without giving up anything in safety or function. The steering is well weighted, and the brakes are good. The C70 comes with a turbocharged, 236-hp Five. It doesn't feel very responsive unless it's revved a lot. A "light pressure" turbo is due for 1999.

Specifications

Dimensions *Length,* 186 in.; *Width,* 72 in.; *Curb weight,* 3380 lb.; *Passengers, front/rear,* 2/2 **Drive wheels** Front **Engines** 2.3-liter 5 turbo (236 hp) **Transmissions** 5-speed manual, 4-speed automatic

Safety information

Side air bags ....Standard
Antilock brakes ....Standard
Gov't front-crash test, driver/front passenger ...NA/NA
IIHS offset crash test ....NA

Reliability history

TROUBLE SPOTS	90 91 92 93 94 95 96 97
Engine	
Cooling	
Fuel	
Ignition	NO
Auto. trans.	
Man. trans.	DATA
Clutch	
Electrical	
A/C	NEW
Suspension	
Brakes	MODEL
Exhaust	
Body rust	
Paint/trim	
Integrity	
Hardware	

Medium car over $25,000

Volvo S90/V90

■ **Trim line:** — ■ **Body style:** 4-door, 4-door wagon ■ **Price:** $34,300-$35,850 ■ **Predicted depreciation:** ○ ■ **Predicted reliability:** ○ ■ The capable 90 series, the last rear-wheel-drive Volvo, remains basically unchanged for 1998. It comes with a 2.9-liter Six that performs enthusiastically. The ride is good, and handling is sound. The front seats are pleasantly firm and nicely shaped. The rear seat is about as hospitable as they get. The sedan has a cavernous trunk; the wagon, an exceptionally roomy cargo area. Traction control isn't offered. A front-drive model will replace this car for 1999.

Specifications

Dimensions *Length,* 192 in.; *Width,* 69 in.; *Curb weight,* 3485 lb.; *Passengers, front/rear,* 2/3 **Drive** **wheels** Rear **Engines** 2.9-liter 6 (181 hp) **Transmissions** 4-speed automatic

Safety information

Side air bags ....Standard
Antilock brakes ....Standard
Gov't front-crash test, driver/front passenger .....◓/◓
IIHS offset crash test ....NA

Reliability history

TROUBLE SPOTS	Volvo 960 Series						
	90 91	92	93	94	95	96	97
Engine		Insufficient data	Insufficient data	Insufficient data	◓	●	●
Cooling					◓	●	●
Fuel					◓	●	●
Ignition					○	◓	◓
Auto. trans.					◒	●	●
Man. trans.							
Clutch							
Electrical					◒	○	◓
A/C					○	◓	●
Suspension					◒	◓	●
Brakes					◒	○	●
Exhaust					●	●	●
Body rust					●	●	●
Paint/trim					◓	◓	●
Integrity					○	○	●
Hardware					⬤	○	◓

C H A P T E R S E V E N

CARING *for your* CAR

CAR-CARE GUIDE

Most new cars these days are less troublesome, easier to maintain, and built to last much longer than cars made a few years ago. It used to be that most cars were ready for the scrap yard at 100,000 miles. Today, with moderate care, a car should be able to go 200,000 miles or more.

Two big reasons for this change: better rust-proofing and the use of solid-state electronics. Manufacturers' rust-through warranties now run five to eight years and 100,000 miles or more. With electronic ignition systems, the traditional tune-up—changing the spark plugs and points and adjusting the timing every six months—is a thing of the past. Some cars can go 60,000, even 100,000 miles before needing new spark plugs.

All the electronics and computers used in autos bring some problems, too. It's increasingly difficult to do your own mechanical work, and even your local garage may lack the sophisticated computer equipment needed to diagnose a modern car's maladies. And problems with electrical systems are a major trouble spot in new cars.

Just because modern cars are more reliable doesn't mean they never break down or that servicing them is cheap. A dealer's service department still socks you for a lot of money for the multitude of electronic inspections and minor adjustments it makes when you bring the car in at its required service intervals.

To get the most miles out of your car, you need to do only three things:

- Drive with care.
- Change the oil regularly.
- Keep the car clean.

GOOD DRIVING PRACTICES

Driving "softly" helps prolong the life of mechanical parts. If your motions are smooth and gentle—no jackrabbit starts, sudden braking, or hard cornering—you'll also save on gasoline and maybe even avoid an accident.

Frequent sudden stops wear the brake pads quickly. Anticipate stops and slow gradually by pressing lightly on the brakes.

Come to a complete stop before shifting between reverse and a forward gear. If your car has a manual transmission, always fully depress the clutch when changing gears. And if you're stopped on a hill temporarily, don't hold the car motionless by using the clutch and gas pedal. Instead, depress the clutch and use the brake to hold the car.

PREVENTIVE MAINTENANCE

Taking good care of a car means checking its systems and performing some routine preventive maintenance regularly. If you notice any unusual noise, vibration, or odor, or if a warning light comes on the dashboard, don't ignore it. Dealing with minor ailments early helps to avoid major problems down the road.

If the car is still covered by the manufacturer's warranty, you don't have to tolerate nagging problems. Take the car back to the dealer promptly and ask to have it put right. The extra trip to the dealer may be inconvenient, but it's far better to have a free minor repair than an expensive major repair later on.

Follow the manufacturer's service recommendations. You'll find the schedule, and the items covered at each service interval, in your owner's manual. Sometimes dealers provide a maintenance schedule that's far more rigorous than the manufacturer's. Go with the manufacturer's, not the dealer's recommendations.

For the general advice we give below, keep in mind that you don't have to do most of this work yourself. An oil-change center will check all the fluid levels, for instance, as a matter of course.

PERIODIC CHECKS

OIL LEVEL. Try to do this when the engine is cold. Or, if you need to check the oil when the engine is hot, park the car on level ground and wait a few minutes. Then pull out and wipe the dipstick and reinsert it. If the level measures below the "add" line, put in enough oil to bring the level to "full." Don't overfill.

TIRE PRESSURE. Check tire pressure regularly—say once a month or before going on a trip. Keep a good tire-pressure gauge in the car. (It will cost under $10 at an auto-parts store.) The owner's manual or a label on the driver's doorpost or in the glove compartment will tell you the recommended tire pressure. Check the tires when they're cold—and don't forget the spare.

TIRE CARE. Check for abnormal or uneven wear every month or two. Uneven wear can be a sign you need to have the wheels aligned. Cuts or bulges in the sidewalls are signs of an imminent blowout. Replace damaged tires right away. To extend your tires' life, rotate them every 7500 miles (more often if you drive the car hard).

KEEP THE BODY CLEAN. Road grime and air pollution can damage a car's paint, so try to wash the car regularly. It's easiest to take the car to a car wash. But if you do it yourself, use ample water to avoid scratching the finish. Hose out the fender wells and undercarriage with a strong spray. If you drive in places where the car is exposed to road salt, do this—or have it done at a car wash—several times per winter. When water beads on the body become larger than a quarter, it's time to apply wax or polish.

EACH OIL CHANGE

OIL. Use the correct viscosity motor oil—the one recommended in your owner's manual. Most automakers recommend you change the oil every 7500 miles. The brand isn't so important, as long as it carries the industry's "starburst" symbol on the label and meets the service grade called SJ (see "It's not just oil," page 228). Unless you drive a lot in very hot or very cold weather or do a lot of stop-and-go driving, expensive synthetic motor oils seem to offer no advantage. Likewise, we see no benefit from using any of the popular oil additives. (See "Choosing motor oil," page 226.)

AIR FILTER. Remove the air-filter cover and hold the filter up to light. If you don't see light, replace the filter.

CONSTANT-VELOCITY-JOINT BOOTS. On front-wheel-drive cars (and some four-wheel-drive vehicles), examine the bellows-like rubber boots on the front axles. If they're cut or leaking, have them replaced.

EXHAUST SYSTEM. It's hard to check the exhaust system yourself because you have to get under the car to do it. If you do, tighten any loose clamps you find, and look for rusted-through parts that need to be replaced. It's probably cheaper in the long run to replace the entire exhaust system all at once rather than piecemeal.

RADIATOR COOLANT. Check the plastic overflow bottle, attached by a hose to the radiator. If the level is below "full," add water and antifreeze in equal amounts. If you need to add water and antifreeze frequently, check for leaks.

AUTOMATIC-TRANSMISSION FLUID. Check the fluid level and color, using the transmission dipstick, when the engine is warmed up and running. (See the owner's manual for details.) If the level is low, add fluid until the dipstick reading is between "add" and "full." If the fluid is brown or black or smells burnt, have the transmission checked by a professional. It probably needs adjustments or repair.

POWER-STEERING FLUID. Check the level with the dipstick (usually attached to the fluid-reservoir cap). If the level is low, top it up and have the system checked for leaks.

BRAKE FLUID. Check the level in the brake-fluid reservoir. If the fluid level is low, top it up and have the system checked for leaks.

BATTERY. Check the battery liquid by prying off the covers or unscrewing the caps; if necessary, add distilled water. If you have a "maintenance-free" battery, there is an "eye" you peer at to check the state of charge. Green or blue means the battery is OK. If the "eye" is black, have the battery tested and charged; if it's pale or yellow, replace the battery.

ONCE A YEAR

BRAKES. Do brake work yourself only if you're an experienced do-it-yourselfer. Otherwise, leave this to a mechanic. Remove all wheels and examine the brakes. Replace excessively worn pads or linings and have badly scored rotors or drums machined or replaced. Have the wheel bearings greased.

CLEAN THE RADIATOR. To prevent overheating, remove debris with a soft brush and wash the outside of the radiator with detergent solution.

CHECK THE BATTERY TERMINALS. Remove deposits with a wire brush, rinse with a solution of two teaspoons of baking soda in a pint of water, and wipe it dry with a soft cloth. Cover vent holes with tape during cleaning so baking soda doesn't get inside. Coat the terminals with a dielectric grease (one that doesn't conduct electricity), available at auto-parts stores.

EVERY TWO TO FOUR YEARS

COOLING SYSTEM. Drain and flush the cooling system. Considering the hassle of collecting and safely disposing of old antifreeze, this is a job usually better left to a local garage.

TRANSMISSION. Check the owner's manual for recommended servicing of the automatic transmission. The fluid—and filter if your transmission has one—should be replaced every 36,000 miles, or more often if the normally pink fluid takes on a brownish tint. In some new models, the fluid and filter can go 100,000 miles or more before they need changing.

BELTS AND HOSES. Replace hoses and accessory drive belts every two or three years, even if they don't show wear. If a belt becomes noisy, have it adjusted promptly.

TIMING BELT. If your car has a timing belt instead of a timing chain, be sure to follow the manufacturer's recommendation about having it replaced—every 60,000 to 80,000 miles in most cases. Details are in the owner's manual.

CHOOSING MOTOR OIL

Oil companies spend millions of advertising dollars each year to convince you that their oil can make your car's engine perform better and last longer. And purveyors of motor-oil and engine "treatments" assert that their products offer engine protection that oil alone can't provide. In CONSUMER REPORTS' most ambitious test project ever, we used a fleet of 75 New York City taxicabs. CONSUMER REPORTS put identical rebuilt engines with precisely measured parts into the cabs at the beginning of the test, and changed their oil every 6000 miles. That's about twice as long as the automakers recommend for the severe service that taxicabs see, but that interval was chosen to accelerate the test results and provide worst-case conditions. After 60,000 miles (which translated into 10 to 12 months of use), the engines were disassembled and checked for wear and harmful deposits. The test conditions were grueling. The typical Big Apple cab is driven day and night, in traffic that is legendary for its perversity, by cabbies who are just as legendary for their driving abandon.

In addition to the taxicab tests, CONSUMER REPORTS had the oils' chemical and physical properties analyzed by an independent lab. At each oil change, a sample of the old oil was analyzed to check its viscosity and to look for evidence of worn metals and other contaminants.

CHOOSING VISCOSITY

One of a motor oil's key attributes is its viscosity, or ability to flow at a given temperature. The two most commonly recommended viscosity grades are 10W-30 and 5W-30. Automakers specify grades according to the temperature range expected in the climate where the car is used. The lower the number, the thinner the oil and the more easily it flows.

In 5W-30 oil, for example, the two numbers mean it's a "multiviscosity" or "multigrade" oil that's effective over a range of temperatures. The first number, 5, is an index that refers to how the oil flows at low temperatures. The second number, 30, refers to how it flows at high temperatures. The W designation means the oil can be used in winter.

A popular belief is that 5W-30 oils are too thin to protect vital engine parts when they get hot. One of CONSUMER REPORTS' laboratory tests measured the viscosity of oils under high-temperature, high-stress conditions and found essentially no difference between 5W-30 oils and their 10W-30 brand mates. At low temperatures, the 5W-30 oil flowed more easily.

Viscosity grade is important, so be careful. Recommendations vary with the make, engine, and model year of the car, so check your owner's manual and be sure to use the proper grade of oil.

CHOOSING BRANDS

If you've been loyal to one brand, you may be surprised to learn that every oil CONSUMER REPORTS tested was good at doing what motor oil is supposed to do. Thorough statistical analysis of the data showed no brand—not even the expensive synthetic motor oils—to be meaningfully better or worse in our tests.

The wear on key metal parts within the engine averaged only 0.0026 inch, about the thickness of a magazine page. Generally, CONSUMER REPORTS noted as much variation between engines using the same oil as between those using different oils. Even the engines with the most wear didn't reach a level where CONSUMER REPORTS could detect operational problems.

Sludge is a mucky sediment that can prevent oil from circulating freely and make the engine run hotter. Varnish is a hard deposit that would remain on engine parts if you wiped off the sludge. It can make moving parts stick. All the oils proved excellent at preventing sludge, perhaps because sludge is more apt to form during cold start-ups and short trips—conditions the test cabs rarely experienced. The accumulations were so light that we wouldn't expect sludge to be a problem with any of these oils under most conditions. Some varnish deposits were heavy enough to lead to problems eventually, but no brand consistently produced more varnish than any other.

All the products tested carried the industry's starburst symbol on their container (see "It's not just oil," page 228). Beware of oils without the starburst; they may lack the full complement of additives needed to keep modern engines running reliably.

According to the laboratory tests, Mobil 1 and Pennzoil Performax synthetics flow exceptionally easily at low temperatures—a condition our taxi tests didn't simulate effectively. They also had the highest viscosity under high-temperature, high-stress conditions, when a thick oil protects the engine. Thus, these oils may be a good choice for hard driving in extreme temperatures.

HOW OFTEN TO CHANGE THE OIL?

The long-time mantra of auto mechanics has been to change your oil every 3000 miles. Most automakers recommend an oil change every 7500 miles or six months (whichever comes first) for "normal" driving, and every 3000 miles or three months for "severe" driving—frequent trips of less than four or five miles, stop-and-go traffic, extended idling, towing a trailer, or dusty or extremely cold conditions. Many motorists' driving falls into one or more of those "severe" categories.

To determine whether frequent oil changes really help, CONSUMER REPORTS changed the oil in three cabs every 3000 miles. After 60,000 miles, those engines were compared with the engines from the base tests of the same oil, changed every 6000 miles. CONSUMER REPORTS saw no meaningful differences.

Modern motor oils needn't be changed as often as oils did years ago. More frequent oil changes won't hurt your car, but you could be spending money unnecessarily and adding to the nation's energy and oil-disposal problems.

For "normal" service, 7500-mile intervals or every six months—whichever comes first (or the recommendation in your owner's manual)—should be fine. Change the oil at least that often to protect your engine and maintain your warranty. Some severe service—frequent cold starts and short trips, dusty conditions, trailer towing—may require a shorter interval. Special engines such as diesels and turbos, which CONSUMER REPORTS didn't test, may need more frequent oil changes.

OIL ADDITIVES

CONSUMER REPORTS also tested Slick 50 engine treatment and STP Oil Treatment each in three cabs. Both boast that they reduce engine friction and wear.

The engine treatments are added with the oil. Slick 50 claims to bond to engine parts and provide protection for 50,000 miles. We used each according to instructions.

It's not just oil

Motor oil does much more than lubricate. It helps cool the engine, keep it clean, prevent corrosion, and reduce friction to improve fuel economy. To do all that, refiners blend in various additives, which account for 10 to 25 percent of the product you buy. The oil industry has devised a starburst symbol (shown at right) to certify that a particular motor oil meets the latest industry requirements for protection against deposits, wear, oxidation, and corrosion. The starburst on the label means the oil meets the latest API (American Petroleum Institute) Service requirements. Service SJ is the most advanced formulation.

Here are some of the additives found in modern oils:

- Viscosity-index improvers modify the oil so its viscosity is more consistent over a wide temperature range.
- Antioxidants prevent the oil from thickening when it runs hot for extended periods.
- Dispersants keep contaminants suspended so they don't form deposits in the engine.
- Detergents help prevent varnish and sludge on engine parts and neutralize acid formed in the engine.
- Rust and corrosion inhibitors protect metal parts from acids and water formed in the engine.
- Pour-point depressants help the oil flow in a cold engine, especially in cold weather.
- Foam inhibitors collapse the bubbles churned up by the engine crankshaft. (Foam reduces lubricating effectiveness.)
- Friction modifiers strengthen the oil film and prevent unlubricated contact between moving parts.
- Antiwear agents provide lubrication when oil is squeezed out from between moving engine parts.

The engines were disassembled and checked for wear and deposits. There were no discernible benefits from either of these products.

Consumer Reports sees little reason why anyone using one of today's high-quality motor oils would need these engine/oil treatments. One notable effect of STP Oil Treatment was an increase in oil viscosity; it made our 10W-30 oil act more like a 15W-40, a grade not often recommended. In very cold weather, that might pose a risk of engine damage.

BUYING ADVICE

Buy the viscosity grade recommended in your owner's manual, and look for the starburst emblem on the container. Expensive synthetic oil (typically, $3 or $4 a quart) worked no better than conventional motor oils in our taxi tests, but they're worth considering for extreme driving conditions—high ambient temperatures and high engine load or very cold temperatures.

WHERE TO GO FOR AN OIL CHANGE

Choosing the right motor oil is only the first step. Someone has to change the oil regularly. Should you economize by doing the work yourself? Should you go to the local service station? The car dealer? A quick-lube center?

Consumer Reports own tests plus the experiences of some 900 Consumer Reports readers provide some answers to those questions. Readers in 1996 were asked how often they change their car's oil, who does it, and how satisfied they are with the service. Shoppers were sent in several parts of the U.S. to 55 local quick-lube centers to assess the service and to collect oil samples Consumer Reports could analyze.

WHERE SHOULD YOU GO?

The car owners we surveyed used these four options in roughly equal measure:

SERVICE STATION OR GARAGE. Many local garages compete with quick-lube centers by charging $20 to $30 or so for an oil change.

NEW-CAR DEALER. Some dealers offer regular oil changes for little or no extra cost with the purchase of a car. Some new-car dealers offer a "one-price" oil change that's competitive with the prices charged by quick-lube centers. But without such an arrangement, expect dealer-performed oil changes to cost about $30. Car dealers were also the slowest and least convenient, according to our survey.

DO IT YOURSELF. People change their own oil not only to save money (oil and filter together can cost as little as $10), and to know the job was done right.

If you handle your own oil changes, be sure to dispose of the used oil properly to prevent it from polluting the environment. It's best to take the oil to a local service station that accepts used oil, or to a municipal household hazardous-waste collection center. Whatever you do, don't pour the oil down the sewer or discard it with the rest of the household trash.

QUICK-LUBE CENTERS. These operations promise to get you in and out in as little as 10 minutes; 90 percent of CONSUMER REPORTS' surveyed readers reported that they waited less than half an hour. Cost: $15 to $35. Although about three-quarters of readers were highly satisfied with quick-lube centers, service stations and car dealers earned even higher scores.

QUICK-LUBES: HOW RELIABLE?

Quick-lube centers promise a lot for a little—change the oil and filter, top off other fluids, check the tire pressure, perhaps even vacuum the car's interior, all in about half an hour.

To check the centers out, CONSUMER REPORTS shoppers in California, Florida, Illinois, and Texas took cars in for an oil change at quick-lube centers. The shoppers visited outlets run by Jiffy Lube, Kmart, Wal-Mart, and others.

CONSUMER REPORTS didn't visit enough centers often enough to rank the centers from best to worst. But there were patterns in the service:

THE SHOPS VISITED DIDN'T CUT CORNERS. The oil they dispense from a drum is comparable to the oil you can buy in one-quart containers. The shops also did a good job of filling oil and other fluids to the proper levels.

HOWEVER, THE SHOPS DO MAKE MISTAKES. The most common one that any servicer can make: using the wrong viscosity grade of oil for the car. Many oil-change centers maintain computerized data on which oil grades are recommended for specific makes and models. But in the cases where CONSUMER REPORTS could compare the received oil grade with the grade the car's owner's manual listed as preferred, the quick-lube shop used a different grade half the time.

You might not be able to tell if your car got, say, 10W-40 instead of 5W-30. But the engine may not always be adequately protected if it has the wrong grade of oil in very hot or very cold weather.

THE SHOPS ARE USUALLY FAST AND ECONOMICAL. They took 10 minutes to more than an hour for service. Average time: 35 minutes. Average cost: $23.

SERVICE VARIES. Some centers change the oil and filter, period. Others include a variety of services.

About one in five readers who used a quick-lube center complained that it tried to sell unwanted services. A few readers (8 percent) said the centers didn't perform a necessary service—changing the oil filter.

RECOMMENDATIONS

Change the oil yourself only if you have the tools and equipment, can safely dispose of the used oil, and feel that it's worth the hassle to save about $15. Otherwise, any of the commercial alternatives can do an adequate job. Use a garage or the dealer when you also need other work done at the same time. Choose among quick-lube centers according to price and service—and be sure you tell the center what grade of oil your car needs. Discount coupons are common; you seldom need to pay full price.

Glossary

ABS. Antilock braking system. A computer-controlled braking system that senses when a wheel is starting to lock up and skid, and rapidly pumps the brake on that wheel. The ABS computer may also selectively use the car's braking system to slow the wheels on cars with traction control.

ACCELERATION TESTS. Consumer Reports conducts a number of acceleration tests. All but the 45-65 mph passing test are clocked from a standstill with the engine idling.

ACCESS. A Consumer Reports judgment of how easy it is to get in and out of a vehicle's seats.

AERODYNAMICS. Design elements concerned with wind resistance. Aerodynamic designs are supposed to reduce air drag when the car is moving, thus improving performance and fuel economy and reducing noise.

AIR BAG. A cushion that rapidly inflates to protect an occupant in a frontal collision. Dual air bags are now standard in all passenger cars and most light trucks. Side air bags are showing up in more and more cars.

ALL-SEASON TIRE. A tire designed for year-round use; standard equipment on most passenger cars.

ALL-WHEEL DRIVE. A type of four-wheel-drive system that remains (or can remain) permanently engaged. It may work without the driver having to move a lever or switch. It uses a center differential or some equivalent mechanism to distribute power to the front and rear wheels.

ANNUAL FUEL. To get an idea of what a year's worth of fuel would cost for a given car, Consumer Reports calculates how many gallons of fuel a car would use to travel 15,000 miles, then multiplies that by national average gasoline prices: $1.20 per gallon for regular; $1.30 for mid-grade; and $1.40 for premium.

ANNUAL QUESTIONNAIRE. A questionnaire sent annually to Consumer Reports subscribers. This survey provides data based on readers' real-life experiences for our Frequency-of-Repair charts, dealer satisfaction, and other reliability information.

A-PILLAR. The roof support on either side of the car's windshield.

ASPECT RATIO. The ratio of a tire's sidewall height to its cross-section width. The middle number in a three-part tire-size description (the 60 in a tire that's sized 175/60R-15).

ATC (AUTOMATIC TEMPERATURE CONTROL). A climate-control system that requires you to select only the temperature. The system automatically chooses the ducts, fan speed, and mode (air conditioning, heat, defrost, etc.) needed to reach and maintain that temperature. Also called "automatic climate control" or "automatic climate system."

AUTOMATIC-LOCKING RETRACTOR. Also known as ALR. A design that keeps the safety belt cinched tight—essential for securing a child safety seat (standard on 1995 and later models). The ALR is built into the shoulder-belt portion. It's activated when you pull that portion of the belt all the way to the end of the reel, listening for a click, then let it rewind. Systems without an ALR may require a separate locking clip to secure a child seat.

AUTOMATIC RESTRAINT. See Passive restraint.

BELTLINE. An imaginary horizontal line just below the window openings on a car body.

BIO-SID (SIDE-IMPACT DUMMY). A crash-test dummy used for side-impact crash-testing. Bio-SID is a type used in the U.S.; Euro-SID is used in Europe.

BODILY INJURY LIABILITY INSURANCE. Coverage that pays for injuries to another person or persons injured in a car accident.

BODY HARDWARE. Components attached to body parts, such as window cranks, seat tracks, and trim.

BODY INTEGRITY. A tally of squeaks and rattles and parts that fall off. One of the automobile trouble-spot areas covered in CONSUMER REPORTS' Annual Questionnaire.

BODY-ON-FRAME. A method of car and truck construction, rarely used in modern passenger cars, in which the body panels are attached to a chassis frame.

BODY STYLE. The body configuration that defines the vehicle type—sedan, wagon, coupe, convertible, hatchback, minivan, pickup, or sport-utility vehicle.

BOOSTER SEAT. A safety seat for a child too large for a baby seat but not big enough to sit safely on a standard car seat.

B-PILLAR. The central post supporting the roof, located behind the car's front doors.

BRAKING TESTS. CONSUMER REPORTS tests brakes a number of ways, including checking for brake fade with repeated use; measuring minimum stopping distances on wet and dry pavement; checking whether stops are straight (including a tough wet-divided pavement test where the track is slicker under one side of the vehicle than the other); and gauging pedal effort and feel. Braking distances apply only to CONSUMER REPORTS test conditions.

BUMPER-BASHER TESTS. CONSUMER REPORTS uses a heavy hydraulic ram to inflict 3- and 5-mph impacts on a car's front and rear bumpers to see how well they can withstand low-speed collisions. After the prescribed series of blows, the damage, if any, is assessed.

CAFE. See **Corporate Average Fuel Economy.**

CAMBER. A wheel-alignment term describing the tilt of a tire inward (negative) or outward (positive) from a vertical plane.

CAMSHAFT. An engine shaft fitted with lobes called cams. As the shaft rotates, the lobes push open the intake and exhaust valves in sequence. Some cars have Double Overhead Camshafts (DOHC), while others have a Single Overhead Camshaft (SOHC).

CAPITAL COST. In auto-leasing terminology, the vehicle price that the customer and the dealer agree to base the lease on.

CAPITAL-COST REDUCTION. An auto-leasing term for the down payment made at the start of the lease.

CARGO VOLUME. For station wagons, minivans, and sport-utility vehicles, the usable cargo volume, measured in cubic feet. CONSUMER REPORTS measures cargo volume with an expandable pipe-frame "box" that is extended to the maximum length, width, and height that will fit through the rear hatch and allow the tailgate to close.

CASTER. A wheel-alignment term. Caster adjustments pull the wheel fore or aft of a vertical line perpendicular to the axle. Think of a furniture caster where the wheel trails behind the leg slightly as the furniture is moved.

CATALYTIC CONVERTER. An emissions-control device in the exhaust system that removes unburned fuel from the exhaust stream by burning it.

CENTER HIGH-MOUNTED STOP LIGHT. CHMSL. A brake light located in the center, and high on the rear, of a vehicle.

CENTER-LOCKING DIFFERENTIAL. In full-time all-wheel-drive systems, a third differential, in addition to the ones on the front and rear axles, that distributes the power to the front and rear. Normally, it allows the front and rear wheels to turn at the different speeds necessary to corner on dry pavement. On slippery surfaces, it locks all four wheels together, either automatically or manually, for greater traction.

CENTRAL LOCKING SYSTEM. For cars with power door locks, a system that locks or unlocks all doors at once. Typically, you turn the key in the driver's door or press a button on a key-fob transmitter.

CFCS. Chlorofluorocarbons. A class of chemicals once used as refrigerants in air-conditioning systems. Most of the world has reduced or banned the use of CFCs because they are thought to harm the Earth's ozone layer.

CHASSIS. A car's platform, with its suspension, steering, and brake hardware.

CHILD SAFETY SEAT. A seat for young children, secured with safety belts. Some are built into the rear seats. See also **Integrated child seats.**

CITY DRIVING, MPG. CONSUMER REPORTS derives a city-driving fuel-use figure by driving tested models, equipped with a high-precision fuel meter, on a special stop-and-go "city driving course" at CONSUMER REPORTS' auto-testing track.

CLEARCOAT. The transparent topmost layer of many modern cars' paint finish. Intended to create a long-lasting, lustrous appearance.

CLOSED-END LEASE. An auto lease in which the customer isn't required to buy the vehicle at the end of the lease or to make up any shortfall in its residual value.

COLLISION COVERAGE. Auto-insurance coverage that pays for damage to your car regardless of who is at fault.

COMPOSITE. Any plastic material, such as foam, fiberglass, carbon fiber, or urethane. Composite materials are often lighter in weight than the materials they replace, such as steel.

COMPREHENSIVE COVERAGE. Insurance that compensates you if your car is stolen or vandalized.

COMPRESSION TEST. A service check that measures the compression in an engine's cylinders. It is used to determine wear on the piston rings and valves.

CONTROLS. The knobs, levers, buttons, and slides that operate a car's various functions and accessories, such as lights, wipers, and climate controls.

CONVENIENCE SCORES. A composite of CONSUMER REPORTS judgments of access, ergonomics, visibility, and cargo area or trunk space.

CONVEYANCE FEE. An arbitrary fee imposed by car dealers, allegedly to cover the cost of preparing a car's paperwork prior to sale. Also called a document fee.

CORPORATE AVERAGE FUEL ECONOMY. CAFE. A U.S. government mandate that automakers' production cars must meet certain average fuel-economy goals by certain dates.

COUPE. A closed two-door car.

C-PILLAR. The rearmost roof-support pillar.

CRASH PROTECTION. A score based on a CONSUMER REPORTS analysis of the government's 35-mph crash-test results. The five-point score assesses the likelihood of moderate, severe, or fatal injury to a driver and passenger.

CRUISING RANGE. CONSUMER REPORTS estimates a car's cruising range by measuring the miles per gallon a tested model achieves on a specific 150-mile test trip, multiplying that by the fuel tank's refill capacity, and subtracting a safety margin of 30 miles.

CRUMPLE ZONE. Portions of a car's structure designed to crumple in a collision to absorb the energy of the crash.

CURB WEIGHT. The weight of a vehicle with all fluids topped off but no occupants or cargo.

DAYTIME RUNNING LIGHTS. DRL. Headlights that come on whenever the car is running, a safety feature that makes a car more visible to others.

DEALER INCENTIVE. A discount offered to a car dealer by the factory, generally for a limited period.

DEALER-INVOICE PRICE. Also referred to as dealer cost, it's the price a dealer must pay the factory for a car. A dealer may receive an incentive, or discount, from the factory, as well as a "holdback," a percentage of the car's wholesale price. These effectively reduce the dealer's actual cost.

DEPRECIATION. A vehicle's loss in value over time.

DESTINATION CHARGE. A fee charged by the factory to deliver a car to a dealership. This charge is non-negotiable.

DIFFERENTIAL. A gear set usually located on an axle that allows the outside wheels to turn faster than the inside wheels when the car rounds a curve. Four-wheel-drive and all-wheel-drive vehicles have two differentials, one for the front axle, one for the rear. On some full-time all-wheel-drive vehicles, a third (center) differential on the drive shaft runs between the front and rear axles. See also **Limited-slip differential.**

DISC BRAKES. An effective brake design now universal on a car's front wheels, and generally on the rear wheels as well. The discs, also called brake rotors, are round plates attached to the wheel hub. When the brakes are applied, hydraulically powered calipers squeeze the discs to slow the car.

DISPLACEMENT. A measurement of the volume displaced by the pistons. Formerly expressed in cubic inches, now more commonly in liters.

DIVIDED-PAVEMENT TEST. A CONSUMER REPORTS wet-braking test in which the asphalt is slicker under the left wheels than under the right wheels.

DOCUMENT FEE. A fee imposed on car buyers by dealers, supposedly to cover the cost of processing the paperwork. Also called a conveyance fee.

DOOR TOP TO GROUND. This Consumer Reports measurement, from the top of the door opening to the ground, gives an idea of how easy it is to get in and out of a vehicle. About 50 inches is a reasonable minimum for an average-size (5-foot 9-inch) adult.

DOUBLE OVERHEAD CAMSHAFT. DOHC. An efficient engine design in which the valves are opened and closed by a pair of camshafts located over the cylinder head.

DOUBLE-WISHBONE SUSPENSION. A type of independent suspension in which upper and lower support pieces somewhat resemble wishbones.

DRIVETRAIN. The combination of the engine, transmission, driveshaft, and differential. (The transmission and differential are combined in a "transaxle" in front-wheel-drive cars.)

DRIVE WHEELS. The wheels to which the engine transmits its power (the front wheels in most modern cars).

DRIVING POSITION. The position of the driver behind the wheel. Consumer Reports assesses comfort, seat adjustability, reach to the pedals, visibility over the hood, and other factors in its judgment of driving position.

ELECTRONICALLY CONTROLLED TRANSMISSION. ECT. An automatic transmission that uses electronic devices to determine shift points. In some, a switch allows selection from two or three modes, such as Power, Normal, and Economy, that change the shift points.

EMERGENCY HANDLING. Consumer Reports tests all its cars to determine how they behave when reaching their cornering limits, as when swerving around an object that suddenly appears in the road ahead. The test consists of making a rapid double lane-change at higher and higher speeds until the vehicle knocks over one or more of the traffic cones that outline the course.

EMERGENCY-LOCKING RETRACTOR. ELR. A safety-belt design that allows a shoulder belt to pay out freely but that locks immediately in a crash or a sudden stop. See also **Automatic-locking retractor.**

ENVIRONMENTAL PROTECTION AGENCY. EPA. The U.S. government agency charged with regulating air quality. EPA regulations govern many aspects of automobile performance, from emission standards to fuel economy.

EPA FUEL ECONOMY. The EPA requires automakers to conduct a specified test to estimate every new model's fuel use in the city and on the highway. It's usually given as two numbers separated by a slash, for city/highway mileage, and is posted on a new car's window sticker.

EURO-SID (SIDE-IMPACT DUMMY). A crash-test dummy used for side-impact testing. Bio-SID is a type used in the U.S.; Euro-SID is used in Europe.

EXTENDED WARRANTY. Also called an extended service contract, this extra-cost service contract picks up where a car's basic warranty leaves off. Not worth the money, especially given 3- to 10-year warranties by manufacturers.

FACTORY-TO-CUSTOMER REBATE. Usually heavily promoted, this is a refund paid to the purchaser of a new car. You can wait and get the check directly from the automaker, or you can sign it over to the dealer as part of the down payment.

FACTORY-TO-DEALER REBATE. A discount the dealer may occasionally get from the manufacturer, and may or may not pass along to the car buyer. Knowing about the rebate gives you more room to deal.

FINAL-DRIVE RATIO. The ratio of the number of rotations of the engine for one rotation of a wheel, in high gear. Sometimes expressed as simply the differential's reduction-gear ratio. In general, a low number means better fuel economy but slower acceleration. Ratios vary from about 1.7 to 4.5. A number close to 3 is typical.

FOOTREST. The place on the left side of the driver's foot well for resting or bracing the left foot. Sometimes it's a raised rubber pad or "dead pedal."

FOOT ROOM. The space for a car occupant's feet in each seating position.

FOOT WELL. The space for the legs and feet of front-seat occupants.

FOUR-WHEEL DRIVE. A system that makes all four wheels driving wheels. Variations abound. Most primitive are part-time systems, selected with a switch or lever, and with manually locking hubs. They connect all four wheels so all go the same speed. Such systems are not suitable for use on dry pavement. Full-time four-wheel-drive systems—or all-wheel-drive systems—can stay engaged at all times if desired. Some are engaged permanently; some you engage with a switch or lever. They use a center differential or other device to distribute power to the front and rear wheels. When such a system senses impending wheel slip, it can lock itself temporarily, linking together both axles to increase traction.

FREON. DuPont's brand name for a chlorofluorocarbon refrigerant known as CFC-12. Formerly used in auto air-conditioners, but now limited or banned by international treaty for environmental reasons.

FREQUENCY-OF-REPAIR. A report card on a car's trouble history, derived from hundreds of thousands of responses to CONSUMER REPORTS' Annual Questionnaire. This survey of subscribers asks respondents about problems they've had with their vehicles in the previous year, in trouble spots ranging from the engine to the paint. The scores in the charts show the proportion of respondents who said they had serious problems.

FRONT LEGROOM. The distance from the heel of a driver's accelerator foot to the seatback with the seat adjusted all the way rearward.

FUEL INJECTION. A method of delivering fuel directly into an engine's intake port. More efficient and precise than the old-fashioned carburetor. These days, the trend is toward electronically controlled fuel injection with one injector per cylinder, sometimes called multiport fuel injection.

GAP INSURANCE. Guaranteed Auto Protection. A type of extra insurance for people who lease their car. It covers the difference between the book value of the car and whatever is owed on the lease. It's important coverage if the car is destroyed or stolen fairly early in the lease term, when one has normally paid less on the lease than the amount by which the car has depreciated.

GOVERNMENT CRASH TESTS. The U.S. government conducts 35-mph frontal-impact crash tests on several dozen cars and light trucks each year. CONSUMER REPORTS analyzes the data from those tests and assigns the vehicles crash-protection scores according to how survivable the crash appeared for the "driver" and "passenger" dummies.

GROSS VEHICLE WEIGHT RATING. GVWR. The curb weight of the vehicle plus the maximum load it is rated by the manufacturer to carry.

HATCHBACK. A practical design often found on small sedans and coupes, in which the trunk lid and back window lift as a unit, hinged at the top.

HEADLINER. The interior covering of a car roof.

HEADROOM. The distance from an occupant's head to the inside of the roof, or headliner. In CONSUMER REPORTS, the clearance above the head of a 5-foot-9-inch male tester.

HIGHWAY DRIVING, MPG. CONSUMER REPORTS measures fuel use on the highway by driving tested models, equipped with a precision fuel-metering device, at least six times up and down a four-mile stretch of flat, smooth highway.

HORSEPOWER. A measurement of an engine's power output. One horsepower is the power needed to lift a 550-pound weight one foot in one second.

INDEPENDENT SUSPENSION. A suspension system in which the left and right wheels can move up and down independently of one another.

INFANT CARRIER. A child safety seat designed for infants. Some seats are designed to face rearward; these should not be used in the front seat of a car with a passenger-side air bag.

INFLATION PRESSURE. The pressure in a tire, usually measured in pounds per square inch, psi. In the metric system, it's measured in kilo-Pascals, kPa.

INJURY-CLAIM RATE. The frequency of insurance claims that involve personal injury. The data used by CONSUMER REPORTS are compiled by the Highway Loss Data Institute, an insurance-industry-sponsored organization affiliated with the

Insurance Institute for Highway Safety. Consumer Reports presents them two ways. The first is a judgment of a given car's injury rate compared with all other cars. The second compares a car's rate of injury with other cars in the same category (sports cars, sedans).

INSTRUMENTS. The gauges and indicator lights that tell you the status of a car's operating condition—speed, engine revs, and so forth.

INSURANCE INSTITUTE FOR HIGHWAY SAFETY. IIHS. A research and lobbying group devoted to auto-safety issues and funded by the insurance industry.

INTEGRATED CHILD SEATS. Permanently installed child seats that fold out of the seatback, normally in the rear center position in a sedan or in one or two of the middle seating positions in a minivan. Sometimes these are designed as booster seats for children who have outgrown a small child seat.

INTERCOOLER. A device that cools intake air as it leaves a turbocharger or supercharger before the air is blown into the engine air intake. Cooling makes the air denser and hence richer in oxygen, which allows the engine to develop more power when the fuel/air mixture is ignited.

KEY-FOB TRANSMITTER. A transmitter on the car's key ring, used for locking or unlocking the car from a short distance away. Many are infrared-controlled. Some use radio waves and have a longer range. Some can arm or disarm a car's security system.

KEYLESS-ENTRY SYSTEM. A system for locking and unlocking doors without using a key. Remote key-fob transmitters are one version; electronic combination locks are another.

LATERAL GS. A measure of sideways forces (gravities) developed as a car rounds a corner. Used by Consumer Reports as one indication of road holding or grip: The more lateral Gs a car can maintain without skidding or spinning out, the better. An accelerometer measures such forces.

LEGROOM. Space for a car occupant's legs. In Consumer Reports, front legroom is the measurement from the accelerator's heel point to the back of the front seat cushion, with the seat adjusted all the way back on its track. With rear fore-and-aft, which measures knee room, the measurement is taken with the front seat adjusted for 40 inches of front legroom.

LIABILITY INSURANCE. A form of automobile insurance mandatory in nearly every state. It covers personal injury or damage inflicted on others by your car.

LIFTOVER. The distance you must lift an object off the ground to swing it into a trunk or cargo bay. A high trunk lip makes loading inconvenient.

LIMITED-SERVICE SPARE. A narrow and sometimes undersized tire used as a temporary spare. It's lighter and takes up less space than a regular tire but is designed to be used for only a limited time and at moderate speed.

LIMITED-SLIP DIFFERENTIAL. A device that helps prevent the drive wheels from skidding or losing traction. It diverts power from a wheel that is slipping to the opposite wheel on the same axle. Not as effective as traction control.

LIMIT OF ADHESION. The point at which the tires are about to lose grip on the road surface. This influences a car's overall handling and emergency-avoidance capabilities.

LIST PRICE. The manufacturer's asking price for a new car, also called sticker price or manufacturer's suggested retail price (MSRP). It's generally negotiable.

LOAD INDEX. In tire labeling, this number indicates the maximum weight a tire is rated to carry. On a tire labeled 185/60R14 82H, the load index is the 82. Index numbers, from 65 to 104, correspond to load capacities from 639 to 1984 pounds.

LOCKING CLIP. An H-shaped clip used to tie off the safety-belt slack when you mount a child safety seat or infant carrier in some cars. Cars that do not have automatic-locking retractors or switchable retractors require a locking clip to secure a child seat.

LUGGAGE CAPACITY. Consumer Reports measures luggage capacity by loading a car's trunk with as many rigid large Pullman cases and small weekend cases as will fit. A number like 4+2 means four Pullmans, two weekenders.

MACPHERSON STRUTS. A suspension system often used with small cars, chosen for its space-saving quality and relatively low manufacturing cost. Typically, a MacPherson strut is a reinforced shock absorber that doubles as a support strut.

MANUFACTURER'S SUGGESTED RETAIL PRICE. MSRP, or sticker price. See **List price.**

MAXIMUM LOAD. According to the car's manufacturer, the maximum weight of passengers and cargo that the vehicle can safely carry.

MEDICAL-PAYMENTS COVERAGE. Coverage for medical payments for a car's driver and whoever else happens to be in the car should it be involved in an accident, regardless of who was at fault.

MONEY FACTOR. A term from auto leasing analogous to the annual percentage rate charged on a loan. It's usually a decimal, like .0041. Convert it to an approximate percentage rate by multiplying it by 2400.

MUFFLER. A component in a vehicle's exhaust system that is designed to quiet the engine's exhaust noise.

MULTIGRADE OIL. Oil that lubricates effectively over a wide range of temperatures. Also called "multiviscosity oil."

MULTI-LINK SUSPENSION. A type of independent suspension that uses multiple links (usually steel arms) to maintain maximum road contact of the tires.

NATIONAL HIGHWAY TRAFFIC SAFETY ADMINISTRATION. NHTSA. Part of the U.S. Department of Transportation. Among other things, NHTSA runs crash tests, regulates traffic safety, and analyzes safety-related defects that may result in a recall.

NEW CAR ASSESSMENT PROGRAM. NCAP. Often referred to simply as "government crash testing," it is one of several crash-test programs run by the National Highway Traffic Safety Administration. The standard NCAP test primarily gauges the effectiveness of a car's occupant-restraint systems. Cars are crashed head-on into a rigid barrier at 35 mph. Instrumented test dummies record the crash forces, and the NHTSA assigns a score that indicates the likelihood of severe, moderate, or fatal injury. CONSUMER REPORTS does its own analyses of the crash data and assigns crash-protection scores based on those studies.

NO-FAULT INSURANCE. An auto-insurance concept, adopted in differing versions in about a dozen states. In a no-fault state, auto-accident victims are compensated for medical expenses by their own insurer, regardless of who was at fault in the accident. By contrast, the traditional system, known as the tort liability system, requires accident victims to sue (or have their insurance company sue) the other driver to gain compensation.

NO-HAGGLE PRICING. You pay the price on the window sticker, or on the placard drawn up by the dealer, just as you would when buying a toaster in a department store.

NOISE. A CONSUMER REPORTS judgment of a car's interior noise. Based both on objective measurements of loudness recorded on various road surfaces and on subjective impressions of our auto engineers.

NOTCHBACK. Any sedan with a trunk, as opposed to a hatchback, whose trunk is integrated with the car's interior.

OIL VISCOSITY. A number relating to the ability of oil to flow. Viscosity varies according to temperature.

OPEN-END LEASE. An auto lease in which the customer agrees to buy the vehicle at the end of the lease. Most leases these days are closed-ended, which is preferable.

OPTIONS. Extra-cost accessories, such as leather upholstery or an upgraded sound system, that do not come as standard equipment in a given car model's trim line. Options are often bundled together as options packages.

OPTIONS PACKAGES. Groups of options bundled together and sold as a unit, often at a discount. For instance, a "convenience package" might include power windows, locks, and seats and a tilt steering wheel. An "all-weather package" might include a heavy-duty battery, heated seats, and a more powerful heater and rear defroster. Packages are worthwhile if you want most of the included equipment. If you don't, you may be better off ordering the items you want separately.

OVERALL MILEAGE. CONSUMER REPORTS calculates overall mileage by taking equal portions of city, expressway, and 150-mile-trip mileage and deriving an average miles-per-gallon figure from those measurements.

OVERALL RATIO. The ratio of the number of rotations of the driveshaft for one rotation of a wheel, in high gear. In general, the lower the ratio, the better the fuel economy but the slower the acceleration. Ratios range from about 1.7 to 4.5. A number close to 3 is typical.

OVERALL SCORE. A composite test score assigned by CONSUMER REPORTS' engineers to each car tested. It includes some 20 judgments of performance, comfort, convenience, and fuel economy—but not reliability. Overall scores are derived the same way for each car within a class, such as sports cars or large sedans, but the scores are scaled differently between classes to reflect the intended use of the vehicle. That way, sports cars aren't penalized for lacking a rear seat, and minivans aren't awarded huge bonuses for having more cargo area than sedans.

OVERDRIVE. A high gear ratio, less than 1:1. Overdrive lets the engine turn relatively slowly, and hence quietly and economically, at highway speeds. The fourth gear in a four-speed automatic transmission, the fifth gear in a five-speed automatic transmission, and often both fourth and fifth gears in a five-speed manual are overdrive gears.

OVERHEAD CAMSHAFT. A camshaft located on top of an engine's cylinder head, a design that, in principle, allows faster valve operation and higher rpms than a pushrod engine produces.

OVERSTEER. A handling term describing the tendency of a car's rear tires to lose grip in a hard turn, resulting in a tighter turning radius than intended.

PACKAGE SHELF. The shelf behind the rear seat in a sedan or coupe. We don't recommend storing packages there.

PASSIVE RESTRAINT. Any structure or device that automatically helps restrain car occupants in a collision. Devices include air bags, door-mounted belts, belt pretensioners, padded knee bolsters, and so forth. Air bags are also called Supplemental Restraint Systems (SRS).

PAYLOAD. The maximum weight in people and cargo that a vehicle can safely carry, as specified by the manufacturer.

PEDAL EFFORT. The amount of effort applied to the brake pedal to stop a car.

PERCENT WEIGHT, FRONT/REAR. CONSUMER REPORTS weighs cars to determine their weight distribution, front and rear. A 50/50 distribution is the theoretical ideal—and very unusual.

PERFORMANCE SCORES. In CONSUMER REPORTS, performance scores refer to a tested vehicle's acceleration, brakes, transmission, and routine and emergency handling. Performance scores are distinct from scores for comfort, convenience, fuel economy, safety, and reliability.

PERFORMANCE TIRE. A tire designed for safe operation and good traction in aggressive driving—qualities that sometimes come at the expense of noise, short tread life, and poor traction in snow.

PERSONAL-INJURY PROTECTION. PIP. An auto-insurance term. In no-fault states, PIP covers your medical costs and other accident-related expenses, such as lost income, regardless of who is at fault.

PLOW. See **Understeer.**

P-METRIC. A commonly seen tire-sizing convention using metric and inch values. Example: P215/70R14. "P" refers to passenger car tire. The 215 is the tire's cross-section width in centimeters; the 70 is the ratio of sidewall height to width (aspect ratio); and the 14 is the wheel diameter, in inches.

PREDICTED RELIABILITY. In CONSUMER REPORTS, a projection of a car's future reliability based on its recent reliability history, as reported in surveys of CONSUMER REPORTS readers. We use a five-point scale, ranging from much better than average to much worse than average.

PRETENSIONER. A device that senses when a collision is happening and instantly reels in any slack in the safety belts.

PROPERTY-DAMAGE LIABILITY. Part of a standard auto-insurance policy, covering any damage your car does to someone else's property.

PUSHROD. One of the rods in a piston engine that operates the valves. Used in overhead valve engines.

QUARTER PANEL. A car's rear fender.

R-134A. Refrigerant now used in auto air conditioners. Less damaging to the environment than the chlorofluorocarbon (CFC) refrigerant it replaced.

RACK AND PINION. A steering mechanism in which a gear at the end of the steering column, the pinion, engages a toothed bar, the rack, which is connected to the front wheels. Turning the steering wheel makes the rack move from side to side.

RATINGS. In CONSUMER REPORTS, Ratings are a rank-ordering of products based on overall quality. The overall scores used in auto Ratings include performance, comfort, convenience, and fuel-economy scores, but not reliability.

REAR LEGROOM. The distance from the rear seatback to the front seatback, with the front legroom set at 40 inches.

REBATE. A partial reimbursement given by a manufacturer to either the purchaser or the dealer. Used by car companies to promote sales.

RECALLS. Campaigns organized by the manufacturer to call in designated vehicles for repair of some defect, usually safety-related. Recalls are sometimes requested by the government.

RECOMMENDED MODEL. In CONSUMER REPORTS, a vehicle is Recommended if it has done well in our tests and is expected to be at least average or better in reliability.

REDLINE. A point on an engine's tachometer indicating the maximum rpm the engine can safely withstand.

RELIABILITY. A report card on a car's trouble history, derived from hundreds of thousands of responses to CONSUMER REPORTS' Annual Questionnaire. Subscribers are asked about serious problems they've had with their vehicles in the previous year, in trouble spots ranging from the engine to the paint.

RESIDUAL VALUE. A leasing term that refers to the projected dollar value of the car at the end of the lease term.

RIDE, FULL LOAD. In CONSUMER REPORTS, a judgment of ride comfort when the vehicle is fully loaded with people and luggage, according to the manufacturer's stated load capacity.

RIDE, NORMAL LOAD. In CONSUMER REPORTS, a judgment of ride comfort when the vehicle is carrying just a driver and one passenger.

RIDE HEIGHT. The distance between the ground and some specified part of a car's undercarriage, such as the oil pan.

ROAD CLEARANCE. The distance between the ground and the lowest part of a car's undercarriage likely to strike the pavement, such as the oil pan or differential. Also called ground clearance.

ROCKER. In an engine, a pivoting arm, like a seesaw, that transfers motion between the camshaft and a valve. When a cam lifts one end of the rocker, it forces the other end down.

ROCKER PANEL. The body panel running beneath a car's doors.

ROLLING RESISTANCE. A measure of how easily a car rolls—a function of how much friction the tires and other components exert. Low rolling resistance increases fuel economy.

ROLLOVER STANDARDS. Safety standards that specify the minimal allowable roof-structure integrity in a rollover collision. Existing government standards use a static roof crush test. In the test, a car's roof is slowly loaded with weight. The standard specifies that the roof must not compress more than a certain amount.

ROUTINE HANDLING. In CONSUMER REPORTS, a judgment of how a car corners and steers in normal driving conditions.

RPMS. Revolutions per minute. The number of times per minute a car engine's crankshaft revolves. Sometimes called "revs." The dashboard instrument that counts the revs is the tachometer.

SAE. Society of Automotive Engineers. A professional association of engineers that sets and adopts certain industry-wide engineering standards, specifications, and test procedures.

SAFETY SCORES. In CONSUMER REPORTS, a series of safety-related scores and judgments of safety equipment like air bags, safety belts, head restraints, child restraints, and so forth. CONSUMER REPORTS also scores crash-protection based on government crash-test data.

SEDAN. As used by CONSUMER REPORTS, a four-door passenger car.

SEQUENTIAL ELECTRONIC FUEL INJECTION. SEFI. A fuel-injection system using one electronically controlled injector for each cylinder. Older systems used throttle-body fuel injection, in which a single injector fed all cylinders.

SHOCK ABSORBERS. The suspension parts that damp ride motions as the vehicle goes over the road. Within a shock absorber, a piston rides up and down in a cylinder filled with thick fluid or compressed gas. It counteracts the vertical movement allowed by the springs. When the car hits a bump, the piston tries to force its way through the fluid. As the fluid resists the motion of the piston, the shock absorber prevents the car body from moving up and down as far or as quickly as it otherwise would.

SHOULDER ROOM. As used in CONSUMER REPORTS, front shoulder room is the width of the car's interior, measured just below the windows, from the inside door trim to the opposite door's inside trim. Rear shoulder room is measured similarly, trim to trim across the car.

SIDE AIR BAG. An inflatable passive restraint designed to protect occupants in a side collision. Different designs are mounted in the side of the seatback, or in the door, or just above the door top.

SIDE DOOR BEAM. A reinforcing beam that strengthens a car door in case of a side impact.

SIDE-IMPACT DUMMY. An instrumented test dummy designed for testing in a side-on collision. Bio-SID is a type used in the U.S.; Euro-SID is used in Europe.

SINGLE OVERHEAD CAMSHAFT. SOHC. An engine in which a single camshaft located above the cylinder head operates both intake and exhaust valves. Compare with double overhead camshaft.

SKID PAD. A paved circle used to test road-holding. At CONSUMER REPORTS, the pad is about 200 feet in diameter. By driving faster and faster around the pad until the car slides out of its lane, a test driver using a g-analyst instrument can gauge a vehicle's grip or road-holding ability.

SLUDGE. An engine deposit that can prevent oil from circulating freely.

SPEED RATING. With tires, an alphabetical rating indicating what speed the tire can safely maintain. Common speed ratings are, in order of increasing speed, S, T, H, V, and Z.

SPOILER. A horizontal wing or faring attached to the front or rear of a car, often on the trunk lid. At race-car speeds, a spoiler helps keep the car planted on the ground. At highway speeds, a spoiler is merely an affectation.

STANDARD 208. A U.S. government crash-test standard every vehicle must pass before it can be sold in the U.S. The test is a 30-mph frontal impact, with instrumented test dummies representing unbelted car occupants. See also **New Car Assessment Program.**

STANDARD EQUIPMENT. Equipment included in the basic price of the car, such as power steering and radio. Higher trim lines tend to include more standard equipment.

STEERING FEEL. A judgment of how well a car communicates to the driver what the front wheels are doing. Steering feel is one component of handling.

STEERING RESPONSE. A judgment of how quickly a car responds to the steering wheel.

STICKER PRICE. The nominal price of a new car, posted on a standard window sticker. Also known as MSRP, or manufacturer's suggested retail price. (The sticker's format is dictated by government regulation and is uniform for all new cars.) The "top sticker" price, at the top right corner of the sticker, lists the cost of the basic car and its standard equipment. The "bottom sticker" price adds to that the prices of any options present, as well as the destination charge.

STOPPING DISTANCE. In CONSUMER REPORTS braking tests, the distance it takes to stop the car from a set speed (usually 60 mph).

SUPERCHARGER. A device that provides more power by forcing more air into the engine's air intake. A supercharger is a blower that's mechanically driven off the engine.

SUPPLEMENTAL RESTRAINT SYSTEM. SRS. The term used by most automakers except General Motors to designate an air bag. (General Motors calls it a supplemental inflatable restraint, or SIR.) The word "supplemental" indicates that it is not a substitute for safety belts but meant to supplement the belts.

SUSPENSION. The system of pivoting arms and springs that suspends the body over a car's wheels. See also **Independent suspension.**

SWITCHABLE RETRACTOR. A safety-belt design that aids in securely mounting a child safety seat.

SYSTEM. The components that provide the sparks that ignite fuel in the engine, including the coil, distributor, and spark plugs.

TACHOMETER. An instrument that counts the engine's revolutions per minute. In manual-transmission cars, it helps indicate when you should shift gears. If present, the "tach" is usually next to the speedometer.

TAIL WAG. The tendency of a car's rear end to lose grip and slide sideways as the car is cornering. Also called "fishtailing" or "oversteer."

T-BONE CRASH. A side impact where one car hits another straight amidships.

TOE-IN. Toe-in and toe-out are wheel-alignment terms. If the front edges of the two tires on an axle point slightly toward each other, it's called toe-in. If they point slightly away from each other, it's called toe-out. (If you look down at your shoes, and the toes are pointed toward each other, that's toe-in. If your shoes make a V, that's toe-out. The same principle applies here.) On front-wheel-drive cars, the front tires are often adjusted to be just slightly toe-in, which helps compensate for the effects of torque steer.

TOE-OUT. See Toe-in.

TORQUE. Rotational force or twisting power, measured in foot pounds. What you feel taking off from a standstill is mostly torque. What you feel when passing at speed is mostly horsepower.

TORQUE STEER. With front-drive cars, the tendency of the front wheels to pull to the side during hard acceleration.

TORSIONAL STIFFNESS. A car body's resistance to twisting motions.

TOURING TIRE. An ambiguous term indicating a tire that is designed for good performance at moderately high speed. Ideally, a touring tire combines the versatility of a standard all-season tire with some high-performance characteristics.

TRACK. A car's width, measured from the center of one tire's contact patch to the center of the opposite tire's contact patch.

TRACKING. The ability of a car to maintain a straight line with minimal steering corrections.

TRACTION CONTROL. A system that helps prevent wheel spin. Some use the antilock-brake system computer to detect when a drive wheel is starting to break loose, then selectively apply brakes to that wheel. Others also throttle back the engine, adjust the transmission, or take other steps to slow the wheel.

TRANSAXLE. A combined transmission and differential found on front-drive cars.

TRANSFER CASE. In four-wheel-drive vehicles, a gearbox that allows power to be delivered to both front and rear wheels.

TRANSMISSION. The gearbox that takes power from the engine's crankshaft and delivers it to the driven axle(s) or the driveshaft. With a manual transmission, you use a clutch pedal and shift lever to change gears. An automatic transmission changes the forward gears automatically. A five-speed manual or four-speed automatic is the typical setup in most modern cars.

TRANSMISSION SCORE. In CONSUMER REPORTS, a judgment of how smoothly and effectively the car's transmission shifts.

TREAD-WEAR INDEX. A number indicating tread life, derived from a government-specified test of tread wear. The index number is embossed on the sidewall of passenger car tires, along with traction and temperature ratings. The tread-wear test is based on a "reference tire" that has a tread wear of 100. A tire rated at 200 should in theory last twice as long; 300, three times as long. These days, a rating of 150 is very low, while a rating of 450 is quite high.

TRIM LINE. An automaker's designation of a specific model with a certain level of standard equipment that comes with it. The trim-line names separate the base car from upper trim levels. For instance, DX, LX, and EX are the names of trim lines for the Honda Accord. LX, SE, and SHO are trim lines for the Ford Taurus.

TROUBLE SPOTS. In CONSUMER REPORTS, this refers to one or another of 16 specific areas in which readers are polled about problems they may have had with cars they own. Scores for individual trouble spots (e.g., engine, clutch, body rust) are the basis of a car's reliability history.

TURBOCHARGER. A device that uses the exhaust-gas stream to power a blower that feeds extra air into an engine, giving it more power.

TURBO LAG. The delay in the time it takes to get the turbocharger up and running after you depress the accelerator.

TURNING CIRCLE. As measured by CONSUMER REPORTS, the clearance needed to make a U-turn.

TURNING RADIUS. Half the turning circle.

UNDERINSURED-MOTORIST INSURANCE. Coverage that pays for your injuries if you are injured by a driver who has insufficient or no insurance to cover you.

UNDERSTEER. The tendency of a car to plow ahead as the front tires lose grip in a turn, and to resist turning when the steering wheel is turned.

UNIDIRECTIONAL TIRES. Tires whose tread pattern is designed to get optimum traction only when the tire is mounted to roll in one direction.

UNINSURED-MOTORIST INSURANCE. Coverage that pays for your injuries if you are injured by a driver who has insufficient or no insurance to cover you.

UNIT BODY. A car-construction design that does not employ a separate chassis frame. Instead, the floor, roof, pillars, and reinforcements in key areas comprise the main structural platform.

UNSPRUNG WEIGHT. The weight of car components not supported by the springs: the tires, wheels, axles, and brakes, plus half the weight of the driveshafts and springs themselves.

VALVE TRAIN. The engine valves, and anything attached to them, such as rockers, push rods, camshafts, and associated linkages, that makes them move up and down.

VARIABLE-ASSIST STEERING. A power-steering variant that feels light at parking speeds but heavier as the car approaches highway speeds so as to provide more road feel.

VARNISH. A hard, damaging engine-oil deposit.

WHEELBASE. The length of a car from the center of the front wheel hubs to the center of the rear hubs.

Car index

USING THE INDEX

These pages list all the cars previewed in the *New Car Buying Guide*. When the last road test is relevant to the new model, we have listed the issue of CONSUMER REPORTS containing the full test report. Reports marked with an asterisk (*) were not tests of that car, but of a similar model.

Also noted are all cars for which full test reports are available by fax or mail. To order, call Consumer Reports by Request at 800 789-3715. You can use MasterCard, Visa, or American Express. Most reports are $7.75. Reports marked with a dagger (†) are $4.00. Add $2.00 outside the U.S. When you call, have ready the report's fax number, your charge-card number, and the card's expiration date. If no fax number is listed, a full report was not available as we went to press.

MODEL	PAGE NO.	LAST FULL REPORT	FAX NO.
Dodge Dakota †	113	7/97	5591
Dodge Durango	114	5/98	9661
Dodge Grand Caravan*	115	7/97	9589
Dodge Intrepid	116	7/98	9673
Dodge Neon	117	3/96	9457
Dodge Ram 1500	118	9/96	9499
Dodge Stratus	119	12/95	9433
Ford Contour	120	8/96	9493
Ford Crown Victoria*	121	7/98	9673
Ford Escort	122	1/97	9539
Ford Expedition	123	6/97	9575
Ford Explorer	124	6/97	9575
Ford F-150	125	9/96	9499
Ford Mustang	205	—	—
Ford Ranger	206	—	—
Ford Taurus	126	1/96	9447
Ford Windstar	127	7/97	9589
GMC Jimmy*	128	5/98	9661
GMC Safari	129	7/96	9489
GMC Sierra C/K 1500*	130	9/96	9499
GMC Sonoma	131	11/95	9434
GMC Suburban	206	—	—
GMC Yukon*	132	10/96	9508
Honda Accord	133	2/98	9651
Honda Civic	135	3/96	9457
Honda CR-V	134	11/97	9622
Honda Odyssey	136	10/95	9431
Honda Passport*	137	5/98	9661
Honda Prelude	206	—	—
Hyundai Accent	138	9/95	9429
Hyundai Elantra	139	1/97	9539
Hyundai Sonata	207	—	—
Hyundai Tiburon	140	8/97	9597
Infiniti I30	141	2/96	9456
Infiniti Q45	207	—	—
Infiniti QX4	207	—	—
Isuzu Amigo	208	—	—
Isuzu Hombre	208	—	—
Isuzu Oasis*	142	10/95	9431
Isuzu Rodeo	143	5/98	9661
Isuzu Trooper	208	—	—
Jaguar XJ8	209	—	—
Jeep Cherokee	144	11/97	9622
Jeep Grand Cherokee	145	6/97	9575
Jeep Wrangler	146	11/97	9622
Kia Sephia	209	—	—

MODEL	PAGE NO.	LAST FULL REPORT	FAX NO.
Kia Sportage	209	—	—
Land Rover Discovery	147	8/95	9421
Land Rover Range Rover	210	—	—
Lexus ES300	148	3/97	9558
Lexus GS300/GS400	210	—	—
Lexus LS400	210	—	—
Lexus LX470	211	—	—
Lexus RX300	211	—	—
Lexus SC300/SC400	211	—	—
Lincoln Continental	149	11/96	9513
Lincoln Navigator	212	—	—
Lincoln Town Car	150	6/98	9672
Mazda 626	151	2/98	9651
Mazda B-Series	212	—	—
Mazda Millenia	153	5/95	9401
Mazda MPV	152	7/96	9489
Mazda MX-5 Miata	212	—	—
Mazda Protegé	154	3/98	9657
Mercedes-Benz C-Class	155	3/97	9558
Mercedes-Benz CLK	213	—	—
Mercedes-Benz E-Class	156	11/96	9513
Mercedes-Benz M-Class	213	—	—
Mercedes-Benz S320	213	—	—
Mercedes-Benz SLK	214	—	—
Mercury Cougar	214	—	—
Mercury Grand Marquis	157	7/98	9673
Mercury Mountaineer	214	—	—
Mercury Mystique	158	10/97	9618
Mercury Sable	159	2/97	9549
Mercury Tracer*	160	1/97	9539
Mercury Villager	161	7/96	9489
Mitsubishi 3000GT	215	—	—
Mitsubishi Diamante	215	—	—
Mitsubishi Eclipse	215	—	—
Mitsubishi Galant	162	5/97	9572
Mitsubishi Mirage	163	1/97	9539
Mitsubishi Montero	216	—	—
Mitsubishi Montero Sport	164	6/97	9575
Nissan 200SX	165	5/96	9471
Nissan 240SX	216	—	—
Nissan Altima	166	2/98	9651
Nissan Frontier	216	—	—
Nissan Maxima	167	1/98	9644
Nissan Pathfinder	168	10/96	9508
Nissan Quest*	169	7/96	9489

MODEL	PAGE NO.	LAST FULL REPORT	FAX NO.
Nissan Sentra	170	6/95	9416
Oldsmobile 88	217	—	—
Oldsmobile Alero	217	—	—
Oldsmobile Aurora	171	6/98	9672
Oldsmobile Bravada	217	—	—
Oldsmobile Cutlass	172	10/97	9618
Oldsmobile Intrigue	173	1/98	9644
Oldsmobile Silhouette*	174	7/97	9589
Plymouth Breeze	175	8/96	9493
Plymouth Grand Voyager	176	7/97	9589
Plymouth Neon*	177	5/96	9471
Plymouth Voyager*	178	7/96	9489
Pontiac Bonneville	218	—	—
Pontiac Firebird	218	—	—
Pontiac Grand Am	218	—	—
Pontiac Grand Prix	179	2/97	9549
Pontiac Sunfire	180	5/96	9471
Pontiac Trans Sport	181	7/97	9589
Porsche Boxster	219	—	—
Saab 9-3	219	—	—
Saab 9-5	219	—	—
Saturn	182	3/98	9657
Saturn SC	183	8/97	9597
Subaru Forester	184	5/98	9661
Subaru Impreza	185	9/97	9603
Subaru Legacy	186	5/97	9572
Suzuki Esteem	187	3/96	9457
Suzuki Sidekick	188	6/96	9478
Suzuki Swift*	189	9/95	9429
Suzuki X90	190	6/96	9478
Toyota 4Runner	191	10/96	9508
Toyota Avalon	192	7/98	9673
Toyota Camry	193	5/97	9572
Toyota Celica	220	—	—
Toyota Corolla	194	3/98	9657
Toyota Land Cruiser	220	—	—
Toyota RAV4	195	11/97	9622
Toyota Sienna †	196	3/98	5662
Toyota Supra	220	—	—
Toyota T100	221	—	—
Toyota Tacoma	221	—	—
Toyota Tercel	197	9/95	9429
Volkswagen Golf	198	5/96	9471
Volkswagen Jetta	221	—	—
Volkswagen New Beetle	222	—	—
Volkswagen Passat	199	2/98	9651
Volvo C70	222	—	—
Volvo S70/V70	200	9/97	9603
Volvo S90/V90	222	—	—

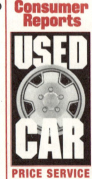